Praise for *Accused*

"Sexual abuse of children is a serious crime, and should be dealt with fairly and carefully. Over the years attempts to bring offenders to justice have often been abusive in their own right. Cases built by so-called experts pressuring children through suggestive and leading questions, combined with overzealous prosecutions, have led to the debacles we experienced in California in the McMartin case, and in the Kern County prosecutions I reviewed when I was California Attorney General. They should have created a warning, a yellow light, to be careful when dealing with child witnesses. When those warnings are not heeded injustice can result, and the lives of the accused, when innocent, can be irreparably damaged. Tonya Craft's own story, and the jury's findings of Not Guilty on 22 counts, more than twenty years after the California cases, proves once again that when dealing with allegations of this sort, the best practices we learned the hard way need to be front and center. Will we ever learn?"

—John Van de Kamp, Former California Attorney General

"I've been a lawyer since 2001, and I've known Tonya Craft since 2010. Nothing prepared me for the power of this book and its markedly human perspective of the realities of being criminally accused. Tonya reveals the strength of her own character and gives the reader a look beyond legalities and into the heart of a caring mother. *Accused* is a must-read, a true tour de force."

—R. Champ Crocker, Cullman Attorney named one of the Nation's Top One Percent by the National Association of Distinguished Council

"Tonya Craft found herself in an unspeakable situation that rocked her world. Through the grace of God and her tenacious spirit, today she is a trusted expert highly sought by the falsely accused and those who defend them. You will be amazed at the power of forgiveness and its impact on an impossible situation."

—Jan Silvious, author of *Foolproofing Your Life* and *Same Life, New Story*

"*Accused*, the true story of a Tonya Craft's fight against the criminal justice system, is much more than a blow by blow account of a woman facing a prosecutorial steamroller. It is also a deeper journey of the heart, and how the power of forgiveness is greater than the bitter root of false accusation."

—Robert Whitlow, bestselling author of *The Confession*

Accused

Accused

My Fight for Truth, Justice, and the Strength to Forgive

Tonya Craft

with Mark Dagostino

BenBella Books, Inc.
Dallas, Texas

The facts presented in this narrative have been pieced together from testimony in the trial, public record, and interviews and research done by the authors. See the author's note for more information.

BenBella

BenBella Books, Inc.
10300 N. Central Expressway
Suite #530
Dallas, TX 75231
www.benbellabooks.com
Send feedback to feedback@benbellabooks.com

Printed in the United States of America
10 9 8 7 6 5 4 3 2 1

Library of Congress Cataloging-in-Publication Data
Craft, Tonya, author.
  Accused : my fight for truth, justice and the strength to forgive / Tonya Craft with Mark Dagostino.
     pages cm
  Includes bibliographical references and index.
  ISBN 978-1-941631-73-7 (trade cloth : alkaline paper) — ISBN 978-1-941631-74-4 (electronic) 1. Craft, Tonya—Trials, litigation, etc. 2. Trials (Child sexual abuse)—Georgia—Catoosa County. 3. Kindergarten teachers—Georgia—Catoosa County—Biography. I. Dagostino, Mark, author. II. Title.
  KF225.C73 C73 2015
  345.758'02536—dc23
                         2015020101

Editing by Vy Tran
Copyediting by Stacia Seaman
Proofreading by Amy Zarkos and Michael Fedison
Text design by Aaron Edmiston
Text composition by PerfecType Typesetting, Nashville, TN
Cover design by Sarah Dombrowsky
Cover photo by Doug Strickland
Printed by Lake Book Manufacturing

Distributed by Perseus Distribution
www.perseusdistribution.com

To place orders through Perseus Distribution:
Tel: (800) 343-4499
Fax: (800) 351-5073
E-mail: orderentry@perseusbooks.com

Significant discounts for bulk sales are available.
Please contact Glenn Yeffeth at glenn@benbellabooks.com or (214) 750-3628.

To my two children, my husband, and my parents.

"Then you will know the truth, and the truth will set you free."
—John 8:32 (NIV)

Contents

Author's Note xiii

Prologue xv

PART I—The Promise 1

PART II—The Marathon 81

PART III—The Fight. 235

PART IV—Freedom 377

Epilogue: Revelations 395

Acknowledgments 403

Notes 407

About the Authors 413

Author's Note

What you're about to read is my story, told from my point of view. The details are drawn from my memory, bolstered by hundreds upon hundreds of court documents, transcripts (from depositions, interviews, court proceedings, and testimonies), taped conversations, the recollections of my close friends and family, portions of the gavel-to-gavel media coverage of my case, and a complete review of the videotaped proceedings from the in-courtroom camera that stood watch over my trial. Wherever possible, exact quotes are preserved and repeated in these pages; in cases of past exchanges and more casual conversations, I've preserved the words and most certainly the meanings of the conversations to the absolute best of my recollection.

In order to protect their privacy, the first names of all children mentioned in this book have been changed.

Some of the details in these pages are quite graphic in nature—not by choice, but because they represent the truth of the subject matter with which I came forcibly face-to-face. While I've chosen to mute some of the more colorful language that emerged during the tense moments behind closed doors during my ordeal, there may still be occasional moments that will shock and dismay some readers. I hope the inclusion of those details serves a much higher purpose in the end. It is not my intent to shock. It is my intent to reveal the truth of the horror that unfolds when false allegations are allowed to move forward. I hope the details of my story will push us all to work harder to seek the truth in our daily lives and to demand that truth come first in our legal system. I believe that the greatest truth begins in the presumption of innocence that every human being deserves—and flourishes through the redemption and forgiveness that every human being is capable of giving and receiving through faith.

Prologue

The night before they made me break the most important promise a mother can make, I woke up startled by the sound of my baby crying.

"Ashley?" I called to her.

Before I could get my feet over the side of the bed, I heard her little feet pattering down the hallway. "Mommy! Mommy!" she yelled.

"Baby, what's the matter?"

"I had a dream," she said as she crawled into my arms.

"About what, sweetie?"

"I had a dream that I was jumping on the trampoline and David walked around the corner of the house, and he said he was home and was never going to leave again."

I wasn't expecting that. Some nightmare, some monster, maybe. But not that. I pulled my daughter close and started crying right along with her.

David was my husband of ten months. He was the most loving stepfather to Ashley and her older brother, Tyler, that I ever could have imagined. He had swept into my life and brought the three of us more joy than we had known in what felt like forever. Then six weeks before this night, he walked out the door.

Ashley was only in kindergarten and had already been subjected to two failed marriages—first me leaving her daddy, and now her stepdaddy leaving me. The pain I'd been through no longer mattered. This whole situation was not fair to my kids. It wasn't right. The fact that she woke up crying in the middle of the night over how much she wanted her stepdaddy back just about broke my heart.

I didn't let myself cry for long. I knew that wasn't what she needed. Not from me. Not then. We'd had enough tears. What Ashley really needed was to get some sleep. After all, it was May 29. The kids had finished their last day of school, and we'd all be enjoying our first-day-of-summer celebration the very next morning. None of us could wait to get to the community pool. I loved my summers with the kids. Always had. *Always would.*

God, I thought. *I love my kids so much. I feel so blessed just to have them in my life. Thank you.* I welled up with this warm, powerful feeling of connection. A feeling I'm pretty sure only mothers truly understand.

"I'll never leave you, Ashley," I whispered. I pulled my head back just enough to see her precious little face as I held her. "Ashley, look at me. You know Mommy loves you. I'll never leave you."

She nodded and stopped crying.

"Sweetie, y'all couldn't get rid of me if you wanted to!" I said, and she laughed a little. But then she got this scared look in her eyes.

"What if someone took you away?" she asked.

"No one could take me away, Ashley. And even if they did, I'd come right back."

"But, Mommy, what if someone took you all the way to Australia?"

Ashley's imagination never failed to surprise me. I had to think of a good comeback. "Well . . . then I'd find a kangaroo and climb on his back and hop all the way back to you," I said. She laughed a little more at that, and suddenly it was a game.

She asked me what I'd do if the wind blew me "all the way to Antarctica!"

"I'd climb on a polar bear and ride him right into your arms."

"What if you jumped into the pool and when you came up for air you were in the middle of the ocean?"

"I'd just grab the tail of a big blue whale and swim all the way back to you!"

"But, Mommy, what if we were in the forest and a wolf tried to take me away from you?"

"Well . . . I would transform into a giant grizzly bear and battle with that wolf until you were safe and sound again."

"No matter what?" Ashley said.

"No matter what."

Ashley gave me a great big hug and I held her close. There's hardly a better feeling in the world than being able to comfort your child.

She looked up at me again. She was smiling. So was I.

That's when I looked my baby girl in the eye and made that promise that still haunts me to this day. "Ashley," I said. "I'm never going to go anywhere. I promise."

Part I

The Promise

Chapter 1

N o matter what anyone tries to tell you about the long hours and low pay, one of the great perks of being a teacher is getting summers off to spend with your kids. The three of us didn't have a schedule. We could laze around the house, or take day trips, or have friends over. Other parents had to work, so I was happy to have their kids come over anytime, too. And there aren't many things that go better together than kids and water, so I'd take the whole gang swimming every chance we got.

May 30, 2008, a Friday, would mark our first trip of the season to the community pool.

Tyler and Ashley had already packed up all of their paraphernalia and were playing with it on the front porch when my friend Tammy came by on her way to work and dropped off her son, Hunter. The three kids had finished up an early lunch and were now chomping at the bit to get out the door. I was the one stuck on Georgia time, making them wait while I went to my bedroom to put on my bathing suit. I had just finished pulling on my shirt and shorts when I heard the doorbell ring. It couldn't have been three seconds later when all three of the kids came bounding into my room together.

"Mommy, there are two men on the front porch, but we didn't open the door because you said to always come get you first," Tyler said. I was thrilled to see that my lectures on not opening the door to strangers had actually gotten through to them.

"Thank you for remembering," I said as I walked out.

I'll admit I was a little annoyed at the intrusion. I'm not a big fan of door-to-door anything. I could see two men through the window wearing button-down shirts and suit jackets. As I opened the door I recognized one of them. The dark-haired one. He was the father of a little girl who went to the school where I worked. He looked a lot like Ashley and Tyler's daddy. Could've been his twin brother, actually. They looked so much alike that it gave me a start whenever I caught a glimpse of him in the hallways at school—and it gave me a start that morning.

"Can I help you?" I said.

The other man pulled his jacket back, revealing a badge. "Can we talk to you for a minute?" he said. I remember thinking he looked more like a Sunday school teacher than a police officer.

"What's this about?" I asked, as all three kids squished into my legs behind me.

"It might be better if you come out and close the door."

I told the kids to go play. "We'll leave in a few minutes." Then I stepped out just like he asked. The kids didn't go play, of course. They stood right next to the door with their faces against the window, just as curious as could be.

"I'm Tim Deal," said the light-haired one.

"And I'm Stephen Keith," said the one who looked like my ex.

"We're going to ask you a few questions."

It felt like a script. As if they had rehearsed this.

I said, "Okay."

"I see your license plate," Detective Deal said. "Are you a teacher?"

My car had an educator's plate on it. "Yes," I said. Looking over, I noticed their car parked right in my driveway, a regular-looking sedan with no police markings at all.

"Where do you teach? What grade?"

I found it a little surprising that the dark-haired man, Detective Keith, didn't recognize me from school. Chickamauga, Georgia, is about as small-town as small town gets, and our school was almost like a private school where everybody knew everybody. But they kept asking these sorts of questions as if they didn't know who I was.

I finally asked again, "What's this all about?"

"We need to ask you a question about your daughter and some touching."

My heart sank. I was frightened to think something might have happened to my little girl. And then it occurred to me what they must have been talking about. *But how would they even know about that?*

Two years earlier, Ashley had been playing with her friend Chloe McDonald when all of a sudden Chloe's mom, Kelly, went hysterical. She lost it because the girls had been "touching" each other.[1] I'll never forget the way she said that word: *touching*. It made my skin crawl.

"No kid would do something like that unless they had been molested," Kelly had said. "I would know, because my husband was molested."[2]

The girls were only three or four years old at the time. Chloe's mom couldn't even explain what she meant by "touching" because she hadn't witnessed it. It made no sense. Still, I took it seriously and did everything a mom could. I even took Ashley to her pediatrician to be sure that nothing inappropriate had happened. The pediatrician found nothing out of the ordinary. And of course I kept an eye on Ashley for any changes in behavior. But there hadn't been any. The biggest consequence was that Chloe's mom and I stopped hanging around each other much after that. It had certainly never been brought to the attention of the police. Still, when Detectives Deal and Keith asked me about "my daughter" and "touching," that was what jumped to mind.

"Yes," I said. "There was a situation a couple of years ago. I've taken care of that."

"You've taken care of touching kids?" Deal said.

"I—what? What do you mean?"

"You've been accused of molesting three little girls."

I stopped breathing. I stared at him. It was such an unbelievable thing for him to say. I didn't know what to do.

"Are you kidding me?" I asked.

It was very clear they were not kidding. There was nothing about their demeanor that implied anything but seriousness. I just couldn't think straight.

"No, ma'am," said Keith.

"Well, what do you mean? Who would say such a thing?"

That's when Deal spoke the names of my accusers, out loud, for the very first time.

"Chloe McDonald," he said.

I tried not to react. I was shocked that my first instinct was correct. Why on earth would that day in May of 2005 be addressed now? And why would anyone be accusing *me*?

Then he said the second name: "Brianna Lamb."

I was horrified. Brianna was seven, and I'd had an issue with her mother ever since my daughter's birthday party a few months earlier. Brianna and her friend Lydia Wilson were saying some things to Ashley that I didn't think were very nice, so I scolded them. Politely. Like any parent or teacher would have done, I'd said, "That was a very unkind thing to say. How would you feel if someone said that same thing to you at *your* birthday party?"

Brianna stopped talking to me after that. She used to come down to my classroom after school every day and play with Ashley like she was her little sister. She stopped doing that, too. I couldn't understand why her reaction was so strong. Worse? My scolding had rubbed Brianna's and Lydia's moms the wrong way. I'd managed to tick them off more than once in the past few months, both in school and out, to the point where those women had gone around town after Ashley's birthday party telling people, "Tonya messed with the wrong families!" and "Tonya's gonna pay!"[3] It was awful. I was honestly worried they might try to get me fired. I knew they had the pull to do it, too. The Wilsons seemed to be the wealthiest, most influential family in the whole county.

Is that what this is about? Do those two want to get me fired? Did their trash talk somehow get back to the police?

It was amazing how quickly my mind raced through that whole scenario. It was a horrible flash of fear that these women who didn't like me might have said something terrible happened to their children just to hurt me. Just to wreck my reputation. But I dismissed it just as quickly as it came.

No one would do something that awful.

Then Detective Deal said the name of my third accuser: "Skyler Walker."

I was speechless. Skyler Walker was the daughter of one of my very best friends. There had never been a lick of animosity between us or our children.

"We've interviewed these kids, and they said that you touched them, so we need you to come down to the police station . . ."

They've interviewed these kids? I felt like my mind was lagging a few steps behind. *I thought they didn't know who I was?* My legs felt weak. *What does this have to do with my daughter? Didn't he say they had a question about "my daughter" and "touching"?*

I usually handle crises really well in the middle of 'em. Only afterward do I break down and let all the emotions rush in. But these men had me all confused and sick to my stomach before I fully understood what they were trying to tell me. I felt like I couldn't keep up with their words.

They said I needed to come down to the Catoosa County Police Station "immediately" so they could interview me "and then do a polygraph."

"A polygraph?" I said.

The heat on that porch was stifling. Those three sets of eyes were still peering at me through the window. These two men kept telling me what they "needed" me to do, with this calm demeanor that suddenly felt intimidating and strange, as if they were sweet-talking me into buying a used car or something. I had watched enough *Law & Order* to know that I'd better cooperate—and also to know that I'd better be careful. I didn't want to make matters worse. I wanted to cooperate. I wanted to get to the bottom of this and clear my name as quickly as I could. I couldn't believe I was being accused of something so terrible. *Me. A mom. A teacher who loves working with kids.* But I also wanted to be careful not to say anything that could be twisted or misconstrued. I hadn't done anything wrong. *Somebody must've mistaken me for somebody else, or misunderstood what somebody said, or something.*

"Do I need some sort of legal counsel?" I asked.

The two men stopped and looked at each other. "That won't be necessary," they said. According to the detectives, it would be "easier" and "better" to just come down to the station, to "clear this all up and get it over with."

I was the only adult there. I had kids to take care of. "I'll need to call my parents to see if they can come watch the children," I said. "They live up in East Ridge, so it might take a while." I insisted that I had nothing to hide, that this whole thing was crazy, that as soon as I could, I would come down to the station. "I'll even take the polygraph if that's what you need, as long I can bring an attorney—"

Saying that word was like throwing a match into a pit full of fireworks.

Suddenly both men started shouting at me, yelling about my "obvious guilt" and "lack of cooperation."

"Now we *know* you did something wrong!" Deal said.

My heart started pounding so hard it physically hurt in my chest.

"If you won't cooperate," Deal barked, "we'll be back here with an arrest warrant!"

"I'm not saying I won't cooperate—"

"We even talked to your soon-to-be ex-husband, and *he* said you're a child molester."

"What?!"

David would never say such a thing. *They talked to David?* I don't care how mad he'd been when he left; he would never, ever say that.

I felt my eyes well up. I closed them and tried to think. "That can't be," I whispered to myself. "It can't—"

"Are you saying you didn't do this?"

Deal's words snapped me to attention.

"That's exactly what I'm saying," I said. I looked him right in the eyes. I held back my tears as best as I could. "Look, I will cooperate with everything. I will do just as you've asked me to. I'll come down to the station. I'll be happy to talk to you. I just think it's a good idea to have an attorney present—"

"If you won't cooperate, we're going to arrest you!"

At that point I'd had enough of their yelling. Their anger was making *me* angry. I hadn't done anything wrong. I hadn't done anything at all! It suddenly occurred to me that they couldn't arrest an innocent person, so I put my panic aside and got real calm and direct. For a moment I got back to being me.

"Y'all do what you need to do," I said. "I'm going to go call my parents now."

Deal squinted his eyes and looked at me, hard. He pulled out a business card and handed it to me. "Make sure you call me when you're on your way," he said. "Remember my name. Detective Tim Deal. As in, *Let's Make a Deal.*"

I took the card and said, "I think I'll remember it better like *Deal or No Deal.*"

That's when the two of them stepped off my porch, got into their car, and drove away.

As I watched them disappear from view, I could hear my own pulse in my ears. I stood there clutching that business card in my right hand and rubbing my thumb back and forth over the surface of it. I felt dizzy. My mind tried to process what had just happened. I looked down and saw my son's dirty sneakers on the porch. An hour ago that porch had been filled with laughter. A few minutes ago we'd been getting ready for our first day of summer. I'd been getting dressed for our day at the pool. Now I was—

Wait. What just happened?

I started shaking. I leaned one hand against the door frame to hold myself up.

Do they really believe I did something to those girls? Who else did they talk to? Who else has been talking about this? How many people know about this? Did something happen to those three girls? Did someone molest them, and for some reason they—

Then it hit me. All at once.

Oh my God. They think I'm a monster.

Chapter 2

B ack in 2005, when I first came to work in Chickamauga, Georgia, I coulda sworn I'd stepped foot into a real-life version of *Mayberry R.F.D.*

You hear about places with only one stoplight, where life's a little bit slower and everybody knows everybody. How many of us ever really get the chance to live and work in one? Driving my old GMC Yukon up to that one red light in the center of downtown, with its old brick buildings and little Western-style storefronts that look as if they were plucked off an old movie set, I felt like I'd finally hit the jackpot. I was so excited about getting a job teaching kindergarten at Chickamauga Elementary that I spent hundreds of dollars of my own money to set up my classroom that summer. I bought a nice comfy rug for the children to gather on. I made up a sign that said "Welcome Home to Kindergarten." I bought a whole new set of stamps with letters on them, plus books on tape and cans of shaving cream so the kids could practice writing letters on their desks with their fingers in the messy sort of way that kindergarten-age kids absolutely love. I'd accumulated lots of fun classroom supplies in all my previous years of teaching, too, and I brought them all in to make my classroom feel like a true home away from home for my students.

People might not think teaching kindergarten is the toughest job in the world, but it sure is a far cry from babysitting, I can tell you that. It took exhausting amounts of work every night and weekend. And I loved every second of it. In fact, I loved it so much I decided to pursue my master's degree in teaching even before I started my new job. It would stretch my night and weekend time like crazy over the next couple of years, but to be quite frank, as a single mom, I needed the salary bump that master's degree would get me. And seeing those smiling faces every day, knowing I was making a difference, knowing I was getting a chance to improve myself and my ability to teach those kids while getting to start my life over in such a beautiful school, in such a beautiful town, made all of the sacrifice worth it.

I was still living in Tennessee for that '05–'06 school year. After finally emerging from a horrible divorce over the previous couple of years from my ex-husband, Joal—the father of my two children—I'd lived in my parents' house for a few months. Then I was lucky enough to find a town house on the street just behind my parents' that I could rent for a while with the luxury of knowing my kids could safely run over to Grandma and Pop-Pop's anytime they wanted, or anytime I needed. That was another wonderful thing about Chickamauga: It may have been in a whole different state, but it wasn't even twenty miles south of the very house where I grew up in East Ridge, a quiet suburb of Chattanooga on the Tennessee-Georgia line.

One of the first people I met in Chickamauga was Sandra Lamb. From the very first moment on the first day of school, Sandra was there. She was always *there*. You couldn't miss her! The tall, flashy brunette in blinged-out designer jeans. Throw in her son and daughter and a well-to-do husband named Greg and they were the picture-perfect All-American family. Her cute-as-a-button blond daughter, Brianna, was in my class. Brianna was an aspiring actress, and Sandra shared all sorts of excitement over the developments in that little girl's acting career. The way they talked, it seemed Brianna was headed for Hollywood stardom.

Sandra stepped right up as one of the classroom moms before I even asked for volunteers. She seemed to already know just about every other parent who walked through the door and was always flitting around the hallway saying hi to everyone before and after school.

She was quite the character, but having Sandra take a shine to me as her daughter's teacher provided a big leg up in the community for me: She introduced me to just about everyone she knew with a big smile and the most glowing words. "Tonya is the greatest friend and teacher in the world!" she'd say, which always left me red-faced, but I couldn't have asked for a nicer introduction in a small town.

My son, Tyler, was lucky enough to attend Chickamauga Elementary when I started teaching that year even though we were living up over the border in Tennessee. It was one of the wonderful perks of the job. Some wealthy people from other towns would fill out applications and pay to have their kids attend Chickamauga—even though it was a public school. That's how good a reputation it has. But as a teacher there, my kids were allowed to attend the school. Tyler was placed in a classroom right across the hall from mine. Ashley's two years younger than Tyler, so I enrolled her in a nearby preschool and looked forward to the day when all three of us would be in the same building five days a week.

Outside of the classroom, fall means football season, and those Friday night games under the lights would be the first place I'd do much socializing. Tyler started hanging out with a little boy named Evan during the games. Evan happened to be one of my students, and his friendship with my son led me to grow close to Evan's mother, Kim Walker. She and I just hit it off, which was funny to me, because most of my friends tend to be older than I am. Kim was young. She'd had Evan when she was around eighteen years old, so she must have been all of twenty-three when we met. I was in my midthirties. Yet there was just something about me and Kim that clicked. Maybe it was an athletic thing. She played softball. I played softball. Kim had a daughter named Skyler who was Ashley's age, and let's face it: Friendships in adulthood revolve a whole lot around each other's kids. Having sons and daughters who get along means the grownups can sit and talk while the kids play. Tyler and Evan and Ashley and Skyler got along beautifully, and that was a blessing like no other.

One of Sandra Lamb's friends, Kelly McDonald, had a son in my class, too. And as luck would have it, Kelly's younger daughter, Chloe, was a preschooler just like Ashley. Kelly was a hoot. She reminded me of Sherri Shepherd on *The View*, all charismatic and spunky, only she's white and had short, spiky, frosted-blond hair. Anyway, right near the beginning of the year, Kelly offered to pick up Ashley at preschool and drive her to my classroom at the end of the day. She had to drive right by there anyway, but I insisted on paying her to do it. Turned out, she needed the money. So it worked out great for everyone. Tyler would come over to my classroom at the end of the day, and Kelly would drop Ashley off when she picked up her son, who became friendly with Tyler. Sandra was always hanging around with Brianna after school, and Brianna just loved to play big sister to Ashley. All in all, the social life and kid arrangements seemed to be working out just perfectly.

The way I saw it, we were all supporting each other through those hectic, crazy days when your kids are just starting out in school and it's all you can do to keep your head on straight before collapsing into bed at the end of the day.

What's that phrase? "It takes a village to raise a child"? Well, Chickamauga sure felt like a big part of the "village" of my life to me. Working in that town felt a little bit like I'd stepped back in time. I liked that feeling.

Chapter 3

As I watched that unmarked car round the corner and disappear, I tried to pull myself together. My heart was pounding and my head still spinning when I finally opened the front door to find the kids standing there all chomping at the bit.

"Mommy! Mommy!"

"Who were those strangers?"

"When are we going to the pool?!"

I couldn't handle it.

"Kids, please! Y'all go up to the bonus room. I have to take care of some adult business, okay?"

They started in with the whining and complaining and I just yelled, "Go!"

I hardly recognized my own voice. It sounded like it came from outside my body. It must have scared them, because all three of them turned and ran up to the playroom over the garage without another word.

My mind was still spinning. *Did Sandra and Kelly make this up? Who would do such a thing? Who would use their own child to make an accusation like that? No one could be that evil. I don't care how much they hate me!*

I took a breath and tried to gather my thoughts. How on earth is a person supposed to know what to do in a situation like this? All I could think was I'd better call my parents. They have always been there for me. No matter what. They would be there for me through this—whatever *this* was.

I picked up my cell phone ready to dial my parents, but in the confusion and panic of the moment, I couldn't stop thinking about the third girl those detectives had mentioned: Skyler Walker. *Why would Skyler accuse me of something like this? Where would she get such an idea?*

I was short of breath. I wanted to lie down. But I couldn't. Before I knew it, I had dialed Kim Walker's number. While her phone rang I kept pacing around, and the anger and confusion and fear came bubbling up like lava. When she finally picked up, I exploded at her: "What the hell is going on?"

Without me having to explain one word, Kim knew what I was calling about.

"I'm so sorry, Tonya," she said. She started crying. "I wanted to tell you, but the police said not to say a word." The tears came pouring down my face, too. *Has one of my very best friends turned on me? Does she hate me for some reason, the way Sandra Lamb and Kelly McDonald and Sherri Wilson do now? It can't be. It just can't.*

I asked her, "Did those detectives interview Skyler?"

"They did interview Skyler," Kim said, "but Skyler said that nothing inappropriate had happened. The police said her name wouldn't even come up in this. I don't understand why they would've said something."

"If Skyler said I did nothing wrong, then why did the police say she was one of my accusers? Did *you* tell them I did something to her?"

"No! Of course not, Tonya!"

"They accused me of molesting her, Kim. Don't lie to me. Tell me what's going on!"

"I don't know! It doesn't make any sense to me."

I was so confused and angry I just blew up. "How could you not tell me this was going on behind my back?" I shouted. "With friends like you, who needs enemies?"

I hung up on her. Seething. Heartbroken by my friend's actions. It felt like my whole world was crashing down.

I heard the kids playing upstairs and I panicked again.

My God. What if they're on their way back here to arrest me right now?

I didn't want to risk the kids overhearing any more of this, and certainly didn't want to risk having my children see me put in handcuffs and shoved into the back of a police car. So I carried my phone outside to the front lawn and dialed my parents. I needed help. *Now.*

I was bawling again when my mom picked up.

"Mom, I need you and Dad to come over to the house. Right now." She wanted to know what was wrong, but I couldn't speak over my sobs. She couldn't understand what I was saying. "Just come. I need you. Now!"

I hung up breathing like I'd just run a marathon. I thought of Hunter, upstairs with my kids. His mother, Tammy, needed to know. She was at work. I hated the thought of bothering her there, but I had to tell her what was going on. Plus, she was closer to my house than my parents. *Maybe she can get here faster*, I thought. I needed somebody, anybody, just some adult to be there with me.

I was crying so hard when Tammy picked up the phone that she couldn't understand a word I said. I must have terrified her because she yelled at me, asking if the kids were hurt. I caught my breath enough to say, "No." She asked if *I* was hurt. "No! Just please come *now!*"

That's when my legs finally gave out and I fell to the ground, sobbing.

Time seemed to swirl together. I can't tell you if it was one minute or ten minutes later when I pulled myself together enough to stand up and have a clear thought.

I need to call an attorney.

I'd been working with an attorney on a whole other matter related to my ex-husband and his new wife, so I had her number in my phone. I dialed her, but there was no answer. I left her a message. I waited a few minutes and then tried her again, this time leaving a more frantic message. I can't even begin to tell you how frustrating it is to get voice mail when your whole life is on the line.

Why can't I get a hold of her?

Then I suddenly got hit with the thought of something else those detectives said: They had talked to my "soon-to-be ex-husband," David. My husband. The husband who'd left me. The man whom Ashley had come to me crying about just last night. *He wouldn't abandon me through this. He just wouldn't. I need him.* I called his cell phone. David always had his cell phone on him. He didn't pick up. I left a message. I called the number again. I left another message. I called again, this time leaving an angry message. Four days earlier David had left me a message saying simply, "I love you." We'd been talking a little bit about him moving back in. He loved my kids. My kids loved him. *I* loved him. He might have been mad at me, but he knew what kind of person I was, and he knew what kind of mom I was. *Did he really tell those detectives I was a child molester?*

I called again, this time furious and spewing a flurry of words that shouldn't come out of any God-loving Christian's mouth, ever. I knew for a fact that he had that cell phone in his pocket. He always did. He always answered. Always. I stood there staring at my phone in a daze, wondering why he was avoiding my calls, just staring until I felt a tug on my arm. I looked up. It was Tammy. I hadn't seen her drive up. I must have been in some kind of shock because I could see her lips moving but I couldn't hear a word she was saying. She finally grabbed my shoulders and shook me. She put her hands on my face and looked right at me and yelled, "Tonya, calm down and tell me what is going on!"

I managed to start speaking. I told Tammy everything. I told her what I'd been accused of. I concluded with the fact that my own husband wasn't picking up my calls. That's when my mother and father pulled into the driveway. Tammy didn't know what to say. By the time I was through, she looked as if she were in as much shock as I was. She ran inside to check on the children while I tried to figure out how to explain it all again to my parents. Speechless, I stared at the two of them for the longest time: my mother, who was always so strong, and my father, who had worked so hard to give my brother and me everything we ever needed our whole lives.

Finally, I said it: "They said I've been accused of molesting three little girls."

My beautiful mother's face fell in horror like I've never seen. My mom doesn't have a filter, and a flurry of angry words spewed out of her mouth. Her instincts about how certain people must have made up this lie to try to hurt me were the same kind of instincts I was having, and she let me know it in no uncertain terms. My poor daddy didn't say anything. His shoulders slumped over like his heart was going to give out right there. Honestly, I'd never seen them so distressed in my entire life. I don't think there's anything in the world I could have told them, including that somebody had died, that would have shaken them like this did.

During one of my calmer moments I remembered that I knew another local attorney. David and I had hired him to help Tammy get through her own divorce the previous year, and just a month earlier I had spoken to him about some questions I had regarding my ex and his new wife and their care of my daughter, Ashley. *How did my life become so complicated that I know more than one attorney?* I called his office, half expecting to suffer through another voice mail message when I surprisingly got through to him.

"Tonya, what's going on?" he said.

As calmly as I could, I relayed the whole story, still standing there in my front yard. I swear I could hear the sound of that doorbell ringing in my ears. I was scared to death that if I went inside, I'd hear the doorbell again and see those detectives again. I was frightened that I'd hear the bell and be dragged off to jail on this horrible charge, accused of molesting these children when I'd done nothing wrong. When I'd done nothing at all.

I grew more panicked as I spoke it out loud again. I told the attorney that the detectives wanted me to come down to the police station for an interview and a polygraph. I told him that they threatened to get an arrest warrant and come back for me. "For all I know they could be on their way right now!"

He kept telling me that it would be okay, that he would handle it. He asked me for the names of the detectives and I pulled out that business card and gave him the number for Tim Deal. The attorney stayed calm through the whole thing and said he would place a call to Detective Deal for me. "But first," he said, "I'm gonna call Buzz."

"Who?"

"Buzz Franklin. He's the district attorney. Just to see if I can get to the bottom of this whole thing. I should be able to get some answers for you, Tonya."

This attorney was a local guy. Well connected. He knew people. I was sure he could help.

"Thank you," I said. "*Thank you.*"

For the first time since it all began, I felt calm for more than a few seconds.

It wouldn't last.

Chapter 4

I've never been annoyed by the commotion and liveliness of kids. The noise and chaos of a classroom or a house full of children never bothered me. I *like* being around kids. I babysat as soon as I was old enough to do so. I taught Sunday school. I became a teacher because I love teaching kids. At the end of the school day, I would often let my children invite friends over—the more, the merrier—knowing they would all entertain each other, freeing me to do other things.

Of course, just about the only "other thing" I ever had time to do as we rounded the corner into 2006 was study. I was back and forth to graduate school every Monday through Thursday evening after work. The kids stayed with my parents while I was in class, and I had a slew of papers to work on. I was determined to complete my master's program in a year and a half. I was also determined to do it with a high grade point average. That's just how I am. If I'm going to do something, I go for it. I give it my all.

My schedule didn't leave a whole lot of room for socializing away from the kids, aside from the times they were at playdates or sleepovers. Especially during the week, and especially when baseball season started up in February.

Tyler's always been a little tall for his age, and he's definitely got the combination of both my genes and my ex-husband's when it comes to being athletic. Ashley does, too, for that matter. She'd show off her skills in tumbling class, being the energetic four-year-old she was. And between tumbling classes, baseball practice two nights a week, and baseball tournaments on the weekend, all while driving back and forth from our town house in Tennessee, I felt like I was running a children's taxi service sometimes.

We all made new friends through baseball, though. Tyler was on a team with a boy named Aaron Potter, who was a year younger and wouldn't be going into kindergarten until the following year, but they really hit it off. I hit it off with his parents, too. Mike and Dee Potter were a wonderful, down-to-earth couple who lived just a mile or so from the school, and all of our kids got along beautifully—Ashley and the Potters' daughter, who was quite a bit older than both of my kids, had sort of a big sister/little sister, or maybe babysitter-child, relationship. As spring heated up, they invited us over to their pool just about every weekend, and we had cookouts together. It was wonderful.

Kelly McDonald's son was on Tyler's baseball team, too, which worked out really well: Kelly's daughter, Chloe, and Ashley could play together while the boys played ball. The McDonald kids would come over to play at the house now and then, too.

The Lambs weren't in the picture quite as much at that point. I don't think there was more than one night during that whole school year when Brianna Lamb came over and joined Ashley for a sleepover up at our town house in Tennessee. But I was happy to have her that one time she did come over. Ashley loved going over to the Lambs' big house with its fancy pool in the backyard, too. She would sleep over there now and then. There was a closeness to this whole community.

The Walker children were always around. In fact, hanging out at the Potters' pool together made me like Kim Walker even more than I had before. Her kids would wind up coming over for sleepovers, and in time I got to know her husband, too. Even though she was so young, I could be myself around Kim. I noticed early on that it wasn't quite like that with Kelly or Sandra.

To be frank, Kelly's behavior was all over the map. That spunky personality of hers could turn unkind, bordering on nasty at times. She made remarks about other people that made me uncomfortable. Sandra would do that, too. I had an uneasy feeling about her, but she was such a "Tonya fan" that I brushed it off. It felt good to be the object of her praise in school and around town. Who wouldn't want to be talked up in all sorts of glowing ways by a woman who seemed to be so well-known throughout the community?

In the spring, I decided to start looking around at houses in Chickamauga. I told everybody I knew that I was on the hunt, just in case anybody knew of a nice place opening up. That's when something funny happened that I've thought back to time and again. The principal at the school pulled me into her office one day and said, "Don't do it."

"Don't do what?" I asked her. She and I seemed to see eye to eye on almost everything when it came to education, so I wasn't sure what she was talking about.

"Don't move here," she said.

"What? What do you mean?"

"Do not move here. It's the most drama-filled place—just do not buy a house here," she said. "It's just—you do what you're told here, and if you didn't grow up here, you're always going to be an outsider. I won't be the principal here forever. I'm not going to conform to what everybody wants. They don't like it. And they get rid of people who don't conform to their ways."

I remember thinking that she must have been exaggerating. People exaggerate all the time just because they've had one bad experience or something. So I listened but I didn't really pay attention to a word she said.

In May of 2006, I bought a comfortable little three-bedroom house. It was beautiful. It was brick in front and had tan siding on the sides and back with green shutters, in a brand-new development on the edge of town. In fact, a small part of the development crossed the border out of Walker County, where Chickamauga is located, and carried over into Catoosa County. That's where my house was—not that it would make a difference, as far as I knew.

We were the first people to buy a house in that whole development. I bought it with no cosigner, either. For the first time in my life I had a home in my name, and my trusty old SUV was paid off, too, which made me proud.

I can hardly explain how excited Tyler and Ashley were to have a new house to call their own. Not to mention how excited I was to be setting down some roots that felt solid.

Before I drifted off on our first night in the house, I sat there and watched my kids sleep, just as peaceful as could be. For the first time in ages, I felt like I was home.

Chapter 5

After getting off the phone with the attorney, I managed to stay calm for a little while. I went back to telling myself it would all be okay. *I haven't done anything wrong. They can't arrest you if you haven't done anything wrong.*

I talked the whole thing through calmly for a while with Tammy and my parents, and I eventually decided I should get the kids out of there. They didn't need to see or hear any of this. I directed my father to go take the kids for ice cream. The kids loved their Pop-Pop and would jump at the chance to go out for ice cream with him. Joal was scheduled to pick them up in a couple of hours anyway for his weekend visitation, so my dad could just have him pick the kids up at his house instead. It made sense.

My mom insisted she would stay behind. She knew I needed her.

As Tammy helped usher the kids into their bedrooms to change out of their bathing suits, Ashley started crying. She demanded to know what happened, and of course none of us would tell her. What could we say?

The attorney finally called back just as the kids came out the front door. I blew by them with the phone to my ear, rushing inside and closing the door behind me so I could find some quiet. I realized I didn't say good-bye to Tyler and Ashley. I didn't give them a kiss or tell them I loved them. Even though I knew they'd only be gone for a little while, it bothered me that I didn't stop to kiss my children good-bye. It all happened so quickly.

"I've made a whole bunch of calls on this, Tonya. The first call I made was to Buzz Franklin, the DA, and I have to tell you, he had never heard the name Tonya Craft. He had no knowledge of a case against you whatsoever," he said.

"What does that mean?"

"Well, that's what I wanted to know and what *he* wanted to know. So he said he was going to make some calls and get back to me. I also left multiple messages for Tim Deal, who has yet to call me back, and tried some other sources. But Buzz finally called me back just a minute ago—"

"And?"

"And . . . he said that there were too many holes in the case, and that an arrest warrant would not be issued."

"Oh, thank God. Thank God."

"So you're gonna be okay. All right, Tonya? Nothing's going to happen to you. You're not going to get arrested. I don't have all the answers, and I wish I had more to tell you. But at this point, I'm confident that nothing is going to happen immediately, and that you and I can meet on Monday morning and work this all out. Okay?"

I took a deep breath.

"Okay," I replied.

As we set up an appointment for first thing Monday, I looked up and saw that my mom and Tammy had both come back into the house. I gave them a little smile and nodded, like it was all going to be okay. They seemed relieved. I seemed relieved.

My mom got me a glass of water. Tammy gathered up Hunter, gave me a great big hug, and said she'd call in a little while to check on me.

Before she got out the door, though, the phone rang again. I got a bad feeling.

"Hello?"

"Is this Tonya Craft?" the man said.

"Yes."

"Why are you not at the police station like you said you would be?" He started yelling. "I can only presume that your absence means you're guilty?"

"Can I ask who this is?"

"This is Detective Tim Deal, Tonya, and your lack of cooperation can only mean one—"

"Detective, I told you I am more than willing to cooperate, to come in for an interview, even take a polygraph as long as my attorney is present, and my attorney has left numerous messages for you—"

"I do not work for your attorney. I have no obligation whatsoever to return his call. Ms. Craft, I just want to enlighten you to the fact that if you refuse to cooperate with an interview with myself and Detective Keith at this time, it will result in your immediate arrest."

"I want to cooperate, if you'll just call my attorn—"

"I am not concerned about your attorney. I am only concerned with you, and you have now left me no choice."

The next thing I heard was a dial tone.

I freaked out. My mom and Tammy insisted I call my attorney back. So I did. "He's bluffing. There is no arrest warrant, and there won't be. Don't worry, Tonya! We will work it all out on Monday!" he said.

His tone was nonchalant, almost jovial. Yet "worry" didn't begin to describe what I was feeling. *Why would a detective lie to me? What does the attorney mean by "he's bluffing"? Is this some kind of good cop/bad cop thing like you'd see on TV? What in the world is going on?*

I felt weak. I decided to go to my bedroom to lie down, and Tammy followed me in.

"Were the kids okay when they left?" I asked her.

"Tyler seemed fine, but Ashley . . ."

"What?"

"She was crying."

I could see Tammy was extremely upset. "What, Tammy? Tell me."

"The tears were just streaming down her little face, you know? I told her everything was going to be okay, but she started sobbing and screaming, 'No, it *won't* be okay! No, it *won't* be okay!' She kept screaming the whole time your daddy drove them away."

Tammy started crying and I just couldn't take it. I lay down and curled up into the fetal position and cried, too. Time seemed to slip away as I lay there on my bed. I couldn't sleep. I couldn't get up. I just lay there, shivering, wishing it would all go away.

I tried to stop myself from thinking the worst. I told myself over and over, *It's gonna be okay. It has to be okay. My babies are going to be okay. This'll all be cleared up Monday morning. This'll all get worked out Monday morning—*

That's when the doorbell rang. Again.

Chapter 6

"You did *what*?!"

Kelly's shout startled me. It was the afternoon of the last day of the 2005–06 school year, just after we'd moved into our new house. Ashley and I were over visiting with Chloe and her mom. Ashley and Chloe had been playing quietly together in Chloe's bedroom, and Kelly had just gotten up to go see what they were doing, but her scream sounded really hysterical. *Oh, brother. What'd the girls do now?* I wondered. Then all of a sudden I heard Chloe scream bloody murder. I ran in to find Kelly beating her child with a belt.

"What is going on?" I shouted, but Kelly just kept yelling at her daughter.

"I told you not to do that!" she yelled while she whacked her. Chloe was squalling something awful.

That bedroom couldn't have been twenty steps from where Kelly and I were watching TV and talking in the living room of their little farmhouse. Kelly and her husband, Jerry, who worked as an EMT, tended the farm in exchange for free rent and some additional pay. The big piece of land it sat on was owned by a local doctor. It was a nice setup but a ton of work for Jerry, who was also training to work on a medevac helicopter. I always wondered how he managed to do it all.

Anyway, Ashley was crying, and I couldn't get an answer from anyone about what happened. Kelly just plain lost it.[4] I couldn't imagine what Chloe could have done to elicit that kind of a response. I didn't want my daughter caught up in the middle of it, so I decided to get her out of there.

Ashley cried almost the whole ride home. I don't think she'd ever seen someone's mother get that mad before, and Ashley certainly had never been treated in that manner. I tried to ask her to tell me what happened once we got home, but she did what a lot of kids do when they see grownups getting angry: She shut down, shrugged, and avoided my questions. So I just did my best to calm her down. Once she was quiet, I went into the other room and called Kelly.

"Chloe and Ashley were *touching* each other," Kelly shouted through the phone. "Down there!"

I was surprised of course, and concerned—what mother wouldn't be? But all I could think was, *You hit your child with a belt because of that? And screamed at her?*

"Chloe said that Ashley was pointing at her, but Ashley's the one who started it, Tonya. Ashley started it," Kelly said, real insistent.

"Well, hold on now. Kids are kids, and kids blame each other for things. Did you see what happened?"

"No, but I'm telling you, she had to learn this from somewhere. Kids don't just do this sort of *touching* unless they learned it somewhere. Clearly Ashley's been molested, Tonya. I should know, because my husband was molested when he was a child."

I was appalled by what she said. *Why would she reveal something that personal and sensitive about her husband? What does that have to do with this?* Ashley was four years old. Chloe was right about the same age. Kelly herself said she didn't see what happened, and even if she did, all I kept thinking was that it's not that unusual. Kids sometimes touch each other at that age. Any teacher has to learn about this stuff in their education classes because it's a part of childhood development. Kids get curious about their own bodies, they touch themselves, and sometimes they touch each other as a way to explore and learn about the human body, too. It's a normal course of development even if it makes people uncomfortable to think about, and it's up to us parents and caretakers to respond accordingly and to teach children what's appropriate and what's not. So if these girls really were touching each other "down there," then we certainly shouldn't be going into hysterics and making it a bigger deal than it was.

I tried to talk to Kelly about all of that, but she wouldn't listen. "Ashley's been molested," she insisted. "Mark my words."

I was speechless. It was Kelly who yelled at Chloe, "I told you not to do that!" *Why is she so adamant that my daughter started this if her daughter had obviously done something like this before?* I certainly wasn't going to try to turn this around on Chloe, and Kelly was still in such a semihysterical state that I could tell there was no reasoning with her. Plus, I didn't think blaming either child would have done any of us any good.

I didn't dismiss Kelly's accusation about Ashley. It made me sick to my stomach. *What if something happened to her and I don't know?* So as soon as I got off the phone I called our pediatrician, and the next day I took Ashley in for an exam just to be sure. I didn't want to turn a blind eye or overlook anything that might be wrong with my baby girl. Thankfully the doctor said she saw no signs of anything abnormal. She asked Ashley questions and gave her a thorough physical while I waited outside the room. When I came back in, she said she saw nothing out of the ordinary. Then she told me what I already knew: that sometimes children do these things, and it's up to adults to explain appropriate behavior and to draw the line at privacy and keeping our hands to ourselves.

I called Kelly and told her all of this, and she still wouldn't let it go.

"No kid would do something like that unless they had been molested," she kept insisting, and yet she didn't take her own daughter to see anyone for an exam. As far as I know, she didn't talk to any counselors about it or do anything to help Chloe in those next few days. Instead, she just stayed angry and kept laying the blame on my daughter.

That's when I backed off my friendship with Kelly McDonald. I didn't say, "I'm never going to talk to you again." I didn't make a big scene or talk about it with other people. I just backed off. Seeing the way she handled that whole thing, from the belt to the blaming, led me to determine that she was not a person I wanted to be around, and she was clearly not a person I wanted my children to be around, either.

I tried to let that incident go as best I could. I was focused on my studies, and I channeled my energy into running. I loved going for runs down the tree-canopied street outside our development, along those beautiful roads toward downtown Chickamauga, through majestic fields with the hay bales all caught up in the glow of the summer sunshine. When the kids were around, I'd stay home and run on the treadmill in the garage, using that physical push of my body as a time to clear my mind, to focus, and very often to pray. Aside from the Kelly and Chloe situation, I felt happier than I had been in as long as I could remember.

I had grown so close to the Potters that they asked me if I'd be interested in watching their children that summer. Mike and Dee both worked full-time, and they knew I didn't have another summer job. "You can watch them at our house, and bring your kids, and play in the pool all day," Dee said. "And we'll pay you, of course. We'd have to pay someone, so why not you?"

I was honored that they'd trust me with their kids like that, but I absolutely refused to get paid for it. Hanging out at a pool with other kids around to entertain my kids all day, I felt like I should be paying *them*!

The Potter kids would come to my house sometimes, too, and once in a great while, we'd go to the community pool, where all of the kids could play with lots of other friends from school who'd inevitably show up on the hot days. And whether it was the sound of the cicadas or the smell of the barbecue, that summer was one of my best summers ever.

The Potters and I hung out together when the kids weren't around, too. We even took an impromptu trip to Las Vegas one weekend when my kids were with their father. We shared a room due to my lack of finances, and the whole thing was a blast.

It all worked out so well that Mike and Dee asked if I'd be willing to let their kids hang out at my house after school in the fall, too, just until one or the other of them got out of work and could swing by and pick them up. There wasn't a moment's hesitation on my part. My door was always open, and I told them to just pop on in if I didn't hear the doorbell or something. As the school year went on, my home started to feel a little bit like Grand Central Station, there were so many kids and parents coming and going every afternoon.

I first met Tammy in the fall of 2006. Her son, Hunter, arrived in my classroom about three weeks after the school year had started. The principal called me in and said, "There's a little boy that's going to be here and it's a not-good situation. The parents are separating, and I thought you would understand what he is going through and have the personality to handle this."

I talked with Tammy frequently about how Hunter was adjusting and shared with her that my children had been through similar circumstances, so we had a common bond. Our friendship grew quickly.

When Tammy couldn't afford after-school daycare for Hunter, I offered to have him come over to my house after school every day. It truly became like a second home to him and to Tammy, too. The kids got along so well that we decided Hunter should stay with us during the workdays that following summer, too. One more kid in the house just meant more fun for Tyler and Ashley, as they mingled with the Potters and Kim Walker's kids. The fun never stopped!

Brianna Lamb was still coming to my classroom to hang out with Ashley almost every day after school before Sandra came to pick her up. Even though she'd moved on to first grade, I'd wind up seeing and talking to her and Sandra for at least a few minutes here and there on an almost daily basis during the whole 2006–07 school year.

Outside of school, Sandra and I still didn't really see each other. We would talk on the phone, and we'd invite each other's children over for the kids' birthday parties and things like that. But that was all.

I never would have imagined in a million years that before the '06–'07 school year was over, Sandra Lamb would introduce me to the love of my life.

Chapter 7

I jerked my head up to the sound of that doorbell, and the first eyes I met were my mother's. I could see her reaction to the terror in my face, and for the briefest moment, I pressed my eyelids shut as tight as possible, praying this was all just a nightmare. When I opened them again, I saw Tammy's silhouette in the bedroom doorway. Finally, together, the three of us walked to the front door.

Sure enough, it was them: Detective Tim Deal, Detective Stephen Keith, and someone I had never met before—an imposing presence of a man who towered over them and towered over me. There was no "hello" this time. No "sorry to bother you again, ma'am." No niceties whatsoever.

"Are the children home?" Detective Deal asked me the moment I got the door open.[5]

With all of the composure I could muster, I simply replied, "No."

That's all it took to uncork his rage. "So you're hiding them? Let me warn you that refusing to advise me of their current whereabouts is only going to get you into more trouble!"

As calmly as I could, I said, "Detective Deal, you did not ask me their location. You only asked me about their presence in my home. I'm more than willing to tell you where the children are. I was merely answering the question presented to me."

My calmness ticked him off even more. All of a sudden Deal's glare was full of fury and his face turned bright red as he pointed a finger at me and started warning me about how my "uncooperative nature" was going to result in my "arrest."

When his tirade concluded, I told him where my two children were. I told him that my ex-husband, Joal Henke, the children's father, would be meeting my own father to pick them up for his "normal weekend visit" after their trip to a local ice cream shop—at which point Detective Keith

28

spoke up and said, very specifically, "Joal knows nothing about this situation, and we're not going to tell him about it."

Wait a second. How does this detective know my ex-husband's name if he hasn't spoken to him? And he's on a first-name basis with him?

That's when they introduced the third visitor on my porch, a man by the name of Brandon Boggess. As I raised my eyes to look at this man who, no exaggeration, stood six foot five—maybe more—they told me he worked for DFACS, the Department of Family and Children Services. Much to my relief, this towering man had the first set of compassionate eyes I had encountered among these strangers that day.

"Is it okay if I come in?" Mr. Boggess asked. For some reason, without hesitation, I stepped aside and nodded. When the two detectives shifted their weight forward like they were going to follow him into my house, though, my instincts kicked in. I got this image in my head of Detective Munch on that TV show *Law & Order: SVU*—that quirky character who would get inside someone's house and just ramble aimlessly and sift through the inhabitants' personal belongings in search of clues. I quickly moved right into the pathway of those two men.

"*You* are not welcome into my house without a warrant," I said.

To this day I cannot explain how I got up the courage to do that. Somehow, deep down, I knew the damage that could be done by allowing them entry into my home. I just didn't trust them. But, boy oh boy, did that make them mad. They kept trying to convince me I *had* to let them in. Detective Deal even demanded access "to ensure the safety of Mr. Boggess"! Was he serious? He wanted to protect this giant of a man from me and the two other women in my home, whom he completely dwarfed in size? Mr. Boggess himself seemed taken aback by the idea of my being a "possible threat." He assured the detectives he was not in harm's way.

With that, they both backed off a bit, but they still insisted that I leave my front door open so they could "ensure Mr. Boggess's safety."

"Otherwise, you'll be under arrest," they said.

I had never had a run-in with the law in my entire life. Other than a few speeding tickets, my record was clean. I had no idea what my rights were or how far their tentacles actually reached. So I complied and left my front door open. The day was sweltering and I vividly remember the sweat rolling down the detectives' faces as they made threats from my porch. Their annoyance increased with each moment they spent in that heat.

Mr. Boggess had a completely different demeanor than those two. He talked to me calmly. He tried to explain the situation. We sat there for what felt like hours while he talked me through it. The fact was there was an accusation. More than one accusation. It was his job to make sure my children were safe, and he asked if I, as their mother, could understand the importance of that.

"Yes, of course," I replied.

Then he started talking to me about authorizing a "safety plan," just until everything got figured out. Because it was a Friday, and the offices that handle these situations wouldn't be open over the weekend, he basically wanted me to sign a piece of paper saying I would have no contact with my children until they were both interviewed on Monday, June 2, 2008. They needed to interview the kids to make sure that there was nothing going on in my home and that my children were not in any kind of danger. As a teacher, I'd been trained in this kind of stuff. It made sense that they'd want to protect the children when an allegation had been made against somebody—against anybody. I just wanted to know what I'd been accused of, how it happened, who said what—anything that I could wrap my head around. I repeatedly told them I hadn't done anything and certainly hadn't done anything to my own children. My home was as safe as could be, and I loved my children more than life itself. None of that seemed to matter.

"But the children aren't with me this weekend, anyway," I said. "They're with their father. You're welcome to call him. I'm sure he can keep them an extra night if it's necessary, until they can be interviewed. If you'd just talk to my attorney, he said we can get this all worked out on Monday morning. I'm sure of it."

Of course, my attorney was nowhere to be found. I kept calling and calling during this whole exchange, and he either wasn't available or simply chose not to pick up my call. I was forced to deal with this seemingly impossible situation on my own.

Mr. Boggess kept trying to explain, over and over, that the safety plan was necessary. It just didn't make sense to me. *Wouldn't it make more sense to say I can't have any contact with the three girls who supposedly accused me of molesting them? What does any of this have to do with my children?*

The more I talked and the more I tried to understand why I needed to sign this so-called "safety plan," the more irritated those two officers on the porch seemed to get.

"If you don't sign it, your children will be picked up in a squad car and taken to a foster home!" one of them yelled.

Mr. Boggess would always wait patiently when my tears would begin to flow, and then as soon as I could collect myself, he would resume where he had left off.

Following hours of unbridled confusion, I resolved myself to the only option I thought I had. Naïvely, I held fast to the fact that I had done nothing wrong. Knowing I had to do *something*, I maintained a mistaken confidence that the system would not fail me: a mother, a respected school-teacher, an innocent woman.

My hands trembled so violently I could barely maintain a grip on the pen he gave me. I signed the paper stipulating that I could have no contact whatsoever with my two precious children before Monday. No phone calls. No visits. No hugs. No kisses good night.

Mr. Boggess thanked me. He said he would be in touch after the interviews on Monday. Then he got up and left. The detectives left with him, without saying another word.

My home—which had just been filled by more turmoil and confusion than I'd ever known in my life, which just a few hours earlier had been filled with laughter, love, and the sounds of my children and their friend playing together—was suddenly eerily quiet.

All I could do was picture my kids having to sit down and answer unnecessary and horrendous questions about things they shouldn't even be aware of. About their own *mother*. All I wanted to do was to call them, to hear their sweet voices. I stood at the door with my back to the room, afraid to turn around to face my mother and Tammy. The quiet was awful.

I swear the only sound I could hear was the sound of my heart, breaking.

Chapter 8

After my divorce from Joal, I'd resolved that I was never going to get married again. I had done some dating. I had met a couple of men who got close enough to come hang out with me and my friends over a barbecue or over at the Potters' pool on a Saturday afternoon. But nothing was serious. I wasn't anywhere *close* to wanting to settle down with anyone. Frankly, I didn't have time or interest, and I certainly didn't have a "need" for a man in my life full-time.

Still, Sandra Lamb insisted she wanted to fix me up with someone, and it was her husband, Greg, who spoke up one evening and said, "What about David?"

"Oh my gosh, he'd be perfect for you!" Sandra said. David was a friend of Greg's, a real nice "country boy" who's an executive vice president of a very successful business, they told me. I rolled my eyes and almost told her to forget it. Everybody was always trying to fix me up with somebody they thought was "perfect" for me. They never came close.

I had also resolved that I would never, ever go on a blind date.

Never say "never," I suppose. My schedule was busy, and I only had every other weekend without the kids, so it took a while to set up. But in April of 2007, I wound up going out to dinner with Sandra and Greg Lamb and a man named David Craft. The three of them came together and picked me up at my house, and wouldn't you know it: I fell head over heels for the man.

We saw each other just about every single day after that first date.

David definitely was a good ol' country boy, just like they described. He had sandy-blond hair, and he loved bass fishing more than just about anything else in the world. He had skills manning the barbecue, which he used to impress me. (His bacon-wrapped filet mignon is to die for!) He was polite and well mannered. He also happened to be one of the most caring, gentle, kind, and generous men I'd ever met in the whole wide world.

And the Lambs weren't lying when they said he was a successful, self-made man. He'd started by sweeping the floors in the business he was in, a company that sold industrial ovens to all sorts of businesses all over the world. He'd worked his way up through every job in the company until he was finally named executive vice president a few years back.

He had a beautiful house up in Soddy Daisy, about ten miles north of where I grew up. He had a nice bass boat (his pride and joy). He could afford to take me to the sorts of restaurants that Sandra and Greg liked to go to, so the four of us started to hang out together quite a bit. It was fun. You never would have known David had money by looking at him. He wasn't flashy at all. He was humble. "Down-to-earth" is a phrase people use too often, but that's really just how he was.

We fell in love almost instantly, and it didn't take long before I introduced him to my kids. They fell in love with him, too.

Sandra was so thrilled that the two of us hit it off, and so proud that she had played the successful matchmaker, that she took us on as one of her "projects." Sandra always seemed to have "projects," whether it was remodeling her house—because, well, it was just remodeled four months ago and it needed updating—or seeing to it that David and I would live happily ever after.

Don't get me wrong. When David and I started dating, it was clear as day that the two of us were going to wind up getting married. Sandra just sort of jumped right in and pushed things along. She went to look at a ring with David. She actually saw my engagement ring before I did! She organized the whole wedding herself and insisted that we get married at her house. She decided she was going to be my maid of honor, and she had such a strong personality that I said, "Okay!" *If you want to plan my whole wedding, that means I don't have to do the work. I'm good with that!*

I was surprisingly ready to jump in with both feet, and that's certainly what I did with David. We met in mid-April, and we set a wedding date of July 7—07/07/07—which had a nice ring to it.

Chapter 9

I felt dizzy. My mother and Tammy grabbed hold of me and led me to the sofa, where we all sat silently for what felt like ages. I suppose they didn't know what to say after the day's events. My throat was too constricted to speak. I sat in shock, trying to grasp some kind of understanding of this nightmare my life had just turned into.

When my dad came by to pick up my mom, she was reluctant to leave. I told her I would be okay, even though I doubted that very much. But Tammy promised to stay the night after she dropped Hunter off at his father's for the weekend, so my mother agreed to go.

Tammy left soon after with Hunter, who had tears streaming down his face. He didn't understand what was going on, but even a kid could tell that something devastating had happened in that house that day. After waving good-bye, I walked back into my house alone for the first time since those men first showed up. I felt like a ghost of myself. I didn't know what to do. There was nothing I could do. No one else I could call. I made my way to Tyler's bedroom. I looked over and saw Froggie, the stuffed animal that my son slept with every night. I grabbed hold of it and clutched it in my arms and wept.

Eventually I walked out and collapsed onto the couch. I didn't move until the ringing of my cell phone snapped me back to attention. I looked at the clock. It was 7:21 P.M. The screen displayed the number of Ashley and Tyler's stepmother—the same mobile phone Ashley would sometimes use to call me when she was at her father's for the weekend. I desperately wanted to answer, but I couldn't. I had placed my signature on that deplorable piece of paper forbidding me to have any contact whatsoever with my own children. So instead I sat there clutching the phone until it stopped ringing. Then I waited and waited, anxiously hoping to hear the "ding" that meant I'd received a message.

"Ding!"

With shaking hands, I lifted the phone to my ear and I heard my six-year-old baby girl, Ashley. Whispering. Almost like she was hiding and trying not to be heard: "Hey, Mommy. I love you. Bye. I won't be seeing you for a very long time. Love you. Bye."

Chapter 10

Looking back, I guess it seemed a little over-the-top to have a "beach wedding" around a pool in a backyard in Georgia. It took a dump truck full of sand to pull off the look. But with Sandra making all the plans and David writing all the checks, I was happy to just let it unfold while I tried to stay focused on everything else that was going on in my life.

As July 7, 2007, came around, I was ready to enjoy myself—and to finally become Mrs. David Craft in the eyes of friends, family, God, and my children. It was a beautiful afternoon that flowed into quite the party that night. With the twinkling lights and tiki torches, it really felt like a beautiful beach getaway. All the kids (except for Brianna, since it was her house) eventually went for sleepovers elsewhere as the DJ turned up the volume. Everything in my life was so good at that moment that I decided to really cut loose. I drank more than I should have. Vodka and red-raspberry Crystal Light with water was my drink of choice—and I swear before I could empty a glass, Greg Lamb would come along and put another full one in my hand. Toward the end of the evening, I'm pretty sure he was skipping the water part.

At one point, David and I jumped right into the pool with all of our clothes on. A whole bunch of other partygoers jumped in, too. The thing I remember most about the whole evening is how much laughter there was. Everyone seemed to have a great time.

Thankfully we didn't have to worry about driving. We'd made arrangements with the Lambs to spend our wedding night in one of the guest rooms at their sprawling house. Still, I shouldn't have consumed so much alcohol. I wound up getting sick in the middle of the night. I didn't make it to the bathroom and left a red stain on the Lambs' carpet. I was mortified. David rented a portable carpet cleaner the next day, and when the stain didn't come out, we insisted that we'd pay to replace the carpet. But Sandra and Greg wouldn't hear of it. Sandra just laughed and laughed when she learned what I'd done. It seemed as if my behavior that night didn't bother her in the slightest. It bothered me, though. I was incredibly disappointed in myself, but I think Sandra enjoyed the funny story she got out of it, and it certainly didn't deter her involvement in my life. She even tried to convince us to buy a house right up the street from her.

I didn't want to uproot our kids from the perfect little life we'd created in Chickamauga, and David seemed perfectly comfortable with downsizing and moving in with the three of us. Lucky for me, my kids were comfortable with that idea, too.

When fall came, life only got better. I swear every night at our house was a party. Not literally, of course. I was always strict about my kids getting their homework done and eating a good dinner, and we always had a million things going on with the kids' schedules. But somehow with the four of us in that house, life was always *fun*. We used to sit and watch *Dancing with the Stars* as a family before the kids went to bed some nights. Tyler and I would get up and do our best Mel B and Maksim moves, trying to mimic the spins and dips they were doing on the dance floor, and then Ashley and David would get up there and do their best Hélio and Julianne, and we'd trade off and score each other, and of course we really couldn't do any of those moves so we'd wind up falling down and laughing like crazy.

I felt so blessed. You hear a lot about the difficulties of blending families after a divorce and remarriage. With us it was never difficult.

Maybe God knew we were going to have enough to deal with without having to deal with that, too.

The fall of 2007 kicked off beautifully in my work life as well. I dolled up my classroom all over again and met a whole new crop of kids and parents. Ashley was a kindergartner by then, so both of my kids were in the same school right down the hall from me and able to walk to my classroom at the end of the day.

I happened to have the daughter of Sandra Lamb's best friend in my class that year: a little girl named Lauren Wilson. Lauren's parents had actually requested me to be her teacher because of all the glowing things Sandra had to say about me. The principal told me that, which I thought was a bit strange. Parents aren't supposed to handpick their kids' teachers, but it seemed she'd obliged the Wilsons' request right away.

Lauren's mother, Sherri Wilson, and Sandra were like peas in a pod. Sherri stepped up the exact same way Sandra did to serve as a classroom mom before I had even asked for volunteers.

The thing about Sherri is that her last name preceded her everywhere she went. The Lambs might have been well-off, but the Wilsons had both money *and* power. They were one of the most powerful families in the whole region. The Wilsons owned Angel Ambulance Service, the ambulance company that served all of North Georgia and all the way up over the Tennessee border into Chattanooga. Sherri's husband, DeWayne, also happened to be the county coroner. The Wilsons were an old Chickamauga family, and from what I understood, they had millions upon millions of dollars' worth of contracts with the county. They even owned the local funeral homes. So the Wilsons had their hand in everybody's business, from life right on through death.

Brianna Lamb was a second-grader at that point, and she was good friends with Sherri's older daughter, Lydia, so that whole bunch of children would wind up hanging out in my classroom after school sometimes.

The thing is, just as I probably wouldn't have been friends with Sandra Lamb under any other circumstance, I probably wouldn't have been friends with Sherri Wilson, either. There was something about the combination of Sherri and Sandra that didn't sit well with me. It's almost as if they brought out the worst in each other, like they were tryin' to one-up each other at times in the way they spoke about other people. I couldn't help but wonder what they might be saying about me when I was out of their presence.

And heaven forbid anyone ever said anything critical about their children. Their children seemed to be off-limits to any sort of reprimand—and that is difficult when you are the teacher or adult who might ever have to correct them.

For the most part, though, Sandra's and Sherri's talk would just go in one ear and out the other. I didn't have any reason to focus on it. I was just a happy-go-lucky newlywed, blissfully enjoying everything and everybody. I was happy to have Sherri's help in the classroom and happy to see our kids getting along.

I use that word a lot when talking about those days: "happy." That's what I was. I was happy.

Chapter 11

*H**ey, Mommy. I love you. Bye. I won't be seeing you for a very long time. Love you. Bye.*

I listened to Ashley's message over and over. I couldn't stop. I couldn't understand why she would say something like that. When you don't have much to go on, you cling to things and try to dissect them and discern every little bit of information you can.

When Tammy returned after dropping Hunter off at his father's, I said, "You'll never believe the message that Ashley just left me." I repeated it to her word for word and then bombarded her with my thoughts on its oddities.

"Tammy, that detective said very clearly that Joal knew nothing about these allegations. Why would Ashley say she's not going to see me for a long time if somebody hadn't told her that? And why would they tell her? Joal must know something. He must! And what did he tell my kids? And why was she cryin' so hard when she left this house? Did she know something was happening even then?"

Tammy did her best to help me calm down. She tried to say I might be getting worked up over nothing, and maybe I should just take a step back. So I played the message for her so she could hear it for herself, and after hearing Ashley's voice she agreed with me.

"You're right, Tonya. It makes no sense," she said. "Somebody must've told her something."

We continued to analyze and scrutinize every aspect of every word I'd heard that day as the night progressed. Tammy also tried unsuccessfully to get me to consume even a small amount of food. My stomach would reject anything edible before it would reach my lips. The rest of the night devolved into a blur. I am aware that I spoke with my mother several times, and that I also phoned another very close friend of mine, Diana—who was not only shocked when I told her what was going on but also immediately jumped in to help me scrutinize the situation. I appreciated her directness and willingness to help.

Diana was a dear friend from Tennessee who had known me for a few years longer than Tammy—longer than any of these new friends from Chickamauga. To have her support in the middle of that first night meant the world to me.

As the night went on, I'd fall asleep, then wake in a state of panic. I was fearful that one of those times I'd doze off only to find law enforcement back at my door, busting in with a search warrant or arresting me after all. At some point well after midnight, I grabbed a permanent marker and wrote my attorney's phone number on both palms of my hands. Tammy wrote the number on both of her palms, too, in case she was the only one with immediate access to a phone line.

Every hour felt like days, and I couldn't imagine how I'd possibly make it through the weekend.

<hr>

"I think we should call some people," Tammy finally said in a hushed tone at the breakfast table on Saturday morning. I still couldn't eat or drink. I couldn't swallow. "Just some of your closest friends. To come over and pray for you. To pray about what's happening, and most of all to pray for your children. What do you think of that?"

Suddenly there was something uplifting and purposeful to focus on. Tammy made some calls, and that afternoon, seven friends showed up at my house. Seven people whom I had come to trust and love. None of them knew exactly why they had come. They just showed up because I needed them—yet each person who entered my house seemed to sense the unspeakable atrocity of the situation. The heaviness that permeated the air as I welcomed everyone was awful. Everyone took a seat in my living room and sat there, silently, until finally I sat down on an ottoman, tucked my feet underneath me, wrapped my arms around my body, and fixed my gaze on the floor while trying to gather the strength to say what I needed to say.

"I have been accused of sexually abusing three little girls," I said. "I wanted you to hear this from me before you hear it from anyone else. I want you to know that I didn't do it. I didn't do anything that could be misconstrued like this. I did nothing of the sort. I am innocent."

It was the first time I had uttered that phrase out loud.

"The detectives who showed up at my front door yesterday threatened to arrest me, but they didn't. As far as I know, a person cannot be arrested when they haven't done anything wrong. So I'll be okay. I've contacted an attorney and I have faith that the truth will come out, and this will all get worked out on Monday morning, but I'm having a real tough time right now. All I ask is that you pray for the truth, and pray for my babies—"

The tears flowed when I spoke of my children. I looked up for a moment and saw tears on just about everyone else's faces, too.

"Tyler and Ashley don't deserve to be put through this. So please pray for them, okay?"

Everyone had questions, of course. But no one seemed to question my innocence. No one who knew me, no one who cared about me, could possibly think I had actually done something to harm a child. Any child. I took some comfort in that. We talked, we cried, and we prayed.

As the day progressed, one by one, my friends had to leave to get home to their families and back to their lives. In my agony it felt as if the entire world were standing still. It was difficult for me to accept that life around me was still going on. Diana and Tammy both stayed with me into the evening and persuaded me, finally, to eat a little something.

Diana realized how worried I was about my children and how this would affect them. She insisted I get in touch with an attorney she knew through church up in Tennessee. An attorney named Clancy Covert. Diana put us in touch on the phone that day, and I told him most of what had happened. We made an appointment for Monday afternoon—hopefully late enough that I'd have already met with my local attorney and heard back from Brandon Boggess about the interviews with my kids, so I could bring them back home. So much would be happening that Monday, it was overwhelming for me to think about. It's difficult to keep track of a schedule when you're so panicked you can barely force yourself to eat.

Diana saw how distressed I was and she asked if I'd like to come spend the night at her home on Sunday. "You could just come back with me after church," she said. Tammy would have to go home and take care of Hunter that night, and I'll admit I was scared to death about staying in my house alone. I was terrified those men were going to come back and arrest me, so I was very thankful for Diana's offer.

"My home is your home," Diana said. "Stay as long as you want to."

"Thank you," I replied. "I'm sure it'll just be for one night. But thank you."

Chapter 12

On our first Christmas as newlyweds, David helped me buy the kids more presents than I'd ever seen under a single Christmas tree. I'd always taught my kids the true meaning of Christmas and the value of giving more than receiving. Just the Christmas before, I had noticed a homeless man sitting off by himself at the gas station. I brought my kids home and we fixed up a hot dinner plate for that man, and we drove right back to the gas station and gave it to him. Tyler had asked, "But, Mommy, aren't you scared of him?" And I'd explained that I wasn't.

"We're all here to help each other out on this earth," I had told him.

I'd always done things like that with the kids all year long, not just at Christmastime. Still, as a single mother who didn't make very much money and who had to skimp on gifts the three years prior, watching my kids' faces light up when they laid eyes on all those presents under our tree on Christmas of 2007 filled my heart.

I had David to thank for so much of the new happiness in my life. It's almost like he was the reward God gave to the kids and me after my divorce from Joal—for making it through the challenge of starting over.

My relationship with Joal is one of the most difficult things to talk about in my life, in part because I was still married to my first husband when Joal and I initially got together. I'm not proud to admit this, but I've actually been married three times. The first marriage was simply a matter of marrying too young. I married my high school sweetheart. My parents knew it was a mistake. On my wedding day, right before he walked me down the aisle, my daddy made a last-ditch attempt to get me to call it off: He offered me a large sum of money not to go through with it.

I was so young and bullheaded that his offer just made me more determined than ever to prove him wrong. The simple truth of the matter is that I was in love, and my first husband loved me with all his heart. I know that. But over the course of those first few years out of high school, I grew up. I changed. He didn't. I never had harsh feelings toward him. I loved him and he loved me, but the relationship was not a healthy one.

I had taken my love of sports and turned it into a love of fitness in my early twenties. Fitness competitions were all the rage at that time, and I found myself entering and placing pretty well in my fair share of them. Being a part of that glamorous fitness world was a complete escape from the Tennessee country life—and the Tennessee country boy I married. So when a charismatic man named Joal Henke came around, he charmed me. He told me he was part owner of the gym that was now my sponsor for the competitions, and we wound up spending a great deal of time together.

Looking back on it, I don't know if what Joal and I shared was ever truly love. It was passion. It was fascination. It was fun. Why I thought that was enough to make a marriage work, I don't know. It turned out that he didn't own the gym. For some reason I let that lie go, the same way I let go of rumors that Joal was a ladies' man—I simply chose not to listen.

Three months after we got married, just as soon as we started trying, I got pregnant with Tyler. It seemed meant to be. Joal was thrilled. When I got pregnant with Ashley two years later, though, Joal was not as enthusiastic. Things went south between us pretty quickly.

Somehow, my leaving Joal seemed to be the greatest insult he'd ever endured. He seemed to turn every bit of hatred he had in the world on me. I would face his wrath through a long, drawn-out, bitter divorce proceeding for nearly two years of my life—the two years right after Ashley was born in 2002.

The bitterness wouldn't end when the divorce was finalized, either. Joal finally signed off on my divorce agreement after being faced with some information my private investigator turned up, but then once it was over, I felt as if Joal kept taking digs at me. I'd heard that he was talking about me behind my back. It seemed to me that he tried to manipulate my children into thinking I was a bad person. But there came a point when I decided I would face his words and actions with as much dignity and grace as I could.

One day at the park, I witnessed a divorced couple yelling and screaming in front of their crying children, and I made a vow right then and there: "I will never, ever have my little kids' tummies hurt just because their dad and I are in the same room."

It wasn't easy. But I often told people, "I don't care what Joal does. I'm only responsible for my actions and reactions."

I managed to pull it off so well that the first time my friend Dee Potter met Joal, she thought the two of us were still married! I'm not saying I'm perfect. Clearly, I'm far from it. My relationship with my new husband, David, wasn't "perfect," either. We had all the normal ups and downs anybody else has. But compared to the awful marriage I'd been in before and the gut-wrenching divorce I'd been through, my life with David sure felt pretty close to perfect. I had just about everything I had ever wanted or even dreamed of wanting. And I was thankful for it.

Best of all, I had love.

———————•———————

Wouldn't you know it? The first big crack in my otherwise peaceful little snow globe of a life came the very next month—on January 18, 2008, to be exact. It was the day of Ashley's sixth birthday party.

With David's help, I went all out compared to Ashley's previous birthdays. She and her friends all gathered at my house, where my friend Shanica Lewis volunteered to get the girls glammed up. Shanica had done my hair and Ashley's hair for my wedding. She and I had become really close by then, and so had our children.

We hired a big stretch limo to pick Ashley and her girlfriends up once they were all made up, and we rode together to get ice cream in downtown Chattanooga. Then we came back for pizza and presents, and all the girls changed into pj's for a big sleepover.

Both Lauren Wilson and her older sister, Lydia, were at that party. Lydia is closer to Tyler's age, but it didn't feel right not to invite her. And since Lydia was close friends with Brianna Lamb, and Ashley and Brianna still played together after school sometimes, we invited Brianna to come along, too.

The party itself was a hit. All the kids had fun. The parents had fun. The few who stayed got a chance to hang out and talk in between cake and ice cream and presents. I've got picture after picture of all the girls playing and jumping around and smiling, including the older girls, Brianna and Lydia. The plan was for all the kids to spend the night, to make it a big slumber party. But as I walked up the steps near the bonus room where the kids were playing at one point, I heard Ashley crying. Brianna and Lydia were there with her.[6]

"This is a *baby's* birthday party," one of the girls said.

"We just wanted to come ride in the limo, and we weren't planning on spending the night anyway," said the other.

That's when I stepped in. I dealt with this sort of stuff in kindergarten every day, and I handled it the same way I would in school. I squatted down to their eye level and I said, "That was a very unkind thing to say. How would you feel if someone said that same thing to you at *your* birthday party?"

Both the girls had a bit of an attitude about it: "Well, I wouldn't care," and, "If someone wants to go home, they can just go home if they want to."

"Well, I know you say that," I said to them, "but we need to say things that are kind, and we need to consider how it feels to Ashley."

The girls didn't take too kindly to my correcting them. They asked if they could call their moms to get picked up early, so they could go stay at Lydia's house instead. I let them use the phone. I also told Ashley, "I know your feelings were hurt, but we're fine now. Let's let it go and go play." Ashley listened and went back to having fun. In fact, all the girls went back to playing, including Lydia and Brianna—right after they made their phone call.

I had a feeling that wasn't the last I was going to hear about it. I went downstairs, and Shanica was still there, and David was there, and I said to them both, "All right. I did it. I just ticked off the two most influential people in Chickamauga." What I meant was that I knew as soon as those girls went home and told their moms that I'd got onto them, their moms were going to get mad. Not at them, but at *me*. That's just how they were.

A little while later, Sherri Wilson came and picked Lydia and Brianna up, and we all said "bye" and that was that. There was no apparent drama. There were no tears or anything. Lauren Wilson (the younger of the Wilson sisters) even stayed for the sleepover.

After that night, Sandra Lamb never spoke to me again. Brianna stopped coming down to my classroom after school. When I saw Brianna in the hall, she wouldn't speak to me. In fact, there were times when that little girl would glare at me. I figured it would eventually blow over, but then Sherri Wilson called me and said she wanted to know why I'd "yelled" at her children. She wanted to know why I'd apparently told them that they weren't welcome back at my house ever again.

I said, "Sherri, does that sound like anything I would ever say?"

I tried to tell her what had really happened, but Sherri was mad. She didn't believe me. I said, "Sherri, I'm not going to argue with you. You heard the kids' version. I'm telling you from an adult's perspective what happened."

Sherri was still my homeroom mom at that point, and she quit coming into my classroom. So suddenly I was left without help in the mornings at school. All because I asked her daughter and Brianna Lamb not to be unkind to Ashley.

David was shocked at how right I was in my assessment of the situation. I tried not to let it bother me. In some ways, maybe it was better this way. As I'd gotten to know them better, I wasn't really comfortable with either of those moms.

But I'll be honest: When someone stops speaking to you, no matter who it is, it bothers you. I wished I could explain it to them and smooth everything over, but I knew from experience that there wasn't any talking to either Sandra or Sherri when they were angry.

What I didn't realize was just how angry they were gonna get.

Chapter 13

I only packed one change of clothes.

This would all get "worked out" on Monday morning. To me, the only possible interpretation of that statement was that I'd be back home with my babies by Monday night, and this whole unimaginable nightmare would be over.

That's what I kept telling myself as Tammy drove me to church to meet up with Diana. I couldn't drive. I was too scared I'd get pulled over and arrested for some reason. My emotions were still all over the place.

Walking into City Church, I wondered what people thought of my constant stream of tears. I took comfort in the fact that no one besides Diana and Tammy knew the awful thing those detectives had said I was accused of. I wasn't looking for sympathy or assistance or anything any person in that congregation could have offered that day. I wasn't even looking for comfort in the words of our pastor. The only reason I was there was to find strength in God. In my heart, no matter how many times I tried to convince myself it would all be okay, some part of me understood that I could not withstand this burden that had been placed on me all by myself. I prayed to God for strength.

I guess I didn't realize how deeply God had already been working in my life by providing my friend Diana. I would realize soon enough, though. That spunky church lady was so caring and mothering to me that people would sometimes ask if we were mother and daughter when we were out getting our nails done or something, even though she's only eight years older than me. She didn't like that very much, but we would laugh about it every time. I don't think it has anything to do with how she looks. She doesn't look old! There's something about the grace she exudes that just makes her seem motherly.

Diana took me back to her house, where I stepped into the lovely home she kept. I said hello to her husband, Michael, and their teenage son, Josh.

I put on a good face as she showed me to the guest room in the back of that house, tucked deep into a neighborhood around lots of corners and away from any main roads. I hoped no one could find me for a while. Other than Tammy and my parents, I didn't tell another soul where I'd gone. Not even my attorney. It just felt like the right thing to do.

I wasn't going to risk another ring of the doorbell.

After spending time at church, I showed up at Diana's full of grand notions and a renewed confidence in a legal system that promised "justice for all." We sat and prayed together, and I even ate a little dinner.

Then my attorney called to inform me that the interviews of my children would be postponed until Tuesday, due to "a change of staff members at the CAC."

"The what?"

"The Child Advocacy Center," he told me.

"So I have to wait a whole other day because of some staff change?"

"Unfortunately, that's just the way it is," he said.

"That safety plan I signed through Monday gets extended, just like that?"

"It does, Tonya. You just need to cooperate. Be patient, okay?"

It wasn't okay. I hung up the phone and relayed the whole conversation to Diana, who listened like an angel and then gave me the space I needed. When I'm really upset sometimes, I don't want anyone hugging me or touching me. I just want to be left alone. I went to the guest room and closed the door.

I went to bed that night panicking again. After all that hope, knowing at the very least there was a plan to get some answers and put this behind me, now I had no idea what Monday would bring and could hardly imagine waiting through another twenty-four hours. Worse, I had no idea what my kids were being told about the situation. I knew they'd be asking all kinds of questions. I kept thinking back to Ashley's message. I had a bad feeling that Joal was already messed up in this somehow. It was more than a feeling. I *knew* it. It was clear that he had been told about the allegations, at the very least, and, if my gut was right, that he was actually a part of all of this. I was terrified about what he might say or do to make things worse.

I hadn't done anything. I kept telling myself that my innocence would surely shelter me from any lies anyone might make up. Those detectives couldn't have any evidence against me when there wasn't any evidence to be found. I naïvely thought that would protect me.

Chapter 14

Mid-February was the time of year when we started having meet-ings with parents to discuss whether their children might need to be retained or placed in Pre-First—a wonderful, child-centered program that Chickamauga offered for kindergarteners who weren't quite mature enough either emotionally or academically to handle the transition to first grade the following year. It wasn't a done deal at the first parent-teacher meeting. It was more of a heads-up so that parents weren't surprised by the news at the end of the school year and so that maybe we could find new ways to help the children work toward some goals.

One of the families I had to call in that February of 2008 was the Wil-sons. Lauren was only four years old at the start of the kindergarten year. The assessments made by me and other professionals showed she would benefit from Pre-First rather than going on to first grade, so we called in Sherri and DeWayne to talk about it.

It was the first time I had conversed with Sherri since her phone call after the birthday party incident, and instead of taking the news thought-fully, like most parents do, she and DeWayne got angry. At *me*.

"You're just doing this because we're not friends anymore," Sherri said.

She accused me of trying to "socially devastate" her child.

Lauren had been working with a specialist at school. There was all kinds of documentation. I didn't arbitrarily pick Lauren out for this, and a final decision hadn't even been made, but their take on it was "There is no *way* you are getting away with this. No daughter of ours is going to *Pre-First!*"

Sherri Wilson said "Pre-First" like it was a cuss word.

Over the course of the next couple months, the Wilsons kept repeating that sentiment—not only in meetings with me and the specialist and the school counselor but also to the new principal of Chickamauga Elemen-tary. The old principal—the one I had gotten along with so well, the one who had told me "don't do it" when she heard I was looking to buy a house in Chickamauga—had moved on just like she said she would. She'd told me she felt "pushed out," and I was starting to think that maybe she was.

The new principal was a Chickamauga native and was friendly with the Wilsons. She made it clear to me that I should just let Lauren go to first grade. "No," I said. "She's not ready. You've seen her documentation. You know this isn't me trying to hold Lauren back. She needs some time to mature."

The principal nodded but wouldn't budge. "It's not worth it. Just make it easier on everyone," is what I heard her say.

"If this family was living in the trailer park, we wouldn't even be having this discussion," I commented. "If Tyler or Ashley were being put into Pre-First and I came in here and pitched a big enough fit, would you just pass them, too?"

I wasn't one to talk back very often. I take things in stride. But when something is worth standing up and fighting for, I have a tendency to speak my mind, and I had to do what the assessments indicated was right for that child.

It seemed to me that the principal was furious at me for my assessment, and clearly so were the Wilsons. I bucked the system—and they *were* the system. The Wilsons were used to getting whatever they wanted. People simply didn't stand up to them.

I did.

<hr />

It's hard enough to deal with one fire at a time. I wish somebody would explain to me why so many of life's fires always come in twos, or threes, or fours, or more.

Right at the time this whole situation was unfolding with the Wilsons, my daughter, Ashley, said something to me that caught me completely off guard.

"You and Mommy Sarah are different," she said.[7]

Sarah is the young bride that Joal had taken after we divorced. She was Tyler and Ashley's new stepmother—a woman so young that she had actually been one of my students in Sunday school years earlier.

"How so?" I asked, thinking Ashley would say that Sarah was taller or played basketball better than me.

"Because she does not have hair down there," Ashley said.

To say her words shocked me doesn't do it justice. I was floored.

I simply nodded and said, "Oh." I'd learned enough in all of my training as a teacher not to overreact when a child says something shocking,
especially in a realm that involves anything of a sexual nature. You don't
want the child to shut down or stop talking, and you don't want to put any
thoughts into their head that might not be there already. So I did my best
not to overtly question her about how she knew this about her stepmother
or to make her feel uncomfortable about it no matter how uncomfortable
it made me feel. Clearly she wanted to get this off her chest, so I let her talk.
And talk she did.

It turned out that Ashley had been taking baths and showers with her
stepmother.[8] *What on earth is Sarah doing showering with my daughter?*

Keeping calm when your child tells you something like that is not an
easy thing to do. I bit my tongue so hard it almost bled, especially when she
spontaneously told me that her dad "sat on a stool in the bathroom, outside
the shower" when they were in there.

Ashley was six. I had bathed with her myself until about six months
before that moment. I'm her mother. It's normal. And it's normal that she
would notice the difference between the way her mother looks and the way
her stepmother looks. I just didn't think it was "normal" or at all appropriate that she was showering with this woman.

I didn't want to tell her she *shouldn't* shower with Sarah. I didn't want to
make Ashley feel bad about doing something that wasn't her fault. I would
never automatically think something improper was happening with my
daughter at her father's house, either. It just made me very uncomfortable.

So before I made a big deal about it, I asked a few colleagues, rather
quietly, what they thought of somebody's stepmother taking showers with
a little girl. Not one of them thought it was appropriate.[9] Every one of them
made the face I'm sure I did before trying to hide my feelings about the
situation from Ashley.

Approaching the subject with Joal would be tricky. I knew that. I was
afraid of his reaction. I was concerned that he would deny it and become
angry, and it would cause a huge rift in our relationship as parents.

As I've already mentioned, Ashley and Tyler only stayed with Joal every
other weekend, so I took a little time to think about this, and I decided I'd
better not bring it up right away. I thanked Ashley for telling me, and I
reminded her that she could talk to me about anything. I did that in a general way, not directly tied to what she told me, just as I did with Tyler, and

just as I had done with both of them for as long as I could remember. They knew I was there for them. Always.

Then the subject got a whole lot more complicated. Ashley came home after one weekend at Joal's and told me that she'd learned how to shave her legs—from Sarah. Ashley had just turned six. *There isn't a six-year-old girl on the planet who needs to know how to shave her legs*, I thought.

"Well, what did she show you?" I asked.

Ashley talked about soaping the leg all up, and just shaving in one direction, 'cause the razor's real sharp and you could cut yourself if you moved it side to side, and being careful around the knee—"and then you have to make sure you pull back the skin when you shave around your vagina," she said.

I was floored. Ashley knew the word "vagina." I had always taught my kids appropriate anatomy. But I had to do everything in my power not to show Ashley the horror I was feeling at the thought that Sarah was showing hers off in the shower.

"Um . . . tell me more about that," I said.

"I helped her."

"You helped her? How?"

"With the razor."

Showering was one thing. If she had let my daughter "help" her shave her lady parts, that would set off a whole *sea* of red flags for me.[10] I didn't want to alarm Ashley, though. "Well . . . just be real careful that no one gets cut with a razor, okay?" I told her.

I didn't know what else to say. I really didn't.

I remember telling David that night, "I don't know what to do. This isn't right."

"Just call Joal up and tell them they need to stop," he said.

David still didn't seem to get it.

"I can't confront him like that. He'll say I'm lying. He'll say I made it up," I said. "I swear to you, if he thinks I'm accusing him or Sarah of something, he'll turn around and accuse me of doing something right back."

"Well, then I don't know. Just hope it doesn't happen again."

David seemed a little nonchalant about it. I didn't like that.

"I'll talk to the school counselor tomorrow. I'll see if maybe Ashley can talk to somebody. I can't just go forward without substantiating these allegations or Joal will turn this into a horrible fight and we'll never hear the end of it. I won't do that to the kids."

The next morning I went to the school counselor, who agreed that I was right to be concerned and also agreed that I should proceed very cautiously before making any allegations based on Ashley's words alone.[11] She had a friend who worked for the Department of Family and Children Services (DFACS), and she actually placed a call over there just to ask whether it was "normal" behavior to be showering and shaving like that with a six-year-old. The DFACS rep said, "That's inappropriate behavior."

As we all know, kids get confused. Kids tell stories. Kids say things out of context. Even our own kids, whom we think we know so well, sometimes say things that their little imaginations have made up all on their own. Any child psychologist with a credential to his name knows that, and most people who work with kids realize it, too. So I wanted to get some more objective advice about this and get someone qualified in this area to ask Ashley about it.

I called the Walker County sheriff for advice. I knew his wife from church, and he had his child investigator call me back. I was told that Ashley would have to repeat her story on the record before any charges could be made. I wasn't sure I wanted to put Ashley in that situation. I wasn't sure if there were any "charges" that needed to be filed. That's a lot of pressure to put on a kid. I wasn't looking to hurt Joal or Sarah with any of this. I just wanted to make sure my baby was okay.

I spoke to Ashley's teacher about it. I spoke to some friends who had experience with abuse, including a therapist friend who works with adult victims of child abuse. She recommended that I should talk to an attorney and that I should think about hiring someone nonbiased to interview Ashley. I wanted to make sure I did everything right, and although it seemed to be taking an excruciatingly long time, I took a one-step-at-a-time approach to getting to the bottom of it before accusing anybody of anything.

I prayed about it, and I kept going back to that promise I made never to fight with Joal in front of the kids. The whole thing ate me up inside. I wasn't sleeping well. I drove poor David nuts with all my wavering back and forth about what the next step ought to be, but he also wasn't being as caring as I thought he ought to be.

Amidst the tension of everything that was happening with Ashley and trying to get to the bottom of it, the tension of everything that was going on at school, and the pressure I felt from the new principal to conform, on top of juggling the kids, and baseball, and tumbling—I was stressed. And sometimes when I'm all stressed out I can be a bit of a pain in the tush. I realize this. I don't think David fully realized it because he had never lived with it before, but he sure realized it then.

Ashley started having severe stomachaches and other odd symptoms when she came back from her visits with Joal. That worried me. I hated seeing my baby sick and in pain—but what if it was a sign of something more? I wound up paying all sorts of extra attention to Ashley that spring. When her stomach was hurting, I'd lie with her in bed and sometimes fall asleep at her side. It got to a point where David started complaining that I wasn't spending enough time with him. He said that he felt I was "neglecting" him.

One night when he was particularly whiny about it, I said to him, "I'm your wife, not your momma. If you need a momma, there's the door!"

I know that wasn't the nicest thing to say, but I had a lot on my mind. I just assumed that David would stand by me and we'd get through all of this together. We were married. He was the love of my life. I knew he loved me back. What more was there to talk about?

Chapter 15

I was out in the garage, running on the treadmill, when I learned that my husband had left me. It was Friday, April 11, 2008.

"When are you coming home?" I asked David over the phone.

"I'm not," David said.

I jumped my feet off to the sides with the belt still whizzing by beneath me. "What do you mean?"

My friend Tammy was standing right there. She had just come over to pick up Hunter. She saw the look on my face and quickly went back inside the house.

"I'm not coming home. I'm done, Tonya."

His words shattered me.

"The kids are here," I said. "Tyler's got a ball game. What do you mean?"

"I'm just done," David said.

Tammy came back out and looked at me with this look of despair. I was so hurt I simply hung up the phone without saying anything.

"His closet is completely empty," Tammy said.

My husband's closet is empty?

There was no note. He hadn't called first or left a message. Nothing.

I can't explain how I got through the rest of that day. It's all a blur. I had things to do. I took Tyler to his game. I made dinner. I just did what I had to do and didn't breathe a word about that phone call to the kids or to anyone else. Tammy was the only one who knew.

The next morning, I called David again. "Can we talk about this?"

"There's nothing much to talk about," he said.

How could there be nothing to talk about?

"What should I tell the kids?"

"I don't know," he said. He was so distant I almost didn't recognize the sound of his voice. It was like he had already disconnected from our lives. He seemed emotionally dead.

"We need to sit and tell the kids together," I said, "don't you think?"

"No."

Maybe I was so caught up in my own life, and Ashley, and school, that I just didn't see it. I didn't see how he had progressed from the loving husband and father figure to this distant, cold person on the phone who'd left me without a word of warning. *How could I have missed the wall he was building up, when clearly that wall was gigantic?*

When the phone call ended, I decided not to tell the kids anything. I prayed that he'd come back, for their sake if not mine. I painted a smile on my face and went on with my days. When the kids asked where David was, I told them that he had to go away on a business trip and he wasn't sure how long he'd be gone. That was actually true. The trip didn't start until a few days after this, but David had to go all the way to Israel for a client. So I didn't have to lie to my children. I just had to hide some of the facts from them, and that alone broke my heart. I spent the whole weekend in a fog of confusion and heartache. The kids had made cards for David's birthday that Sunday, and I just kept up a happy face and stuck to my excuses. I told them we'd celebrate when he came back.

David and I had met just after his birthday a year earlier. We'd only been married for ten months. *We should be celebrating*, I thought.

Once the kids were in bed that night, I pretty much cried myself to sleep. Then I woke up Monday morning, alone, knowing I somehow had to find the strength to go battle the world by myself.

We had another meeting with the Wilsons to discuss Lauren's progress on Monday, April 14—"we" being the principal, the school counselor, the paraprofessional who worked in my classroom, and me. I was a bit of an emotional wreck going into that meeting. DeWayne and Sherri were highly upset. While we laid out a solid educational transition plan for their daughter, I teared up—not because I was afraid of them or upset about the situation with Lauren but because I was thinking about David and Ashley. All of a sudden DeWayne Wilson stood up, grabbed a book, and flung it forcibly across the table. It nearly hit me in the chest.

"Somebody dropped the ball!" he shouted. "Somebody's gonna pay! And we all know who *that* is!"[12]

He scared me. I left the meeting really shaken up. I must've looked weak in their eyes to be crying like that. But I still didn't budge when it came to recommending the correct course of action for Lauren. If I relented just because I'd made someone angry rather than staying focused on what was best for the child, I thought, I might as well retire right then and there.

After school on that very same day, I finally went to see a local attorney to discuss the showering situation with Ashley. It had taken me a while to get the appointment, so I couldn't cancel no matter how awful I felt. It was too important.

I sat down with him, one-on-one, for the very first time at his office in Catoosa County, and we discussed everything Ashley had told me. I didn't know much about that attorney at that point, other than the fact that David and I had paid him a lot of money to help my friend Tammy get through her divorce. He looked like a lawyer should look, with his lawyerly suit and tie. He agreed that I shouldn't proceed with filing any kind of a complaint until I had more to substantiate Ashley's claim. He also wanted me to make sure there wasn't anything more to the story. I had suffered that thought too many times to count, so to hear it from another human being made me sick to my stomach.

The attorney also clarified for me that I wouldn't be able to file any kind of a complaint about this in Georgia. Joal and Sarah lived in Tennessee. The abuse, if that's what this was, took place at their home. Therefore, I would have to file in a court up there if the time came.

He recommended an attorney up in Tennessee, a woman, and I told him I'd call her. I did. Of course, it would take a couple of weeks for me to get in to see her, too. Everything just kept stalling on me that spring.

The Wilsons refused to meet with me after the last meeting. Any other meetings that were held to discuss Lauren's future were held without me— even though I was her teacher.

This is also when word started to get back to me about the things Sherri Wilson and Sandra Lamb were saying about me around town.[13] I began to be very concerned that my job might be in jeopardy. I kept thinking about my former principal's warning about living in Chickamauga. *Are these die-hard Chickamaugans going to get me fired?*

Everything had been going so well for me at school until then. I could hardly believe how fast it all seemed to unravel. I kept asking myself, *How did this happen?*

The tension from the whole thing was bad enough that I started quietly looking around to see what teaching jobs might be opening up in surrounding towns. I had a feeling this wasn't going to end well. I felt like I ought to prepare myself for the worst.

I felt that way about the situation with Ashley, too. I finally got in to see the attorney up in Tennessee at the beginning of May, and we decided on a course of action, which was to have Ashley sit for an interview with a qualified forensic psychologist to see if we could really get to the bottom of what was going on at her dad's house. Finding someone qualified to do that kind of an interview with a child turned out to be quite a task. I made a ton of phone calls and researched online for hours and hours. I wasn't going to let just anyone interview my daughter about something so personal and potentially disturbing. This was just as big a deal to me as finding the right surgeon or specialist for my child if she had something physically wrong with her.

In fact, during that period just after David left, she actually *did* have something physically wrong with her: Ashley started suffering awful stomachaches and diarrhea. It got so bad that she developed a rash all over her bottom and under her privates. It irritated her so much that she couldn't sleep, so I put a little udder balm on that rash one night—it's an old-fashioned medicinal balm that is actually used on cow's udders, but it works wonders on rashes and skin irritations. It's one of those things a Southern grandmother would recommend, and it works like a charm. I tried to get Ashley to apply it herself, since she was old enough to do that sort of thing on her own, but she couldn't do it, so I finally told her, "Bend over," and I did it for her. I had used it for diaper rash plenty of times when the kids were little, and I hoped it would work just as well on Ashley at that age. I had a feeling it would.[14]

I was worried that her health could be a reflection of what she told me about those showering incidents, which was another reason I wanted to get her interviewed as quickly as possible by someone whose reputation was beyond reproach. This was serious stuff. I needed Ashley to speak to a qualified expert who could get to the absolute truth.

I had also managed to make it through almost an entire month without telling the kids that David was gone for good. He and I had been talking on the phone, and I kept holding out hope that he'd come around, so I kept putting it off. It was Mother's Day when Tyler finally started crying about it. "He's not ever coming back, is he?" Tyler asked through tears. I guess he knew, instinctively, that David never would have missed Mother's Day unless something was wrong. I told Tyler the truth, and then I told Ashley the truth, too. Both kids cried something awful, and so did I.

It was just about the worst Mother's Day I could imagine. Or so I thought.

———————◆———————

Finally, in mid-May, I found a qualified child psychologist and forensic interviewer to speak with Ashley. It would cost me an arm and a leg to hire that woman, which David complained to me about during one of our phone calls. But I wasn't going to mess around with this. It had to be done right. I made the earliest appointment I could, which was for June 12. It seemed like a long time to wait, but like I said, I was preparing myself for the worst, and making sure that interview was impeccably done meant a lot to me. I wasn't about to accuse somebody of something if they hadn't actually done anything wrong, but I was determined to protect Ashley with everything in me.

David and I saw each other a few times and talked on the phone now and then over the course of that May. But he didn't move back in. He didn't make any promises that he would, either. I don't think I had ever felt more alone in my life.

On the third Saturday in May, with just a week to go before the kids and I planned to tackle our first-day-of-summer celebration at the community pool, I sat in my house and wallowed in my own misery. Not just about David, but about everything. I felt lost. My whole life was a mess. And while I prayed to God to give me the strength to get through it and to bring my family back together again, I remember laughing to myself, too.

"Well," I said right out loud. "At least it can't get any worse!"

Chapter 16

After everything in my life unraveled so explosively on May 30, 2008, every thought, every action, every word, every moment that unfolded in the following days felt heightened. I wrestled with every decision I made. I worried, constantly, that with one mistake I could find myself in an even more horrific situation—if that was even possible.

I knew I needed help. So even though the interviews with my kids were being delayed, I kept my appointment to see the Tennessee attorney, Diana's friend Clancy Covert, on Monday. Once again, I had to sit there in front of a stranger and explain what had happened to me that weekend from start to finish. Only this time, as I sat there telling this attorney about the allegations that had been made against me, I also discussed the concerns I had regarding Ashley. I had waited too long to truly do something about the situation, and with everything that was going on, I simply couldn't wait any longer.

I brought Clancy up to date about the steps I had taken to deal with it, including setting up an interview with a professional child interviewer so I could get some totally unbiased information before I went ahead and made a stink about anything. That interview was scheduled to occur on June 12—ten days from that very Monday as I sat there explaining it.

With criminal allegations pending against me in Georgia, Clancy explained that Joal could file an emergency custody request with the court to keep the kids away from me. It killed me that I wasn't with my kids on Monday: I couldn't imagine not seeing them for one more day, let alone the weeks or months that a custody dispute might take in civil court. Here I had been quietly harboring questions about what Ashley said about her stepmother, and the "system" was treating their father's house as a place of safety and refuge while I stood falsely accused of something I didn't do! It made absolutely no sense to me, and I kept kicking myself for signing that safety plan. I never should have agreed to it. I certainly wouldn't agree to something like that again.

I wanted my kids back. I wanted them in my care. I wanted an investigation to move forward into the goings-on at Joal's house. And all of that needed to happen immediately. My one-step-at-a-time approach didn't apply anymore.

Clancy made calls with me right there in his office to make sure he handled my case correctly, and he promised to do all the paperwork that night so my requests could be filed as soon as the courthouse opened in Chattanooga in the morning.

———◆———

I woke up in the cocoon of a bedroom at the back of Diana's house on Tuesday with a knot in my stomach so thick and gnarly I swore it was going to cut right through my body and spill my insides all over the floor. I didn't want to move. I was terrified to get out of bed. I was just as terrified that I was going to fall back to sleep and miss a phone call with news—about anything.

When I finally did get up, I looked in the mirror and couldn't believe how drawn my face looked. Four days without a single full meal had taken a toll on me. My body was starting to look the way my heart felt.

I thought about something Clancy Covert had mentioned the previous afternoon that made a lot of sense to me. He gave me some advice on what I ought to be doing to prepare myself for whatever was going to happen with these allegations down in Georgia. He said that I ought to be putting a timeline together of everything I could remember about any time I had ever spent with those three girls the detectives said had accused me: Brianna Lamb, Chloe McDonald, and Skyler Walker.

"But Kim—Skyler's mother—told me that Skyler didn't accuse me of anything," I'd told him.

"That's important, then. Was she around you a lot?"

"Yes."

"Was she around these other kids?"

"Yes, all the time."

"Then that'll show up in the timeline, and that'll help your case."

The more I could remember about every time I'd ever been around those girls, he said, and especially any time I'd spent alone with those girls, the better my chances of refuting anything that they might have told the detectives.

"I don't recall ever being *alone* alone with any of them," I'd told him, "unless they walked into the kitchen, or if Ashley went to the bathroom while we were watching TV together in the living room. Like, normal stuff. Chloe McDonald only slept over one time, at a party we threw for the kids. Brianna only slept over at our town house one time that I can recall, too, and there were always other kids there. In fact, the one time Brianna slept over, Tyler's friend Braden was there—my friend Courtney's son. And David was around during any kids' sleepovers that would've happened in the last year."

"Well, that's a pretty good start. All those witnesses, that corroboration, that could be used to refute any claims they may have made, right?"

I got it. I saw his point. So that Tuesday morning I started going over some of those dates and times with Diana's help. She took notes and did some digging on her computer to help me remember certain dates. I wasn't really sure how helpful that exercise would be, or whether I'd even need it since I hadn't done anything wrong, but at least it gave me something to do while I waited for the phone to ring.

I think the most excruciating and unnerving part of the whole ordeal was that I had no idea what was actually said about me. *What have I actually been accused of? And why won't anybody tell me?* It was awful. My imagination ran wild. Whatever they said about me wasn't true. I knew that much. But all that really meant was that they could have said *anything*. I hated not knowing. If I knew, at least I could have dealt with it in my own mind. I might have had some inkling of whether these children had been fed some set of malicious lies, or whether they had taken something out of context, or misconstrued something, or whatever. Instead, my mind was left to worry and fret over every little scrap of what little I'd been told.

Of course, I was also terrified about how my own kids were now being dragged into this whole thing. I tried not to obsess over it, but it felt impossible to stop.

Then my phone rang. It was Clancy. He'd done it: He'd filed my complaint at the juvenile court in Chattanooga, demanding an investigation into the living and bathing arrangements at Joal and Sarah's and demanding that my children be returned to my custody.

"Thank you. Thank you so much, Clancy. When will I hear something back?"

"The court should act on it quickly, so we should know more by this afternoon. Just stay calm, okay? Any word on the interviews?"

"No, nothing yet."

"I'm going to make a call to DFACS and speak to Brandon Boggess on your behalf, if that's okay with you. Since the interviews will directly impact this custody case, I want to make sure everybody's in the loop and make sure he calls me when the interviews are finished."

"By all means, yes. Please. Let me know whatever you find out."

"I will. As soon as I know anything, I'll call you."

"Thank you, Clancy, for all your help. You're a godsend. Thank you."

I knew both Tyler and Ashley were supposed to be interviewed that morning, but I didn't know what time. The relief I felt knowing that this attorney was going to stay on top of it was something I could hold on to. Having two attorneys on board, with my local attorney working on it from the Georgia side, was a relief as well. I wasn't sure how I was going to pay for it all, but my parents had stepped up and said they would help with whatever I needed. I hadn't spoken to my husband through this entire ordeal. David hadn't picked up his phone even once, and he never returned any of my messages. I felt like crying every time I thought about him, but I couldn't. I had too many other things to worry about.

Waiting on news about my children that morning was by far one of the most agonizing waits of my life. I kept looking at the clock. Diana and I prayed together, asking God to see those kids through and to keep them strong under whatever questioning they were forced to endure. We prayed for guidance. Most of all, we prayed for the truth to come out.

A good couple of hours ticked by before my phone rang again. It was Clancy.

"Well, I have what I think is some very good news. I spoke to a couple of people and the interview with Ashley is complete, and she apparently didn't say anything about you that could be seen as criminal."

"Oh, thank God. Thank God," I said. Diana took my hand across the table.

"Does this mean it's over?" I asked.

"The investigation? No. Not necessarily. You should speak to your Georgia attorney about that. You said he was in touch with the DA's office, right?"

"He and the DA are apparently buddies. At least, that's what he led me to believe."

"Then he should be able to find out more now that the interviews are finished."

I hung up with Clancy and immediately got on the phone to my Georgia attorney. He said it was news to him that the interviews were complete but promised he'd make some calls and get back to me. While I waited, Clancy called back.

"Sorry to call back so soon, but I'm down at the circuit court and I just received word that your ex-husband filed an emergency motion to keep the kids in his custody pending the outcome of the case against you in Catoosa County."

"What? Can he still do that?"

"Technically, the court should not have accepted it because we filed your complaint in Juvenile Court a good two hours before he filed his motion in Circuit, so that should override it."

"What?" I asked. I had no idea what he was talking about. With every passing word, I realized how little I knew about the court system. Outside of my divorce proceedings, I had never had reason to learn.

"It's technical, but no. He can't do this. We just may need to get in front of a judge to convince the court to remove his request."

I was mad. The fact that Joal filed something like that confirmed to me that he *did* know about the "case" in Catoosa County. *How much does Joal know? How long has he known? When did he get involved?* My mind started spinning and I worried about how urgently I needed to get my kids out of that house.

"How fast can you make that happen? I want to see my kids, Clancy."

"It will take a little time."

"But by 'a little time' you mean today, right?"

"Tonya, I'm afraid these things sometimes move slower than we'd like, but I'll push to get a hearing as soon as possible."

"Like, today?"

"That is very, very unlikely. I'll do my best, but realistically, this could take a few days."

"How the heck can he take the kids away from me when I haven't been arrested? I haven't been charged with anything. I haven't *done* anything!"

"I know. Let me see if I can get a judge to look at it today, okay? I'll do my best."

I tried to calm down. I knew it wasn't Clancy's fault.

"Thank you," I said.

I relayed all of this to Diana and she simply could not believe how messed up the whole system was. How can the court just take your kids away based on *nothing*? Especially based on the words of a disgruntled ex-husband? And especially now that Ashley had been interviewed and said nothing about me that was criminal or even inappropriate? What in the world was going on?

My Georgia attorney got back to me that afternoon and told me the same thing that Clancy told me: From what he had found out, my daughter hadn't "revealed" anything that would be described as "criminal" in her interview about me. Tyler's interview didn't reveal anything harmful or negative about me either.

"But I'm afraid that's not going to be the end of it," he said. "I finally heard back from Tim Deal."

"The detective?"

"Yes. I worked on a murder case that he investigated not too long ago, and my client pled out. Her plea didn't include any jail time and Tim wasn't too happy about that."

"So what does that have to do with me?"

"Well, Detective Deal vowed to 'put that girl away for life,' and he failed. And in the message he left me, he swore to me that 'this one won't get away.' Meaning you. Those were his words. So I just don't see him giving up on this case."

"That's horrible! What is this, some kind of vendetta? How can a detective be biased against me based on some other case and some other crime? That doesn't make sense! Not to mention, what case is he talking about? I mean, what exactly have I been accused of? Can somebody please tell me that? Please?"

My own attorney couldn't answer my questions. It seemed that no one could answer my questions. I couldn't get answers, literally to save my life. I felt like I'd hit a brick wall. I didn't know how to get through it, or over it, or even under it. I was stuck.

That state of disbelief, disorientation, and absolute limbo was right where I would remain for the next ten days. For ten straight days I made phone calls and visited my attorneys' offices and showed up in court in Tennessee thinking we were going to have a custody hearing, only to be sent home. I went without kissing my kids good night. I continued to live off the good graces of Diana and her husband, Michael—who ran down to get me more clothes and other necessities from my house in Chickamauga, and who stayed positive and reiterated what I wanted to believe in my heart.

"There's nothing to worry about, Tonya," Michael kept saying. "They can't arrest you when you've done nothing wrong. You're going to be fine. It's just taking some time to sort through it all, that's all."

I went to bed each night with more worry than the last. My anxiety climbed higher with each passing hour. I tried to distract myself by building my timeline, digging through notebooks and calendars and classroom activities and after-school schedules, hoping to piece together everything I could recall about the previous three years of my life, especially the times I had been around those children who had supposedly accused me—or *not* accused me, in the case of Skyler Walker.

Diana helped me sort through all kinds of photos to categorize them and add them to my timeline—even my wedding photos, which included shots of a smiling Brianna Lamb standing right beside me at the Lambs' pool.

"How can anyone who knows me think I molested that little girl or any other child?" I wondered aloud.

"They can't," Diana said.

I can't stress enough how dedicated Diana was in helping me get through this and helping me to focus on the tasks at hand so I wouldn't lose my mind while I waited for resolution.

Finally, after suffering through another weekend without answers, my Georgia attorney called me back with a "proposal" from the detectives and the ADA (the "assistant district attorney," he explained) who was now working my case. They wanted me to come in for a polygraph, he said, just like they'd wanted me to do on that very first day, only this time they would allow him to come along. The long and short of the ADA's offer was this: If I passed the polygraph, they would conclude the investigation. If I failed it? The investigation would continue.

My attorney expressed some doubts about the whole idea, but I was unwavering in the fact that I had done nothing improper to any child. So I agreed to go ahead and take the polygraph. They set up an appointment for Wednesday, June 11, 2008—the day after my son's ninth birthday. It was also, coincidentally, one day before Ashley was scheduled to go to the appointment I'd set up before all of this started, so an unbiased forensic psychologist could get to the bottom of what might be going on at Joal's house.

It was right on Tyler's birthday that we finally got in front of a Tennessee judge on the custody case, too. Joal didn't show up. I wasn't able to look him in the eye or to get any sense of what was going on with him or to understand why he might have filed that motion to take the kids from me. Instead, only his attorney was present. I never missed a court appearance, hearing, or anything that involved my two children. *How could he just not show up?*

Well, it turned out Clancy was right: Juvenile Court trumped Circuit Court in our case, so the judge tossed out Joal's "emergency" motion and ordered that my children be returned to my custody as soon as possible. All I could think was, *Yes!*

I was frantic to see my children and so relieved that something had finally gone in my favor, but I was also aware of just how much trauma those kids had been put through. It was late in the day when that order finally came down. It was Tyler's birthday, and the last thing I wanted to do was to cause him more pain than what he had already been put through. So with Clancy's nod, I decided that I would wait until my polygraph was concluded the next morning and this whole ordeal was truly behind me before I would pick up my son and daughter. We relayed that news through Joal's attorney. It ripped my heart to shreds that I wouldn't see my son on his birthday and that I wouldn't see my daughter for even one more minute. Yet I thought it was the right thing to do. For all of us.

I went to bed believing that missing my son's birthday would mark the "last of my worst days," and I sprang out of bed on June 11 with a renewed sense of optimism. Diana, Michael, and even their son, Josh, were taken aback by my confidence that morning. I dressed in a suit that I felt exuded professionalism. When the time came, we rose to exit the front door on the way to the polygraph—and then my cell phone rang. It was my attorney.

"Where are you?" he asked.

"Just leaving," I said.

"Don't. Stay right where you are. They've issued a warrant for your arrest."

His words completely knocked the wind out of me. I honestly could not breathe. I could feel the color draining from my face as blackness closed in around my eyes. My ears started ringing.

"What's wrong?" Diana asked. "Tonya? Tonya, what's wrong?!"

My legs gave out. I leaned back against the wall and slid down to the floor as my attorney kept talking. I kept the phone pressed to my ear and listened as best I could. I could see Diana's face. She looked terrified. She picked up her phone prepared to dial 911 to get an ambulance for me—and she would have, had I not hung up with my attorney and finally acknowledged her.

"Breathe, Tonya! Breathe. Please."

I took a breath. It felt like my body weighed 400 pounds. It was all I could do just to sit up.

"What happened?" Diana begged.

Slowly and barely audibly, I told her: "There's a warrant out for my arrest. The police went to my house last night. They were planning to pull me right out of my house, in the middle of the night."

"I don't understand. What about the polygraph?" Diana asked.

I stared at her in pure disbelief.

"There isn't going to be a polygraph. It was just to get me to come down to the police station so they could arrest me."

"What?"

"That's what my attorney told me."

"Why?"

"The local media's all there. They've all been alerted that a teacher's going to be arrested for molesting children. It's a big story. They apparently wanted to put me in handcuffs and put me on display. A perp walk, he called it."

"That's outrageous! Tonya, that's not possible. How in the world—what else did he say? What on earth are we supposed to do?"

I kept talking, but it all felt separated—like the words were just floating around me. My breathing was so shallow that I felt light-headed and dizzy.

"I need to call my parents," I said. "We need to post a bond. He said I don't have a choice in this. I have to turn myself in."

"Turn yourself in? To who? The police?"

"At the jail," I said. "In Catoosa County. I'm going to jail, Diana. They're arresting me. I'm going to jail."

Chapter 17

I placed a call to my mom from the floor of Diana's kitchen. I asked her to sit down, and I told her about the warrant for my arrest. I told her that I was okay and that no one knew where I was, so I was pretty sure I'd be able to turn myself in at the jail without making a big spectacle of myself all over the evening news. But I also told her that the only way I'd be able to come home that night was if we posted a cash bond. A big one.

My mother agreed to put up whatever money was needed, no questions asked. Thankfully her mother, my grandmother, had been a penny-pincher her whole life. She'd left my mother an inheritance that we would be able to tap into. I hated to use my mother's inheritance for this awfulness, but I was also thankful that it was there. I'm not sure what I would have done otherwise.

A whole series of phone calls ensued between my parents and my attorney, and my attorney and the ADA on my case, and a judge apparently, until they finally settled on a prearranged bond. The bond was for $50,000. For $50,000, I would be allowed to turn myself in at the Catoosa County Jail, where I'd be booked and fingerprinted and then released—as long as I followed certain bond conditions. *What is a bond condition? What does that even mean?*

Finally it was all arranged. My parents went down to the Catoosa County Courthouse in Ringgold with a cashier's check and handed it to a secretary in an office on the second floor. My attorney got a call saying everything seemed in order, so he called me up to tell me I should head down to the jail to turn myself in.

"Will you meet me there? Or should we come to your office and drive over together? How should we do this?"

"You'll be fine. You'll be in and out in a matter of minutes."

"Wait, you're not coming?" I said.

"It's just a formality. Everything's arranged; the bond is set—"

"Do you really think this is going to be a formality? Look, this may seem like a formality to you, but this is the most awful thing I've had to do in my whole life. I'm paying you, and I expect you to be there to make sure everything goes the way it's supposed to go. So do you want to meet me there, or do you want me to come by your office?"

That local attorney sighed, audibly, into the telephone. "Well, all right. I don't think it's necessary, but I understand why you're upset. I'll meet you down there. We should do it soon, though."

We settled on a time. I called my parents and they said they would meet me in the parking lot outside the main entrance to the jail—a hulking, modern concrete structure that stands out like a sore thumb on Highway 41 down in Ringgold. Suddenly this whole thing was real. We had plans. In a matter of a half hour, I'd be walking into a jail and getting arrested for a crime I had not committed.

My well of tears seemed to run dry as I sat in the passenger seat of my Yukon, as Diana took the wheel and pointed us south for the longest twenty-minute drive of my life.

Thankfully there was no media in the parking lot as we pulled in, and I gasped for air. My heart was pounding something fierce, and my dad was crying as I hugged him and my mom. My attorney walked ahead and held the door for us.

Walking into that lobby, it was clear that everybody knew who I was. The media had been alerted, so I shouldn't have been surprised that the officers at the jail would be expecting me—and I felt they all looked at me as if I were exactly the monster those detectives made me out to be.

The officers took me inside. The door slammed shut, and my parents stood there on the other side of the window watching as those officers put me in handcuffs. They read me my rights and walked me back into the part of the jail that no innocent person should ever have to lay eyes on.

My attorney had already explained to me the basics of what was about to happen. I knew they would show me the warrants for my arrest. I would have to acknowledge that I had read those warrants by signing a piece of paper. I might be asked out loud if I understood the charges against me, and all I was to say was "Yes." That was it. I wasn't supposed to engage in conversation, because anything I said "could and would be used against me in a court of law." I understood that. I also understood that I didn't want to make anyone mad in there. I thought I ought to be respectful, and I didn't have a problem with that. The officers in that jail weren't the ones who had wronged me.

I'll never forget the feeling of those handcuffs being closed on my wrists. They were tighter than I imagined they needed to be. The metal was cold, and they hurt something awful. I thought of movies where some cop would twist those cuffs and yank on them to force some perp to the ground, and it made me queasy.

The cuffs weren't on for very long—just long enough to walk me back to a holding cell. But I had to rub my wrists when they took them off.

There were a couple of other women in the cell with me and a whole bunch of men in the cells around us. They all looked tough to me. I tried to avoid eye contact, and I stayed silent when one of the women asked me, "What are you in for?" The holding cells lined the walls on either side of a great big room, with a desk set up on a platform right in the center.

I'm not sure how long I was in there, but it sure was a lot more than the "few minutes" this whole thing was supposed to take. It was hours. After a while someone came and ushered me and a few others out of our cells to face our charges. They lined us all up against a wall to get our mug shots, where we waited for what felt like another hour.

Next thing I knew someone pointed a camera at me and snapped my picture without much warning at all. I guess they didn't want us to smile. I'm sure I couldn't have mustered one even if they'd forced me to.

It was a strange feeling standing there after that, waiting to see my arrest warrants. Part of me was scared to death and part of me was chomping at the bit to see them. *I'll finally have some answers!* When the arrest warrants were laid before me, I read them as quickly as I could—these black-and-white forms with names and dates and details scribbled on them in someone's messy handwriting. I wanted to memorize everything I could, to take away any detail that might give me some sense of understanding, or any bit of information I could use to help put an end to this nightmare.

There were three warrants with Brianna Lamb's name on them, one with Chloe McDonald's—and one with Ashley's. *My daughter, Ashley.*

The warrant accused me of committing "an immoral/indecent act in the presence of/with/upon the person of/to Ashley Henkey—"

It infuriated me that they were charging me with this awful crime and yet they couldn't even spell her name correctly. Her last name is Henke. *Henke!*

"—a child under the age of 16 years, by touching the primary genital area with the intent to arouse/satisfy the sexual desires of said accused/child."

I felt nauseated. I'm her *mother*. It was all I could do not to cry and throw up. *How could Ashley possibly think I molested her? Why would my baby ever say such a thing? What have they done to her?*

I read the warrant in Chloe's name, and it had the exact same wording as Ashley's.

Then there were the three warrants under the name Brianna Lamb. One accused me of "touching" her, just like the other warrants did. One said the same thing again, up until the part about her being "under the age of 16," and then said, "by having said child fondle the defendant's breast." And the last warrant accused me of an "aggravated" immoral/indecent act: It said that I, Tonya Craft, "did intentionally penetrate the sex organ of Brianna Lamb with a finger without the consent of said person." I gagged. I had to close my eyes and catch my balance just to stop myself from making a scene right there in the jail. The thought that anyone would falsely accuse me of something so heinous absolutely terrified me. It didn't matter what the motive was; it didn't matter how it had happened. Just the fact that my name was on a piece of paper saying I had done something like that to a child—it took everything I had not to throw up.

When I opened my eyes again, I saw something that made no sense. All of the warrants said the date of the incidents were "between 12:01 A.M. and 11:59 P.M. on the 1st day of January, 2008." I wasn't with Tyler and Ashley on New Year's. I wasn't around those other children, either. My children were with Joal and Sarah. To me, that was *something*. That was proof right there in writing that this whole thing was false. I still felt sick, and I was worried to death about what would happen next, but that one obvious fact stood out like a sore thumb. *I can prove I'm innocent*, I thought, just like you'd see on TV or in the movies. I was pretty sure it would be just about all we would need to clear this mess up. I could not wait to tell my attorneys about it.

"Do you understand the charges that have been made against you?" an officer asked.

"Yes," I said, just as I'd been told.

"Then sign here, acknowledging that you've read the warrants."

I signed my name. Then they moved me into a room to get fingerprinted.

As I stood there waiting and waiting—again—I thought about what I'd heard from both of my attorneys. Ashley hadn't accused me of anything "criminal" during her interview with DFACS. *So where did this charge come from? Did they interview her again? God, please let her be okay.*

I felt that Joal was involved. I felt it. I felt it when Ashley left me that hushed message on May 30. *But why? How did this happen? When did this all get started? Was it his idea? Is he doing this just to hurt me? Have he and Sandra and Kelly been talking? Did all three of them put the girls up to this? Or did the girls even say these things? Could a warrant be written on the basis of something a parent said? How do I not know these answers?*

"Step forward."

The female officer manning the fingerprint machine motioned to me. I remember she had brown hair. She was chatty. She started talking about her dogs and asked me if I had any pets. I wanted to be polite, so I answered, very succinctly.

"My kids have two dogs," I said.

"What kind?" she asked.

"Miniature Schnauzers."

"What are their names?"

"Buddy and Candy Cane."

Given the seriousness of what was going on, it struck me as odd that an officer would be trying to carry on conversations like that.

They don't use ink in this day and age. It's more like a scanner that they press your fingers into. It records your fingerprints into a computer system. For some reason it wasn't working right. It took her forever. When she finally got it working again, she looked at my charges, and then she looked up at me.

"These are some pretty serious charges," she said.

"Yes, ma'am," I answered.

"I have to ask you: Did you do this?"

"No, I did not," I said.

She looked into my eyes and said, "Well, I tend to believe you."

That was what finally broke me. I started squalling right there. Tears came raining down my face. To have somebody with a badge on give me a little bit of encouragement simply meant the world to me. I didn't belong there and I thanked God that at least one person seemed to see through the mistake of it all.

They put me back in the holding cell for a while longer, and then finally they put me back into handcuffs and escorted me out, right back to that area in front of the door where I could see my parents still waiting, patiently, in the cold, stark lobby. The officer who took my fingerprints happened to walk into the hallway just as I was being uncuffed.

"Good luck to you," she said.

"Thank you."

With that, they opened the door and I fell into the arms of my mom and dad. I cried to the point of shaking.

My parents told me that my attorney had gone back to his office and asked that we come see him as soon as I was released. Diana had left, too. Apparently some media outlets showed up and were asking around trying to catch a glimpse of me at the jail. Quick-thinking Diana ran out to my Yukon, started it up, drove it right up to the front door of the jail, waited until the media people spotted her, and then took off. She led them away on a wild goose chase so they wouldn't be there when I came out that door. God bless Diana. And God bless my parents for their patience and kindness.

We got into their car and drove straight over to my attorney's office. He and I sat down and went over everything. I brought up the discrepancy in the reports concerning the timing on New Year's Day, hoping that would be a huge step toward getting these charges dismissed so I could move on with my life. But he burst that bubble in an instant.

"The time and date is just a formality. No one really pays attention to that stuff. If a child says someone touched them, the expectation that they'll get all the details right doesn't matter. It's a violation, and that's all that counts," he said.

The details don't matter?

"Also, the digital penetration charge—that's serious. That's aggravated," he said. "That's bad."

"What does that even mean?" I asked.

"A conviction on aggravated sexual assault of a child could mean life in prison."

I went cold. It honestly felt like my heart stopped beating. Not just from the words themselves, but the way he delivered them. I didn't even really know what the word "aggravated" meant in a case like this, and suddenly he was talking about convictions and life in prison. And it sounded as though he were saying it like it was a foregone conclusion.

———————◆———————

At some point in that blurry, awful aftermath of the arrest, the attorney showed me the actual bond that had allowed me to leave the jail. It was the first time I saw the conditions of my release in print:[15]

ORDER SETTING BOND

The above-styled matter having come before this Court upon Defendant's motion for bond, upon consideration of the charges in this matter, the Defendant is hereby released on bond in the amount of $50,000.00. Furthermore, the defendant shall not have contact, directly or indirectly, with any minor, except her natural children, in which case, supervised visitation shall be allowed through Four Points in Lafayette, GA. The Defendant retains the right to petition the court for a modification of this agreement.

SO ORDERED, this 11th day of June, 2008.

Judge, Superior Court,
Lookout Mountain Judicial Circuit

"What does that mean, 'directly or indirectly'?" I asked my lawyer. "And what is this 'Four Points'?"

"It means that you can't have any contact with children," he said.

"Okay, but what is 'indirect' contact?"

He seemed baffled. He read it over again and said he wasn't exactly sure.

"Is this normal? Is this what normally happens to people when they're accused of something?"

"I can't say it is, no," he told me. "The 'indirect contact' part of it is very unusual. But look, we'll go back to court as soon as we can and get it all sorted out. It may take a couple of weeks, but it won't be a problem."

"Well, what am I supposed to do in the meantime?"

It suddenly struck me that Diana's son, Josh, was only sixteen. *Does this mean I can't legally stay at her house anymore?*

"What the heck is indirect contact?" I asked again. It was so vague it was terrifying. "Does that mean if I call my friend Tammy and her son picks up the phone and says something to me, is that indirect contact? Does that mean I'd go to jail? Is this their way of setting me up so they can throw me behind bars no matter what?"

My attorney thought I was being paranoid and asked me to keep calm. He legitimately seemed to think this would all get worked out in a quick hearing. I tried to take his word for it, but the longer we sat there, the more I panicked.

Where am I going to go if I can't stay at Diana's? I couldn't afford a hotel or a rental. I didn't want to rent anything in my name anyway, for fear the police or some reporter would come find me. Other friends had offered to let me stay with them, but just about all of them had kids, and I didn't want to burden anyone else. My friends had said I wouldn't be a burden, but I sure *felt* like a burden. I didn't want to put that on anyone else. I felt bad enough putting all of this on Diana and her family.

The more I thought about it, the more the bond felt like a jail sentence to me. If I couldn't be in the presence of anyone under eighteen, did that mean I couldn't go into a gas station to pay for my gas or to a park or to the grocery store—anywhere where there might be children or teenagers—without fear of being arrested and thrown in jail?

I kept asking myself over and over again, *How can I be punished like this when I haven't done anything wrong?*

"What if this drags out through the summer? If I can't be around minors, I can't go back to my job. What will happen to my job?"

"We'll petition the court and get this modified before that ever happens. We'll get back in front of Van Pelt before the month's out," he said.

Van Pelt was apparently the name of the judge on my case.

I went back to the question of this "Four Points" place down in Lafayette, where the bond said I could see my kids. My attorney explained that Four Points was a state-run facility that allowed parents in difficult cases to see their children. He said the rules are really strict. So strict that even murderers and convicted abusers of all sorts were allowed to see their children under the supervision of that facility.

"So, you're telling me that this bond basically lumps me in with a bunch of murderers and abusers, even though I haven't been convicted of anything?"

It seemed that he was a little taken aback by my tone.

"I think we'll be able to get that changed, too," he said. "It shouldn't take long. I don't think you should even make an appointment at Four Points. That's not where you or your kids belong. I think we should just go back to court and try to get some sort of normal, supervised visitation set up."

By that point, I didn't feel like talking anymore. I didn't want to argue about anything. I didn't want to get mad. I was exhausted. I was frustrated. I felt humiliated and defeated. So we left. My parents took me back to Diana's, where my friend consoled me and tried to get me to eat some dinner. Lucky for me, her minor son, Josh, was out of the house for a couple of days, staying at a friend's, so I'd have at least twenty-four hours or so to figure out what in the heck I was going to do for a new living arrangement.

Diana kept trying to get me to consume a little something as we turned on the five o'clock news that night. For some reason I thought the media wouldn't make much of a spectacle of this since they hadn't captured my "perp walk."

I couldn't have been more wrong.

My mug shot filled up the whole screen. I wasn't just *a* story. I was the *top* story: "A Chickamauga kindergarten teacher accused of molesting three children." They didn't name the children, of course. They only named *me*. Tonya Craft. They showed the picture the police had taken of me at the jail just a couple of hours beforehand. They showed it over and over, with my hair disheveled and that awful, sad, fallen look on my face. I couldn't believe how awful I looked. It didn't even look like me.

The news went on. They showed a different picture of me that I did recognize—it was one of my wedding pictures! Sandra Lamb had arranged for all of my wedding photography. The finished photos were actually delivered to her house. She was the only other person besides me who had copies of them. She had looked at my wedding pictures before I did.

"Sandra Lamb must have given them that picture," I said to Diana. Then the news showed another picture of me, this one in my classroom. It only showed me from the shoulders up, but I recognized that I was wearing candy cane pajamas in the photo—the exact pajamas I had bought for our class pajama day, just before Christmas, the year that Brianna Lamb was in my class. "Sandra must have given 'em that one, too."

After that, they cut to some video footage they took right in front of my house, which I hadn't seen in nearly two weeks. The camera zoomed in as the reporter kept talking about the charges against me, and there on the front porch I saw my son's dirty sneakers—the very same sneakers Tyler had taken off just before Tim Deal and Stephen Keith rang my doorbell.

For some reason the sight of those sneakers broke me down again. I fell apart. I ran back into the bedroom, closed the door, and collapsed in a heap.

Before that day, I suppose I was like most people in the world who look at a mug shot on the news and just assume the person must be guilty of something if they were arrested. *Innocent people don't get arrested.* At least I think that's what I would assume. I never even really thought about it. Seeing a mug shot of some child molester just made me cringe.

Now I *was* that mug shot.

How can they do this? How can they say my name and show my picture and show my house? Where I live? Where my children live? When I'm innocent!

I knew as I lay there that I could never go back to that house. Ever. It would never be the same. It would never feel safe. I was so sad and furious all at once, I felt as if I would crumble into pieces on the floor. I wished with everything I had that it would all go away. And in my mind, I yelled at God: *Why is this happening? How can you let this happen?*

I stayed in that room and didn't move. For hours.

My phone kept ringing. I turned it off. I didn't listen to any of the messages. I was afraid of what I might hear. I couldn't take any more attacks on my character.

I eventually got up after everyone else was asleep. I got on Diana's computer and watched the same news video, and all the different news broadcasts from all the local stations from Chattanooga to Atlanta, over and over again until the sky was brightening and the birds were singing outside. Every time I saw my house and that porch and those sneakers, it broke my heart all over again.

At some point, though, I stopped watching in pure sadness—and I started taking notes. I opened up my laptop and started looking back through some of my old pictures. If they were going to use photos against me, I needed to find every photo I had that showed who I really was. I had made photo books for all of the parents at the end of each year in Chickamauga. I thought it was a nice keepsake. There were lots of photos taken in my classroom. I decided to dig those out to verify the timing of that pajama-day photo.

Verifying the timing of that photo pretty much solidified my belief that Sandra Lamb was involved in this whole thing. The news broadcast even featured an anonymous quote from one of the parents of the children who had accused "Miss Tonya" of molesting them: "My daughter's a strong girl and will get through this." It sounded to me like something that Sandra would say. I thought that information might be useful to my attorneys. I paid close attention to what the reporters said the charges were, too, and how the reporters described me. I was sickened by the words of the superintendent of my school system and those of a neighbor who spoke about me, someone I barely knew.

How can they say these terrible things about me? How can they tell the whole world that I'm a child molester?

I wrote down all sorts of thoughts about what I needed to do. I added a few notes to the timeline I had been working on with Diana's help. I printed out some blank calendar pages and started filling in some dates. I also marked down how many days it had been since I'd seen my kids: 13.

As the sun came up over the horizon, I finally resolved to try to get some sleep. Stepping back into Diana's spare bedroom, I thought back to that moment, not a month earlier, when I sat at home on a Saturday night, missing David and feeling awful about everything in my life—that night when I laughed at the thoughts I was having, and I said out loud to my empty home, "Well, it can't get any worse than this!"

Life certainly *could* get worse. A *lot* worse. There was nothing I could do now to remove the image of my mug shot from the minds of thousands, maybe millions of people, and especially right there in the town where I worked and lived—where I'd grown up. Now that the allegations were out there, there was no way to make them go away. The toothpaste was already out of the tube. Heck, it was squished all over the counter. You ever try to put toothpaste back into a tube? You can't do it. The damage would only get bigger when the newspapers hit the next day and when the talk-radio shows in the area got a hold of this story. I knew that. I knew what I would think myself if I saw the mug shot of an accused child molester on the front page next to my morning cup of coffee: I'd think, *That person ought to fry!* Wouldn't we all think that? It's human nature. So none of what came before that moment really mattered anymore, did it?

I had prayed to God for guidance ever since this started. I had prayed to God for guidance right there at Diana's kitchen table just that morning, when I thought I was on my way to take a polygraph that would put an end to this entire investigation.

Well, I have to say: God delivered.

As I pulled the shades in that guest bedroom and laid my head on the pillow in the quiet moments before the rest of the world would wake up and continue living, God let me know what counted most. I closed my eyes with a sense of purpose and clarity the likes of which I'd never felt in my life.

From that day forward, there would only be one thing that mattered: finding a way to get back to my babies. That was what I had to stay focused on—fulfilling the promise that every mother makes to her children, the promise that I had made to Ashley so devotedly on the night before our world fell apart. The promise I'd made to both of my children to always be there.

I have to find a way to get back to my kids.

I knew in my heart there was only one way that was ever going to happen. No matter what it took, no matter what sacrifices I had to make or what obstacles I had to climb over or what distances I was required to travel, I needed to prove—to the whole world, if necessary—that I hadn't done what those arrest warrants said I did. I needed to prove my innocence, wholly and completely, without any doubts whatsoever.

In order to get back to my children, I needed to clear my name.

Part II

The Marathon

Chapter 18

The next morning, nearly the moment I turned my phone back on, my mother called. "Turn on the radio," she said. "You need to hear what they're saying about you."

"Mom, no. I can't take any more. I really can't."

"Trust me, Tonya, you need to turn this on. Right now!"

I turned on the local talk station that everyone listens to and heard a female caller saying, "My kids had Tonya as a teacher and I'm telling you, there is no way that woman could hurt a child. Somebody is making this up!"

"Diana, come listen to this," I said. I turned up the volume. I sat on her kitchen table with my feet on the seat of a chair, and we listened as caller after caller phoned in with words of support for me. People complained about the court in Ringgold, mouthed off about their experiences with the police in Catoosa County, and said they simply didn't believe the charges against me.

After that, I finally listened to the messages on my phone, and much to my surprise, they weren't full of hatred. They were full of love and support. I had messages from friends and the parents of some of my students and more—all saying they knew these allegations couldn't be true and offering to help in any way they could.

I cried tears of thankfulness.

A little while later, Tammy came by to help me figure out what to do about my living situation. She'd already spoken with Diana about it that morning, and thankfully these supporters I had around me were able to think and act and come up with plans in those times when I was too overwhelmed to even think anymore.

"Don't your parents have an RV?" Tammy asked me.

"Yeah."

"Couldn't you just park that somewhere and live in that for a while? Just 'til this gets sorted out?"

"I suppose so, but where?"

My parents kept an old motor home parked in their driveway. They barely ever used it anymore. I was sure they would let me stay in it. There was just one problem: They'd already tried to see the kids, with Joal fighting them every step of the way, so I couldn't stay in the RV in their driveway and put that potential visitation at further risk. They didn't have a spot in an RV park or anything, and I didn't want to risk being seen by too many people anyway. Then Diana thought of a place where I could stay—and it turned out I wouldn't have to move very far from where I already was.

My parents drove their vintage, tan-and-brown 1980s Residency over and parked it in Diana's driveway. Diana's husband, Michael, ran an electric line and even a cable television line out the back of their house so I could keep it up and running and even watch some TV if I wanted to. I swear, their kindness, patience, and thoughtfulness knew no bounds.

I'll never forget what it felt like to sleep in there that first night, though. This wasn't a vacation. This wasn't some outing I chose to take. I was in that motor home because it was the only place I was allowed to sleep. The old blue carpet and pastel interior designs were a step up from what I'd face if I went to prison, I realized. But in many ways, I was already there. It felt like the walls were closing in as I lay on that bed, knowing that Josh would be home that night and that I'd have to wait for him to leave the house the next morning before I could safely go inside and take a shower. The timing of my day-to-day routines no longer belonged to me. The decision over something as basic as where I laid my head was no longer mine. Even with as much support as I had, and as grateful as I was to have found a solution to the urgent question of where I could sleep without being in "direct or indirect contact" with anyone under eighteen, I don't think I had ever felt quite as alone as I did that night in June. I longed to hold my kids. And while I couldn't understand where the feeling was coming from, in my loneliness, I longed to be held by my husband.

I opened my eyes and sat straight up in bed. I'd been dreaming. I dreamed that I stood before my ex-husband, Joal, the father of my children, and said to his face, as firmly I could, "I want you to look me in the eye and tell me that you honestly believe I molested those girls. Look at me and tell me that you believe I molested our daughter."

Then I woke up. On previous nights I had dreamed about confronting Kelly McDonald in the same way, and another time Sandra Lamb, and another time Sherri Wilson. I'd never had recurring dreams of any kind until after my arrest. In my heart of hearts, I wished I really *could* confront whoever was behind it all.

Why? I wondered. *Why would allegations like this even come up? Why would they start? Who would get such an idea in their head to say something so horrible about somebody and to use children to make it happen? Is there a chance that they really believe something happened?*

It's the not knowing that can drive a person mad. Not knowing what those girls said, or who said what, or when, or where, or to whom. I would pull myself back and try to stop thinking about it, but then another question would pop up and my mind would consider it.

I needed answers. I needed to understand. So I got up and Googled "false accusation of child molestation" on my trusty black laptop. That single search returned more than a million pages of news reports, consultants, help groups, documentaries, attorneys, private investigators, and more. A *million*. I was completely overwhelmed. I started clicking through page after page, just scanning the headlines and the subjects and the pictures.

I dug in with everything I had.

Of all the research I had ever done as a teacher or a student, I knew this would be the most important I would ever have to do. I knew how to study. I knew how to do this. I had waited long enough—maybe too long—to apply my own skill set to my own awful situation. I didn't even know exactly what I was looking for as I sat there in front of that computer that night. I just knew that I needed to go to school on this subject.

Chapter 19

"This is going to be a straightforward hearing. Nothing big. Nothing to worry about," my attorney told me.

I stepped foot into the Catoosa County Courthouse in Ringgold, Georgia, for the very first time on June 25, 2008. I suppose it looks like a lot of other courthouses in a lot of other small towns: a big brick building that's been standing there for almost a century, almost right smack dab in the center of downtown, with a lawn out in front, some neatly placed sidewalks, and a metal detector that greets you just a few steps inside what can only be described as a drab, outdated entryway. The inside of that courthouse, with its scuffed, industrial-looking tiled floors and dull paint, seemed oddly devoid of sunlight. There were some windows, of course, but it just seemed like no light got into that building at all. The fluorescent fixtures buzzed in the hallway on the second floor, where I sat on a bench outside of a little courtroom to talk things over before we went in.

I was nervous as all get-out. My father had picked me up and driven me over and waited right there with me. I had Clancy come down just to observe, since whatever happened here could directly affect the custody case in Tennessee. He wouldn't be allowed to act as my attorney since this was a different state and my local attorney hadn't agreed to co-counsel. But I felt good knowing Clancy was there.

The goal of this bond modification was to get the court to specifically allow me to see my kids under "normal" circumstances instead of going to Four Points. We would use that decision to go back to the Tennessee courts and compel Joal to cooperate and give me some time with them. I needed to see my children.

We also wanted to loosen up some of the other restrictions—especially the part that said that I couldn't come in "indirect" contact with anyone under eighteen. Our argument was that my record was entirely clean, and that I was a schoolteacher, so the restriction would affect my employment. He planned to argue that I had never been arrested, let alone accused of hurting anyone ever before. It was therefore unfair that I was being punished and faced the potential loss of my employment, my sole source of income, when I hadn't been convicted of any crime. And that was exactly what was going on, too. I'd already received word from the superintendent at Chickamauga that they were planning a termination hearing based on these allegations.

We would also argue that the part about indirect contact should be removed completely and the part about being around other "minors" should be modified to say that I couldn't be "alone" with any minors. I understood that restriction, as much as I hated it. I could see why it made sense, given the charges. Intellectually, at least, it was palatable—and it was certainly fairer than what that judge had ordered initially.

A few minutes before we were scheduled to go in, my attorney asked me to "sit tight" so he could go speak to Judge Van Pelt before we got started. I said, "Okay."

I sat there. And sat there. A good ten or fifteen minutes went by. I kept looking at my watch. The hearing was supposed to have started already. Clancy went inside to see if anything was happening, and he came out a few minutes later to tell me that my ex, Joal Henke, and Sandra Lamb were both in the courtroom.

"What?" I asked him. "What are they doing here?"

"They're sitting right next to each other, whispering and giggling. If I didn't know any better, I'd think they were a couple."

I was flabbergasted. Joal and Sandra didn't even know each other. *What are they doing in that courtroom together?*

I got all fidgety and panicky. I didn't know what to do. *Should I go in there? What happens if I'm not in the courtroom on time? Will that hurt my case? Where is my attorney?*

Then all of a sudden, my attorney came out.

"Well, that's that," he said. He kept on walking.

"What do you mean, 'That's that'? Don't we have to go in?"

"Nope, it's all decided."

I grabbed up my purse and my notebooks as quickly as I could and tried to follow him. "What do you mean? When can I see my kids?"

"He left it at Four Points but bounced the ultimate decision back to Tennessee."

"So nothing changed?"

"Not really."

He would not stop moving. He headed down the stairs as I hurried after him.

"Well, what about the other part? What about the indirect contact?"

"He left it in there. He loosened it a bit, but it's still there. Look, I'm sorry it didn't work out the way we wanted, Tonya. Call me Monday morning. I'll have a copy of the bond in my hands then, and we'll discuss it, all right?"

I'd followed him all the way down the stairs and out the front door to the sidewalk while he said all of this. Then he jumped in his car and drove off. I was dumbfounded.

How could all of that happen when I wasn't even present?

In meeting after meeting, I'd felt that this attorney had been dismissive of my feelings. I tried to ignore it, as women are so often forced to do, but I felt small around him, like I wasn't being heard. Just a few days earlier, in the middle of all of this awfulness, he'd handed me divorce papers from David without any warning. Without so much as a simple "I'm sorry." *How can someone who shows so little sensitivity for my situation and my emotional state possibly fight for me?*

The moment at the courthouse was the last straw. In the middle of everything else I was going through, I now had to find myself a new lawyer. Pronto.

Devastated doesn't begin to describe my emotional state after that bond modification went south on me. I felt homeless and imprisoned at the same time. I felt like I didn't have anybody fighting for me anymore, except for Clancy, and there was nothing he could do about anything on the Georgia side of my ordeal. I felt lost and alone. I needed my husband. I'd laid eyes on the divorce papers. Actually held them in my hands. They were real. David believed the marriage was over. Yet, I lay there in that stupid motor home and prayed to God to bring David back to me.

"Please, God," I prayed again and again. "Please, let us reconcile."

On Monday, as promised, my attorney gave me a copy of the bond modification, and I just stared at it for the longest time. It didn't make anything simpler. All it did was make things more confusing and more convoluted. Instead of being one paragraph now, it was two pages long. The first page looked like this:

ORDER MODIFYING BOND CONDITIONS

The above-styled case having come on before the Court upon the Defendant's request for a modification of bond conditions, after hearing the argument of counsel, the bond order is hereby modified as follows:

1.

The Defendant shall continue to have supervised visitation with her minor children through Four Points in LaFayette, Georgia. However, it appears to the Court that there is a pending custody and visitation action pending in Hamilton County, Tennessee. The Defendant may seek to address and litigate in the Juvenile Court of Hamilton County, Tennessee, or any other court of competent jurisdiction, the issue of custody and visitation of the minor children provided that any order entered as to such shall be immediately presented to the District Attorney's Office in Catoosa County. If the District Attorney's Office shall have any concerns with the order entered, the District Attorney may request this Court to modify the bond conditions to address the concern and a full hearing shall be conducted if necessary.

"So, the court gave me the right to fight for my kids up in Tennessee, but then gave itself the right to oversee whatever happens and to put new restrictions on me if it doesn't like what Tennessee decides?" I asked.

The attorney said I was reading that correctly.

This is the second page:

2.

Pursuant to the agreement of the parties, neither the Defendant nor the father of the children or any supervisor of visitation, shall not discuss with the children the facts of the criminal case, their potential testimony, or similar information concerning the criminal case.

3.

Pursuant to the agreement of the parties, the Defendant may attend family functions where other minor children are present. However, all contact with such children shall be supervised by another adult being present throughout any contact or visitation.

4.

Pursuant to the agreement of the parties, the Defendant shall have no contact, whether directly in person or indirectly through any means of communication, with any child under the age of eighteen. However, it is recognized that in attending normal public events such as church, grocery stores, and shopping centers, the Defendant may have incidental contact with children. In such a situation, the Defendant shall be civil and courteous to the child but shall promptly remove herself from the company of or communication with such children.

SO ORDERED, this 25th day of June, 2008.

RALPH VAN PELT,
JUDGE, SUPERIOR COURT
LOOKOUT MOUNTAIN JUDICIAL
CIRCUIT

It was also signed by my attorney, and then there was a third page that was signed by the DA, Buzz Franklin. The whole thing just flabbergasted me. First of all, it said over and over that "the parties agree," when I wasn't even present. *I didn't agree to any of this!* I'll admit I was grateful that the court was going to allow me to attend family functions and that the order made at least a little bit more sense when it talked about having indirect contact with children, but it was still pretty vague. It seemed to me it was still open to interpretation—that if I wasn't "prompt" enough in removing myself from a minor's presence, then someone could have me arrested. It still begged the question of what would happen if one of my friends' kids happened to answer the phone if I called. In fact, this seemed to clarify that I couldn't have direct or indirect contact by "any means of communication." That made me extremely nervous, and my attorney's assurances that those scenarios wouldn't lead to my arrest didn't set my mind at ease at all.

I walked away from that meeting knowing what I had to do.

Chapter 20

When you no longer have your work, your home, or your family—when you're no longer taking the kids to school, cooking, cleaning, getting groceries, running around to sports, or making plans for next week or next month or even tomorrow—there are a whole lot of empty hours in the day that get consumed by whatever you're thinking about. For someone whose life is going on as planned, having none of those things might seem like a dream. Like a vacation. It's not. It's a horrible, horrible way to exist, especially when you're consumed by the fear that you're going to spend the rest of your life in prison—and worse, not ever be able to see your children again.

The only way I could function was to focus on tasks that needed to get done. And the task that needed doing the most as July came around was to find myself a new lawyer. I made calls and read articles and looked up "Georgia's best lawyers" online. I even tried to set up an appointment with Bobby Lee Cook, the attorney who inspired the TV show *Matlock*. But another attorney seemed to be running his practice in Lafayette nowadays, and it turned out that one of the four judges who serve Catoosa County was Bobby Lee Cook's daughter. The potential for small-town conflicts and cronyism made me too uneasy to pursue it. The thing that had worried me most about my local attorney was a distinct feeling that he wasn't strong enough or aggressive enough to go up against these other locals that he dealt with every day. It wasn't a personal thing. I just didn't feel that his advice or his tepid stance or any of his actions thus far had been beneficial for me or my case. I needed an attorney with enough distance and autonomy and backbone to fight, and fight hard.

I finally reached out to two Atlanta-based attorneys named Cary and Scott King. They were a father-son team who came highly recommended. I called them as soon as I heard their credentials, and while their weekdays were full, Cary King heard my urgency and agreed to come into his office on a Saturday so I wouldn't have to wait. I liked him already.

I asked if Clancy could come to the meeting with me, and Cary didn't have any problem with that. He said it might be helpful to have him there. I liked that answer, too.

Clancy gave me some more homework before that meeting: to create separate timeline folders dedicated to each of the families involved in the allegations. So that meant a timeline folder dedicated entirely to Brianna Lamb—detailing when I'd first met Sandra and Brianna, and every time I could remember that Brianna had been to my house or that Ashley had been to their house for a sleepover, etc. Same for Kelly and Chloe McDonald. Same for the Wilsons. Clancy was absolutely convinced that if we could put all of this together, we could prove to a court that the abuse described in those warrants couldn't have happened—no matter what dates they put on them. What each of those detailed timelines would show was that I simply couldn't have been alone with Chloe or Brianna for more than a few moments, ever. Almost anytime I was around either of them, there were other witnesses present. The timelines would also show the completely normal relationship I had with my daughter and show just how much time David and Tyler were in the house with the two of us as well.

I spent the better part of that week entirely focused on creating those timelines and putting them into separate binders. I pasted calendars all over the walls of the motor home to help me visualize the dates and keep everything straight. I stayed up almost forty-eight hours straight that Thursday and Friday before the meeting with Cary to get it done. It felt good to be working and accomplishing something that I felt would help my case.

Our appointment was at Cary's office down in Atlanta on July 11—exactly one month after my arrest. It was intimidating at first, walking into a gigantic high-rise and trying to find their office. But I got a good feeling the moment I walked through their door.

Cary King had a gentlemanly look about him, with glasses, dark wavy hair, and a salt-and-pepper beard. Although he's not nearly old enough to be my grandfather, he had a sort of grandfatherly way about him. He seemed experienced and sure of himself and caring in a way that felt genuine, not forced. He listened deeply to what I had to say. And believe me, once I got going, I would not shut up. I told him all the ins and outs of everything that had happened, from the very beginning.

I was right in the middle of it when we heard someone else come into the office. It was Cary's son and business partner, Scott, a balding man in his thirties with a shaved head and a confident stride about him. Scott just happened to stop by that morning, but Cary called him in. "You have got to hear this," he said. "She couldn't make this stuff up!"

I went back and started at the beginning, and Cary listened to my entire story again with a deep sense of caring and worry for me as I talked about the detectives ringing my doorbell, my arrest, and the fact that I hadn't seen my kids for forty days and forty nights. Scott listened just as closely but seemed more incensed by the minute. It felt like he wanted to knock those detectives' teeth in for the way they'd handled this case. I got the distinct feeling that he wanted to kick Joal's teeth in, too. I liked his fire.

I had done enough research to know that Cary and Scott had handled cases involving allegations of child molestation in the past. I wasn't sure exactly how many of those cases they'd handled, but considering how incapable I felt my previous attorney was, I already felt better in their hands. I liked the fact that they were based in Atlanta, a solid two-hour drive and a cosmopolitan world away from Chickamauga. And I really liked their tenacity.

I think the thing they listened to most clearly was my resolve to clear my name. I didn't just want to "win my case" and get my kids back. I wanted everyone—my kids included—to know that I did not do this. My local attorney once told me that in order to win my case in court, "we'd only need to get one jury member." A lot of defense attorneys feel that way: As long as there's "reasonable doubt" and one jury member goes your way, you get a hung jury. To some attorneys that is a victory. Well, I didn't just want to prove beyond a reasonable doubt that I didn't do this. I wanted to prove beyond *any* doubt that I didn't do this.

Reaching for the lowest bar was not acceptable to me. Cary and Scott made it clear it wasn't acceptable to them, either. They actually sat there at that very first meeting—on a Saturday, mind you—and went through the timelines I brought in. They paged through the two-inch binder full of motions and orders from the criminal and custody hearings we'd already been through. They praised me for my hard work and praised Clancy for coming up with the idea of making those timelines in the first place.

Then Cary asked me point-blank: "Did you do this?"

"No," I said.

"Did you do any part of this?"

"No."

"Did you do anything that could be misconstrued as this?"

"No!"

I wasn't clueless about what could or could not be misconstrued as the improper handling of a child. I taught school. I'd had training on these matters. I was more aware than the average person, and I applied those lessons in my daily life. If Ashley had friends with her when we went to the pool, I wouldn't even wrap a towel around them because I wouldn't want anything to be misconstrued. I worked at a daycare center when I was in college and we always made sure someone else was present whenever we changed a diaper. I had not done one thing that even remotely resembled inappropriate touching with any of these girls or anyone else. I was sure of it.

Toward the end of the meeting, Cary looked at me and said, "I believe you. And you know what? They're going to *know* I believe you."

There are things in life you just know. It's a peaceful feeling when it happens—this very intense peace that you feel, like, "Okay, this is it." With Cary and Scott, it was just a fit. I never questioned if they were right from that day onward. I knew they were right. It wasn't all rainbows and roses. We'd get into some major disagreements in the coming months and fight like family around the dinner table. But in my heart I felt God had brought me to them.

On Monday I typed up a letter dismissing my former attorney. He wrote back to me a few days later. He kindly returned most of the retainer we'd given him, and I knew he didn't have to do that. I was grateful. He said he was "very disappointed" that I didn't have more faith in him. I wanted to write back and tell him what I *really* thought. But I didn't. It wasn't worth any more of my anger or my time. To use an old cliché, I had bigger fish to fry. My parents wrote yet another check in order to retain Cary and Scott, and I finally felt like I was building a top-notch team of cooks in my metaphorical kitchen.

Chapter 21

The rest of the scorching month of July was spent prepping for my job-termination hearing in Chickamauga on August 15; continuing to fight for the right to see my children under "normal" circumstances; continuing to fight Joal to let the kids see my parents, their friends, and anybody else they'd been ripped apart from (in addition to myself); and trying to make sense of the absurdity of my imprisonment in the motor home in Diana's driveway. There were times when I needed to take a shower when Josh was home, and that poor boy would wind up standing around in the blazing sun in the yard while I went inside the house to clean up. *How long is this going to go on?*

It was during this period when I first learned that my children were being forced to see a court-ordered therapist named Laurie Evans. Evans worked at the Children's Advocacy Center, right next door to the courthouse in Ringgold. This one therapist was seeing my son as well as *all three* of the little girls who were involved in my case. I'm no expert, but that seemed absurd to me. *Wouldn't the prosecution want independent verification of what those girls were supposedly going through? Why would they want to have to rely on one therapist to make the case for all three girls?*

One of the first goals my new team of attorneys set was to gather all the information we could get our hands on in order to figure out what was really going on behind the scenes. We wanted transcripts of each of my accusers' interviews. We wanted to see the actual videotapes of those interviews—and we knew they were required by law in the state of Georgia to videotape any interview with a child. We wanted phone records from the detectives and from the accusers' parents. But we wouldn't be able to even *request* any of those things until after an indictment came down. So we went above and beyond the criminal case and used my divorce case with David to subpoena phone records from David and from Sandra Lamb. We used the custody case in Tennessee to subpoena phone records from Joal and Sarah, too, and started putting paperwork in motion to demand depositions from the parties in each of those cases.

My attorneys warned me that the process would not be a quick one.

The only saving grace seemed to be my upcoming termination hearing. I know that sounds funny, but with the way the school district had filed their case against me, they had opened the door to the calling of witnesses. We prepared subpoenas to send to Sandra Lamb, the Wilsons, the McDonalds, to David, and more. We also planned to subpoena teachers and colleagues to testify that there had never been any problems with me and that in fact I was a great teacher and an asset to the community. But a big part of what we hoped to gain during that termination hearing was knowledge about the criminal allegations, of which we still knew so little.

My heart broke every time I thought about my classroom. The superintendent specifically forbade me from going onto school grounds or participating in the usual routines of my employment whatsoever that summer. They wouldn't even let me back into my classroom to pick up my things. I had hundreds, maybe thousands of dollars' worth of supplies I had purchased with my own money in that classroom. David had bought me a beautiful set of cabinets and a new desk for that room as a gift, which I cherished. Knowing that I couldn't touch any of those things opened a hole in my heart almost as big as the hole I had for the belongings that still sat in my home—all those little objects and photos that provide a sense of comfort and familiarity in the place where you live. I hoped that by bringing in all of those witnesses and making my case in front of the Chickamauga School Board, they would at the very least see the mistakes of their ways, put me on administrative leave until the case was finished, and perhaps let me in after-hours to pick up my things.

While those preparations and that whole subpoena process was under way, my attorneys went back to the very origins of the case against me. They looked at the fact that the detectives and the ADA had told my original attorney that if I passed a polygraph test, the charges would be dropped—and we decided it would be in my best interest to go get a polygraph of my own. We began a search for the most-qualified polygraph examiner we could find—someone whose reputation could not be questioned. By anyone.

The thought of it terrified me. How was I going to sit there and answer questions without my nervousness overtaking everything and making me look guilty?

At the same time, we went ahead and hired a private investigator to start finding out more about the circumstances of the allegations. I followed the advice of Scott and Cary and we hired a man named Eric Echols, a P.I. with impeccable credentials and a stellar reputation for getting to the bottom of things. Eric came aboard with a healthy skepticism; I could tell. He didn't presume I was innocent. It wasn't until he listened to what I had to say, and then did a little digging himself, that he came to the conclusion that the allegations against me were false and that his abilities as an investigator could be put to good use to help me prove it. We assigned him a huge task to begin with: background checks on all of the key players involved in my case, including ADA Chris Arnt (the assistant district attorney assigned to my case, whom I hadn't even laid eyes on yet), the detectives (Stephen Keith and Tim Deal), and even my own husband, David—*everyone*. Then we put together a list of names for him to subpoena, including some of my friends, acquaintances, and colleagues—hoping to bring them in for a series of videotaped interviews that would illuminate who I really was. Those friendly interviews would be sworn in and witnessed in a manner that would make them acceptable in a court of law. We had to dot every "i" and cross every "t," and we knew it.

Eric was also tasked with serving subpoenas to Joal and Sarah and a whole host of my new "adversaries." We didn't expect those would be easy to get, but Eric was skilled at delivering court orders and getting cooperation from the uncooperative. I put a lot of trust in the fact that he would be out there doing what I needed him to do while I continued my personal battle for survival.

Finally, as August came around, we found the best polygraph examiner we could find—and he just happened to be located right in Atlanta. Charles Slupski was his name. He was a graduate of the US Army Polygraph School and a former instructor at the Department of Defense Polygraph Institute. He founded the American International Institute of Polygraph. He was the guy who *taught* people how to do this. He was just what I wanted and needed. He was beyond reproach. It would cost a small fortune to get him to administer a polygraph himself, but at this point I knew it was worth it. After all, you get what you pay for. My dad had always hammered that phrase home with me, and boy, oh boy, did I understand it now. If I was going to cut corners, it wouldn't be with this.

We set an appointment for August 8. I was ready to go prove my innocence. I got up and had coffee with Diana that morning, and we both got into her car for the drive to Atlanta. That's when the panic attack hit. The racing heart. The cold sweats. The trembling. The fear.

"Diana," I cried. "What happens if I fail?"

Chapter 22

 My panic attack never let up.

Mr. Slupski kept me locked in a room for hours, grilling me over and over again with those wires and straps on me. It was torture. The whole time I thought for sure my shaking and sweating had falsely pointed toward my "guilt."

Mr. Slupski's face remained expressionless the whole time, even when he finally gave me my result: "Tonya, you passed the polygraph." I burst into tears. I stepped out of that torture room weeping, with my head held down, my face smeared with makeup. Cary and Diana looked anxious at the far end of the hall. "What's wrong?" they asked. They didn't understand. Mr. Slupski had delivered the news of my "stellar outcome" to them a few minutes before he revealed the news to me. I couldn't put it into words at the time, but expecting me to be happy after enduring that experience was like expecting someone who had been viciously violated to "just be happy that it's over."

Plus, it *wasn't* over. I still had a possibility of failing. I'd have to come back in a few days for "part two" in order for Mr. Slupski to confirm his findings. I felt like I'd just completed the first round of chemotherapy—something that I hoped and prayed was good for me, but that made me sick nonetheless. I fell fast asleep as Diana drove me home.

We wound up postponing the second half of that polygraph exam. The very same day it was supposed to happen, we walked into the Juvenile Court in Chattanooga prepared to resolve the matter of seeing my children, only to have the judge argue once again that it wasn't in their jurisdiction. We had to move everything over to Circuit Court and schedule another hearing—for September.

Joal had gone ahead and enrolled my kids in a school in Tennessee. I was worried sick that my daughter may still be showering with her stepmother.[16] Because of our filings in Tennessee, an investigator had supposedly knocked on their door to check into the allegations—but then walked away after Joal said that everything at home was normal. The investigator didn't talk to Ashley, Sarah, or anybody else.

I was a wreck.

"I need to see my kids," I told Cary as we sat in his car in the parking lot afterward. "I'll go to Four Points. I don't care if they treat me like a monster in that facility. I can't take it anymore. I need to see them!"

"We'll set up an appointment," Cary said as I broke down and dissolved into a shell of myself right in front of him.

As we drove up to the Chickamauga Elementary administration building on August 15, we saw camera crews out front and hordes of people. When we rounded the corner to find a place to park, I spotted a dark-haired man in a suit standing off by himself, talking on a cell phone beside the building. I wondered if he was the attorney for the school board. There were more police vehicles there than I could possibly count, and the number of uniformed officers walking around made it look like there'd been a bomb threat or something.

Why is this happening? I wondered. *Why does it need to be this way?*

After they aired my mug shot on TV, school superintendent Melody Day suggested to me that I should resign. She suggested that would be "best for everyone." I unequivocally stated I had done nothing wrong and had nothing to hide. She did not seem to like that very much. How it turned from a private matter into a public spectacle, though, I have no idea.

Seeing all of those townspeople gathered out front, I could only imagine that I'd have some pretty ugly words tossed at me on the way into that building. I took a few minutes to prepare myself. Finally, with my team surrounding me, we walked toward the front door—only to find a whole bunch of *supporters* filtering up the steps. No one shouted anything nasty at me. Instead, all I heard was, "You go, Miss Tonya!"

"We're here for you, Tonya!"

"Stay strong, Tonya!"

An officer stood there at the doorway vetting everyone who came in. He was sort of like an usher at a wedding, only instead of asking if guests were with the bride or the groom, he asked, "Are you *for* or *against*?" When people answered, they were shuffled into one room or another.

It floored me that so many people would come out to support me. I closed my eyes and thanked God—and when I opened them, I spotted an old friend: Kim Walker. Kim was the young woman I'd yelled at on the phone the day those detectives first rang my doorbell. Seeing her caught me off guard. I glared at her something awful.

It was almost time for the hearing to begin, and a whole bunch of authorities swarmed the building trying to create some sense of order. The hearing room filled up as they finally let my supporters in, and my attorneys donated their own seats to people who had no place to sit. Everybody who wasn't seated was kicked out of the room. They either stood in the hall or went outside to join a prayer circle that somebody told me had formed on the front lawn. *Who ever heard of a prayer circle to support someone accused of child molestation?* I thought. I was truly moved.

There was one supportive face missing from that crowd, though—the one face I had most hoped to see right behind me that day. I guess I half expected him not to show up, despite the subpoena. The school board's attorney had made a last-minute filing that morning to ensure that we wouldn't be able to call any witnesses related to the criminal case. It sure felt fishy that word got around to the witnesses in time for them to not show up. Still, David's absence stung. I really thought he'd turn up for me. I looked down at my wedding ring and silently prayed, once again, "God, please let us reconcile or please let me stop loving him."

Suddenly the hearing was called to order and the entire building stuffed full of people quieted down.[17] My attorneys spoke first, asking for a continuance to address the eleventh-hour changes we'd been presented with that morning. The school board denied the request. Instead they went ahead and called Superintendent Melody Day to testify.

Ms. Day got up there and testified that she had no knowledge of any facts that would support the charges against me. She also stated that she had never seen me behave inappropriately in any way toward a child. She agreed with my attorney's assertion that no one had ever reported *any* inappropriate behavior by "Miss Craft."

"She is a very good teacher," she said. According to her own testimony, her first knowledge of my allegations came from the media.

Then they called ADA Chris Arnt forward to testify. He was the man I had seen on a cell phone outside the building—a stocky man with a wide nose, dark eyes, and an odd hairline scrawled across the top of his forehead like it was drawn by a child's shaky hand. I was suddenly face-to-face with the man who was heading up the case against me. It's hard to describe how that felt. I could barely look at him, but I couldn't take my eyes off him, either.

The cynical side of me could not ignore the fact that he and everyone else in the DA's office would be up for reelection that November. *Is that what this is about? Am I just a pawn in a political campaign?*

The ADA got up there in front of all of those people and recounted the fact that I had been arrested on felony charges of inappropriately touching three girls, all of whom were students at Chickamauga Elementary. He didn't use the word "allegedly." It didn't seem to matter that the alleged "touching" had not happened at the school. It did not seem to matter that we were requesting an administrative leave without pay until the outcome of the case was determined and that therefore I wouldn't have contact with anyone at the school. It didn't seem to matter that none of the allegations had been proven or that I hadn't even been indicted. Nothing seemed to matter. The whole "hearing" was nothing but a formality to a foregone conclusion.

ADA Chris Arnt was the last witness the school board allowed.

After the briefest deliberation imaginable, the school board delivered their finding: terminated.

I'd predicted that outcome all along, I suppose, yet somehow it didn't hit me until I heard the actual word. My lawyers assured me they would file an appeal, but I knew in my heart that appeal would be denied. Cary King went out in front of the cameras as soon as it was over and proclaimed my innocence to the world, saying we would "prove" my innocence when my case came to trial. I doubted the truth of the latter part of his statement more than ever on that terrible day.

Chris Arnt went outside in front of those same cameras and told them that justice had been done there that day—and that justice would be done when Tonya Craft was put behind bars.

I climbed into the car with Scott and Clancy and wondered what was taking Cary so long. I just wanted to leave.

"You'll never guess who just pulled me aside," Cary said as he got in.

"Who?"

"Your friend Kim Walker."

"Oh yeah? What did she want?" I asked.

Turns out Kim wasn't against me. She came there to stand with my supporters.

"What?" I said. "What did she say?"

"She teared up," he said. "She wants to help. She said, 'I *know* Tonya didn't do this.'"

Kim had been mixed up in this thing from the beginning. I had assumed she was on the side of Sandra, Joal, Kelly, and the Wilsons. If I was wrong—and apparently I'd been wrong—then she knew what had happened and might be able to help us. Her daughter, Skyler, was there when this all began. Her daughter had been questioned by the detectives. If she was willing to forgive my judging her in haste, Kim could potentially help me understand how this all began.

"That's good news," I said.

"It's extremely good news," Cary added.

A part of me felt terrible. If I had judged Kim in haste, then she needed to hear my apology. Kim is one of the sweetest people I have ever known. I hoped and prayed that she and I might be able to be friends again.

I didn't get more than a few seconds to savor that feeling of relief, though.

As the car pulled away, and I saw those camera crews packing up, the hard truth of what had just happened in that building hit me like a kick to the stomach. Teaching had been my God-given passion. It was, in the truest sense, my life's work. And in a matter of minutes, based on nothing but allegations, that school system had just tossed my entire career—one of my very reasons for living—out the window.

Chapter 23

There were days when I woke up wishing that I hadn't woken up at all—feeling angry at God for not taking me in my sleep just to stop the pain. I was in that state when I went to see Mr. Slupski again on August 27.

I shook. I broke down. I left in tears. I walked out of the building as quickly as I could. I was sure that I'd failed that second polygraph. This time, I'd have to wait for days until an analysis was completed in order get my results.

I was also in that state when I went to visit Four Points, to make all the preparations to finally see my children in that highly supervised facility. My interview there was as grueling as the polygraph. They made me feel like a monster. I hadn't been convicted of anything whatsoever, but the people at that facility barked orders at me about how I wouldn't be able to have any physical contact with my children. I worried about how damaging it might be for my children to see me under those conditions, and I asked God once again why I was being punished when I had not done a thing.

I was tucked back inside the motor home with the shades drawn when the email from Mr. Slupski finally arrived. I left it unopened on my laptop for hours. I'd learned a few things since I'd gone in for the first polygraph. Things that left me too scared to look. For instance, in the state of Georgia, no one in law enforcement can be hired until they pass a polygraph. If polygraphs are considered a reliable test before handing someone a badge and a gun, then clearly if I failed that test, the prosecution would be salivating to use it against me. If I failed, it was my understanding that it would stand as "proof" of my guilt. I felt like I'd just dug my own grave. I wished I'd never taken it.

At some point, I decided it would be better to know my fate than to wonder, so I got off the bed and opened the email. I scanned the document from the top, as quickly as I could. When I finally reached a section called "Findings," I noticed that I had been holding my breath that entire time. I closed my eyes. I filled my lungs. I exhaled slowly. I tried to calm down. Then I looked and saw the words that mattered: "a conclusion of **No Deception Indicated** . . . Tonya H. Craft **was being truthful.**"

The bolds and underlines are exactly how they appeared in that report.

My attorneys would of course think those findings were wonderful. Me? I knew I'd been telling the truth all along. Seeing that report, all I could think was, *Why do I need this? Why have I been put through this?*

I couldn't even muster up a smile.

I had agreed at the outset of these allegations to take a polygraph with the examiner in Catoosa County. All I asked was to have my attorney present. I'd agreed to it on the very first day those detectives first rang my doorbell, and I'd agreed to it again through my attorney ten days later—only to have that offer rescinded and a warrant issued for my arrest. Now I'd finally gone and done what they wanted, and I stood there doubting whether any of it would matter.

My body was failing me. I felt sick and exhausted. I was hardly doing anything but sleeping and praying. And then things got worse.

First, Joal refused to take Ashley and Tyler to Four Points even though there was a court order directing as much. Additionally, ADA Chris Arnt placed one phone call to Four Points and somehow quashed the possibility of me seeing my children in that facility. One call and it was over.[18]

Then my dad's mom died. My sweet grandmother, Mabel. I wasn't allowed to attend her funeral. There would be children there. My bond said I would have to remove myself from the presence of any children as quickly as possible. My attorneys said I simply should not go.

I used to say to people, "If something ever happened and I couldn't be with my kids, you might as well bury me." I swear, the death of my grandmother made me wish that I could've followed her into the ground. I would never consider taking my own life, but I felt in my heart that death would have been easier than spending the rest of my life in prison.

I hid myself in the motor home. I refused to eat. I refused to answer my phone. I blocked out the world and tried to make myself disappear. For days.

Diana came in and took photos of me lying in bed, practically comatose with the shades all down. She wanted to document everything I was going through. They were worried to death, and none of their kind words or even Diana's home cooking made me snap out of it. Finally, her husband, Michael, came in and got mad at me.

"Okay, Tonya," he said. "You've had your cry. Now it's time to put your big-girl panties on and get out of that bed. Do you hear me?"

Michael's about the gentlest man you could ever meet. He'd stayed pretty quiet throughout this whole ordeal. He stood behind Diana, and I wondered sometimes if he was secretly mad at her for taking me in and putting his family through all of this. But he'd never said a harsh word, ever. His tough talk startled me.

The thing is, he was right. They say you never know what you're capable of until you're put to the test, and clearly this test was not over. I needed to go get my kids back. I needed to get up and find a way to get strong again.

From the corner of my eye, I saw him looking at me, waiting for a response. He shook his head when I didn't move.

"Tonya—I have something very important to tell you," he said.

"What?" I asked.

"I love you," he said. That took me by surprise, too. Then he turned to go.

"Michael," I called.

"Yeah?"

I lifted my head and propped myself up. "Would you do something for me?"

"You know that I will. What is it?"

"Can we go get my treadmill?"

Chapter 24

On September 13, Michael and Diana drove me down to Chickamauga in their pickup truck with a trailer on the back. It was the first time I'd stepped foot in my house since I'd first come to Diana's for "just one night" on June 1. It felt like I was walking into a dream, stepping back into some long-ago life that didn't exist anymore. I looked at the pictures on the walls and some of the photos in little frames on the tables and everywhere of what had been my family. One second I would stare at my kids' smiling faces and feel flushed with joy, and the next it'd be too painful to look at them. I decided to take some of those photos back with me, just so I could look at them when I wanted to—or when I needed to.

It struck me as strange that the house had just sat there, basically untouched. *Why have they never searched my home? Surely they could have gotten a search warrant in all that time. If they believe that I'm a child molester, wouldn't they want to search my house? Search through my photos? Seize my computer? Something?*

I made a mental note to myself that I'd better back up all of my computer files in case anyone ever came after my trusty black laptop.

I tried to focus on the task at hand and get out of that house as soon as possible. The whole time I was in there I kept worrying that the doorbell was going to ring. I kept worrying that someone would report that we were there, and that somehow they'd find a reason to come out and arrest me.

We had another friend meet us at the house to help with the lifting, and they managed to get my treadmill, my elliptical, the free weights, and all the rest of that heavy equipment loaded up in a few painstaking hours. We set them up in Diana's garage on the very same day. Diana took a picture as I stepped foot onto that treadmill for the first time in months.

I don't think I had realized quite how important it was to me before. That treadmill had been my therapist and psychologist. Instead of lying on a couch telling some stranger my innermost thoughts and struggles,

I would pound away on the treadmill—and talk to God. For years, that's where I'd found my peace, where I pushed my body as hard as it could go while I had my private internal conversations.

I was apprehensive as I turned it on. I started real slow. Then I pushed my speed up a little bit. My legs got sore in no time at all, but I didn't stop. I pushed myself, faster and faster. I woke the next morning in agonizing pain, but I pushed myself through it and ran again. I prayed to God with every stride I took. I prayed for Ashley. I prayed for Tyler. I prayed for my life. I prayed for Sandra Lamb, and Sherri Wilson, and Kelly McDonald, and even ADA Chris Arnt. I prayed for Joal and Sarah, too. I prayed for them to find peace, to find wisdom, to find truth, and to let go of whatever demons were driving them to make the appalling choices I thought they were making. I prayed for Chloe. I prayed for Brianna, too. I prayed that nothing had happened to those little girls, and I prayed that they'd find the strength to get through the awful pressure that they must be under.

Then, even after all that time, even after all that hurt, I prayed once again for reconciliation with my husband, David.

The running made me hungry, so I ate Diana's food. The next day I ran on the treadmill some more. Then again the next day. And again. A few days later, I worked up the courage to take a run around Diana's neighborhood. I let myself feel the September chill in the air, and I noticed the different hues of the sky. I got on the phone and talked to my attorneys, and I talked to Kim Walker, Dee Potter, Tammy, and Shanica Lewis. I talked to P.I. Eric Echols about the interviews we'd conducted and brainstormed about whom we should interview next. I started doing some research again, typing away on my little black laptop deep into the wee hours of the morning.

I began to wrap my head around the fact that I would need to keep working in order to build my defense. I started feeling less than horrible about the case we'd built so far and the fact that I had actually made some progress along the way. I had a solid team of attorneys now. I had more allies in the community than I'd once believed. The more I heard from them, and the more they opened up on the record, the more fishy this whole "investigation" against me became. I realized that I still had lots of questions that I needed to find answers to, and that *I* was the one who needed to lead the search.

After all, who had more at stake here than I did? Who was going to fight harder for me than *me*? This fight wasn't even *about* me, in the end.

This fight was about my children. I needed to rescue them from this horrible ordeal.

I got so fired up one night that I said to Diana, "You know what? I didn't *mess with the wrong families.* They messed with the wrong mother's *kids!*"

Diana seemed thrilled to see me charged up again.

From that day forward, I ran. I was sure I would continue to collapse now and then. I was sure I would continue to have plenty of down days. In the back of my mind, I also knew that there would be a very long road ahead. This was going to be a marathon longer than anyone could anticipate. I just prayed that every time I got knocked down, I would somehow find the strength to get back up.

And I ran, and I ran, and I ran.

———————————

As my strength improved that month, so did my understanding of some of the circumstances that led to the charges against me. We'd managed to set up a series of on-the-record, videotaped interviews with colleagues and friends who all provided valuable information. My P.I., Eric Echols, conducted the interviews with one of my attorneys and a court reporter present—as official as could be. (And as expensive as could be. I often asked myself, *How does anybody defend themselves against these sorts of charges if they don't have these sorts of financial resources?*)

Dee Potter, whose kids were still enrolled at Chickamauga, turned out to be full of valuable information. She still saw Kelly and Sandra and everybody who was involved in this on a regular basis. She knew more than I realized. She had also been one of the friends who had heard Sandra spouting off about me at the ball fields.[19]

Kim Walker was a huge fount of information for us as well. She told us—on the record—that she had been threatened and bullied into *forcing* her daughter to talk to the detectives about me.[20] She helped us to get a handle on when the allegations first seemed to arise, too. They were prompted in part by something her daughter had allegedly written in sidewalk chalk over at Sherri Wilson's house one day. Something that rubbed both Sherri and Sandra the wrong way. Her little girl supposedly wrote the word "sex." Apparently those parents got all upset about it, and they wound up grilling Skyler and Brianna about a game they'd allegedly been playing with my daughter, Ashley. They apparently called it the "boyfriend-girlfriend game." It involved the girls kissing each other on the cheek, and it may or may not have involved some touching. It was very unclear. All I could think was I wished someone had spoken to me about it at the time, because I have no idea if Ashley was really involved in such a game or not.[21] I never got the chance to ask her myself.

Kim said the allegations against me built from there, after Sandra spent three days grilling Brianna about whether or not something more had happened—and whether I'd "done something" to her daughter.

Kim also shared that Sandra and Kelly had coached their children on what to say about me before their interviews with the detectives. Both of those mothers tried to insist that Kim "remind" Skyler about what I had supposedly done to her as well. It was shocking, sickening, but incredibly valuable information.[22]

My attorneys assured me that all of those interviews were very good news.

On September 27, I went along with Eric to a series of interviews we'd set up at a local hotel. We used a hotel so it would be neutral ground for everybody involved. The fact that I got a room at that hotel for the night was a fluke, really. It came included as part of the rental rate for the conference room we were using. I certainly wasn't going to turn *that* down. It would allow me a little bit of reprieve from the motor home: a real bed, a real bathroom, and some luxurious bedding.

The interviews flowed smoothly and drew to a close around dinnertime, so Eric and I decided to grab a bite before he headed back to Atlanta. There was a favorite chain restaurant of mine nearby called Bonefish Grill that I hadn't been to since this all began, so we decided to go there, just the two of us.

As we walked in, I noticed lots of glares thrown our way. I think I know the reason: Eric is African American, and I'm Caucasian. We were in the Deep South. Judgment ensued. I found it almost entertaining. I wondered if the people staring knew who I was. *If they knew the charges that have been made against me, would they be more incensed by those accusations or by the fact that I'm standing next to a black man?*

My mood was almost light as we sat down. I was determined to benefit from this rare opportunity for a good meal out with some good company.

All that changed seconds before the food arrived. I looked up—and I saw David. My husband, David. He saw me, too. He was walking right toward us. He glanced at Eric, looked at me, and then rolled his eyes and laughed a little bit. He *laughed* and then kept on walking.

I froze. Eric immediately noticed my mood change. I'd gone from talkative to mute in two seconds flat. He asked me several times what the matter was before I finally responded.

"That was David," I said. I said it with a gamut of emotions. I didn't know what emotion I should feel.

"We need to leave," I said. I stood up and walked out. Eric called a waitress over and boxed up our food as I rushed outside to catch my breath. He drove me back to the hotel. He walked me to my room. I was silent the whole time. So was he. I don't think he knew what to do. I certainly didn't know what to do. The flood of emotion was awful. I stared into space as if no person was present in my body.

Eric sat in a chair and I sat cross-legged on the corner of the bed until he finally spoke a few simple words. "Tonya, this will all be okay," he said—and I lost it.

"How do you know this will all be okay? Can you guarantee me I will not go to prison for something I did not do? My husband just walked by me and *laughed*. What is funny about this situation? Tell me!" My tirade continued as Eric sat with his index fingers touching one another, covering his mouth. He listened patiently until I finally said, "Just leave, because you don't care either!"

Silently he rose and walked out the door. He texted me when he left and said he was there if I needed him.

I collapsed onto the bed and sobbed—for the loss I felt, for the humiliation I felt, for my suspicion that David was probably on the phone with Sandra Lamb right at that moment, laughing about how his wife was out to dinner with a "black man."

I was angry at Eric for not being able to fix it. I felt rejected by David for turning his back on me again and finding some sort of sick humor in my pain. And once again, I saw no conclusion to any of this other than my life being spent behind bars. Each and every time I thought I was as depleted as I could get, something else came along and ripped my heart from my chest.

I lay in that hotel room for hours without a wink of sleep. Finally, at 4:32 A.M., I tore myself out of bed, packed up my things, threw them into my car, and sped back toward the motor home.

As I pulled onto the interstate, four police cars came rushing up behind me. Lights flashing. Sirens blaring.

"What now?!" I screamed as I pulled over into the breakdown lane and dropped my head onto the steering wheel. The sound of the sirens got louder and louder. The screeching, whining, overlapping pitch of them rose higher and higher, assaulting my ears, and then fell away as the cars rushed by me and sped on down the freeway.

I looked up. I sat there for a few minutes, wondering if there would ever be a time for the rest of my life when I would see a police car and not panic. I suppose that was a good thought to have. Maybe there was still a slight glimmer of hope somewhere inside, some small part of me that still believed that not every second of the rest of my life would be spent behind bars.

Chapter 25

As I entered month five of not seeing my children, with absolutely no communication from anyone as to how they were doing either in school or out, I pushed all three of my attorneys to get more deeply involved.

It took us at least two court orders over a two-month period just to get the kids' new school to release my children's records. Subpoenas were sent to Laurie Evans, the court-ordered therapist who had been seeing Ashley and Tyler on a regular basis (as well as Chloe and Brianna), demanding her appearance in court for depositions. We brought in experts to make assessments of not only my home but my parents' home as well, to clear them for visitation and also for taking custody of the children regardless of whether or not I would be able to see them myself. We attempted to get court-ordered evaluations of Joal and Sarah's home, to ensure that the kids were living in a safe environment. Given the number of times we had to go back to court to accomplish anything, it seemed to me that we were facing obvious stalling tactics from the other side.

Laurie Evans, the kids' therapist, the one person who perhaps more than anyone should have been working "in the best interest of the children," was in my view about as bad as it gets. On the day of her first scheduled deposition, she faxed my attorneys and demanded an up-front fee of hundreds of dollars for her time before she would appear. I had them send her a check. I didn't want any excuse for her not to show up. She cashed the check, and we set a new date, and then next time around she pulled the same thing, sending a fax again and demanding more money.

I had Eric try to unearth some background information on that woman as fast as he could. Something wasn't right. All of a sudden, I wondered what this woman had to hide. *Who is she? Is she even qualified to be dealing with my children?*

On top of it all, we knew that the grand jury was convening in Catoosa County and that any day now an indictment could come down. Under normal circumstances, that wouldn't have been a big deal. My attorneys all told me that because I had already been arrested and had already been released on bond, "You will not get rearrested when those indictments are issued."

I told my attorneys that was hogwash.

"Believe me, if they have the chance to arrest me and put me through a perp walk for any reason whatsoever, they're going to do it," I said.

Cary and Scott both insisted that wasn't true. "Look, even if there was a new charge against you at this point, what normally happens is there's a phone call made to the DA's office, the new charge is tacked on to the other charges, an adjustment is made on the bond if necessary, and it's all handled with a phone call to the judge," Cary said.

"No, *you* look," I said. "There is nothing *normal* about my case. If you think an indictment's coming down, you need to tell me so we can deal with it on our terms, not theirs. There is no way I'm going to let them throw me in handcuffs in some public place and parade me around on the news."

"Tonya, that is not going to happen. Don't be so paranoid," Scott said.

I shot him a look that might've knocked a weaker man over.

No indictment would come down that fall, or even that winter. I would be forced to wait, never knowing when that boulder would drop off the cliff and land on top of me.

I don't know if I would have made it without my City Church family, and specifically Pastor Chapman.

When I first started living in Diana's driveway, I'd refused to go to church. I was scared to go anywhere because of the "indirect contact" order on my bond. I was scared to death that I'd walk into that church and people would jerk their kids away and walk out. I'd said to Diana, "What if that happens?"

Diana and Michael had been going to City Church much longer than I had. They were deacons. It was like a second home to them. Yet they said to me, "Tonya, if that happens, we will get up and walk out with you and never go back again." Their dedication to me helped convince me to try. And in fact, on the very first day I walked into that church, the opposite of what I feared might happen happened. Everybody was beyond wonderful.

As time went on, my friends and supporters held fund-raisers at that church to help me deal with my legal expenses. Pastor Chapman and his wife attended and wrote me a check out of their own pockets. I'm telling you, that church did what you dream of when you think of the Church and faith and what it's supposed to be all about. When it came time to put up or shut up, they put up.

My friend Jennifer gave me a different sort of support around that same time: She gave me a key to her town house. Jennifer is single and lived nearby with her sister. She told me I could stay at her home anytime I needed to. I could come and go as I pleased. Anytime, day or night.

There were times that fall when the motor home grew icy cold, and at 2:00 A.M., when I couldn't take the cold anymore, I'd jump into my SUV and drive over to Jennifer's just to lie on that couch and warm up.

I'd always hated being cold. I couldn't stand it. Now I felt cold on the inside and out, and I hated it even more.

Chapter 26

Iglared at David. I kept glaring at him across the conference table. It was the first time he'd made eye contact with me since that night at the restaurant when he'd laughed and walked away, and now he sat there with this confused, uncomfortable look on his face, as if he didn't understand why I was glaring.

David's deposition took place in a conference room at attorney Larry Stagg's office on November 5. Stagg, the man David hired to represent him in the divorce, also happened to be Sandra Lamb's family attorney. *Coincidence?* We were set to depose Sandra Lamb on the very same day that Stagg was set to depose *me*. In truth, my biggest concern wasn't any of those depositions. My primary purpose for being there wouldn't come until after all three depositions were over.

Cary King began by asking David a bunch of financial and personal-information questions—the kind of stuff you'd expect in a divorce. But it didn't take long for Cary to switch gears and ask if David was aware of the criminal charges that were pending against me down in Georgia.

Of course he's aware, I thought. *He's been talking to Sandra the whole time, and I have my suspicions that he's been talking to Joal, too.*

The thing was, when we asked whom David had been talking to about the charges, he said that he had talked to two detectives. I had forgotten that the detectives said they talked to David on the day they rang my doorbell. I had never confirmed whether or not that actually happened. "The police called me and needed me to come in and answer a few questions," he said, "and I went in, 'cause I didn't have anything to hide."

David doesn't like to get caught up in anything. He doesn't want to pick a side. He prefers to stay out of arguments. That can be a good trait to have. It's not a good trait when you're trying *not* to pick a side in defense of your wife who's just been accused of molesting children.

117

Contrary to what those detectives told me on my front porch, David denied telling the detectives, "I think she's a child molester."[23] But he also didn't say, "She didn't do this!" He didn't openly defend me. It was more like he was trying to ride the fence on the questions. David said he told them I was a good mom, but when they asked why he had left me, he told them that I hadn't been giving him enough attention. In fact, he said I'd been paying too much attention to Ashley because I was upset about something that was going on over at Joal's house (a red flag that the detectives completely ignored).

Cary tried fishing around for some more details about how the investigation around me began, but we could tell pretty quickly that David didn't have a lot of information to share. As far as how much he had been talking to Sandra, or to Joal, I couldn't tell. We still hadn't gotten a hold of his phone records at that point, so all we could do was take his word for it. He said that he had spoken to Sandra on "quite a few" occasions and that he had only spoken to Joal "to see how the kids were doing."

What? I thought. *He can't stand Joal!*

I knew there was no way he would ever call Joal just to "see how the kids were doing." It didn't make sense. *And if he cares so much about the kids, why isn't he making a declaration about my innocence? Or my guilt, for that matter, if he believes I've done something?*

When we asked for David to get more specific about how many times he had talked to Sandra, he said it was "too many times to count." *Just as I suspected.* But when we asked what they talked about, he said he didn't remember. *Isn't that convenient!*

David's deposition wrapped up with me feeling like I'd learned almost nothing and without my getting the satisfaction I wanted to get from looking him in the eye. I was frustrated. I don't know what I had envisioned happening exactly, but I definitely envisioned something more than that.

My own deposition came next, and David's attorney seemed to focus on asking me questions that were only tangentially related to the divorce. Almost everything seemed to focus on the charges against me and seemed to be fishing for information about what I knew and didn't know. I answered honestly—all the while knowing that they would try to use anything I said against me if they could.

All I thought about the whole time was that David, my husband, still looked like he was more confused than angry or hurt or guilty or any of the other emotions I thought he'd exhibit that day. He was still in that room, sitting down at the far end of the table now.

It wasn't until we took a small break and everyone else filtered out of the room that he looked at me and said, "So, how you been doing?"

"Excuse me?" I spat. "I think you know *exactly* how I've been doing!"

David didn't bother asking anything else after that. He left the room and had a little powwow with his attorney. When we all came back from break, David's attorney asked me, "How is it that you think David should know how you've been doing?"

"Because he's been talking to Sandra Lamb and Joal Henke," I said.

The attorney seemed suspicious when I said that. He asked how I had known that. He even implied I had already looked at David's phone records.

"No," I said. "I just know my husband." Both David and his attorney seemed taken aback by my response. The rest of that deposition went round and round, and none of it mattered to me. I barely remember what they asked me.

We all took a break for lunch, and when we came back in, that was when I laid eyes on Sandra Lamb for the first time in months. I was completely taken aback by the conservative attire she wore to that deposition. I'd never seen her in anything so conservative for as long as I'd known her. Clearly she was ready to put on a show for the camera, I thought.

She seemed to put on a show for the attorneys, too: Just before we started, Cary came to me and said, "Tonya, I know you didn't do anything, but Sandra's attorney asked that you not sit next to her." Apparently Sandra was worried that she might feel compelled to do me physical harm if she had to sit too close to me.

That was fine by me. She sat down at one end of the table with her attorney to her left, and I sat at the other end, basically directly across from David. That was the first time I noticed David looking at me with these sort of puppy-dog eyes. As if he felt bad for me. I couldn't read his exact emotion, but it almost seemed pitiful.

Sandra kept shooting me looks the whole time we were in there. My attorneys later wondered aloud if Sandra and David were having an affair. I told them they were nuts, but I understand why they might have interpreted the combination of David's looks and Sandra's attitude in that manner. She kept shaking her head at me, tipping it from side to side like some teenage girl trying to show some attitude to a rival in the hallway at school.

At times, Sandra seemed distracted from the questioning. Some questions had to be asked more than once. It looked to me like she was losing her train of thought. I'd see her look at David rather than look at the questioner. Her testimony directly contradicted some of David's testimony from just an hour earlier, too—including how many phone calls they'd made to each other. David had testified it was "too many to count," while Sandra testified it was "at the most once a month," which would have meant a total of about five times.

The funny thing was, I felt kind of sorry for Sandra. It was strange to feel that alongside my anger toward her, but it was the truth. I felt sorry that her whole world seemed to be such a mixed-up mess.

As we all stood up to leave the room at the end of that long day, I walked right up to David and said, "Can I talk to you a second, just you and I?" Sandra appeared visibly agitated, but David said, "Sure," and the two of us went into a private room upstairs and closed the door.

This was it. It was the moment I had been praying for. I needed to look him in the eyes, to tell him I love him, and to let him know I didn't want a divorce. I knew that if he could look me in the eyes and tell me that he wanted a divorce to my face, I would sign the papers and walk away, knowing that I'd done everything I could to save my marriage.

"I want to read something to you," I said, and I read him a letter and a poem I'd written just for that occasion. I basically laid my whole heart on the table. I let him know that I had been praying for him to come back. After I read it, I told him straight up, "I love you. I don't want this divorce. I had to file my side of it in order to fight for me and Tyler and Ashley and to get Sandra in here for a deposition. I know you think I'm being difficult, but I'm doing what I have to do in order to fight for my kids. I love you. I'm going to look you in the face and say that so you know it, and if you still want a divorce, it's yours. I'll give you anything you want. If you want this ring right now, you can have it."

The attorneys knocked on the door a few times during all of this: "Y'all okay in there?"

I wasn't sure if we were okay or not. David didn't say much at all. He looked as if he were in shock or something. He didn't seem emotional but didn't seem unemotional, either. When I was all done talking, I felt kind of stupid. I'd poured my heart and soul out to him and he just stood there looking at me and didn't say anything.

We left without a hug or even a handshake.

"Oh, Tonya," Cary said in the parking lot. "He still loves you. Did you see the way he was looking at you?"

I felt really confused. David didn't say, "Yeah, let's sign the divorce papers; it's over." But he didn't say, "I love you, too." So I didn't know what to do.

Those depositions happened on a Friday. On Saturday, I slept. On Sunday, I woke up and ran on the treadmill. "Okay, God," I prayed. "I can't take this anymore. If this is supposed to be over, just let it be over. If not, then let me know that we need to reconcile!"

I went to church that morning. When the choir was singing, there were volunteers up at the front and you could go up there and pray with them. I wound up praying with a man whom I'd never seen before and who clearly didn't know anything about my situation. Even the media reports hadn't mentioned my pending divorce, so there was no way he could have known.

I went up to the rail and I told him, through tears, "I'm just having a really, really rough time. I'm confused about some things. If you can, just pray for peace because I've got none in my life right now."

That's when he stopped me and said, "I really feel like I'm supposed to tell you something."

I looked at him.

"I am a reconciliation coach for people who are on the brink of divorce," he said. "What I do is help couples reconcile. I feel like I'm supposed to tell you that."

"What?" I said. It really freaked me out that he used the exact word I'd been praying about: "Reconcile." *Wow, God. You really did it this time.*

I thanked that man and walked away wordlessly. When I left church, I told Diana all about it. I prayed that night and woke up absolutely convinced that I needed to follow this lead. I remembered that man's name was Brad, so I tracked him down through the church directory, and I called him, and I set up an appointment for Tuesday. That was when I told him my whole story. His jaw just about hit the floor. "That's *you* on TV? I *heard* about that story!" he said.

The reconciliation I'd prayed for was here. I knew it. I felt it. I let that word and this connection fill me up with hope. I desperately wanted Brad to give me an answer, to tell me how to make it happen: "God wants you to do A, B, and C!" He didn't do that, of course. Nothing's ever that simple. We just talked and he prayed with me, and he told me that I "would know what to do."

I left that Tuesday meeting and did nothing but pray the whole night.

On Wednesday, my friend Jennifer picked me up to take me to the gym for a proper workout, like we used to have in the old days.

In the car, I started to wonder, *Do I let it go?* David hadn't contacted me. Not a word. I'd poured my heart out to him and he hadn't so much as sent me a text in response. Yet on that day, in my heart, I felt like God was telling me, "You need to call him." I know when it's God talking to me because I argue with him. Usually what he wants me to do is *not* what I want to do myself. *No! David needs to be the one to call me!* I argued. *There's no way I'm calling him first!*

I thought I might text him or something, but I swear I had this overwhelming feeling telling me, "You need to call him and you need to call him right *now.*"

As we pulled into the gym parking lot, I told Jennifer, "I need to make a phone call. I'll be there in a minute."

Jennifer would have taken my phone away if she'd known I was calling David. I watched her walk in. I dialed. David's phone kept ringing. I prayed I'd get his voice mail. That would have been a whole lot easier than talking to him directly.

He picked up.

"Hey," I said.

He said, "Hey."

"How you doing?"

It was really awkward.

"Is there any way that we could sit down and talk?" I asked.

He said, "Yeah."

He said he had a fishing tournament on Saturday and said he'd call me after that. Then we kind of said "bye" and hung up. He didn't sound real excited about it. In fact, his tone really bothered me. But I decided to wait. The ball was in his court now.

On November 14, 2008, my parents sat in a parking lot, waiting at a designated meeting area to pick up Tyler and Ashley. They were so excited. Joal had finally agreed to a court order in Tennessee to let the children see their grandparents. At first he had agreed to let me see the children as well, but then he went out of his way to have the Georgia court step in to stop it.[24] I would have to wait until a December 11 proceeding at the court in Ringgold,

Georgia, to fight that order, and the fact that my parents were about to see my children without me that day was the only thing clouding their spirits—until the seconds, minutes, and hours passed with no Joal and no children.

Joal never showed. My parents called me. Devastated.

I called my attorneys. My parents called their attorney. We were compelled to get the court involved yet again. Their lawyer and my lawyers had to file the first of multiple contempt charges against Joal in Tennessee. He would continue to ignore various court rulings over and over.[25] Here I was facing life in prison for a crime I did not commit in Georgia, and yet it seemed to me that Joal could blatantly ignore court orders without fines or jail time, and no one in the system seemed to care.

I waited all day that Saturday. I waited until dark. The fishing tournament was clearly long over. David never called.

I told Tammy what was going on and she came over and dragged me to Outback Steakhouse. Jennifer came to meet us, too. I was thankful for their support at a moment when I felt like my husband had rejected me all over again.

I fell asleep that night crying and praying for this chapter of my life to just plain end.

Then on Sunday—a full week after my moment in church with the reconciliation coach—David finally called and asked if I still wanted to talk.

I took a deep breath and said, "Yes."

I decided to bring a tape recorder with me to David's house that day. I loved him, but I didn't trust him. Not yet. I had gone out and bought myself a little digital tape recorder. I carried it just about everywhere I went. I'd leave it running in my purse whenever I talked to someone. Sometimes I'd find a way to hide it in a pocket. Sometimes if I was wearing the right kind of shirt, I'd stick that little digital recorder right in my bra. I bought an adaptor and recorded every single phone call I had with anyone who had anything to do with the case. When one tape recorder got full, I'd buy another, and another. Then I learned to download the files to my computer and to back them up online. Sometimes I'd run two or three tape recorders at the same time during important meetings.

I also read up on the laws concerning taping conversations. There are some states, referred to as "two-party states," which require people on all sides of the conversation to be aware that a conversation is being recorded. It's illegal to record somebody's conversation that you're not a party to in many states. That's just plain spying. So I never did that or anything close. Instead, I only recorded my own conversations with others, and I only did so in so-called "one-party states." Lucky for me, Tennessee and Georgia are both one-party states—which means as long as one party to the conversation (like me) knows it is being recorded, no one else has to know, by law.

Having tape recordings of as many of my conversations as possible would give me the backup I needed, in case anyone tried to twist my words or use a conversation against me in some way. If I could have, I'd have started wearing a little video camera on a necklace to record everything I did and everywhere I went, just to make sure nobody could make up any more lies about me.

Recording my husband may seem like an awful thing to do. For me, at that time, all I was doing was protecting myself. I still didn't really know which side David was on.

I drove myself up to his beautiful house in Soddy Daisy. We said hello and walked into the living room. He lay back on his old couch, which was one of the few pieces of furniture he still had in that place, and I sat on the carpeted floor—and we talked. Once again, I told him that I loved him. He didn't respond in the enthusiastic way I'd hoped, but since we were talking, I decided to tell him absolutely everything that had happened to me. Turned out, there was a lot that David didn't know. He was pretty oblivious to what was going on with me. He cried for me. We cried together. Somehow we even managed to laugh together. He hugged me. He held me. And the next time I said "I love you" on that very same afternoon, he answered: "I love you, too."

It was surreal for me. I had prayed so hard for that and wanted it so badly. It was the first truly good thing that had happened to me since all of it started. I'd been carrying the weight of ten elephants on my shoulders, and in that moment, one of them got lifted off.

We kissed each other so much that my lips were raw for days afterward. Not lustful kissing—just sweet kissing. Just love. It was one of the most incredible nights I've ever had.

The next morning, David revealed something that blew me away.

"That Wednesday, before you called, I got up that morning and got out of the shower and I prayed for an hour," he said. "I said, 'God, I can't do this anymore. If we're supposed to get back together, please have Tonya call me today. And it can't be a text or an email or anything else. If she doesn't call me by the end of the day, then we're done. I'll sign the divorce papers.'"

Our reconciliation was more of a "God thing" than I'd even imagined.

David and I were back together from that moment forward.

My mom didn't take the news real well. Nobody I knew took it well when I first told them. No one could understand how I could take him back after he'd abandoned me.

It didn't matter if anyone else understood. I understood.

The thing was, David felt he had been manipulated. Sitting in on the deposition of Sandra Lamb hit him hard. He sat there and listened to her contradict him, he told me. After his conversations with Sandra, David was under the impression that I had sold my engagement ring. Yet there I was, wearing that ring in the deposition. Seeing that ring on my finger was like shining a light on the truth of the situation. He felt like a fool. He reassessed everything he'd been thinking since way back in springtime.

They say the difficult times either kill you or make you stronger—they either rip your marriage apart or make it sturdier. It would take a while to know which outcome we were really going to face, but I felt strongly that God wouldn't have brought us back together if it wasn't for the best.

Our reconciliation was the first bright light in an absolutely pitch-black situation. I prayed that there would be more, and soon.

———————

I moved into David's house on Thanksgiving weekend.

I couldn't go to Thanksgiving dinner anywhere because there would be kids around. So instead, I threw myself into unpacking all of my boxes. I unpacked my children's belongings and placed them in the rooms that would be their rooms—while I faced the cold fact that I had now gone six months without seeing either one of them. I cried when I thought about the fact that my kids had gone six months without seeing *me*, and the fact that they hadn't seen their grandparents, either.

The kids' dogs, Buddy and Candy Cane, joined me. They'd stayed at my parents' house for a while, and they'd occasionally shared that lonely motor home with me, but there were times when I couldn't take being around them. They simply reminded me too much of Tyler and Ashley. Once I moved in with David, I finally allowed myself to open up a little bit and to let those dogs show me some of the love that dogs so willingly give to their owners. Letting them jump up on the bed and cuddle up next to me helped to fill a tiny bit of the giant chasm that was left by my children's absence.

The fact is, I held those dogs more often than I held my husband in those early days of our reunion. It's difficult to talk about, but I had a hard time allowing myself to have any kind of intimacy with David throughout the rest of this ordeal.

As glad as I was to have him back in my life, I still felt betrayed by David. I prayed about it all the time. I just wasn't sure how to completely forgive him.

We'd subpoenaed David's phone records as part of my divorce filing, and David just gave them to me after I moved in with him. Lo and behold, my instincts were right: There were dozens upon dozens of calls both to and from Sandra Lamb's cell phone—many lasting well over an hour. I went through and highlighted the numbers and cross-referenced them with my timelines, and it seemed clear as day to me that David had been giving her information—whether maliciously or not—that was used against me.

That hurt.

It was more than that, though. The intimacy problem wasn't as much about David as it was about me. I had been accused of being a monster. I was treated like a monster whenever I came face-to-face with the system that was supposed to be working on my behalf under a presumption of innocence. That constant berating gets to a person, no matter how innocent they may be. I felt dirty. I felt uncomfortable in my own skin. Being intimate with my husband just felt wrong.

I felt I had no right to experience anything good for myself. Period.

Chapter 27

We finally compelled the court-ordered therapist, Laurie Evans, to come to a deposition on December 3. The courts in Tennessee barred me from attending and from being privy to any information gathered during that deposition.

I felt like a blindfolded boxer with my hands tied behind my back, standing in the ring with an opponent who could openly pummel me with no restrictions whatsoever. All I could do was sit and wait and worry.

Once Evans's deposition was finished, two things happened that made me worry even more. First, I was informed that my parents would not be allowed to act as sole supervisors during any possible visits that I might be granted with my children. My mom and dad would no longer be allowed to visit with my children on their own, either. The court determined, based on whatever Evans had said, that my parents would need to be "supervised." And their supervisors would have to be approved by the court *and* meet with Joal's approval.

Just to clarify this scenario, which is absolutely as ridiculous as it sounds: Let's say Tyler were to come spend time at my home. It had already been determined that my father or mother must be present to "supervise" Tyler's visit. Now, because of something that "came to light" during Evans's deposition, somebody else would also have to be there to "supervise" my parents.

Joal could never stand my mother.[26] And it didn't take a rocket scientist to guess that he may have made some sort of accusation about her to this therapist.[27] Joal and Laurie Evans were talking all the time during that period. On their cell phones. Sometimes after office hours. (Subpoenaing phone records turned out to be incredibly illuminating.)

The second thing that came out of Evans's question-and-answer session was even more distressing. Back in November, we'd managed to get the court to appoint Tyler and Ashley a guardian ad litem (GAL)—an attorney who would theoretically work in the interest of the children and not in the interest of either parent. The morning after Evans's deposition, the GAL filed a motion in Tennessee calling for Evans's immediate removal as my children's therapist.

I kept asking myself, over and over, *What did Laurie Evans do to my kids that warrants "immediate removal"?*

———————

David and I walked up to the entrance of the Catoosa County Courthouse on December 11 with all sorts of fear and apprehension. This was David's first attendance at any proceeding, and he had no idea what to expect. All sorts of friends, family, and supporters greeted us as we walked up, and I think David was surprised to see so many people standing up for me. After all, he'd kept his head in the sand for a long time. I had an email chain now to keep my supporters informed and to ask for their prayers before any big court date. And as far as I could tell, this one might turn out to be the biggest and most important appearance before a judge yet.

The metal detector and the tile floors and the stairway to the second floor were all familiar to me now. I knew my way to the courtroom where I'd previously made the mistake of sitting on a bench while Judge Van Pelt, my attorney, and the ADA decided my fate without me. Only now, I had well-wishers and advocates who greeted me at nearly every step and who filtered into the courtroom to sit on my side.

There were a few people seated on the other side, too. They were chatting and laughing, and some of them shot mocking smiles my way. I thought, *Is that the way people normally behave toward an accused child molester?* One of those people was a mousy-looking woman with long curly hair whom I'd never seen before. She was seated right next to Joal. They were real chummy with each other. I wondered, *Could that be Laurie Evans?*

As we all took our seats, it started to feel less like a hearing and more like a preview of what my trial might look like.

"All rise," the clerk said. Judge Ralph Van Pelt Jr., who had already ruled against me in every way imaginable, swept in and got things under way.[28] Van Pelt had short gray hair and silver-rimmed oval glasses on his round face. He stood about five foot ten, and he seemed fidgety and distracted behind the bench from the moment he sat down. He seemed to be playing with his phone or something while our "opening arguments" began.

As Scott King spoke to the court on the subject of my children, proclaiming why we believed that I should be allowed to see them both in a relaxed, natural setting, ADA Chris Arnt stood up and countered, "Normally what we do on bond conditions in these kind of cases is that you're under the sex offender conditions that you would be if you were convicted."

My blood just about boiled. Even *convicted* sex offenders have the right to see their children at the Four Points facility, and yet they'd stopped me from doing *that*! Cary King placed a hand on my forearm. I controlled my outer sentiment, but my mind kept screaming, *Whatever happened to being innocent until proven guilty?*

The prosecution called their first witness: Laurie Evans. Sure enough, it was that mousy little woman seated right next to my ex-husband. She handed Joal her purse and a manila file folder as she stood up to take the stand.

I looked at this woman, and I looked at that judge—a man who had never even laid eyes on my children—and I kept wondering how on earth they had the ability to know what was best for Tyler and Ashley. I wanted to scream: *What is Tyler's favorite color? What is Ashley's favorite bedtime story? When did Tyler take his first steps? When did Ashley first say the word "mommy"?*

Chris Arnt got up there and asked Evans a bunch of questions, and I swear Judge Van Pelt looked like he couldn't care less. He didn't seem to make eye contact with anyone from that bench. He kept fidgeting. *Is he even listening?*

The only thing that seemed to grab his attention were the two heartbreaking conclusions Evans came to on that witness stand. First, she said that my children did not want to see me. *That cannot be true. God, please, that cannot be the truth.*

Then she flat out recommended that I not be allowed to see my daughter or my son under any circumstance whatsoever—even in a professionally supervised environment like Four Points.

I swallowed hard. *I will not let them see me cry. I will not give them that satisfaction.* I trusted my attorneys to get up there and obliterate this woman, because I knew I couldn't stand up and do it myself.

Under cross-examination, Evans admitted that all the information she had on Ashley and Tyler had come from what Joal, my ex-husband, had provided. When questioned as to whether she was ethically bound to speak to anyone else regarding my son or daughter, she said that she felt it was "not critical"—so she didn't speak with teachers, nurses, school counselors, babysitters, or anyone with firsthand knowledge of my children. Based on her testimony, it was clear that other than the time that she spent one-on-one with those kids, in a building right next door to this courthouse, everything she knew and everything she stated was fueled by a history that my ex-husband provided.

I wondered, *Don't these people deal with divorced couples all the time? Don't they have any fail-safes in place for the fact that an ex-husband or ex-wife might have an agenda and might not be telling the truth?*

While she was still on the stand, my attorney asked Evans if she was aware that the GAL in Tennessee had filed a motion to have her removed as Tyler and Ashley's therapist.

"No," she said. She seemed shocked, as if this was the first she'd ever heard about it. She testified that she had never seen the motion, so my attorney provided her with a copy.

Joal took the witness stand next. I stared right at him, yet he never looked me in the eye. Immediately ADA Chris Arnt brought up the order that Joal agreed to in Tennessee in November, allowing me to see Tyler and Ashley under my parents' supervision. The order he failed to follow.

As Joal answered, Judge Van Pelt said, "I see which way this is headed. It's one of those 'my lawyers made me do it' things."

As quickly as he began, the ADA concluded by asking Joal if he'd agreed to let me see Tyler and Ashley.

"Not voluntarily," Joal replied. I shook inside with disgust. The prosecutor wrapped his questions up in about two minutes flat.

When Scott got up for cross-examination, Joal tried to place blame for everything on the GAL. When asked why he would sign something he apparently didn't agree to, he said, "I felt that the guardian ad litem would do their job and say something."

Joal Henke and Laurie Evans were the only two witnesses the prosecution had.

The judge ordered a break for lunch.

───────────◆───────────

"The defense calls Tonya Craft," Cary said after we all came back in.

"That's a dangerous call," the judge muttered.

My attorneys and I had already been through the whole don't-put-your-client-on-the-witness-stand argument. Most attorneys are morbidly afraid to place their clients on the stand. The chance that they could get raked over the coals by the prosecution is just too big a risk to take. But I demanded to get up there and tell that judge that I wanted to see my kids. My attorneys had seen enough from me to be pretty sure that I wouldn't crack under pressure—mainly because I wasn't trying to hide anything. There was nothing to crack. I was telling the truth. And believe me, behind the scenes, they tried to crack me themselves. They wanted to know anything and everything unseemly and untoward that I'd ever done in my life so there could be no surprises from the other side. And I'd told them, too. There wasn't much to tell. My life has been pretty tame compared to some people's. I have been far from perfect, but there was nothing that gave any of my attorneys concern.

Later, people would ask me if I was scared getting up there that first time. I wasn't just scared. I was petrified! I was scared that they were going to somehow twist my words or that I'd say the wrong thing, even though I knew that I had the truth on my side and that I was getting up there for the sake of my children.

I told the judge that it had now been precisely 194 days since I had seen my kids. It felt good to be able to speak it out loud. Cary asked me about the fact that Four Points had not complied with the previous bond allowing me to see my children. We delved into the normal, loving relationship I had with my kids before these allegations arose and barely scratched the surface of how awful it had been for me to be without them.

At that point, Cary wanted to push the envelope a bit. He wanted to show the court that something in this whole business just didn't add up. So he delved into the mysterious whispered message my daughter had left me on May 30—supposedly *before* Joal knew there were any allegations against me. Cary asked me about the specifics of that message, in which she told me that she "loved" me and wouldn't be seeing me "for a very long time." It seemed that Chris Arnt and even Joal were taken aback. They had no idea it was coming.[29]

We then presented independent home studies we had done to show that neither my parents' house nor our house was an "unsafe environment." We entered the findings of those studies into evidence so the judge could see them with his own eyes. Cary brought up Joal's testimony that no safety evaluation was done at his home, and he asked me about my opinion of the safety of Joal's home for the kids. That led to a lengthy discussion of the showers that the courts had not resolved throughout this entire ordeal.

Finally, Cary asked me to tell the court exactly what I was asking for, and I spoke as clearly and unequivocally as I could: I wanted to be allowed to see my kids. All I wanted was for the court to go along with what Tennessee had already decided—"To let my parents be the supervisors and let it be in a natural environment," I said. I added that I would be willing to "have complete supervision the entire time just to spend some time with both kids." I didn't want it to happen at Four Points, I said. I felt it created a very unnatural environment for the kids with unfamiliar persons as supervisors, which I did not feel "was in the best interest of Tyler and Ashley."

I used that phrase, "in the best interest of," because that was truly what I was fighting for. I was also starting to catch on to the fact that the court seemed to use that phrase often. I realized in the middle of this that I needed to speak the court's language and to use that language to *my* advantage rather than to sit quietly and get pummeled by it at every turn. I watched. I listened. I learned as we went along. Those prosecutors had kept me in the dark for months, and like a person stricken with blindness, it seemed that all of my other senses had become more acute.

Finally, I told the judge, "I've done everything the court has said and I just want to see the kids . . . in whatever capacity I can see them."

"No further questions," Cary said.

Chris Arnt stood up, and the first words he ever spoke to me were: "This phone message you claim your daughter sent, I suppose you didn't save it?"

"Actually, I did save it," I replied.

"You did?" he asked with a surprised tone.

"Yes. It's in the car. We can't bring our phones in."

"Your Honor," Cary said, jumping to his feet, "I would be more than happy to go out and get her phone out of the car."

Arnt said that wouldn't be necessary and dropped the whole issue like he was trying to swipe a hornet off his nose. We'd clearly taken him by surprise. We knew something he didn't, and we had evidence to back it up. I wondered how deeply it stung.

Sadly, I knew nothing we presented in that courtroom would be enough to make the DA drop my case. There was no way to stop the avalanche now. My case made major headlines in every newspaper and news broadcast in the area, and since Chickamauga was sandwiched in a one-hundred-mile stretch between Chattanooga and Atlanta, there was not one but *two* major media markets chomping at the bit to hear more about this mythical "monster" of a kindergarten teacher who had secretly ruined the lives of three little girls and their families. *There's no way they could drop my case now and save face*, I thought.

That terrified me.

The ADA then questioned me about the allegations Ashley made against Sarah and asked why I did not immediately call the police when she first told me.

"That's why I got a forensic evaluation scheduled, because I wanted an independent third party to make sure that it was a true allegation, that it very much happened before I went to the authorities and completely made an outcry of something that possibly was exaggerated," I said.

I hoped that the judge and the ADA understood my meaning, loud and clear.

He then tried to make it look as if I refused to take Ashley to the evaluation. I had to remind him that my daughter had been taken by Joal days before that evaluation and never returned. I also reminded him that his office had issued the warrant to arrest me one day before that evaluation was scheduled to take place.

He then questioned whether I invented the allegations against Sarah as some sort of desperate response in retaliation for the allegations that had been made against *me*. The rage I felt over his discussion of a blatantly erroneous chain of events made me dig in my heels and stand firm in response to every single question. I thanked God that my penchant for remaining steady in the face of a crisis apparently carried through into a courtroom setting.

"We do have people that can verify my concern with the allegations well before I was arrested or even before the detectives showed up at my house," I told the court. In fact, I told the judge and the ADA that some of those witnesses were present in the courtroom that day. I knew that when I got off the stand, we would be calling our own witnesses to testify. Kim Walker, Shanica Lewis, and Tammy were all there, ready to act as character witnesses, but they easily could have recalled the timing of everything if we asked them. We'd also called a woman named Beth Guthrie, who was the school counselor for both Tyler and Ashley and knew firsthand that I had come in seeking advice about how to handle Ashley's allegations toward Sarah *long* before those detectives ever rang my doorbell.

Arnt seemed to drop that whole line of questioning, too.

He then tried to accuse me of trying to hide my children from the detectives on that very first day they showed up at my house, asserting, "You didn't tell the detectives you had moved them out of state?"

I absolutely did nothing of the sort, and I told the ADA as much. He said the detectives were accusing me of not cooperating and of concealing the children, and I responded with the truth.

At that point, Arnt stepped back and let me off the stand. I was positive that I had refuted, factually, each and every question and allegation he threw my way.

Our four witnesses got up, and each one of them testified to the loving, healthy, nurturing, and normal interactions they'd long witnessed between me and my children. They also spoke to my loving and appropriate interactions with other children. Each one of our witnesses said that they would feel completely comfortable with me around their own children and that they would allow their children to be in my presence without *any* supervisor if the bond were not in place.

I'm not sure that Judge Van Pelt was really listening to any of it.

We then presented a whole roomful of individuals who were all willing to supervise me so I could see Tyler and Ashley. Every one of my supporters who'd sat there quietly and respectfully throughout this long day full of testimony stood up as a willing participant to support me. The court declined to hear from any of them.

We offered three different plans of action and even suggested that any time I spent with Ashley could be videotaped and submitted to the courts. We were more than reasonable, in every way imaginable.

Even then, in his final argument, ADA Chris Arnt stood up and said he strongly opposed "forcing a victim to be in the company of their victimizer."

At that point, the judge informed the ADA that taking such a harsh stance would ensure "increased pressure on the state to get this case tried." I am not sure of anyone else's definition and understanding of "increased pressure," but I'd already gone 194 days without seeing my kids. An indictment hadn't come down, let alone a trial date. Was there *any* pressure on the state before? It felt to me as if there had been no pressure until that moment. No part of Judge Van Pelt's statement made sense to me. Not one word.

Then, after all of that, the judge decided that he wouldn't make a decision that day. Instead, he said he would "sleep on it."

As frustrated as I was, I left that hearing somehow skeptically optimistic. The state had tendered two witnesses, neither of whom offered up any proof or documents to declare why I should not see my children. We had both personal and professional witnesses verifying my testimony and presenting insight into my relationship with Tyler and Ashley. We submitted a multitude of exhibits as evidence. The ADA proffered none. My team had done well.

Hadn't we?

Chapter 28

I waited with the phone either at my side or in my hand every hour after that, for days. Every vibration caused my heart to race and my stomach to heave. I wanted to see Scott's or Cary's numbers pop up. They promised not to call me until we had news.

When the phone finally rang and I saw that it was Scott, I jerked up off the couch.

"Hello?"

"Well," Scott said, "you got *two* of the three things you were asking for." His voice was so jovial that the sound of it brought a smile to my face. "First, the restriction about being around anyone under the age of eighteen has been changed. Now you can be around any child under the age of eighteen as long as another adult is present."

Thank you, God, I thought.

"Second, you get to see Tyler," he said.

For one brief second, my heart soared.

"But you can't see Ashley," he added.

"*What?* What do you mean?"

Scott tried to tell me it was a good thing. "Tonya, you should be happy," he said. "At least you got half of what you wanted."

He was talking about my children. Half of my *children*.

"Are you kidding me?" I said. "Well, why don't I drive right down there and cut off one of your balls, Scott, and then tell *you* to be happy that you've still got one left!"

Our conversation ended shortly after that. I could hear the regret in Scott's voice as we said good-bye. He would apologize to me profusely later on. He said he would remember that moment every time he broke news to a client for the rest of his career. He did not mean it the way it sounded. He just wanted me to try to see the bright side. In my head I knew that, but my heart was too shattered to see it.

My reunion with Tyler happened on my birthday, December 16, 2008. Exactly 199 days since I'd last laid eyes on my precious baby boy.

The goal was normalcy. Familiarity. The visit would be short. Only a couple of hours. So I gathered with my immediate family and a few close friends at O'Charley's restaurant. It's one of those family-style places where birthdays and gatherings tend to happen. It's a place Tyler liked. I thought it would be much easier for him to see me there surrounded by others than it would be to see me in David's house—a house that should've belonged to those kids as much as anyone but at that moment did not. As uncomfortable as this was going to be for me, I knew it would be a hundred times more uncomfortable for Tyler, and I wanted to do everything I could to make it easier.

I also thought the birthday-party atmosphere might help me to forget just how brokenhearted I was at the absence of my daughter. But nothing could do that.

Seeing Tyler walk into that restaurant ripped my heart to shreds. The face that used to look at me with adoration and kindness showed nothing except hesitancy and fear. The boy who used to bound through the door and jump into my arms yelling "Mommy!" did his absolute best to avoid walking toward me at all.

He wasn't particularly shy or disengaged with anyone else. Just with me.

I cautiously reached out to hug him, and I felt his entire body stiffen at my touch. I felt queasy. I sat through dinner in a fog.

Before I knew it, the visit was over. I held in my emotions and put a smile on my face as big as I could possibly muster as the car pulled up. I squatted down and gently hugged my son.

"I love you," I said. He said nothing.

I watched him walk away. I watched him get into the car. I watched his face through the window. He never looked back at me. Not once.

My next scheduled visit with Tyler was on Christmas Eve. Ashley would be visiting my parents that same night. We were all so excited. But at 5:00 P.M., the approved supervisors for that visit—namely my brother and his wife— backed out. There was so much hatred and fear flying around that my own brother and sister-in-law grew fearful that somebody from the other side might accuse *them* of being child molesters, too, as a way to get back at them for helping me out. My brother insisted that he didn't doubt me. Not one bit. But they had their own children to think of and, to put it simply, they got spooked. On Christmas Eve, their nerves got the better of them and they decided not to participate in the visit.

The visit with Tyler could not move forward without supervision. The courts were closed. We couldn't reach anyone. My father got on the phone with Joal and did everything short of begging him for some mercy. My father recorded that phone call at my insistence. In the end, Joal decided to allow Tyler and Ashley to go spend time with my parents—with the caveat that I absolutely could not see Tyler at all. So I sent David over to my parents' house. At least he would get to spend some quality time with my children, while I sat alone at home on Christmas Eve.

I didn't see Tyler for the rest of December. Joal refused to bring him without the appointed supervisors in place, and we would have to go back to court in January to sort it out once again. I would not celebrate a happy new year in any way, shape, or form. To be honest, it felt almost like I'd gone back to square one. I was devastated thinking that a whole new year was about to start. I had no idea when I'd see my babies again. Seeing Tyler that one time almost made it worse.

On December 30, the judge in Tennessee ruled on the GAL's motion to have Laurie Evans removed as my children's therapist. She not only ordered a new therapist for my children, but also she found Evans "non-credible."[30] She ordered her "immediately removed as the counselor" for my kids and barred her from having any further contact with Ashley and Tyler. More importantly, and shockingly, the judge's ruling said, "After reviewing the videotaped/transcribed deposition of Ms. Evans, the Court concludes that Ms. Evans's entire testimony was/is not credible."

"Ms. Evans's testimony concerning her diagnosis regarding Tyler Henke is not supported," the ruling continued. "Ms. Evans's testimony concerning Ashley Henke was unsupported."

What diagnosis? What did she "diagnose" my son with?

I adhered strictly to the judge's orders, as did my legal team, forcing me to remain ignorant of the facts and details of Evans's deposition. But I was furious. *How could this Laurie Evans have been allowed to see my children if she was "non-credible"?* The more we learned, the more it seemed that almost no one was handling this case with any professionalism.

In fact, our ongoing investigations had shown that Detective Stephen Keith, one of the men who had stood there on my front porch accusing me of molesting three girls, was a close personal friend of Sandra Lamb's.[31] His daughter was close friends with Brianna. *How could he proceed and bring this case forward when there was clearly a conflict of interest from the start? Is anyone tied to my case competent? Are any of them capable of handling themselves in a professional manner, at all?*

———————————————

My supporters would email scripture and words of wisdom to me all the time. Now and then, I would take out a bright Magic Marker and write one of them down. I'd tape those colorful passages up around the desk and cabinets in our home office, which was right by the front door, with a great big window looking out toward the street. (That room would become my new work sanctuary, and I resigned myself to knowing that working to prove my innocence and clear my name was my work now. *This* was my full-time job.)

As 2008 came to a close, I remember looking at one of those pieces of paper in my office. I wasn't sure when or why I'd done it, but in orange marker I'd written down Ephesians 1:18–21:

I pray that your hearts will be flooded with light so that you can understand the confident hope he has given to those he called—his holy people who are his rich and glorious inheritance. I also pray that you will understand the <u>incredible greatness</u> of God's power for us who believe him.

The underlining was my own, and I'd outlined this whole next part in wavy black lines, drawing a bold, cloud-like ring around the word "any," making highlight marks around the word "leader," underlining what I thought were the most powerful words in blue marker:

Now he is far above any <u>ruler</u> or <u>authority</u> or <u>power</u> or leader or <u>anything else</u>—<u>not only in this world</u> but also <u>in the world to come</u>!

Sometimes I felt as if all I had to hold on to were those Magic Marker words.

Chapter 29

I opened my eyes. It was dark. Something had pulled me out of my sleep. A movement. A presence. *There's someone in my bedroom.*

I froze. I caught a glimpse of a shadowy figure by the window, barely visible in the glow of the clock radio on the nightstand. I tried not to breathe. I couldn't make out who it was. Then I finally recognized her blond hair in the moonlight streaming through the window.

"Ashley?" I said.

"Mommy!" she whispered. She ran right over and wrapped her little arms around my neck.

"Baby, what are you doing here?" I asked. I held her to me. I felt the warmth of her skin and breathed in the familiar scent of her shampoo. "Oh, Ashley, thank God. Thank God you're here. I love you so much. I've missed you so much."

She pulled her little face back and her baby blue eyes looked right into mine.

"I love you, Mommy—"

That was when I woke up.

It shook me to my core. You don't go back to sleep after a dream like that.

That dream kept coming back, too, over and over. Not quite as often as my confrontation dreams, but often enough. Sometimes I'd lie there awake until David got up and went to work in the morning. On some days, I'd continue to lie there and cry and pray for the entire day. At ten minutes 'til five, I'd roll out of bed, fix myself up, and pretend like I'd been doing something productive.

Nobody knew how bad I was doing. Nobody.

I'd set myself up in the home office in the evening, after dinner—those times when I even bothered eating—and I'd work until bedtime, which was always late, usually well after midnight. Then the dreams would start up all over again, and that pattern would continue, day in, day out, broken only by meetings with my attorneys and court appearances to try to get the new supervisors approved and to try to change the court's mind on the ruling about not seeing Ashley. There might be an occasional dinner or visit with a friend, who would try to keep my mind from overloading. But I would always go right back to the work or the worry.

I took home a copy of the entire Georgia Criminal Code from Scott and Cary's office one day—a book as thick as one of those old-fashioned collegiate dictionaries people used before the Internet came along, filled with the tiniest print you've ever seen. I read it cover to cover, highlighting it like a schoolbook and putting sticky notes on every other page. I consumed the law, and I asked my attorneys about different strategies and statutes constantly. Sometimes the work and the worry would combine together for good.

After the first day of the new year, we arranged for new supervisors and the judge ruled in favor of me seeing my son on a series of occasional overnight visits at my home. I introduced Tyler to his new room the first night he stayed over. I'd set it up with all of his old familiar things—including Froggie, his lifelong bedtime stuffed animal. I showed him Ashley's room, too. I wanted him to know that it was all set up and that I fully expected both of them to be living with me as soon as we could make it happen. I couldn't talk about the case or discuss any of my expectations out loud. But I wanted him to know it.

Ashley would go stay at my parents' house when Tyler was with me. We'd have to have supervisors with us in both places, at all times, which was a major pain to pull off, but every one of us was willing to do anything it took to make sure those visits went smoothly and that nothing would keep those visits from happening again. We had friends and supporters all around us who were more than willing to step up to serve as supervisors. Finally, for a day at a time, every now and then, I'd get to see my son—but not my daughter. Every once in a while I'd get half of my heart back.

I used to always say to Ashley, "Guess what?" And she would grin and say, "I know, Mommy, you love me."

On my 295th day without seeing my daughter, I wrote a note with dry-erase markers on the mirror in her still-empty bedroom—not knowing when, if ever, she might see it:

Ashley
You're my baby girl
You're the one that God
created

No one in this world
could ever be like you

Guess what?
. . . I love you

———————•———————

The more I learned about how the charges against me got started, the more my original gut instincts seemed to bear themselves out. The phone records, the interviews with Kim Walker and Dee Potter, the work of my private investigator, Eric Echols—everything pointed me and my attorneys to some sort of *something* that started with Sandra Lamb and Sherri Wilson and spiraled over to Kelly McDonald and Joal and Sarah, coupled with a system that began by treating me as guilty from the start.

Yet every once in a while I would step back and ask myself, "Why does any of that matter?"

I'd argue with my attorneys about it: "Once three little girls—including my own daughter—get up there and testify that I've molested them in who knows what kind of horrible ways, why would a jury care about whether or not the parents of those kids despised me? Or whether the lead investigator happened to be close personal friends with Sandra Lamb? Or whether Skyler said nothing happened to *her*? Who cares? The only thing that's gonna matter is that those three girls said I did something, right?"

Scott and Cary would both hem and haw over it. They said we would show the court my history and my character. Evidence and witnesses would show how this had all been some sort of planned agenda and would raise enough doubt in jurors' minds to set me free.

I tried to put myself in a juror's shoes, and quite frankly, I doubted whether I'd have listened to any of those arguments. How on earth could I disprove a negative? How in the world were we going to convince a jury that these girls were mistaken—or worse, that these innocent children had been *manipulated* into saying things that weren't true? Who was gonna believe that? I didn't think I would've believed it before all this started, and as a teacher, I was well aware of the stories that kids could spin out of the blue with no prompting at all. Kids made stuff up all the time. They would fill in details and craft whole elaborate stories about things that never even happened. But a jury wasn't going to take *my* word for it. I could imagine convincing a jury that one kid told a wild story just to get some attention, or because her daddy told her to do it, or because she'd been caught in a lie about something else, or for just no reason at all. But how were we going to convince anybody that *three* kids were all making up stories about the same alleged child molester? Namely *me*?

Despite all of their hard work and through no fault of their own, it became apparent to me that Cary and Scott did not have answers to all of those questions. They weren't experts in child behavior. They certainly weren't experts in the factors that lead up to false allegations of sexual abuse. They assured me that they would find experts to come in and testify when we went to trial, but I started to think that we needed an expert to come and help us prepare for what we might face at trial—*now*. More than that, I truly believed that if I was going to prove my innocence, I needed to find the *best* expert—the most knowledgeable, well-researched, well-educated person I could find in the whole country to explain to us, and eventually a jury, how on earth three children could accuse me of something I didn't do.

Once again, I dug deep into my little black laptop. I threw myself into the world of false-accusation cases I found on the Internet. I pulled up media reports on attorneys and academics who had expertise in this area, and I found one guy in California who seemed to be just what I was looking for. I called him—only to find that his phone had been disconnected. *What if the person I'm looking for doesn't exist?* I panicked.

I dug a little deeper and started watching some videos from actual trials. I managed to find one man who had testified passionately and expertly about research having to do with false allegations. He had an unusual name: Demosthenes Lorandos. I hadn't the slightest clue how to pronounce it, but he was definitely a top expert in this very specialized field. Maybe *the* top expert. I read as much as I could find about him and learned that he was a child psychologist with a PhD. Finally, I watched some of his testimony in a child molestation case. I could tell just by watching and listening to him that he knew what he was talking about. He spoke so clearly. He made perfect sense. He explained to the jury in that case *exactly* how a child could be misled into answering questions in a false manner. He made it seem easy to understand. He started to make *me* understand how something like this could happen, just from that one instance of testifying.

I need him on my team. I absolutely knew it.

I tried calling him. I left messages. He never responded. I found an email address for him. I emailed. No response. I prayed some more, and that was when I knew that I needed to go see him in person. There was no way a phone call from me was going to get through to a man of his stature and prominence, so I decided to go knock on his door.

Chapter 30

"Pack your bags. We're going to Michigan."

My mother thought I was crazy. David thought I was crazy. Everyone thought I was nuts to go traipsing off to some far-off state in search of an "expert" who wouldn't return my calls. Nonetheless, my mother agreed to drive me up to Ann Arbor in April 2009.

I piled my binders and flash drives full of information into her gold Expedition, along with a change of clothes or two, and together we made the nearly ten-hour trek to the office of Demosthenes Lorandos. We arrived at our hotel late at night, and I woke up extra early in the morning so I could spend some time on the treadmill at the hotel gym. I reflected on everything that had led me to make that journey and prayed to God that I was doing the right thing as my feet thudded along that whirring belt at a thunderous nine miles per hour that morning. I hopped off completely exhilarated. I showered, I put on my best professional-looking business attire, gathered up my documentation, and off we went.

Ann Arbor is a quaint little college town, and the downtown area is filled with adorable two-story buildings with mom-and-pop shops on the street level. I had a hard time finding the office at first. There seemed to be a number missing as I walked down the sidewalk—and then I saw it. It was just an odd door with a tiny number way up at the top, which led directly to a set of stairs that led up to a humble, yet impeccable reception area on the second floor.

"May I help you?" a kind gentleman inquired from behind a desk.

"Hi, my name's Tonya Craft, and I've traveled all the way from Chattanooga, Tennessee, in order to meet with Dr. Lorandos." (I'm positive I mispronounced his name.)

"Do you have an appointment?" the man asked.

"No, I don't. But if he'd be willing to give me even five minutes of his time, I know he'll want to take a look at my case. I'm fighting for my life and for the lives of my children," I said.

"Well, he doesn't see anyone without an appointment. We can try to set something up and have you come back—"

"I understand. I've been trying to call, and I've emailed, too, and I came all this way just to see him because I know he's the best of the best at what he does. So if you could just tell him that I'm here and that I really would appreciate just five minutes of his time, I'd be ever so grateful."

I don't think he knew what to make of me, especially with my Southern accent.

"Hold on one second," he said, and he placed a call to his office manager. He showed us to a waiting area and after a few minutes, a female staff member made my acquaintance. It was a crisp, sunny day in Michigan, and she asked if we could go downstairs, grab a cup of coffee, and maybe sit outside somewhere to talk. So we did. I gave her the basic rundown on my case, showed her some of the paperwork in my tabbed binders, and told her that everything was cross-referenced with the materials on the flash drive I'd brought. She seemed impressed. I also told her that it was my intention to stay in town until I could have a few minutes of her superior's time.

That's when I held up the silver pendant I'd put on especially for this occasion. On it were etched two tiny pictures: one of Tyler and one of Ashley. "I am here because I am fighting for my life, as well as the lives of my two children," I told her.

She explained to me that Dr. Lorandos wasn't in the office that day and that he might not be in the office the next day, either. But she said she would talk to him, and she promised to call us. So my mom and I went to lunch and then back to the hotel.

Finally, the phone rang, and the office manager said we could come see Dr. Lorandos the next day.

"Thank you," I said. "Oh, and by the way, how do I pronounce his first name?"

"Just call him Doc," she said. "That's what everybody calls him."

———— ❖ ————

Doc turned out to be much more than I'd anticipated. This lanky, balding man with a gray mustache and professorial looks wasn't just a PhD psychologist. He was an *attorney*. He devoured the pages of my binder and sifted through my computer files, astounded at what I'd put together—and not shocked in the least by any of our thoughts about an agenda-ridden group of individuals, or small-town hysteria, or whatever it was that drove my case forward.

"It happens all the time," Doc said. "Some prosecutors charge ahead based on nothing but some parents' allegation, usually pushing the children through faulty interviews to make all kinds of false statements just to back up their claim. The interviewers badger the kids and ask leading questions and don't take no for an answer, until the kids tell the investigators what they *think* the investigators want to hear. They're children. They want to please whatever authority figure's in front of them."

We spent hours in that office.

"You're smack dab in the middle of the Bible Belt down there, aren't you?" he asked.

Of course we were. You could throw a rock in any direction from any point in Chickamauga and hit a fundamentalist church.

"And the parents of the accusers, the ones other than your daughter, are wealthy? Or influential?"

Some of them were, I told him.

"Look, you need me as much more than an 'expert' or advisor. There are three girls that are going to get on a witness stand and say you molested them. *Three!* I'm a trial lawyer, and the best trial lawyer around when it comes to these sorts of cases. You need to hire me as your attorney."

I knew from the research I'd done that Doc's arrogance was warranted. He talked a good game, sure, but he actually knew what he was talking about. I liked the sense of confidence he had. It made me feel secure. And I had a feeling he'd be able to portray all of that confidence to a jury—since, hopefully, a jury would be made up of people like me. (That's the way it's supposed to work, right?)

I reminded Doc that I already had two attorneys in Georgia, plus another in Tennessee, and that I didn't have any intention of replacing them.

"That's fine. From what you're telling me and what you've shown me, they seem like very competent individuals," he said. "But what I'm telling *you* is that you can't win this case without me."

Based on everything I knew, including the gut instinct I felt as I sat there face-to-face with the man, I believed he was telling me the truth. His child-psychology expertise, his depth of experience with alleged sexual abuse cases, and his legal capabilities combined into a presence that seemed powerful to me.

In fact, I knew as I sat there that Doc wasn't just going to be an "addition" to my team—Doc was going to become my lead attorney.

I felt bad that Scott and Cary would have to step down a notch, but at the end of the day, this was a war I was waging. I was the captain at the helm of a battleship, and I was the only one who would go down with the ship if we didn't win this war by proving my innocence. All the rest of them would have the sanctuary of a lifeboat. They would be able to go on with their lives. I wouldn't. I needed to assert my power and save my own ship.

———————◆———————

Mom and I made the long trek back home and started working to get the money together to put Doc on retainer. It occurred to us that we could potentially put up some sort of collateral for my bond and get the court to return the $50,000 cash payment that my parents had made on the day I was first arrested.

My friend Courtney, whom I basically grew up with, caught wind of this and mentioned it to her mother, Frances Woodard, who had known me ever since I was a little girl. Without hesitation, Frances offered to put her house up as the collateral on my bond. Her *house*!

It took us a few days to get all the paperwork together. When my parents first went to the Catoosa County Courthouse to ask for their $50,000 back, one of the clerks looked in the ledger and told them, "I'm sorry, we don't have any record of a $50,000 payment coming in."

My mother was so angry it was all she could do to keep from swearing up a storm at that clerk. Luckily my mom liked to organize things, as I did. She drove all the way home, knew right where to find her receipt, and went marching right back into that courthouse.

"Oh . . ." the clerk said when she saw it. I swear, if my mother hadn't kept that receipt, that money might have conveniently disappeared. That's just my personal feeling on the matter. I didn't trust any of them anymore.

It was early May before we put that money together, but we did it.

David was astonished at how driven I was. He was floored that I got into Doc's office, got him to listen, and got him to agree to represent me. Part of the reason for all of that, I told him, was because of the documentation I had brought with me. The obsessive amount of work I'd been doing on my case had paid off. My successful meeting with Doc made me all the more determined.

"I need two more bookcases," I told David, and two bookcases showed up the next day. From that point forward, David complied with just about every request I made, no questions asked.

Of course, at home was just about the only place I was getting that result. On May 7, we would be heading back to court once again to try to get a bond modification to allow me to see Ashley. We'd also petitioned Joal via the court in Tennessee to allow me to see Tyler on Mother's Day, that Sunday, May 10. I didn't expect any of it to be as simple as asking and receiving. And yet, I was hopeful in that moment. My Mother's Day in 2008 had been spent without my husband. This year would most likely be spent without my daughter. But the thought of being with Tyler, however distant he still seemed, gave me hope.

After all, we'd made good progress in Tennessee. I'd been seeing Tyler occasionally and without incident for three full months. We had Laurie Evans's "non-credible" ruling to argue in front of the judge. I thought our chances of finally getting access to Ashley were better than they'd ever been, and my attorneys agreed.

As my mom took the wheel and drove toward Atlanta for a final pre-hearing meeting at Scott and Cary's office on May 6, the only immediate dread I felt was over the impending discussion of bringing Doc on as lead attorney. I hadn't officially hired Doc yet. We were getting ready to send the money. But as I sat there with my cell phone in hand, staring out the window, feeling lulled half to sleep by the road noise and the blur of the trees going by, I worried that Scott and Cary might feel blindsided by my decision.

That was when my cell phone buzzed. It was David calling. I got a very, very bad feeling.

Chapter 31

"Tonya," David said. "Where are you?"

"About halfway to Atlanta. Why?"

"There's a warrant out for your arrest."

"What?!" I screamed.

It's a miracle my poor mother didn't get into an accident. She kept looking over, trying to understand what was happening. I couldn't take a break to tell her as I tried to listen over the road noise.

The police were at our home. They'd rung our doorbell. They'd looked in our windows. David's brother, who lived right next door, saw them and went to inquire what they were up to. The police called David at work. They accused me of hiding from them.

"I'm not hiding!" I said.

"I know. I told them that you were at a meeting with your attorneys in Atlanta. I told 'em you weren't hiding at all."

I started squalling. "Let me call Scott," I said.

I told my mom what was going on as I dialed, and her face fell so hard I thought she was going to sink right through her seat.

"Scott!" I yelled the moment he picked up. "There are police at my house saying they have a warrant for my arrest. What is going on?"

"Where are you?"

"I'm in the car with my mother, about halfway down to see you."

"Okay. Pull over somewhere. I'll call you right back."

I told my mother to pull off at the next exit and finally told her every bit of what David had told me. I ducked down in my seat and kept looking up at every car that went by, worried it was a cop coming to get me. I was shaking by the time that phone rang again.

"Okay, here's the deal," Scott said. "The indictment came down, and they have another charge. A new charge. It's from Brianna. You shouldn't get arrested for this, but they're going to arrest you. We need to turn you in."

"I told you, Scott. I told you they were gonna do this."

"You did. I know," he said. Then he sighed. "It gets worse."

My skin went cold.

"The parents want you to be put in jail for twenty-four hours, so they're going to hold you there for twenty-four hours before the bond hearing," he said.

"Can they do that?"

"Unfortunately, they can."

"How can a person just have someone thrown in jail for twenty-four hours?"

"Because as the parents of a minor who's a supposed victim of sexual abuse, they're allowed to ask for the alleged perpetrator to be jailed for twenty-four hours, 'for the child's protection.' They could have asked for this the first time you were arrested, but they probably didn't know the law."

The full impact of what he said took a few seconds to sink in.

"Oh my God. Oh my God, Scott. What am I going to do?" I looked at my mom with my eyes full of tears. "What am I going to do?"

"Tonya, you'll get through this," Scott said. "Stop somewhere, okay?" he told me. "You might want to get a bite to eat because you won't get any food for a while."

Scott was practical like that in the heat of the moment, but I couldn't eat. There was no way, I told him. "Then just wait. I'll come. I'll call you when I'm close to the exit and then I'll follow you down to the jail," he said.

I immediately got on the phone with Cary, whose reaction was the emotional opposite of Scott's. He was angry and yelled profanities. I was glad to have both sides of the spectrum as I tried to process the news that I was about to spend twenty-four hours in jail. I needed someone to keep me on course, and I needed someone to share my absolute horror and anger and frustration.

It took Scott nearly an hour to get to us, and by then I'd gone from hysterical to just plain numb.

"I know this sucks," he said. "I know it's not going to be fun. But we have to do this."

I tried not to let myself feel that the whole world had turned against me. I tried not to wonder if God had abandoned me as we pulled into the parking lot of that concrete hell on Highway 41.

We didn't know what this new charge was all about. *How can there be a brand-new charge from Brianna, after all this time, when I haven't been allowed anywhere near her?*

As we walked into that jail's stark lobby, Scott went to talk to the guard at the desk.

He'd explained to me that because this was a twenty-four-hour stay, I would have to change into prison garb, which meant that there would be a strip search and cavity search, and that any way I looked at it this was bound to be awful. I tried not to think about it. He'd told me about a list of approved items they would be able to bring for my "comfort" after I was in my cell, and he assured me they would get me everything I needed. As a woman, I had some pretty specific needs. I just had no idea how badly I'd need them.

I hugged my mom as hard as I'd ever hugged her in my life as the guard came out to get me. They took me back and put me in handcuffs just like they did the first time—right behind that glass door, in plain sight of my poor mother. Only this time, after taking me back to one of those holding cells with a bunch of other prisoners for a while, they took me to a private room. A guard walked in carrying a folded pair of pinkish-colored, prison-issue pants, a matching shirt, and some canvas tennis shoes with no laces.

"You'll change into these after the search," he said.

He stepped out and a female officer stepped in. "Sorry we have to do this, but please remove all of your clothes," she said to me.

I wasn't prepared for it. I knew it might happen, but until it happens to you, there is just no possible way to prepare. I was dressed in jeans and a T-shirt and flip-flops. I'll never forget the icy feel of that concrete floor on the soles of my feet as I began to undress.

"Everything?" I asked.

"Everything," she answered.

I could understand why they'd want women to remove their bras. A person could use the underwire to create some kind of a weapon or something. But everything?

"The panties too?" I asked.

"Yes."

"Will I be able to put these back on?"

"No, ma'am. You're only allowed plain white cotton in here."

My panties had polka dots on them. I didn't see any underwear or socks with the prison clothes they'd left for me to change into.

"I'm sorry, it's—it's my time of the month," I said.

"If you're using a tampon, you'll need to remove that, too," she said, pulling a pair of rubber gloves on her hands as she spoke to me.

"Yes, ma'am," I said, softly. The last thing I wanted to do was to make anybody angry in this place, so I tried to be polite, and I tried not to cry as I followed her orders.

She asked me to open my mouth. She inspected all around my teeth and under my tongue. She felt in my hair. She told me to bend over, and I did, and with hardly any warning at all she stuck one of her fingers up inside of my body—first in one place, and then in the other. I started sobbing so hard my whole body shook.

"I'm sorry we have to do this," she said.

"I know," I cried.

She stepped back. "I need you to spread your legs and squat down as far as you can," she said. It was to make sure there was nothing hidden deeper than a finger could reach. A knife or any kind of object that someone might hide up in some body cavity would hurt or injure a person if they squatted down on it. So I squatted down with my eyes closed and stood back up with tears streaming down my face.

"Go ahead and get dressed," she said.

I found it difficult to balance as I tried to put my legs into those pants. I remember thinking how thankful I was that these clothes, which were kind of like scrubs, were reddish-pinkish in color. I pulled the shirt on and then those shoes, which were almost comically big for my sockless feet.

They moved me into a holding cell with another young woman. She was drunk as all get-out. I knew she would ask me what I was in for. That was the first thing everybody asked. So I decided to beat her to the punch.

"Well," she drawled, "me and this guy had drank four pitchers of beer and four shots of Jägermeister apiece, and I was driving down the road with a Colt 45 in one hand and steering with the other, and somehow— bam!—there was a tree.

"I've lost my license two times," she said.

She asked me if I'd been arrested in Catoosa County before, and I shook my head.

"Oh, well be glad you're in here," she said, "because you get three meals in here. You don't get that in some of the other counties."

She gave me quite the lowdown on the neighboring jail communities, 'cause apparently she'd been in everywhere. I noticed she had scabs all over.

You could see them through the rips in her jeans. I thought it was from the wreck she'd described, and I asked her, "Are you okay?"

She looked down at herself and said, "Oh, I got that from monking."

"From what?"

"Monking. You ain't never done meth, girl?" she said.

"No."

"Really? You never done meth?"

I just shook my head and tried to fathom how in the world I belonged in the same cell as this troubled young woman.

"Monking's when you do meth and then you have sex for like twenty-four hours straight, and you get scabs on your knees and scars and everything," she told me. I didn't really want to hear any more, but I kept asking her questions because I didn't want to talk about myself. Finally the guard came in and blew my silence wide open.

"Miss Craft," he said, "we're fixing to have to move you to solitary for your protection. You were on the news, and some of the prisoners were threatening to do stuff. Anytime there's a child molestation charge—"

"Oh my gosh!" the girl said. She was shocked. "You didn't do that, did you?"

"No," I said. I didn't want to say anything more. I knew I'd have a hearing the next day. I was petrified that they were recording my conversations and that somehow they'd try to use anything I said against me in the courtroom.

"When they bring you to the regular population, don't you tell *anybody* why you're in here. Just make something up," she said, "'cause they're all gonna want to know what you're in here for. And you're kinda small and kinda cute, so I'd make something bad up, like you killed somebody or somethin'. Just to be safe."

She went on and on giving me all sorts of jail-survival pointers. It turned out none of them would apply. They finally came and took her to the general population area, but they took me to solitary confinement. There were two types of solitary cells in that jail, and they put me in the most intensive one, designed for the worst of the worst—for the prisoners who were in there for trying to kill someone. It looked like where they kept Hannibal Lecter in *Silence of the Lambs*, with clear Plexiglas at the front and the back, so that the officers at their desks in the area behind me and anybody walking in front could see me at all times. There was a flat metal slab of a bed, a toilet right there in plain sight, a folded heavy wool blanket, and me. That was it.

The people in the other solitary cells kept yelling and banging on their doors, trying to get my attention: "Hey! Who's in there?" I didn't answer. I went to the back corner on that metal slab of a bed, sat with my knees up to my chin, and covered myself with the blanket, trying to hide from everyone as best I could. The crotch and inseam of my pant legs were soaked with blood. It was freezing cold. I hate being cold. I sat there under the blanket and cried.

I'm not sure how much time went by before they brought me in front of the magistrate to face my charges. Time was just a blur the whole time I was in there. The process was different this time, too. They didn't take me into a room to face a real person; instead, they took me and a few other inmates to a room with a television monitor in it. They told us the magistrate would be on the other end of the video monitor and that he would be able to see us at the same time we saw him.

I tried to ask one of the guards what I was supposed to do. "Excuse me, ma'am. We're having a bond hearing tomorrow on this whole thing, so I'm not sure what I'm supposed to say or not say, and I'd really like my attorneys to tell me what I'm supposed to say before—"

"You don't get to ask questions in here!" she responded. "I don't care what your damn attorneys tell you."

I tried to ask someone else a few minutes later, real politely, but they were rude, too. So I gave up. They put me in front of the TV with the magistrate and they made everyone else sit in chairs on the other side of the room, as if I were dangerous. That girl I'd met in the holding cell was in there at the same time.

"Hey, Tonya," she said, elbowing the girl next to her, like, "That's *her!*"

I gave her a sheepish nod of acknowledgment, and all I could think was, *Obviously she's told everybody what I'm in here for.*

From there it all happened so fast; I don't even remember who the magistrate was. In front of all of those people, he asked me, "Are you Tonya Craft?"

I answered. Then he asked me my age and "Do you have a degree?"

"Yes."

"What in?"

"I have a bachelor's degree in education, and I have a master's degree in early—"

"You have a master's degree?" he said incredulously.

"Yes, I have a master's degree."

Then, in front of all those people, he said, "You're charged with digital penetration of a six-year-old girl." They all started whispering around me. "Do you understand that charge?" he asked.

"Yes."

"How do you plead?"

That question made me real nervous. I didn't want to say anything to jeopardize my case. Was I supposed to even make a plea for this charge that was being tacked on to the original charges? Wasn't this all part of the same thing?

"We have a bond hearing tomorrow, and—"

"I don't care what you have tomorrow. I'm asking you now!"

I finally said, "Not guilty."

"So you understand the charges?" he said.

"Yes."

"Take her back."

I was scared to death. What if by making a plea and saying that I "understand the charges" I had somehow admitted something that could hurt me? Why wouldn't they just answer my questions to reassure me that I was doing the right thing? I felt railroaded.

As an officer escorted me back to my cell, I looked up and happened to notice a sweatshirt, a package of underwear, and a box of feminine hygiene products on a desk beyond my cell. *Oh, thank the Lord*, I thought.

"I think those are for me," I said to the guard.

"Just get back into your cell," he said.

It's difficult to describe just how anxious I was to get my hands on those items. I hoped they would make me feel a little more human again. I hoped they would warm me up.

I stood there waiting as he walked away, and I stared at those items, and stared and stared—and nobody went near them. Finally, it became clear to me that no one was going to bring them to me anytime soon. So I grabbed the blanket and went back into the corner.

I had no idea what time it was. The lights never went out and I couldn't see any sunlight. I looked at the wall next to me and there were tally marks scratched in it. I figured the only way a person could figure out what time it was is if you kept track of the meals. I didn't eat, though. They brought me a dinner tray and left it by the door at some point, and I just left it there. I didn't want to eat or drink because I didn't want to have to use the toilet in front of everybody.

At one point they gave me a manual describing all the rules and regulations of life behind bars, and I read the whole thing, cover to cover, thinking, *I'd better get to know this stuff. This is going to be my life soon.*

How am I here? A teacher. A mother. How am I in this prison cell? Am I going to spend the rest of my life in a cell this size? How do I do that?

Finally, I couldn't hold it anymore. I had to pee. I asked for some toilet paper and they handed me a roll. I tried to hold the blanket up and cover myself while I went, but that's a whole lot harder than you think it is. And you can't hold it up when it's time to wipe. I cried the whole time. I took a whole bunch of toilet paper and wadded it up in my pants to try to stop some of the blood, but that didn't work very well at all.

The cell was next to a big set of doors, so every time I'd start to nod off, those doors would go "Wham!" and wake me up. It was torture.

When one of the workers came by to remove my dinner tray, he looked at the untouched food and asked, "Are you okay?" I swear that boy looked about twelve years old. I didn't answer. I just hid my face in the blanket.

"All right," he said, and he left.

I didn't see another human being until they brought me a breakfast tray sometime the next morning. I didn't eat that either.

David and Clancy came down first thing, and while I wasn't allowed to see David, an officer took me into one of those rooms with the Plexiglas dividers and the phone handsets so I could speak with Clancy. They made everyone get down and stay back in their cells during the walk to that visiting room—supposedly for my protection. It made me feel like more of a monster. As soon as I stepped out of my cell, I asked about the items on the counter, and they ignored me once again.

Clancy made a point to tell me that he and David had stopped at Walmart the night before to get me everything they were allowed to get me—the white cotton panties, the feminine hygiene products, a sweatshirt, and a sports bra. He asked if it was satisfactory. I let him know that they hadn't given it to me yet.

"You're kidding," he said.

"Do I look like I'm kidding?"

I was a wreck. But we talked, and a few minutes later one of the guards said, "Your other attorney's here." Clancy left and Scott came in, and we talked practicalities—about the fact that I'd be taken from jail directly to my bond hearing by the police that afternoon. Finally, the guard said, "How many attorneys do you have? Because a third attorney's here to see you!"

I remember the visit with Cary the most because I picked up the handset and Cary said, in this soft, caring voice, "How you doin'?"

"I don't know. How do you think I'm doing, Cary? I'm in a solitary cell, I didn't do anything, I'm bleeding, and there's panties sitting right over there that I need and I can't get to them. So how do you think I'm doing?"

"I'm sorry, Tonya," he said.

Poor Cary. I completely lost it in front of him.

They took me back to my cell, and I sat there the rest of that morning, right through lunch, until sometime late in the afternoon. Those prison guards didn't bring my personal items to me until ten minutes before I had to leave for the courthouse.

I folded the blanket before I left and placed it on the bed. The guard seemed surprised. I said I was just following instructions. He said he'd never met anyone who had actually read and followed the manual before.

They shackled and handcuffed me to cart me over to the courthouse. I never imagined how tight and painful shackles might be until I had them on me. They hurt. They dug into my ankles something fierce. I could not walk. All I could do was shuffle.

"Everybody down!" they yelled as they escorted me out and shoved me into the back of a police car. The whole time I was thinking, *I did nothing wrong and I'm being treated like the biggest monster in this whole place.*

I don't know how anybody who's tall or thickset could ever fit in the back of one of those police cars. My knees were all up against the back of the front seat. I could barely move an inch.

As they pulled up to the courthouse, I could see the cameras. The press was there. Luckily they took me around the back, but they kept treating me like Public Enemy Number One as they shoved me into the elevator and made me stand with my face to the back wall.

One of the police officers started lecturing me as we reached the second floor. "You keep your eyes to the ground in here. If you look in your parents' eyes, if you look at anybody and you have eye contact, I swear if you do you're on the ground and you're not getting out and you're not getting bonded. You're not allowed to have eye contact with *anybody*!"

I kept my head down. All I could do was glance sideward a bit as they walked me through the side door into that little courtroom presided over by Judge Van Pelt. It was packed all the way to the back, especially on my side, where my attorneys were standing behind the table. *Mom must've called everyone she knows*, I thought. But as they paraded me past the prosecutor's table, I saw that Joal was sitting on their side, and Joal's *father*, and Sandra Lamb, and Sandra's parents, and Kelly McDonald—though I didn't see her husband, Jerry—and a few others I recognized, plus a few people I didn't recognize. I tried not to make eye contact with any of them, which must've made me look like I was walking in shame. I hated that. I wanted to look every one of those people in the eye.

We'd had court dates before where nobody came from the other side, including Joal, despite the fact that the case involved our children. *Now all of a sudden when I'm in shackles and handcuffs they all just happen to show up?* I was fuming inside.

A man I'd never seen before walked to the front of the courtroom and slammed the little flip-door between us before heading to the prosecutors' table. Scott leaned over to me and whispered, "That's Len Gregor. He's another ADA now assigned to your case."

Great, I thought. *Now I've got two ADAs working against me?*

When Judge Van Pelt came in and said, "Please be seated," I took my seat between my attorneys and we went through the motions to get the bond all worked out. The fact was, I'd already been arrested before, we already knew this was going to trial, I already had about as many restrictions as a person could have on them, and I'd been following the judge's orders to the letter since day one. So it all got worked out pretty quickly. I still wouldn't get to see Ashley, though. At that point, it felt like a given. A devastating conclusion, but a given one.

The judge slammed his gavel and told everybody to remain seated until I was out of the courtroom. I stood up, and a police officer came and grabbed my arm. I started shuffling out in front of that whole gallery full of people—and I tripped.

That was when I heard a sound that I would never forget for the rest of my life: the sound of Sandra and the others laughing. I swear I heard a familiar laugh among them, too: the laugh of the father of my children. Not just snickering but hee-haw laughing. At *me*. It was loud, and a whole group of their friends and family around them joined in. The judge didn't throw his gavel down to stop it. It went on and on.

Those shackles made it feel like someone was using a meat slicer on my ankles and both of my Achilles tendons, yet I regained my footing as best I could and headed toward the elevator, humiliated. Even though I'd been bonded out, they still had to take me back to the jail in handcuffs and shackles and put me through a whole official dismissal process before I'd be allowed to leave the jail.

That meant something I didn't see coming. Even though the officers had been with me the whole time, protocol said they had to strip-search me again. So that was what they did. I went back into that room. I stripped down naked as the day I was born, put the soles of my feet on that icy concrete, bent myself over, and went through the process a second time.

I cried just as hard as I had the first time.

I thought about the charge of "digital penetration" that had been made against me. I had yet to face a jury of my peers. I had yet to have my case heard. I had done absolutely *nothing*. And yet there I stood, receiving a grotesque and humiliating eye-for-eye punishment for the very crime I did not commit. Twice.

In the days and months ahead, some people would ask me, "Well, why don't you let this go? Why don't you just pretend like it didn't happen?"

You know what I feel like telling them? *You* go through that and try to pretend like it didn't happen. Just try. Being violated? Being treated like an animal? A person does not forget that. *Ever.*

David picked me up in front of the jail. I hadn't eaten in more than twenty-four hours. I was exhausted but so famished that I couldn't make it all the way home. So we stopped at Karl's, a little Southern-style restaurant on the way back to Soddy Daisy.

David and I didn't talk much initially. He could see how exhausted I was. He could tell how distant I was, so he didn't push it. In fact, the only thing that really got me talking was the memory of Sandra and those others laughing in that courtroom.

"There's nothing funny about it," I remember saying. "If that were me in that courtroom, looking at somebody who I thought molested my child, I would not be laughing no matter what happened. I'd be glaring. But to them? It was just funny to see me in shackles and handcuffs."

David was smart enough to keep quiet and just let me vent. I get crabby when I'm hungry anyway, so my physical condition only exacerbated my rage. I ordered some meatloaf and mashed potatoes with a side of macaroni and cheese. I cleaned my plate before we headed back up to the house.

That night, all I could think about was the cell they'd locked me in. I thought about going to prison, and it felt like planning my own funeral. *How do you prepare to be buried alive? In a cell? To live in that awful space for the rest of your life?* I didn't know how to prepare for that.

The next day, David was rubbing my legs on the couch and he stopped and asked, "What *is* that?"

I looked down and saw what he was talking about: There were scabs starting to form on my ankles where the shackles had rubbed me raw and cut into my skin. I shook my head and tried to hold back the tears.

They'd finally managed to scar me on the outside, too.

Chapter 32

In total, the DA's office charged me with twenty-two counts of child molestation, aggravated child molestation, and aggravated sexual battery. My lawyers said that if I were to be convicted on all counts, I'd be looking at a minimum of 400 years in prison.

I knew I was up against something awful, but there is nothing quite like sitting down and reading twenty-two counts of horrendous crimes with your name on them.

Each count of the indictment started by saying the grand jury "in the name and behalf of the citizens of Georgia, charge and accuse Tonya Craft, AKA: Tonya Henke . . ."

Each count listed a date range during which the supposed "offense" took place. Not one of them had a specific date attached to it.

And each of those counts said I "did commit an immoral and indecent act" to "a child under the age of 16 years."

I did my best to stop my hands from trembling as I read the first page.

The first count said that I "penetrated the vagina" of Brianna Lamb sometime between August 2005 and the 30th day of June, 2006, "the exact date of the offense being unknown to the Grand Jury."

The second count said I did the very same thing to Ashley, my daughter, sometime between the 17th day of January, 2002, and the 30th of June, 2006. *The 17th of January, 2002, is the day that Ashley was born!* (Her name is blocked out in this particular copy, which was put out through local media at the time of my arraignment.)

INDICTMENT	STATE OF GEORGIA	CATOOSA COUNTY

STATE v. TONYA CRAFT, AKA: TONYA HENKE

COUNT 2

IN THE NAME AND BEHALF OF THE CITIZENS OF GEORGIA, CHARGE AND ACCUSE

TONYA CRAFT, AKA: TONYA HENKE with the offense of Aggravated Child Molestation,

O.C.G.A. 16-6-4(c), for that the said accused, in the State and County aforesaid, between the 17th day

of January, 2002, and the 30th day of June, 2006, the exact date of the offense being unknown to the

Grand Jury, did commit an immoral and indecent act to _____, a child under the age of 16 years,

with the intent to arouse and satisfy the sexual desires of said accused by penetrating the vagina of said

child, said act causing injury to said child, said act not being the same act as described in any other

count, contrary to the laws of said State, the good order, peace and dignity thereof.

The third count was about Chloe. It accused me of "touching" her vagina.

Counts four and five were both about Brianna. The fourth one was written exactly like the previous charge about Chloe, saying I'd "touched" her vagina, which was apparently different from "penetrating" her vagina in the first count because each of these counts had a disclaimer near the bottom saying that it was not the same act described in any other count. It seemed confusing to me, that touching and penetrating were two separate acts, but the confusion was nothing compared to the nausea I felt as I read them. Count five said that I, Tonya Craft, "did intentionally penetrate the anus of Brianna Lamb with her finger, a foreign object, without the consent of said victim."

Count six said that I used my finger to "penetrate the sexual organ" of my daughter, Ashley, during the same date range listed in the second count—basically the whole first four years of her life. And the counts went on and on. The date ranges made no sense. Not one of the counts listed *where* any of the alleged incidents took place.

The nausea nearly overtook me. Chloe. Brianna. Ashley. Chloe. Brianna. Brianna. Brianna. Over and over and over.

Unless we could get some of those indictments dropped before a trial took place, a jury of twelve people would have to agree to find me "not guilty" on all twenty-two separate charges in order for me to walk out of that courtroom and back into whatever was left of my life. This wasn't one fight. This wasn't even the *three* fights against the charges of the three girls. My fight for the truth would have to prevail *twenty-two times* in order for me to walk free and get back to Tyler and Ashley.

I'd waited all that time, hoping and praying to finally know what the charges against me might be, but as I sat there reading those pages in Scott and Cary's office, I wished I'd never seen them at all. The charges made me sick, yet they still didn't tell me anything about what Brianna or Chloe or my precious Ashley had told those detectives. I guess it was my own naiveté to think that I'd actually learn something from those indictments. All I learned was that I was facing more adversity than I could have possibly imagined and that I would now have to overcome more obstacles than even my worried mind had managed to believe before that point in time.

When I finished reading those indictments, the first thing I did was thank God that I had found Doc. Before my second arrest, I had felt in my heart that I needed him. Now I *knew* just how badly we needed every shred of his experience and expertise.

I'm pretty sure I was the only one who was happy to have him aboard. When Doc finally flew down the first time to meet the team, he immediately rubbed Cary the wrong way. He rubbed Scott the wrong way. He rubbed Eric the wrong way. It wasn't long after that we hired a well-respected jury consultant, and Doc rubbed her the wrong way, too. No one could see past his arrogance to see the genius he was and the expertise he brought to the table. "Tonya, he's awful," they said. "He's going to send you right to prison."

They assumed that the arrogance he showed in our meetings would carry over to the courtroom and that his attitude alone would tick off the jury and lead them to convict. People I trusted and believed in said, "Tonya, this is stupid. You're screwing up."

I had to sit there in the middle of this battle with my life on the line and find the strength and conviction to say, "You know what? Doc's the best, so this is how it's going to be." God only knows how I found the resolve to do that when I was under so much pressure.

On top of everything else, in the wake of my arrest, my attorneys were tasked with filing a slew of motions on my behalf in Tennessee.

First of all, we had to file a motion for contempt and/or to compel Joal to submit my children for an unbiased forensic evaluation. We did that in May. The Tennessee court had ordered that exam back in April, and Joal had begun the process but refused to complete it.[32] We also had to file a motion to compel the deposition of Joal, because although he had begun it, he refused to finish it. The court had appointed a new therapist to see my children in Tennessee, but I was concerned that therapist was only gathering information from Joal and Sarah at that time.[33] She hadn't contacted me or anyone else I knew to find out about how my children were really doing through all of this. In fact, I showed up at her office, and her office declined my requests to speak to her even though I was paying for her services. So getting Joal and Sarah to complete their depositions and to get Tyler and Ashley in for an unbiased evaluation weighed heavily on my mind.

When I faced my arraignment in Georgia—where I officially pled "not guilty" to all of those charges—the motions we put forth were plentiful. One of the biggest was a "Defendant's Special Demurrer to Felony Indictment," contending that the State's twenty-two counts against me were mostly so vague and repetitious, it was impossible for me to mount a defense. What we said was that the DA's office was essentially forcing me to guess at what I was defending myself from. We also made a Motion for a Speedy Trial, a Motion for Change of Venue (due to small community size and excessive press coverage), a Motion for Trial by Jury (to ensure that my life wouldn't be left in the hands of a single judge), a Motion for Discovery (for any statements I may have made while in custody or any scientific reports they might be using against me), a Motion and Brief for Examination of Physical Evidence (if they had any), a Motion to Opt In to Reciprocal Discovery (which meant we would share documents with the DA's office just as they would share documents with us), a Brady Motion for Information Necessary to Receive a Fair Trial (a technical matter meant to ensure there wouldn't be any surprises in the courtroom), a Giglio Motion for Information Relating to Promises of Immunity to State Witnesses (since, as we all know from TV and movies, promises of immunity can lead some witnesses to skew their testimony in the prosecution's favor), and finally a Demand for a List of Witnesses (so we'd know who the ADAs planned to put on the stand, so we could research everything we could about them and be prepared to refute whatever they might say against me).

The motion for a speedy trial was basically a backup plan, so they wouldn't keep delaying and delaying this to drag it out, but they put my trial on the calendar for September right there at my arraignment. The rest of the motions in Georgia would have to wait until we had a pre-trial motions hearing—and that would take months.

There was some good news that came out of the motions we filed in Tennessee, though. Joal was finally compelled to complete his depositions *and* to bring Tyler and Ashley to complete their forensic evaluations with a new, unbiased interviewer named Ann Hazzard. I could hardly wait for that process to move forward. I couldn't wait to see some unbiased reports by an expert who could tell us how the children were really doing—and who I hoped would get to the bottom of what *hadn't* happened to Ashley with me and what *did* happen at Joal's house.

Chapter 33

In the wake of my second arrest, my friend Diana pushed me to rally some public support for my case. For months she'd been trying to get me to let her put up a website. She even went so far as to register a domain name: TruthForTonya.com. My attorneys (except for Doc) wanted her to hold off because they didn't want to rock the boat. They were nervous about causing a public ruckus. "You don't want to do anything to tick off the judge or the DA," they told me. "You don't want to make matters worse."

Allowing my case to exist in isolation seemed to have only made matters worse. So I finally told Diana to go ahead and do it. It was her site. I never ran it. But I was strict about what she could put on that site and what she couldn't. For instance, she couldn't name any children, including my own. She couldn't put up any pictures of my own kids or anyone else's. She should keep it simple. She should describe the basics of what had gone on and simply ask people to support my desire to seek the truth. Anyone who looked into it could come to their own conclusions. All I wanted was for the public to be made aware of the case and to give my supporters an outlet through which they could reach out to me if they wanted to, without giving out my personal email address or phone number. The site also allowed people to make donations.

Honestly, I didn't think we'd get any donations. *Who in their right mind would donate money to an accused child molester?* But I let Diana post a donation link nonetheless.

Oddly enough, there seemed to be a shift in momentum among all of my supporters once the indictment came down and once we had a potential trial set for September. I'm not sure if it became more daunting or what, but it just hit home with a lot of people around me. The whole thing, which had been so real and so devastating to me from day one, became that much more real and horrifying to those who knew me.

It even seemed to affect David in a new way. He came home from work one day and handed me a little stainless-steel cross with the word "truth" neatly cut into it. He had a high-powered water jet at work that could cut through metal, almost like a laser. It was quite the machine, and it was difficult to use. It took time and skill and patience. And for some reason, he'd felt driven to make that Truth Cross for me with his own hands.

It was a flat piece of metal, about three inches tall and not much thicker than a credit card. It was polished and shiny. David said he wanted me to carry it in my pocket as a reminder—to give me something I could hold on to when it seemed like the truth was never going to come out. Almost like one of those "hope stones" you see people carry sometimes, that they rub with their thumb. I could rub my thumb over the word "truth" and feel the power of that word within the shape of the cross.

I showed it to Diana, and she immediately asked if David could make one for her. Tammy wanted one the moment she saw it, too. My parents each wanted one. Their longtime neighbors across the street wanted a couple. Other friends—Jennifer, Courtney, everyone—started clamoring for them. David wound up making a whole bunch of these Truth Crosses to give to our family and friends, and they all wound up carrying them wherever they went.

At the same time, we started getting dozens of comments, emails, and donations through the website. People actually opened up their wallets—for *me*. People whom I'd never even met. It wasn't a lot of money at first, but every little bit made a huge difference in my life. We set all of that money aside for my case, to be used for travel or unforeseen expenses that might come up.

Finally, Diana asked if we could offer the Truth Crosses on the website, so people could have them as a prayer token. In the coming months, David would make more than a thousand of those little metal reminders, which would be carried by people all over town, all over the region, and all over the country before we were through.

The momentum seemed to carry over into my case directly, too. Eric was having phenomenal success unearthing all sorts of records and facts about some of the key players. We gathered details on the standard operating procedures of DFACS and Four Points and more—all of which seemed to have been flaunted, ignored, or overridden during the course of the "investigation" of these charges against me.

Through our digging, we discovered that Brianna, Chloe, and Ashley had all been taken in for medical exams to look for physical evidence of molestation. We discovered the name of the nurse who had performed those exams, a woman named Sharon Anderson who had testified in many abuse cases in the region. We would use that information to request copies of the exams, of course, but Doc was extremely interested in looking into Sharon Anderson's qualifications and experience as a sexual assault nurse examiner (SANE). It was a shock to me, but Doc said that his research of other cases around the country found many cases of wrongly diagnosed physical examinations for "sexual assault," just as he had found numerous faulty interviews in which children were coerced (whether purposefully or not) into claiming that they'd been abused. In either case, whether medical or verbal, the examinations were performed by so-called "experts," who in reality had very little training and very little understanding at all of the area in which they called themselves "experts."

The thought made me sick. The thought that my own daughter had undergone such a physical exam when I knew nothing had happened to her made me even sicker.

The looming September trial date set everything into high gear, and in many ways, my P.I., Eric Echols, and I were like the dynamic duo of research and investigation. He was the one out there pounding the pavement and knocking on doors—doing work that I wasn't allowed legally to do—while I worked on my laptop, sifted through documents, and did the organizational work it took to set up interviews and decide many of the avenues we would pursue. Eric was dogged in his pursuits, and he believed in me with all of his heart. I couldn't imagine a better partner in crime—or in my case, a better partner to help *undo* the crimes that had been committed against me.

He was one of the most valuable members of my team.

I guess I should've seen it coming.

Chapter 34

"Tonya," Eric said, "you won't believe what just happened."

"What?" I said.

I'd never heard Eric sound shaken before.

"I tried to serve Sandra the subpoena, and she stood in the middle of the road, screaming at me and blocking my way," Eric said. "Then she came over and tried to take my phone. She slapped me in the face through my open window!"

"She also called me a 'black bastard,'" he said.[34]

"She *what*? Are you okay?"

"No, I'm *not* okay!"

"I am so sorry, Eric!"

"I recorded the whole thing on my phone," he said. "I'm definitely going to file a complaint against her."

Eric's words sent a chill right down my spine.

"I got her on video. I had my phone running the whole time. She's done."

The fact that Eric had captured Sandra's behavior on camera would be evidence enough to get the cops and courts to do something in almost any other county. But in Catoosa? The whole thing worried me. I didn't want any more problems. I didn't want anyone on my team to have to fight any more fights than we were already fighting.

Lo and behold, a court date was set for a hearing on whether or not to issue an arrest warrant against Sandra Lamb. It happened quickly. Almost too quickly. I felt those chills again when Eric gave me the news. I felt like something was up.

Sandra walked into the courtroom a few days later without an attorney by her side. I wasn't there. I was told what happened by a number of my supporters who were present for that hearing and by Eric himself. What they all corroborated was the judge came in and said they were there to discuss a matter concerning an arrest warrant for Sandra Lamb, and Sandra stood up and said something to the effect of, "Oh, I didn't realize it was for *me*. I thought it was a warrant for *his* arrest," and she motioned toward Eric. "I don't have an attorney," she said.

That was when, according to what I was told, the judge dismissed Sandra Lamb from the courtroom. He ordered everyone else to clear the courtroom as well—except for Eric. Once everyone was gone, two detectives came in, slapped handcuffs on Eric, and arrested him.

Eric Echols was charged with three counts of intimidating a witness.[35] Oddly enough, it wasn't Sandra Lamb whom Eric was charged with intimidating. It was Jerry McDonald, Kelly McDonald, and Chloe McDonald.

Eric had interviewed Jerry twice during the month of July, once on July 15 and once on July 23—the day before his run-in with Sandra Lamb. Jerry had submitted to those interviews of his own free will, and those interviews were recorded and transcribed.[36] As far as I understood, Eric barely had any contact with Kelly. She had come to the door when Eric stopped by the house to deliver a subpoena for our custody case in Tennessee, and that was it. As far as I knew, he'd had no contact with Chloe at all. And yet he was forced to sit in a jail cell until his poor wife could get the money together to bail him out.

Worse? After this happened, Eric made a decision not to do legwork on my case anymore. I can't say what happened behind closed doors, but Eric refused to come back to Catoosa County for many months after he was put in jail and his bond was posted. He led me to believe that they would not bond him out unless he agreed not to work on my case any further, and I was very apt to believe him based on what I had experienced.

I was horrified. I was concerned about Eric, of course, but I couldn't help but be scared about what it might mean for my case.

"If there's no indictment before trial, we might still be able to put him on the stand," my attorneys assured me. "We'll just need to be careful. They could attack his credibility because he was arrested. Or they could use this against you, to try to claim that you were attempting to intimidate witnesses by sending a man out to do your legwork."

"Are you serious?" I asked.

The whole thing left me shaking with fear. This small-town justice system was even more frightening than I'd wanted to let myself believe. Seeing how quickly a key member of my team was dispatched sent a very powerful message my way: I needed to put more eyes on my case. I thought, *The FBI should know what's going on here. So should the attorney general. So should the governor. So should the press.*

Once word spread about Eric's arrest, we couldn't find another P.I. to work for us anywhere. Nobody wanted to come near my case with a ten-mile pole. Suddenly, I was left with no one to do the legwork I needed. My team had lost one of its pillars.

———————◆———————

As the summer dragged on, I continued to mark the days on my calendar—noting just how many days I'd gone without seeing Ashley: 433, 434 . . . Not one of those days grew less painful than the one before it. All I wanted was for the trial to arrive so I could show the world the truth and hopefully see her again. Yet I also dreaded it every second, mostly because I *still* didn't know what we were preparing to fight. We hadn't received any discovery from the DA's office yet that summer.[37]

Because of that, we weren't ready to go to trial in September. There was just no way. We still didn't know what exactly we were defending me from. We hadn't seen so much as the girls' interviews with the detectives. We didn't want to let the DA's office know we weren't fully prepared. They might have pressed to go to trial as soon as possible. But through some careful negotiations and discussions between attorneys, both sides wound up agreeing to postpone the trial until the next court session. That next session wouldn't happen until March 2010.

Because my attorneys had previously filed a motion for a "speedy trial," the law in the Lookout Mountain Judicial Circuit said we would have to have a trial within three of the rotating court sessions. We had already passed by one session without a trial in July, immediately following the indictments and my second arrest. So by skipping the September session, the court would have no choice but to put me on the calendar and get my trial scheduled for that next session in March. Period. There was no way around it. It was one of the first definite *anythings* I'd experienced during this whole entire process.

It broke my heart to think I'd have to wait that long to try to clear my name, but I also knew that we needed that time in order to continue to build my case.

It broke my heart even more to consider the possibility that the court might not let me see Ashley before that trial. I couldn't think about it. I just couldn't. The punishment felt too cruel to be plausible. Once again, I put my faith in the powers that be. I prayed that someone in power would see how wrong the court had been to keep me from Ashley for so long. *There has to be someone, somewhere in the system, who can see how wrong it is for Ashley, too!*

I couldn't blindly trust a system that had failed me so many times, how-ever. I had to continue taking matters into my own hands. So I sat down and did some more research. One night I stayed up late on my laptop, reading up on a case in Bakersfield, California, in which a whole bunch of people went to prison based on allegations of child sexual abuse that were later overturned. It was awful. These people spent years in prison before they were finally exonerated. One of them was behind bars for *twenty years* before they got out.

A documentary called *Witch Hunt* had been made about the case, pro-duced and narrated by Sean Penn. I ordered several copies of the DVD on the spot. I needed to know what went wrong in that case so I could keep it from going wrong in mine.

Chapter 35

"I need to go to California," I said.

"What for?" David asked.

"Remember that documentary I told you about? About the Bakersfield case?"

"Yeah."

"Well, it came in the mail yesterday and I watched it last night. And then I watched it again. It's unbelievable, David. The film showed how these people went to prison based on horrendous interviews and detectives who had an all-roads-lead-to-Rome attitude, and a hysteria overtook those parents, and how the convictions were eventually overturned because the California Innocence Project and the attorney general dug into it and pulled apart the files and broke down the interviews with the kids and showed how the parents had coerced them, and the detectives had gone right along with it, and—"

"Yeah, but what do you need to go to California for?"

"To see that attorney general. I guess he's a former attorney general now, but I need to talk to him to find out what convinced him to look at that case in the first place, and what it was that made him look into it. Because when I go to the attorney general in Georgia to show him *my* case, I want to have my ducks in a row and know what's going to catch his attention, like—"

"Do you really think an attorney general in California is going to talk to some unknown woman from Georgia?"

"I don't know, but I have to try."

"Why don't you just call him up on the phone, then?"

"I can't just call him, David. It won't work. It's like with Doc. When you're dealing with somebody that promi—"

"That's just crazy talk," David said. "There's no way you're going to get in to see somebody like that, and we can't afford it anyway. I gotta go."

He shut the door just a little too hard for my liking on his way out.

Maybe it was crazy. I guess it *sounded* crazy. It didn't seem crazy to me.

Two days later David informed me that he had to go away on a business trip for a couple of days. He had to see a client, he said—in *California*.

"Well, I'm going with you," I said.

David could tell just by the way I was looking at him that he wasn't going to convince me otherwise. When we realized that David had accumulated enough frequent flier miles for me to make that trip free of charge, I took it as a sign.

I didn't ask David what *part* of California he was flying to. California's an awfully big place. But it turned out that David's client was located in Carlsbad, California, no more than what looked like a thirty-five-minute drive from the offices of the very man I aimed to see.

True to the cliché, LA traffic was horrendous. It took us several hours to make what should have been a forty-five-minute trip from the airport to the address I'd Googled for former attorney general John Van de Kamp. The drive out and back to Carlsbad would be just as bad. But we did it.

It was strange driving through LA, knowing it was the land of Hollywood, where movies are made—and where Brianna Lamb had actually been cast in a role in a film that came out in 2008. The year after she was in my kindergarten classroom, Brianna spent part of several months filming a horror movie. It was a pretty big deal. In it, she played a little girl who had been abused by her mother. She played a part in another film a year or so after that as well, in which she played a little girl in a foster home. I tried to convince myself that the fact that Brianna had played the part of an abused girl for the cameras was just a coincidence—but the irony of it all struck me pretty hard as we sat in traffic, surrounded by all sorts of Hollywood-looking people in their fancy BMWs and Mercedes.

I approached the security desk in that LA high-rise with the same techniques I'd used to get into Doc's humble office in Ann Arbor, Michigan.

"I'm trying to save the lives of my children," I told the security guard, and I held up my pendant with their pictures on it. That seemed to give him pause.

"Hold on one minute, ma'am," he said.

The security guard put me on the phone with the former AG's assistant. She invited me up to her office. I showed her my pendant, and she said she'd get back to me.

I walked into that lobby the next morning carrying my binders and notebooks, and the security guard remembered me the moment I walked in. "I don't know how you did it, but I am glad you got an appointment," he said, guiding me toward the elevator.

Former AG John Van de Kamp was more than I could have hoped for. Polite. Insightful. Courteous. The Bakersfield case had unfolded more than twenty years earlier, yet I asked him all kinds of questions about it, and he answered every one of them. He asked all kinds of questions of me, too, and he looked at my binders full of timelines and highlighted interviews from some of the witnesses we planned to call in my defense—and then he gave me some advice on what to focus on.

In the Bakersfield case, children testified against their neighbors, against adult role models, and even against their own parents. Based on the documentary, it seemed that detectives and prosecutors, and in some cases family members, didn't so much ask questions of the children to find out if anything had happened to them but instead *told* them what had happened to them and then forced them to testify to those lies. With some of the kids, it wasn't so blatant. The interviewers simply used a lot of repeated questions and leading questions to get the children to give them the answers they wanted to hear. It was awful. Some of the children themselves started to crack in the years following the convictions. Some of them even came forward on their own and tried to get the convictions overturned at the local level. Still, the convicted adults—including some of those kids' own parents— rotted in prison anywhere between twelve and twenty years before their convictions were overturned. The only reason they were overturned even then was because of the involvement of a group called the California Innocence Project and because of Mr. Van de Kamp's crusade to see justice properly served once he took a look at the case.

The worst part of the whole ordeal, to me, was that some of the children who had been forced to testify were grotesquely affected by their involvement. According to the film, their participation was no fault of their own. They were just little kids, so the blame clearly lay with the adults and especially the people in power in the Bakersfield legal system, but the guilt that those children placed on themselves led to drug problems later in life, attempted suicides, and more.

I shuddered to think of the destruction that had already been done to my own children. I silently said a prayer for them even as I listened to Mr. Van de Kamp. I said prayers for Brianna and Chloe, too. *No child should be put through this*, I thought.

Mr. Van de Kamp helped reassure me that the fight was worth fighting. He showed me that by focusing on the facts, by focusing on the transcripts and tapes of the actual interviews with the children, and by analyzing the types of leading questions the detectives and prosecutors likely used in order to come up with these indictments, I would have a shot at convincing a jury that I was, in fact, an innocent woman. It was a long shot, he admitted. It would not be easy. But still, I had a shot.

Just that little bit of encouragement alone made the whole trip worth it.

Mr. Van de Kamp also gave me another bit of advice before I left. As much as he hated to admit it, he said, it would be a good idea for me to get some national media attention on my case. That spotlight would help keep the judges and attorneys in line. The fact that the eyes of the country would be on them might make them think twice before pulling anything fishy, he said.

That was right in line with the thoughts I'd had about getting "more eyes" on my case.

I went back to Tennessee emboldened, convinced I could walk through any door I wanted to. So I walked into the office of the attorney general of the state of Georgia—and his assistant wouldn't let me talk to him.

"Everybody says they're innocent," he told me. "Come back after your trial." He did not even look at any of the documents I had so carefully organized.

I walked straight into the office of the governor, too, though I never did get in to see him, either. I had friends and supporters who made a relentless number of calls to both the AG's office and the governor's office on my behalf after that, requesting that they take meetings with me. They called so often that when I would call to try to set up an appointment, they would ask me to "please" make my supporters stop calling.

I would say, "Well, why don't you just see me for fifteen minutes, and I promise the calls will stop." It was all for naught. But I didn't let that deter me. I figured that even if I didn't get in, even if they didn't take any action, those high-powered people now had my case on their radar. They knew who Tonya Craft was and could never deny they had heard of me or my case.

David sold his bass boat.

It was worth more than two cars put together, and he spent more time and money caring for that thing than he did any other possession he owned. Fishing was his retreat. His solace. His sport. And he sold that boat so I could continue my fight—and continue my travels.

I had a lot of doors left to knock on, in some pretty far-flung places, and I decided to get started right away. I flew on my own to Nebraska to try to track down some of the people who were directly involved in the Bakersfield case. Like a lot of people involved in false-allegation cases, they'd run as far and fast as they could after suffering the devastation. It turned out that some of them ran as far as they could from ever talking about it again, too. I didn't have much luck on that trip. Encountering the sadness and devastation of it, and how far away from their old lives these people had been pushed, was enough of a lesson to keep me focused on proving my innocence—and doing anything I could to help my kids heal once this trial was over.

My new missions would all get put on hold for a while, though, because for all of the traveling I was about to do, some of the most disturbing information I would uncover during my entire investigation was about to get dropped in my lap.

Chapter 36

I'd long expected this was going to be one of the hardest things I'd ever have to face in my life—even while I'd been praying for this day to finally come. So when Scott called me to say a package had arrived containing the first part of the discovery from the ADA's office, I felt like I was going to pass out.

That package contained the DVDs and transcripts of the interviews that Detective Deal and three others had conducted with Brianna, Chloe, and Ashley—the very interviews that had led to the charges against me.

No one said much to me as I walked into Cary and Scott's offices. We all sat down in a conference room. They passed out copies of the transcripts as Scott queued up the first DVD.

For a year and a half, we had been trying to prepare a defense based on hypotheticals because we didn't know what those girls had said. For a year and a half, my life had crumbled into turmoil and despair because of the very words that we were about to hear.

"Are you ready?" Scott said.

"I guess," I responded.

Scott hit play and I turned to the first page of the transcript of the first interview with Brianna Lamb. The interview was conducted on May 27, 2008, at the Child Advocacy Center (CAC), by a woman named Stacy Long.[38] We'd done some homework on her. We knew that she had a master's degree in social work and a BS in psychology, and had conducted more than 1,000 interviews with children in her career.

Seeing Brianna appear on that screen, wearing flowery, preppy-looking pants and pink sandals, I think the first thing that struck me was her demeanor. I expected she'd be upset or something. But she wasn't. She seemed kind of nonchalant. Right when the video first started, she was staring up toward the camera, which appeared to be placed way up by the ceiling in the corner of that interview room, pointed down at an angle toward a kid-sized table with some sheets of paper and a cup full of crayons. Brianna sat on the far side of that little table, so she was facing the camera, and Long sat on the other, so you couldn't really see her face very well.

Right near the beginning, Brianna asked if anyone was going to see the video, and the interviewer basically told her no.

"Nobody can just get that tape and see, okay? It's kept pretty private, okay? So you don't have to worry about that part," she said. "Brianna, the only thing that I need you to do is tell me the truth, no matter what that truth is. Okay?"

"Uh-huh," Brianna answered.

"What does it really mean to tell the truth, though?" Stacy asked.

Brianna responded, "It means to tell you what she really did to you."

I underlined Brianna's answer in the transcript.

I would wind up underlining a whole lot before we were through.

Long asked Brianna if there was anything she wanted to ask her or anything she wanted to say. Brianna's answer was, "Um . . . color." And she grabbed a crayon and started coloring.

"That's the only thing you want to say?" Long asked. Brianna nodded.

"Do you like school?" she asked.

"Uh-huh," Brianna answered.

This banter went on for a while. We watched and read along the transcript, and Brianna didn't talk about me at all. We were all thinking, *She must be fixing to say* something.

Finally, Long asked her, "Okay, Miss Brianna, so how come you are here to talk to me today?"

"Um," Brianna said, taking a pause. It seemed as if she were trying to remember something. "A girl was mean to me."

"When was she mean to you?"

"When I was at her house . . . in Chickamauga."

The interviewer clarified that she was talking about me, Miss Tonya. I immediately thought it was strange that Brianna would refer to me as "a girl." And being "mean" to someone is a far cry from abusing someone. Plus, remember, I didn't live in Chickamauga until the very, very end of Brianna's kindergarten year. I was still commuting from my town house in Tennessee until May of 2006.

The facts didn't seem to matter, though, because Long asked Brianna if I was married, and Brianna said I wasn't. David and I had only been separated a few weeks when that interview was conducted, and I had told virtually no one. It seemed clear to me that she'd heard that from an adult, and I could guess who likely provided her with that information.

Long went on asking Brianna how many times I was mean to her, and Brianna repeated that it was "once." Then she added that it was "at school" as well. Then Long asked, "Where at school did it happen?"

"In the hall," Brianna said.

"Okay, at Tonya's house, where would it happen?"

"Close to the kitchen," Brianna responded.

"Did anyone else see it happen at school or at Tonya's house?"

Brianna shook her head.

"Okay. What was she doing that was mean?"

"She always took me out in the hall at school and told me not to do anything when I didn't do nothing . . . And at her house she, when we were out one day, she got me Taco Bell and—"

Brianna stopped talking, mid-sentence.

"She did what now?" Long asked.

"Got me Taco Bell . . . to be really nice. And, um, she . . . she, um . . . she uh . . . we were in the kitchen one day, and she started kissing me on my head and my neck and my shoulder."

"Okay," Long said.

"And she'll never give me any food and I was hungry."

"Okay," Long said. "So one day in the kitchen . . ."

"Uh-huh," Brianna said.

"Okay. Would . . . did she say anything when that happened?"

"She said it was okay for her to do it."

"Did she say anything else other than it was okay for her to do it?"

"Uh-uh," Brianna said, shaking her head.

"Did anything else happen? Was she mean to you in other ways?"

"Um . . . uh-uh," Brianna said, again shaking her head.

So, up until this point she'd said I'd kissed her on the head and shoulders—which I'd never done—but that was all. When asked if I'd done anything else, she said very clearly, "No." But Long kept pressing.

"Did she do anything else that you didn't like?"

Right here, Brianna switched gears and started talking about Ashley wanting to play the boyfriend-girlfriend game. She said that she didn't want to play it, and that Ashley threatened to tell on her if she wouldn't do it. (Ashley is two years younger than Brianna.)

When asked how you play "boyfriend and girlfriend," Brianna answered, "You would, like, kiss on the cheek like that."

"Anything else?"

"Um, she um, um . . . [pause] stuck her hand down my pants and she told me to do it back to her," Brianna said—again, rather nonchalantly—as she continued coloring with a yellow crayon.

Long went on to ask her about what happened when Ashley's hand was supposedly down her pants. Brianna insisted that Ashley's hand was "on top" of her "panties," and that there was no touching of skin, ever. Yet Long kept asking the question, over and over in different ways—about whether Ashley touched her privates directly and whether she touched Ashley's privates directly when she touched her back. Brianna answered repeatedly, "Uh-uh."

Long then asked, "Where did Ashley learn that?"

"Um, I don't know," Brianna said. "She must have learned it from her mom."

"Why do you think that?" Long asked her.

"I don't know," Brianna answered.

"Okay, did Tonya ever do anything like that to you?"

"Uh-uh," Brianna said. *As in, "No."* She said it without hesitation, clear as day.

Long continued to ask her about how I was mean to her, and Brianna said I never fed her when she was at my house. She said I fed Ashley but refused to feed her a thing. It made no sense at all to me, because there was always food at my house and it was always available to anyone that was at my home.

"How did all this stuff come up, Brianna?" Long asked.

"I don't know," Brianna said.

"You don't know. You don't know . . . Did somebody ask you about it or did you tell somebody about it, or what? You don't know how somebody found out for the very first time about all of this?"

"Uh-uh," Brianna said.

The longer the interview went on, the more it seemed to me like Stacy Long was digging for specific answers.

"Did you tell your mom anything different than what you told me . . . ?" she asked.

"Uh-uh," Brianna said.

"Was there anything about Miss Tonya . . . did she give you touches?"

Brianna shook her head.

"No? Did you tell your mom that she had?"

"Uh-uh," Brianna said.

"No?" Long responded, seemingly begging for another answer with her voice.

After a long pause, Brianna said, "Well, she did pat me right here"—indicating a spot right below her belly button. When pressed about what she called that spot, Brianna called it her "private."

Stacy asked if the touch had been on top of her clothes or under her clothes; Brianna said it was "on top." Then Long asked her, "Did Miss Tonya ever say things to you that scared you or that you worried about?"

"Uh-uh," Brianna said.

"No?" Long asked, again with what seemed to be a leading tone that made it sound like Brianna had given her an incorrect answer—to which Brianna started talking about me playing loud rap music in my car. *I don't listen to rap, ever!*

Long then circled back to whether Brianna knew about anything that happened between me and other girls, to which Brianna replied, slowly, "Chloe . . . Skyler . . ." Then Long asked about when it happened, and Brianna said it happened in kindergarten. (Neither of them specified what the "it" was they were talking about.)

Brianna brought up the night of Ashley's birthday party and talked about leaving the party and how she was scared that I might be mean to her again if she ever came back to my house. No matter what Brianna talked about, Long kept coming back and asking the same questions about whether I'd ever said something that scared her or ever said something about her "mommy loving her." Brianna answered negatively to every question.

Brianna repeatedly answered "uh-uh" to questions about me, such as, "Did she ever want you to touch her in any way?" and "Did she ever show you any of her private parts?"

"Uh-uh," "uh-uh," "uh-uh," over and over.

When asked whether she was telling Long everything that happened, Brianna answered affirmatively.

"You're not leaving anything out because it's hard to talk about or . . . ?"

"No," Brianna said.

Still, Stacy Long would not relent. At this point, Brianna hadn't said anything whatsoever about being touched under her clothing by either me or by Ashley, yet Long suddenly pulled out a picture of a naked child and asked Brianna to point to where I supposedly touched her.

She again pointed to the area just below her belly button.

"And that was on top of your clothes when she did that?" Long said.

"Yes," Brianna responded.

"Is there anything at all that you want to ask me?"

"Um . . ."

"Nothing at all?" Long interrupted.

"Uh-uh," Brianna said.

Just when I thought the interview might be over, she started right back up again. She asked Brianna if she thought a lot about what had happened to her and if it bothered her. Brianna said it bothered her in her dreams at night.

Long then pressed again about whether there was anything else Brianna wanted to tell her. "It all happened exactly like you said?" she asked.

"Uh-huh," Brianna said.

Even then, it wasn't over. Long started talking about me again and asking about my marriage, to which this little girl responded: "Tonya got married to one guy and he divorced her and then she got married to . . . got married to another guy at our house and he got . . . and then he . . . she was mean to him and her other husband so they left her."

Long asked, "Did you see anything happen between Ashley and Chloe or Skyler?"

I was relieved when Brianna shook her head.

"Okay. How do you know that things happened?" Stacy asked.

"My momma told me," she said.

Instead of asking a follow-up question to find out exactly *what* her momma had told her, Stacy Long circled back to some earlier questions and pressed Brianna again about how many times things had happened between her and Ashley. ("Twice," she said. "No more.") Then she asked a question about whether Brianna had seen any books or magazines that had people without clothes on, to which Brianna said, "No."

Finally, she wrapped things up and took Brianna outside—to where, as we would later discover, her mother was waiting for her.[39]

"This is *bullshit*!" Cary yelled. He was fuming mad. Scott stayed silent and just shook his head. I said nothing. I was too flabbergasted to speak.

The video started up again, and Brianna and Stacy Long both came back into the room. It was unclear how much time they'd spent outside talking to Sandra Lamb since the video stopped and started, but the interview was clearly on the same day,[40] and the transcript was dated on the same day. It appeared to have just been a short break, but as far as the transcripts went, this was called "Interview #2."

"So you wanted to come back and talk to me again?" Long said.

"Uh-huh," Brianna answered.

"Okay—"

"Miss Tonya made me touch her back," Brianna said quickly, placing her hand on her upper chest area, up by her left shoulder.

"Like on top of her clothes or under her clothes or what?" Long asked.

"On top," Brianna answered.

Long asked her about what I had said to her ("She told me to touch her") and whether I had asked her to keep her hand still or to move it around ("Keep it still"), and when Brianna had trouble identifying the body part she said I'd asked her to touch, Long showed her an anatomical depiction of a nude woman and asked her to point to the spot on that figure. Brianna still pointed to an upper-chest area, more toward the shoulder or collar bone than anywhere I might think of as sexual.

"Did she want [you] to touch her anywhere else?" Long asked.

Brianna responded in the negative.

Long then asked if she had "forgot" about that during the first interview or whether she was "a little bit scared" to talk about it—to which Brianna replied that she "forgot" *and* that she was "a little bit scared." So Long told her it was okay to be scared and then repeated the question about what I had said to her at the time.

"She told me I had to or I [pause]—or I had to go home," Brianna answered.

So I'd threatened her with sending her home? Wouldn't she want to go home if something bad was happening to her?

Long repeated the question about whether it was on top of my clothes or under my clothes, to which Brianna replied, once again, "On top." Then she made Brianna repeat when it had happened, and Brianna said once again that it was when she was in "kindergarten."

Eventually, Long asked her, "Anything else you can think of?"

"I get to go to the spa today," Brianna said.

"Where are you going to the spa today?" Long asked.

"You can ask my momma," Brianna responded.

"Nothing else you can think of?" Long added again, and then they both got up and left the room, returning a few moments later to mark the spot where she had touched me on that nude female figure. Apparently they had forgotten to mark the spot.

"And you said it was on top of her shirt?" Long asked for a third time. Brianna nodded.

Long then pointed to that naked figure's breast—clearly *below* the spot they had marked—and asked Brianna to name what body part that was. Brianna answered, "Breast."

Long then left the room again, reentered, and asked Brianna, "When you stayed over at Miss Tonya's house with Ashley . . . did you ever, like, take a bath over there?"

Based on everything I'd read and researched about this subject so far, I thought interviewers were not supposed to make suggestions to kids when abuse allegations had been made. Is Sandra in that hallway? Is she getting her questions from her?

"Uh-huh," Brianna said.

Brianna then went on to describe how I would scrub her with a washcloth on her stomach, "real hard." She pointed to her own stomach. She pointed to the stomach on the nude figure when Long asked her to point to it. But she called it her "private," and then Long referred to it as touching her "private" as well.

Brianna said that she took those baths with Ashley and that I was "gentle" with the way I scrubbed my daughter. I hoped and prayed that Ashley would remember during her own interviews that no such baths ever took place. *There were no baths.*

"When she would wash you, did she wash, like, in between your legs, too, on your private?" Stacy asked.

"*Uh*-uh," Brianna answered, emphatically shaking her head.

"Anything else you want to say?" Long pressed once more.

Brianna shook her head yet again.

"Nothing?"

Brianna said something softly. The transcript read "(INDISCERN-IBLE)." Upon a second listen, it was clear to all of us exactly what Brianna had said. Her words weren't "indiscernible" at all.

Brianna Lamb said, "I don't remember anything."

That was it. That was the end of the first two interviews.

"You have got to be kidding me," I said.

I prayed for every other person who'd ever been charged with a crime in this county.

Ignoring what we believed to be clearly coached answers and the apparent coaching that went on in the hallway in the middle of that interview, Brianna *still* hadn't made any kind of a direct accusation against me that would have warranted criminal charges. She called into question what might have been going on between her and my daughter, Ashley—my daughter who is more than two years *younger* than Brianna. She said some things that may have raised some eyebrows about a grown woman kissing her forehead and shoulder, patting her on the tummy, and whatever that bit was about "making" her put her hand on my upper chest area and keeping it "still" or I'd threaten to send her home. Those things hadn't actually happened, but even if they had, they did not rise to a charge of sexual assault and certainly didn't warrant a charge of "aggravated" sexual assault. I'd read the laws now. They seemed very clear.

"Wasn't this the interview that my first arrest was primarily based on?" I asked.

"Yes, it was," Scott said.

"How can that be, Scott? How is that even possible?" I asked.

"I don't know," he said.

Cary was firmer: "I want to take that DVD and shove it up the ADA's ass!" Our anger, combined with my rapport with Scott and Cary, had all three of us swearing during all of this. My attorneys said that they had never come across an interview like that in their entire careers. But Scott didn't want us jumping to any conclusions about it being coached or biased quite yet.

"Maybe it's the corroboration with Chloe and Ashley that added up to the charges, so let's keep going," he said. "Let's look at Chloe's."

He popped Chloe's interview into the DVD player and we turned to the first page of the transcripts. Chloe's first interview took place on May 29, 2008—one day before those detectives showed up at my house—and her interview was performed by none other than Detective Tim Deal.

From what we'd found out, Deal had completed a forty-hour course in child-abuse cases at one point during his training. Deal's BS degree was in organizational management. He'd had on-the-job training and shadowing, and he worked with EMS. That was it, as far as we could discover.[41]

Oh, and he had what we considered to be a conflict of interest going into this that we didn't know about until Deal pointed it out himself at the very start of the interview: "So . . . what is your name? I know it is Chloe," he said. "I probably remember about the time when you were born . . . I guess I've known your mom and dad for a long time. I used to go to church with them . . . I taught your daddy at Vacation Bible School."

How can a man who personally knows her mom and dad be conducting this interview? There are others trained to interview these kids, aren't there?

He told her three times in a row that she was not in trouble and that she wouldn't get anybody else in trouble by talking to him and telling him the truth. He also told her that he was a policeman—an authority figure if there ever was one in the eyes of most children.

"I talked to your mom just a little bit downstairs and I understand that there is a problem . . . And you're not in any trouble and you're not here to get your friend in any trouble . . . I just need to know the truth. Uh. Do you remember anything about that?" Deal asked her.

At that point, Chloe stopped, stared at the camera, and paused for a few seconds. Her voice was quiet, but the transcript said her next statement was: "Yeah, uh, I just remember a place and, uh, uh, (INAUDIBLE) where they touched me." The word "INAUDIBLE" was written in that transcript. We didn't rewind to listen or anything because it was so early in the interview. At that point we just wanted to press forward and hear what she'd accused me of.

"Well, we can talk about that," Deal went on. "You said the wrong place. Who are you talking about?"

She didn't say the "wrong" place, I thought.

"Ashley Henke," Chloe replied.

She had used the pronoun "they," but then the only name she gave was Ashley's.

"I spent the night with her one time," she added.

Chloe was very clear that she had only stayed over one time and hadn't mentioned anything "happening" at this point, but Deal started pressing her about what happened, how it happened, and what was said. Finally, Chloe responded, "They didn't tell us. They just done it. They just touched me in the wrong places. It was their mom and Ashley."

He asked questions about whether it happened in the dark or the daytime, giving her options to choose from as if it were a multiple-choice test. Then Chloe uttered a complete falsehood[42] that Detective Deal failed to follow up on: "Brianna is really our cousin," she said, seemingly out of the blue.

She then described a sleepover that happened with Brianna, Skyler, Ashley, and herself—after a Halloween party at my house. I thought, *But I never had a Halloween party at my house. There was a* High School Musical *party at our house one time, and I'm sure Chloe came to that party, but there were lots of kids there. David could corroborate that. So could either of my kids.*

Deal then asked about "touching" and whether it was inside or outside of Chloe's pajamas. Chloe responded, "Outside." She didn't say who was supposedly touching her. Then Deal changed from talking about "outside or inside the pajamas" to "outside or inside your underwear." *Chloe didn't say anything about underwear!* I thought.

Still, Chloe replied, "Outside."

He also asked her if maybe "they" (meaning Ashley and myself) had made Chloe touch "them." Chloe replied three times in a row that she had not done that.

Deal then asked her six different times whether Ashley or I had told her "not to tell," and each time she answered, "No." Finally, on the seventh time Deal asked, "Did anybody tell you not to tell or anything?" Chloe finally gave him the reply he seemed to want.

"They told me not to tell anyone," she said, echoing his exact words.

Deal then went on to talk more about Chloe's family, after which Chloe talked for what seemed like a long time about some family vacation time, filled with exact details. *She remembers all of those details without any of the vagaries she seemed to exhibit when it came to discussing when or where this "touching" in the "wrong place" might have occurred.*

Deal then told Chloe where "wrong places" might be: "Well, it's a good rule for boys and girls to know that any part that's covered up by a bathing suit is not a good place for people to touch you . . . That might be okay if maybe Mommy and Daddy or your grandma or grandpa are taking care of you," he added, eventually reiterating that, "any place that is covered up by a bathing suit nobody should touch unless they are taking care of you."

They went off-topic again, with Chloe not saying anything about "touching" and instead recalling all sorts of details about getting her tonsils out. She recalled the exact date of December 10. She recalled the taste of the medicine, and her feelings, and specific items that were involved. She did all of that without repeated questioning or multiple-choice options. It was remarkable to me just how good her memory actually was.

The interview wrapped up a few minutes later with a series of questions by Deal, one of which was: "And everything that we've talked in here today is the absolute truth?"

At the end of his series of questions, Chloe said, "Yeah," but it was unclear to me which of those final questions she was answering.

That was it.

Once again, there was no direct talk of a sexual assault and no indication whatsoever of "aggravated" sexual assault.

Except for the interview with Skyler Walker, in which she didn't accuse me of anything whatsoever, these were the only videotaped interviews that took place before Detectives Tim Deal and Stephen Keith rang my doorbell. Those were the interviews that took place before my kids saw me for the very last time, and before the man from DFACS showed up and asked me to sign a document saying my kids wouldn't be returned to me until the interviews were "completed."

The first interview with Ashley didn't happen until June 3. A second interview with Chloe didn't occur until June 11—one day *after* a judge issued a warrant for my arrest.

"How could my arrest warrant be based on these interviews? There is *nothing there*," I said.

Neither Cary nor Scott had a good answer for me.

———————◆———————

When I'd driven in that morning, I wasn't sure if I'd have the strength to watch Ashley's video. I thought about letting Scott and Cary watch it while I went into another room. But after seeing Chloe's and Brianna's videos, I told Scott to go ahead and pop it in the DVD player. I needed to see it for myself.

Watching my baby girl sit in that chair in an interview room a whole year and a half earlier brought waves of emotion and a hurt in the pit of my stomach like nothing I'd ever experienced before that moment. Hearing her voice, seeing her blond hair, imagining and feeling for myself the discomfort she must have felt to have been put in that situation was unlike anything I'd ever felt as a parent. *Yet her father brought her there to be grilled!*

Ashley's interview took place at a different facility, a place called the Greenhouse, and her interview was conducted by a woman named Suzie Thorne. We'd done our homework on her, too. Thorne had been a detective for eight years. She had undergone some "advanced interview training" (a total of forty hours) and had been responsible for interviewing more than 1,000 children. She was still in the middle of working on a bachelor's degree in criminal justice and forensic psychology. She had only completed two years of that four-year degree program.[43]

How could the system allow anyone without so much as a bachelor's degree in child psychology interview more than 1,000 children?

Ashley seemed agitated from the start. To me, she clearly didn't want to be there, at all. She didn't seem like herself. My easy-breezy girl was visibly uncomfortable, and all I could think when I looked at her was, *What are they doing to my child?*

Thorne began by telling her, "The Greenhouse is a safe place for kids. And nobody here at the Greenhouse is going to be mean to you or do anything bad. Okay?"

That opening statement implies that something "mean" and "bad" has happened to her elsewhere, doesn't it?

Ashley didn't seem concerned with any of that, though. She was more concerned about the camera. "Why are you videotaping it?" she asked.

"That's just what we do here . . . Don't worry about that . . . That's nothing to worry about," Thorne told her.

My baby girl wasn't having it. She kept asking her about the camera and what would happen with the videotape. *I know my daughter, and she clearly wants a straight answer. She didn't get one.*

Thorne pressed forward by saying they were there that day to discuss something that happened with Ashley's "mom" and "lying." Ashley's response to that spoke volumes: "That's what my dad told me," she said. "He asked me a lot of questions . . ."

When Thorne asked where my daughter was living, Ashley said, "I'm staying with my dad, but I used to live with my mom. But she got in trouble with the police."

When Ashley mentioned that her mother had lied about something to the police, Thorne asked her if she knew what I had lied about. Ashley responded that she didn't know. "But my dad told me she lied about something," she said.

Thorne didn't follow up on that and instead asked Ashley who else lived in her house.

Wow. Is she really going to ignore the obvious influence of her father here?
She then asked if her "mom" ever had anyone sleep over.

"With her?" Ashley asked.

"Yeah," Thorne responded.

"Us . . . me and Tyler," Ashley said.

"Okay, uh, how come you are staying with your dad now? Why did you say?"

"Because my mom got in trouble from the police," Ashley repeated.

Then Thorne repeated, "What did she get in trouble for?" and Ashley wasn't having it.

"YOU ASKED ME THAT AND I SAID I DON'T KNOW!" Ashley said, rather forcefully.

"Wow, she really is your daughter," Scott interrupted.

Thorne then tried a different line of questioning. She described places that were okay to touch on a child's body and then asked Ashley if there were any places where people shouldn't touch you.

"Not really," she answered. When Thorne pressed her on it, looking for an answer, Ashley finally answered, "The bottom."

"Okay, well, what's the other one called?" Thorne asked.

Ashley answered her question: "Vagina."

Thorne then said it's "not okay" for anyone to touch the vagina or the bottom and said, "Uh, has anyone ever touched you there?"

"My mom," Ashley said.

"Okay. Can you tell me more about that?"

"Well, she has put medicine on me sometimes and sometimes she washes me," Ashley said.

Thorne then asked Ashley to tell her what that was "all about." *Clearly this Suzie doesn't believe that was all I'd done. So now she's putting my six-year-old child in the position of defending a normal parent/child interaction.*

"She just puts medicine on me," Ashley answered.

Thorne pressed on for details about where and why.

"My bottom because sometimes my belly hurts and I have, like, a problem with my stomach and I have to go to the bathroom a lot," Ashley answered.

"When she does that, where are your clothes?" she asked.

"I just do this," Ashley motioned. "I just pull them down for a minute so she can put the medicine on and then I pull them back up."

Thorne pressed her about why her vagina would need medicine, and Ashley kept answering perfectly straightforward and honestly. The medicine for that was applied just the same way, she said. So Thorne pressed on, asking her what the reasons might be for the stomachaches—asking if they were caused by something that was bothering her or making her sad. Ashley said "no" to all of those things and instead offered up that her dad thought she was "allergic to something."

After what seemed to me like she was trying and trying to get Ashley to say something more damaging about me, Thorne switched gears again and instead asked Ashley what kind of games she likes to play.

"Sisters . . . doggy, mom and kid, and tag, gymnastics, dancing," Ashley answered.

"You said you played, uh, mom and kid and mom and dad and tag and all that stuff," Thorne repeated back to her—only it wasn't a straight repetition. She added the "mom and dad" game, which is something that Ashley didn't say. I caught that right away.

So did Ashley.

As Thorne followed up about the games, she mentioned that Ashley said she played a "mom and dad" game again, and my daughter said, "I didn't mean to say dad. I meant to say kid."

Thorne kept asking about it anyway. Ashley grew more and more upset at the repeated questioning, and it seemed that when Thorne wasn't getting anywhere, she would switch things up. Out of the blue she asked my daughter if she took baths at my house—a line of questioning that wound up with Ashley talking about showering at Joal's house with Sarah and a little razor that they would use. When that line of questioning didn't go as Thorne had apparently hoped, she asked whether Ashley had talked to her father that weekend—and what they had talked about. No further discussion of showers and bathing at her father's house with Sarah. Just me. That was the focus. The agenda.

"Did you talk to your dad this weekend about your mom?" Thorne asked.

"Well, actually, he talked to *me* about my mom," Ashley responded. (Italics mine. The transcripts didn't add emotional accents or emphasis, even when they were clearly present.) "He asked me a few questions . . . kind of like you asked me."

"Well, I don't remember what I asked. Can you help me?" Thorne said.

"You don't?" Ashley said, incredulously. Even at six, she was way beyond that sort of adult manipulation.

After some more questioning from Thorne, Ashley finally said that her father had asked her whether I'd ever touched her. And she said she had told him exactly what she had told Thorne a few minutes earlier: that the only time I had ever touched her on her bottom or her vagina was when I put medicine on her.

Suzie then asked Ashley about what had happened on "Friday."

Ashley said, "That's when my mom got arrested." She whispered the word "arrested." It was difficult to hear, but she said it. This interview happened on June 3, 2008. *So in the course of those four days that she'd been with Joal, just after the weekend when she called me and whispered into my voice mail that she wouldn't be seeing me for a very long time, someone wrongly convinced my daughter that I had been arrested. Gee, I wonder who that was? And I had not been arrested at that point!*

Finally, Thorne started asking about the boyfriend-girlfriend game. She kept repeating her questions, relentlessly, until Ashley was visibly upset and on the verge of tears.

"How come you're getting upset about that game?" Thorne asked.

"Because I just don't like it," Ashley said. "I don't want to talk about it," Ashley repeated, but Suzie Thorne did not stop.

She's grilling her! I started crying. *My baby girl is sitting through an interrogation.*

Thorne finally switched gears, to find out if I had yelled at Ashley and the other children about anything on that Friday. Ashley answered truthfully: "She screamed at us and told us to go to our room."

Thorne pressed, "How come she screamed at y'all?"

"I don't know. She just screamed and told us to go to our room," she repeated.

Thorne kept on her, trying to find out what I may have told her about those men on my porch, and "anything" that happened. Ashley answered: "I didn't even know who they were," she said, referring to the detectives. "Not until my dad told me."

We weren't supposed to be discussing the case with the kids. *Didn't the detectives tell me that my ex-husband had "no knowledge" of what was happening that Friday? Was that all a sham? Was it a lie? Were these people tainting my children against me from the moment they were out of my home? And had my ex been interrogating his own daughter?*

Thorne excused herself to go talk to somebody she "works with." Ashley put her feet up on the chair and started sucking her thumb—an annoying habit but something she did on a regular basis. Thorne left her alone in there for what seemed like a very long time.

When she finally returned, Ashley said, "Why can't I leave now? It's been too long."

"You can in just a minute. We're almost done," Thorne told her. "I've just got a couple more questions because I'm kind of confused on something, okay? Now you do know that . . . that you're not in trouble, right?"

Ashley immediately seemed to get upset again, which made me get upset watching her.

"Ashley, you're not in trouble, and I'm not going to ask you about that again, okay?" Thorne said—I think she was referring back to the boyfriend-girlfriend game questions that got Ashley upset in the first place. "But you're not in any trouble, okay? Okay? Uh, I'm just kind of confused on something though. So can you help me?"

Ashley responded through tears and wails so big that you couldn't understand a word she was saying. But Suzie Thorne did not stop. *How can she continue to grill a six-year-old little girl like that?*

"And you told me your mom put medicine on your bottom because it was hurting? Because your tummy was upset and you said that . . . that you told [your dad] that she touched your vagina?" Thorne said.

"She did," Ashley said through tears.

"Huh?" Thorne said.

"She did," Ashley repeated.

"She did, okay. But why did she touch your vagina?" Thorne pressed, even though she had gotten a clear answer about this before.

Bawling her little eyes out, Ashley said, "She just did. I don't know."

"You said she just did. You don't know why?"

"Uh-uh," Ashley cried. "No, I don't know why."

The interview kept going and going. Eventually, Thorne asked, "Where were your clothes?"

"I said . . . I already told you."

"You said that when she put medicine on your bottom that . . . that she pulled them down," Thorne said.

Well, that's not true at all! Ashley said she pulled them down herself and then pulled them right back up!

"Okay, when she touched your vagina . . ." Thorne continued.

Ashley was beside herself at this point, just squalling at the repeated questioning. "THEY WERE PULLED DOWN. IT WAS THE SAME TIME WHEN I HAD MEDICINE!" Ashley yelled.

"It's okay, calm down, all right. But did . . . what I need to know is . . ."

"I don't want to," Ashley cried.

"Ashley, I'm sorry that you're getting upset, okay? And I'm not trying to . . ."

"I want to stop," Ashley said firmly.

"I'm not trying to upset you, okay?"

"I don't want to talk," Ashley repeated.

"Are you scared that . . . are you scared that you're going to get somebody in trouble?" Thorne said.

"No, I just don't want to talk," Ashley repeated, again.

"Okay, well sit up for just a second and we'll be done, okay?"

"I don't want to," Ashley said.

Thorne tried again and again to get her to calm down and then finally asked, "Do you have any questions for me?"

Ashley, still crying, said, "No."

And at that point, I cried, too.

I went to Scott and Cary's office that day expecting to cry. I expected to be sad. Yet none of us expected what we saw on those DVDs. We expected to hear a litany of horrible things that those girls said had happened. I expected to hear charges and accusations to come flying out of their mouths—specific charges that we'd have to specifically refute. Instead, there seemed to be no specific accusations of aggravated sexual assault or any sexual assault at all. Not a one.

For a moment I allowed myself to think, *Let's get this dismissed! There's nothing here that warrants these charges! You can't have an indictment based on something that somebody said—when they didn't even say it!*

Scott was more thoughtful. He said, "We will file a demurrer. We'll file a bill of particulars. We'll file motions to try to get the particular indictments thrown out."

He then reminded me who we were dealing with and what I'd already been put through. "The problem is, it won't work," he said. "This happens all the time. Prosecutors pack on charges. It happens every single day."

Cary and I both knew Scott was right. The truth didn't seem to matter to the court now. All that mattered was the fight.

"Well, this system sucks," I said. "I'm sitting here with seven indictments against my own daughter, and she said *nothing*."

Scott stayed focused on the trial. He's a trial attorney. A good one. "Look, this is a *good* thing," he said. "This crap is not what we were expecting. We can *use* this. A jury is going to see right through this. We were expecting children full of emotions and all kinds of details. That's what a jury will be expecting, too."

As far as I was concerned, there was nothing good about any of it.

Chapter 37

I stayed overnight in Atlanta, and the next morning we went through the follow-up interviews that unfolded in the days and months after those first interviews.

First up was Chloe's second interview, which happened one day *after* the first warrants for my arrest were issued. For this interview, Chloe again sat down with Detective Tim Deal, and she immediately spurted out a new story—saying that she'd been touched "inside the panties."

Detective Deal asked Chloe why she hadn't said anything about it during the first interview, and he asked her if it was because she was "nervous"—a notion that Chloe agreed to. Deal then excused her for not telling the truth if she was nervous. *Does it matter that when I watched that video, I didn't see any outward sign that Chloe was nervous during her first interview at all?*

Deal immediately pulled out a diagram of a naked child, pointed to the vaginal area, and basically started offering her options: "on top of your clothes or under your clothes?" "in or out?" "front or back?"—and on numerous occasions, this little girl chose *both* options. She simply repeated back the words that he used: "On top and under," she said. "In and out," "front and back." Deal never asked for details or specifics. Chloe had revealed what appeared to be an uncanny ability to remember every detail of getting her tonsils out in her last interview. *It makes no sense that he wouldn't ask her to reveal the details of her stories in this interview. It seems pretty obvious to me that Chloe has no details to share because nothing actually happened!*

As the DVD continued, Deal pressed Chloe about whether she had seen me touch Skyler and Brianna, to which she answered, "Yes." Then a few questions later, she said she "didn't see." She added that she couldn't remember where she was or whether she was in the bedroom where Brianna and Skyler were during the "sleepover" (which neither Brianna nor Ashley corroborated), and she plainly contradicted herself by saying that Ashley was in the bedroom and then saying that she *wasn't* in the bedroom. Yet Deal never asked her to clarify any of her statements.

Deal then finally asked what seemed to be a very straightforward question of Chloe: to tell him where Ashley was while I was supposedly touching Skyler and Brianna.

Ashley was "walking with her mom," she answered. So we were taking a walk. Outside.

How can I be inside molesting two girls in the bedroom while I'm simultaneously outside taking a walk with my daughter?

Finally, Deal asked Chloe if the reason she didn't tell him the whole story during their first interview was because she forgot or because she was afraid. And again, Chloe seemed to take both options: "I was afraid and I forgot everything," she said.

I could not help but to note that Chloe, just like Brianna, had "memories" come back to her after spending time with her mom between interviews.

So why was she more comfortable this time around? Perhaps because of one very important detail that Chloe told Detective Deal during that interview: "Mom said if I done good I could go get a toy."

Sometime later, we'd receive the summaries from each of these interviews as part of discovery. Not surprisingly, the interview summary Deal provided to the DA's office didn't mention anything about Chloe being rewarded with a "toy" if she "done good." In fact, none of the interview summaries by the detectives or the other interviewers included any details whatsoever that might have pointed toward parental influence or to my innocence. Those details were simply left out.

The statements that we considered to be evidence of coaching and the overall outlandishness of the accusations got worse as Brianna Lamb came in for what amounted to a third interview, conducted on June 4, 2008, and then a *fourth* interview that was conducted almost a whole year later, on April 1, 2009.

The third interview was conducted by Suzie Thorne, the same woman who'd interviewed Ashley. The interview was filled with new stories of just how "mean" I was to Brianna in all sorts of different ways. I wasn't just mean to her at Ashley's birthday party. I was "mean" to her because I would never feed her when she came to my house, she said. I was "mean" to her when I pulled her into the hallway at school because some other kids had been calling my daughter "Willy Wonka" in class. *She and Ashley weren't in the same grade, let alone the same class.* I was "mean" to her when I wouldn't let her watch TV and made her leave the room when she stayed over. *There were TVs in the kids' bedrooms, as well as the living room, and the bonus room, and any kids that were over were welcome to watch TV anytime.* She also complained that I made her watch TV with bad words (*not true*) and drove too fast and that one time I told her that she had a weird eye color. *What?!* Oh, and after getting questioned and questioned during the first two interviews about whether I ever said anything about her mom, she added a new bit of "meanness" I supposedly uttered: "She would tell me that my momma was mean and that my momma didn't love me."

The interview was filled with contradictory statements that were never questioned. For instance, during the first interviews, Brianna said more than once that this whole thing had allegedly occurred when she was in kindergarten. In the third interview, she said more than once that it happened when she was in "first grade." Yet the oddest contradiction was probably her answer to the "where it happened" questions. In the first interview, she said "it" only happened in the kitchen. In the follow-up interview, she talked about taking baths at my house and how I'd "scrub her real hard" on the stomach. Then in the third interview, Brianna reiterated, "She would only do it in the kitchen . . ."

I didn't hear Suzie Thorne or any of these interviewers ask anything that sounded like a logical follow-up question about any of this contradictory material. There was never one question about who else was in the home when these events allegedly happened. In all of Brianna's stories about being at my house, there was no mention of the fact that Tyler would have been there. Or David. Or the Potter kids, whom I used to babysit every day. Or anyone else. The interviewers never asked, and Brianna never offered. In fact, unless they gave her an "option" question full of scenarios to choose from, Brianna answered open-ended questions, such as "Did anything else happen?", with the most fantastical stories. She spoke about searching and searching all over for me one day and how she couldn't find me anywhere, only to finally find me out mowing my lawn. *My entire lot in Chickamauga was less than half an acre, and it's open with no trees. It wouldn't be hard to find me. And I don't recall Brianna ever being present when I went out to mow the lawn.* She talked about me working out while she was there, in "short shorts" and a "tank top," and telling her that was how I get strong so I can "hurt people." (*What?*) She talked about jumping on the trampoline and how I forced her to do a back handspring, and she hurt her back. *There's no record of any injury. Even Sandra didn't bring up any such incident. It didn't happen.*

After sitting through three interviews in eight days, after answering ninety questions, Brianna Lamb never made an accusation of digital penetration. There was no mention of any penetration of any kind. *So how is it that her name appeared on three of my arrest warrants? And how could those arrest warrants be labeled with charges of "aggravated" sexual assault?*

Brianna's fourth interview happened eleven months after that third one—eleven months of potential parental influence and "therapy" at the hands of Laurie Evans.

The interview was conducted by a woman who hadn't been part of the case before. A woman named Holly Kittle. So what were her qualifications for the unbelievably sensitive and important job of videotaping interviews with children for the CAC? She had a BS in anthropology. She'd worked as a forensic assistant conducting autopsies for about six years. Then she took a five-day training course called "Finding Words" that apparently told her all she needed to know about dealing with cases of alleged child sexual abuse.[44]

A five-day course.

Kittle spent the first few minutes of the interview discussing seemingly unrelated events with Brianna, until eventually Brianna said something about being upset at school and needing to be pulled out of her classroom.

"Why didn't you feel good?" Kittle asked.

"Well," Brianna said, "last night I told Mommy something that the Evil One did . . ."

"The Evil One." That was me she was referring to. Kittle apparently already knew this because she didn't ask who "the Evil One" was. *After nearly a year of therapy, this little girl is referring to me as "the Evil One"?*

"What did you tell her?" Kittle asked.

"I told her one time I was taking a bath, well, she was giving me a bath and she stuck her finger up my butt. And she wouldn't say anything. She would always just not talk when she did it and see, like, when her daughter, Ashleigh"—Ashley's name was spelled incorrectly throughout the transcript—"was in the bath she wouldn't do it because she would always wash me first and then Ashleigh would get in the bath and she would do it . . . see, like, if I was in the bath she would wash me until Ashleigh would come in there and then she would give Ashleigh a bath. Well, anytime me and

Ashleigh took a bath together, she wouldn't do it. So . . . I don't know if she did it to Ashleigh because she would always wash me first. Anytime Ashleigh would be in the bathroom she wouldn't do it. And so, and so, so I don't know if she did it to Ashleigh, but that's the thing she did to me."

Kittle responded to that flurry of words in what seemed to me to be a very nonchalant tone: "And you said that she stuck her finger up your butt . . . Tell me more about that."

"Well, see, I didn't . . . she just automatically started doing it. And so I don't know . . . and then that's . . . and she would sometimes also stick her finger up my private"—at this point, Brianna made a motion with her arm, kind of pointing upward with her hand out in front of her body and face, above the tabletop—"and that's all she would do to me in the bathtub, but that's all she used to do in the bathtub."

"What is that?" Kittle asked, referring to her hand motion.

"I don't know. She just did that. I don't call it anything," Brianna answered.

"Did that go inside your private or outside your private?"

"Inside," Brianna said.

Brianna had been asked similar questions a total of twenty-three times before that moment and had answered "outside," "out," or "on top" every single time—until this time.

"When she did . . . when she did that inside your private, what did it feel like?" Kittle asked.

"It . . . I didn't like it. Before she did it, she said that you can't say anything. And so . . ."

"What did you say when she said that?"

"She covered my mouth," Brianna said. "I couldn't say anything."

"What did she cover your mouth with?" Kittle asked.

"Her hand."

A number of questions later, Kittle asked Brianna to specify which hand I used to cover her mouth.

"Uh, left," Brianna answered.

"And then, where was her right hand?"

"It was behind her back."

"What?" I said out loud right in Scott and Cary's office.

Kittle went right on: "Did she do anything else with her right hand?" she asked.

"Uh-uh," Brianna said. As in, "no."

I grabbed my head with both hands. "So, do I have a third hand grow-ing out of my belly button or something?"

The whole thing made my brain hurt. Brianna's words made no logical sense to me at all. *How could a person have one hand on her mouth, another behind their back, and be putting a finger in her behind or into her private at the same time?*

Kittle asked Brianna about why she hadn't said anything about this before now, to which Brianna replied she was "scared" she would "get in trouble."

"Who were you scared you would get in trouble from?" Kittle asked.

"My mom," Brianna answered.

She apparently wasn't afraid of getting in trouble with *me*. She was afraid of getting in trouble with *her mom*.

"When this happened in the bathtub, were you in her class?" Kittle asked, switching the focus right back to me, Miss Tonya, "the Evil One."

"Yes," Brianna replied.

So now we're back to this happening in kindergarten?

Kittle, to her credit, tried to get some clarification on that matter. But Brianna's answers only made it more confusing. She talked about my old house, then "she moved to the new house where she did it, where what happened . . . It was, like, down in Chickamauga."

Kittle asked again, "Where did this happen in the bathtub? At what house did it happen at?"

"Her . . . not her old one, her second house," Brianna said.

I didn't live in Chickamauga during Brianna's kindergarten year—the only year she was in my class and the only year that I was her teacher.

Kittle then pulled out anatomical dolls and asked Brianna to talk about what I did. Brianna changed her story significantly from the way she'd described things during her previous interviews. Instead of accusing me of using a "finger," she said I used "fingers," and she showed Kittle what she meant by pressing all of her fingers and her thumb together and making a motion, as if I was sticking my whole entire adult-sized hand up inside her vagina. The fact that a child would even suggest such a thing made me sick.

Holly also asked her when the last time anything happened to her was, and Brianna replied, "First grade." So that would have been through May of 2007. And yet her indictments listed a time frame that went through 2008.

Brianna went on to talk about me throwing her down the steps and smacking her across the face. When Kittle asked her when this happened, she said it was when her mom was waiting for her out in my driveway. *So I threw her down the stairs and this little girl doesn't have a mark on her face, or a bruise on her body, or a broken arm, or even wet cheeks from the tears she cried?* Not to mention none of it had come up in three previous interviews or even in the complaints her mother made to DFACS and others about me.

None of it made any sense. Neither did the timing.

It was April 1, 2009, when Brianna Lamb made these statements on the record that I'd penetrated her in the worst imaginable ways. Yet it took the detectives and the judge and the ADAs more than a month to have me arrested and thrown in jail on that charge. I couldn't help but wonder what held them up for so long. *Was there someone involved who recognized the inconsistencies in the stories? Did someone recognize the obvious coaching? Why wouldn't they have arrested me on these new charges right away? Were they scared? Did they feel they needed the grand jury indictment in order to back up their actions? And was there not even one person involved who questioned whether the deteriorating state of mind of this little girl who was now calling me "the Evil One" deserved some investigation of its own?*

———————————◆———————————

Seeing those interviews fueled my desire to know even more about how forensic interviews are supposed to be conducted with children. I started googling everything I could think of, and I read up on three very famous false-allegation cases: more on the Bakersfield case; the McMartin Case, a daycare case from the 1980s in California in which the children's allegations included wild stories of underground tunnels and lions; and the Michaels case in New Jersey, which resulted in the accused being convicted on hundreds of counts of sexually abusing nineteen children—all of which were overturned after the accused spent many years in prison.

Then, in the middle of one very long night, I came across something referred to as the "mousetrap studies." The researchers in the mousetrap studies—Dr. Maggie Bruck, a psychologist at McGill University, and Dr. Stephen Ceci, a psychologist at Cornell University—took a bunch of little kids around four or five years old and tested the idea of implanting memories through conversation. None of these kids had ever had their finger caught in a mousetrap in real life before. The researchers interviewed their parents and had them sign affidavits and so forth to make sure of it. They started out by talking to these kids about what they had for breakfast and other everyday sorts of stuff. Then, after gaining their trust, the interviewers started talking to these kids about how their fingers got caught in a mousetrap. The interviewers would ask them, repeatedly, "Do you remember when that happened?" The kids said "no" at first. But then, when the question and the topic kept coming up, pretty soon those same kids answered "yes." Then they started telling elaborate stories about their fingers getting caught and how much it hurt and what happened afterward. They came up with all kinds of stories, like, "The ambulance was going, and the sirens were going, and we had to make an emergency stop because somebody ran out in front of the ambulance!" I'm paraphrasing all of this, but the shocking result of the study was more than just "Oh my gosh, you can not only get a child to believe something that didn't happen, but they can be detailed about it and even embellish it on their own."

The *New York Times* took a look at some of these studies in an article by Daniel Goleman, which appeared on June 11, 1993. The first few paragraphs sum it up pretty well:

> The testimony of small children has usually been considered truthful unless proved otherwise. Over the past decade such testimony has led to convictions in many child-abuse cases, and the younger the child, the less likely psychologists have thought it was that information could have been fabricated. But now a series of recent studies has turned this conventional wisdom on its head.
>
> Researchers have found new evidence that persistent questioning can lead young children to describe elaborate accounts of events that never occurred, even when at first they denied them.
>
> The research is at the center of a continuing scientific debate over the vexing question of how much judges and juries should rely on a child's word when that is the only evidence of abuse.

The article explained that an estimated 20,000 children testify in sexual-abuse trials each year, and as many as 100,000 are involved in investigations, many of which lead to plea agreements. It then directly addressed the issue of repeated questioning over a period of time:

> Certain techniques often used by investigators with young children increase the likelihood of false reports, the findings show. One is persistent, repeated questioning over periods of several weeks.

When sexual abuse is suspected, children are typically asked the same questions by case workers, police investigators, and lawyers, as well as parents, before they testify in court.

But that repetition may lead some young children to concoct stories, according to results of a study by Dr. Ceci and colleagues reported last month at a meeting on emotional memory at the University of Chicago. . . .

"The more often you ask young children to think about something, the easier it becomes for them to make something up that they think is a memory," he said.

The worst part to me is that when the researchers eventually told the kids the truth and said, "Okay, your finger didn't actually get caught in a mousetrap," the kids would fight back: "Yes, it did!"

Once a memory is established, children seem to adopt it as a real event. As one might imagine, the effects of this in a courtroom can be chilling.

The studies also claimed that the use of anatomical dolls during questioning (not unlike the ones Holly Kittle had used during Brianna's fourth interview) could lead to false memories and false allegations in some cases.[45]

Basically, what I learned is that it takes extraordinary amounts of work on the part of detectives and therapists and everyone involved to get to the truth when it comes to children. It seems that children want to please any authority figure they're talking to and therefore can modify their answers to fit what they think the authority figure wants to hear. And yet all of the interviews with the kids in my case were filled with obviously leading questions and questions that offered the children a choice of suggested answers (rather than letting the child come up with the answers themselves), plus the sorts of repeated questions that might make any child think, *Gee, I must have answered that question incorrectly, so maybe I should change my answer to try to give the right answer!*[46]

I got quite the education. What I couldn't understand then, and what I still don't understand now, is why so many individuals who deal with children's cases all the time, who have such a massive impact on families and children all over this country, don't seem to take the same time or put in the same effort to educate themselves in these matters before possibly ruining lives through false accusations—and potentially destroying the very children they claim to be protecting in the process.

From my viewpoint, there is something very wrong with a system that allows someone with a five-day training course to conduct forensic interviews with children in a sexual-abuse case. Would a teacher be allowed to educate after a five-day training course? Every parent in America should be outraged at the very idea of that. Even if the abuse is real, how is an interviewer with limited experience or education going to get to the truth of what happened?

In my opinion, there is something even *more* wrong with a system that has the audacity to go ahead and arrest people, to take them to trial and try to put them in prison for life based on those same faulty interviews. In fact, it seems to me that some ADAs don't even read the interview transcripts. If they did, they couldn't possibly move ahead when bad interviews happen. It seems to me that the arrest warrants in these cases are based on the written "summaries" of those interviews, to which there don't seem to be any checks or balances to help discern errors or even purposeful omissions that could be meant to sway the court's bias in the direction of guilt.

In my case, none of the interview summaries seemed to mention any portion of the discussions that might have pointed toward my innocence. *So do ADAs glance over the summaries and then go tell a judge their own summary of the summary they've just read? The whole thing seems like one big childhood game of telephone out on the playground! Only in this game, people's lives are at stake—and, in some cases, few people in the game seem to take the time or make the effort to go back and find out what was really said in the first place.*

Chapter 38

I spent hundreds of hours sifting through phone records as we got them. Joal was quite a talker, so his in particular were filled with an abundance of calls and hundreds of different phone numbers—including the dozens of calls he'd made to and received from Sandra Lamb, Laurie Evans, Stephen Keith, Sherri Wilson, and others involved in my case.[47]

There was one odd number that really stuck out to me, though. It was a New Jersey number that Joal had called more than a hundred times, for long periods of time, and especially around some of the key dates of our custody hearings and even my arrests. I called that number and a woman answered. I tried my best to confirm who she was, but she wouldn't give me any information. The best I could do was track down an address in Newark that was tied to that particular phone number. I wasn't sure if it was truly important or not. Maybe it was a coincidence. Maybe she was an old friend of Joal's I'd never known. Maybe she was a girlfriend or former girlfriend. Maybe she was a psychic or shrink or someone that he was leaning on. I had no idea. I tucked that number and that woman's voice into the back of my mind and tried to focus on the information I *did* have.

Once I had most of the numbers figured out, David and I worked side by side putting everything into Excel spreadsheets and cross-referencing those calls against the calls that showed up on other people's phone records, sorting by phone number, triangulating between all of the various records so I could see what went on. David was much better at putting things into the computer than I was. I'll admit it felt good to work on some of this with him right there at my side. I think the collaboration was good for our marriage—and it was certainly good for my case.

Sandra Lamb's and Kelly McDonald's phone records never showed up, no matter what we did to try to get a hold of them. (Those records wouldn't show up until near the very end of my trial—when it was too late to matter.)

Even without their records, David and I were able to put together the basics of patterns and routines between all of those people.

The facts illuminated through those phone records were enormous to me. For instance, during our deposition of Sandra Lamb, on that same stressful day when we deposed David, Sandra stated that she had never, ever called Kim Walker, and therefore never could have "threatened her" the way Kim had described to us. Well, I might not be able to prove she threatened her because their conversation wasn't recorded, but guess what? Kim voluntarily gave me her phone records, and Sandra's phone number is sure as heck on there—as an incoming call—during the exact time period when all of that hullabaloo about the sidewalk chalk and the parents questioning their kids about the boyfriend-girlfriend game had occurred. It was a fact. Sandra had called Kim.

Basically, what the phone records showed to me is that everybody was talking to everybody—except me.

It was exhausting, but doing all of that work was good for me. I think it was part of what kept me from losing my mind during all of that waiting and all of that time that I was unable to see Ashley and so rarely able to see Tyler.

Keeping track of it all was certainly a challenge. In fact, one night in the middle of all of this I left my trusty black laptop open for a few minutes while I went to the bathroom, and our dog Candy Cane started digging at the keys like he was trying to bury a bone. The keys went flying everywhere.

"Candy Cane! No!" I screamed as I shooed him away.

It took forever to find those keys and snap them back into place. I never did find the "W." It's still missing to this day. One of the dogs must've eaten it. I had to go through everything to make sure I hadn't lost any research. Luckily my files were all okay, but the constant spate of near disaster was almost comical at times.

"Really, God?" I shouted. "*Really?*"

Realizing how quickly things could go wrong made me double my efforts to get everything organized and backed up so nothing important would get lost. I worked with Clancy to put all of my files into a Dropbox account that could be shared between all of my attorneys, so we could see everything over the Internet. I went down to Cary and Scott's office and organized all of *their* files on my case, too. I color-coded and labeled every binder. I had their staff running all over, making photocopies, stapling, unstapling, binding, alphabetizing, and scanning. In the middle of it all, I kept asking Cary and Scott, "How on earth are you going to get to the information you need during a trial if it's not perfectly organized and arranged?" They both said they'd always done just fine. "Well, guess what? You haven't won every case you've ever tried, have you?" I said. "I am certainly not going to be on the losing side of any attorney's record because they won't collate and color code."

They didn't like it much when I said things like that, but when I was fully engaged, God filled me with so much clarity of mind and purpose, there was nothing that could stop me. I wouldn't stay that way all the time, of course. I don't think anyone could. I would stumble and go into free fall and sleep for three days and cry. But when I was up, my hope was that everyone benefitted from the work I did.

In public, acquaintances would sometimes say to me, "You're so strong to keep fighting like this." I wanted to say to them, "Well, what else am I supposed to do? Roll over and just let them put me in prison?"

Chapter 39

In the middle of one sleepless night, I decided to turn my attention to a thick binder full of documents that I'd ignored for weeks—a file marked "Laurie Evans's Divorce Records."

For the longest time I'd thought, *What more could possibly be in those records that would make a difference anyway?* I was relieved that she wasn't seeing my children any longer. *What else is there to know?*

I barely got through the first page before I pulled out my stash of Post-it notes, pens, and highlighters. Laurie Evans had been diagnosed with PTSD.[48] In November 2006, Laurie Evans's attorney filed a motion in her divorce case stating that she was not emotionally stable enough to participate in a deposition due to "severe emotional distress" and PTSD. Yet since July 2006 she'd been employed by the CAC to "provide therapy to children who have experienced traumatic events," to oversee the therapeutic program, and to provide staff supervision and legal consultation. This individual was simultaneously claiming severe abuse and was in therapy for it while she was providing therapy and legal consultation on abuse cases for *children*. Not just my children. Not just Brianna and Chloe, whom she was still seeing, but *lots* of children.

According to the divorce records, which we pulled from public record, which anybody could see at any time, this woman had a diagnosis that placed her on the spectrum described as "severely impaired." It seemed obvious to me that a person in that condition should not be treating children. *Is this the only person whose recommendation led ADA Chris Arnt, as well as Judge Van Pelt, to keep me from seeing my daughter for the past year and a half? This woman is clearly crucial to my case.* I wanted to kick myself for waiting to go through every detail of her history.

My attorneys managed to get a motions hearing set for November 23, 2009. It was the first time we'd be going back to a courtroom in Georgia since spring (despite the constant custody appearances in Tennessee courts), and we had a lot to address. Judge Van Pelt agreed to hear arguments for the demurrer (our argument that the indictments were faulty and not based on charges of any actual merit) that day, as well as our requests for a change of venue, and for more discovery. (Other than the DVDs of the interviews with the girls, the ADAs had sent us next to nothing. We knew there must be more.) Most importantly, Judge Van Pelt would hear our new arguments for modification of the bond—and hopefully obliterate all of Laurie Evans's previous testimony and recommendations about Ashley and Tyler, based on the findings in those divorce records and more.

My attorneys and I felt better prepared going into that motions hearing than we had going into any hearing since the beginning. All of the months of work we'd put in had paid off. Add to that the results of my polygraph exams, which we were finally prepared to enter into evidence, and we felt strongly that Judge Van Pelt would be compelled to drop at least some of the twenty-two counts of the indictment.

There was just one problem. Right before we went into that hearing, Judge Van Pelt recused himself from my case. He gave no reason why he was stepping aside after all that time. My attorneys would try everything they could to find out the reason. *What if a conflict of interest has been tainting his decisions from the beginning? We could have grounds to have all of his decisions thrown out!* Suddenly, the man who had been present from the beginning wasn't going to be there to hear another word.

Would a new judge be up to speed? Would he have read all of the documents before we went in front of him? Or was he, too, going to be operating from the summary of summaries and the seemingly ongoing telephone game provided through the DA's office and perhaps now amplified by Judge Van Pelt himself?

The telephone-game angle of all of this made me extremely nervous, because I still doubted whether Judge Van Pelt had been paying attention to half of what we'd said in his courtroom. We got no answers as to why he recused himself, of course. The legal system seemed to protect its own. We were just expected to go in front of whoever this new judge was and to accept that the scales of justice would be fine and fair and balanced and blind.

The new judge was a man named Brian House—a man I recognized for all the wrong reasons. Brian House had served as an attorney for my first husband during our divorce proceedings. In my eyes it was about as big a conflict of interest as I could ever imagine. My attorneys immediately objected and asked for a recusal. A divorce attorney has access to all sorts of privileged information. He could be biased against me. I felt there was every reason to *expect* Brian House to recuse himself. But he didn't. He wouldn't. He refused, and I had no choice but to walk into that courtroom on November 23 and face what felt like another completely absurd travesty of small-town justice.[49]

There I was, looking at that man whose face I remembered well. He was a bit younger than Judge Van Pelt. He had dark hair that was short and what I would describe as sort of a quirky look about him. He reminded me a lot of late-night television's Conan O'Brien, only he spoke more slowly and in a deep voice with a distinct Georgia drawl. He definitely struck me as a good ol' boy from the start.

I tried to put the apparent conflicts aside as we started that hearing, only to notice that Judge Brian House seemed all aloof and distracted in the courtroom. It also felt to me like my case had just landed in his lap, and he didn't want to rock the boat on anything in this first hearing he was involved in. So here we'd done all of this preparation, spent tens of thousands of dollars and countless hours hoping to gain something from this all-important day, and Judge House seemed to take it upon himself to hardly make any decisions at all.

The decisions he did make were decisions that hurt us. First of all, he denied our ability to enter the polygraphs into evidence. After all the worry and trouble we'd gone to, and the pain I'd been through enduring those exams, Judge House simply ruled them inadmissible. That decision meant they would be inadmissible at the trial as well.

He denied our demurrer and therefore wouldn't consider removing any of the individual counts of the indictment, saying, in so many words, "You'll have your day in court to fight those charges." He did so without hearing all of our arguments, basically cutting Scott off in the middle of his presentation.

He did go ahead and set a deadline for the exchange of the rest of the discovery documents, which was helpful. That deadline would be December 15. (Of course, that deadline would come and go and we'd still be missing a whole bunch of important documents we'd asked for. We'd have to come back to court again later to fight for those.) Then he denied our change-of-venue request.

Finally, when it came time to address the bond—and whether or not to allow me to see my daughter—he allowed us to put a number of witnesses on the stand. Powerful witnesses.[50]

My children's guardian ad litem from Tennessee got up there and testified that I should be allowed to see my daughter.

Frances Woodard, the mother of my lifelong friend Courtney, who had put her house up against my bond, gave some stunning testimony about Ashley's demeanor. The prosecutors (including the lanky second ADA, Len Gregor, who was back in action for this hearing) tried to tell the court that Ashley did not want to see me, that she was "terrified" of me, that she would not speak of me, and that she got upset at the very mention of my name—information that seemed to me to be based entirely on the word of my ex-husband, Joal, and the reports of her former court-ordered therapist, Laurie Evans. But Frances was the woman the court had chosen to serve as my mother's "supervisor" during Ashley's visits with her grandparents. So she got up there and testified to firsthand knowledge of Ashley's demeanor and told that court that in her opinion my daughter was *not* terrified of me at all. In fact, she said Ashley talked about me frequently. When they took her out for Japanese food, she would order white rice, "just like my mommy." In fact, she testified that my daughter missed me and expressly *wanted* to see me!

Then we put up our most important witness of the day: Ann Hazzard, the PhD psychologist who'd spent time doing a new forensic interview with Ashley. As part of her evaluation, she'd interviewed people who worked with Ashley every day at school. She also took time to read the transcripts of Ashley's original interview with Suzie Thorne at the Greenhouse. Dr. Hazzard got up on that stand and testified that she found nothing to support any evidence of inappropriate touching between me and Ashley whatsoever—either in the original Suzie Thorne interview or in her own extensive evaluations. She said her professional conclusion was that nothing inappropriate had happened between me and my daughter. She stated with "full confidence" that I should be allowed to see my daughter immediately and that seeing each other would be "in Ashley's best interest."

Then she stated on the record that she *did* find evidence of inappropriate behavior happening at Ashley's father's house, concerning the showers with Joal's wife, Sarah. She testified that those incidents were "very inappropriate."

I briefly allowed myself to get my hopes up. As far as witnesses go, Ann Hazzard was a slam dunk from our side's point of view.

Judge House listened to all of those findings and all of that testimony—and then promptly decided not to take any action at all. He decided to leave my bond exactly as it was. He decided to leave Ashley in Joal's custody. He then made a comment (which I'm paraphrasing here) saying, in effect, "Well . . . since your client hasn't seen her daughter in all this time, I don't see how a couple more months will make any difference."

I was incensed. I wanted to jump over the table and strangle him with my own two hands. My attorneys protested his decision immediately, and Judge House agreed to "revisit it" if for some reason my trial didn't "go" in March as scheduled.

In one fell swoop, Judge House ensured that I wouldn't see my daughter for at least another one hundred days.

Chapter 40

It wasn't long after that hearing, not long after another difficult Thanksgiving, that the stress and terror of the entire ordeal overwhelmed me one random night around dinnertime. The doorbell rang—and the sound of it sent me into a panic. I hid myself in a closet. David didn't know what to do. He'd never seen me so terrified. I was sure it was detectives come to lock me away for good this time. I sat there shivering, balled up on the floor like some kind of broken shell of a human being.

It turned out it was just some creditor, trying to serve me some paperwork about some unpaid bills. David sent him away—but he had to get my father to help get me off the floor and back to my senses.

I insisted David disconnect the doorbell that night. I never wanted to hear the sound of a doorbell again. Ever.

Another Christmas came and went without my children.

The closest thing I had to a saving grace was that Ashley gave me a Christmas present that year. My mom and Frances took Ashley on a shopping trip up to Gatlinburg one day.[51] Ashley picked out a zebra-striped purse that she told them I'd just love. Then she "insisted" on finding me a pair of shoes to match.

She signed the packages, "To Mommy, Love Ashley." She also attached a one-dollar bill to the outside of each wrapper.[52]

"Make sure she gets those dollars," Ashley told my mom. "It's very important."

My mother had never mentioned anything about my financial troubles. Neither had Frances. Neither had anyone else during Ashley's visits with my parents. But it seemed clear to me that *somebody* was talking about it, and she'd heard it—and she'd cared.

David gave me a special present that year, too: a gigantic version of the Truth Cross. This one was made out of stainless steel that was two inches thick. It stood almost two feet high. He'd been working on it in his shop since mid-November, he told me. It was beautiful. It was stunning, really. A solid, tangible object that symbolized everything, all at once: my faith, my fight, the weight of the burden of truth that had somehow fallen entirely on my shoulders. Everything.

By the end of that second year, the analogy of ten elephants that I'd once used to describe the weight on my shoulders felt small by comparison. Especially after we got more discovery from the prosecution—and when I found the strength to sit down and read the medical records from the nurse's exam that all three of those little girls were put through. The report for Chloe showed no signs of abuse, but the report for Brianna was "extremely suspicious," and the report for Ashley was "suspicious" for sexual abuse as well, which was absolutely devastating for me to read.[53]

The report suggested that my daughter was visibly upset and crying through the whole exam. Joal and Sarah both brought her to that exam, and Sarah actually went in the room with her when she was examined. According to the report, Sarah and a nurse had to restrain her on the table. She was examined with her knees all the way up next to her ears in what's called a "frog-leg position," with nurse Sharon Anderson taking photographs of her privates. Joal signed a paper allowing that to take place. In my mind I was sure—even then—that he *knew* that I had done nothing to her. *How could he allow this to happen?*

I felt like *they* had molested my daughter.

As the new year dawned, I put my hand on that giant Truth Cross and bowed my head and prayed with all my heart. I prayed for the truth, as I always did. I prayed for Tyler, as I always did. But in that moment, I prayed for Ashley more than ever before: "Please, God, please keep Ashley strong. Please let her know how much I love her. Please let her be okay, God. Please protect my baby girl. *Please.*"

———————————————

I woke up in early January more determined to fulfill my research missions than ever before. I told David that I needed to fly up to Minnesota to try to find Laurie Evans's first husband. I'd found Laurie Evans's second husband living more than five hours from our home, and he was surprisingly open

with me about Laurie's history, so I figured I might be able to get some information from husband number one as well.

Paying for my travel was becoming a real issue, though. David was just
about tapped out. I had no income. My parents had blown almost their
entire life savings and inheritance by that time. If it weren't for the generosity of my friends, I'm not sure what I would have done. Diana and
Tammy and Courtney and Jennifer—every one of them helped chip in for
my travel funds.

Trying to save money, I thought it would be cheaper and more efficient
to get all my northern travels done in one trip—to fly from Chattanooga to
Minnesota, and then on to Newark, New Jersey, to research that mysterious number I'd come across in Joal's phone records.

I found myself in the middle of a gigantic snowstorm in Minnesota,
driving the cheapest, and therefore smallest, rental car I could find. At one
point the snow blew so wildly across the highway, it was like a clean, white
sheet had blown off somebody's clothesline and stuck itself to my wind-
shield. I'd never squeezed a steering wheel so tight in my life. The storm got
so bad that I finally had to give up. I called the number I had from the car,
and Laurie's first husband's mother picked up the phone. My conversation
with her was extremely short.

There was definitely no love lost between Evans and her ex-mother-in-
law. But the discussion didn't give me much in the way of new information
that might help my case, and at that point I felt I had no choice but to let it go.

I called David, bawling and terrified as I drove back toward the airport
in that tiny car in those horrible conditions. All I wanted was David's per-
mission to stop and get a hotel for the night and to change my tickets for
the rest of the trip. But he wouldn't give in to me. All he did was talk about
the money and how much we'd already spent.

"You know what, David? Fine," I yelled as I hung up the phone. "But if
I die, it's on *you!*"

The fact was, I didn't have a credit card of my own anymore. I couldn't
make the decision to stay at a hotel or to buy a plane ticket on my own if
I wanted to. At some point—I'm not even sure when—the bank had fore-
closed on my house in Chickamauga. I'd made payments for as long as I
could. I just couldn't keep up. I was too consumed with fighting for my
kids. Nothing was selling in that crashed housing market anyway, and at
some point, I just let it go. So on top of everything else, my credit was
ruined. It felt like everything was ruined. Absolutely everything.

I yelled at God harder and louder than I yelled at my husband on that awful, stormy afternoon. "What did I do? Tell me! Why is this happening? Why?" It was the same old set of questions. I just never seemed to get a direct answer. The only answer I ever got back was that I needed to stay focused on my kids. *Keep fighting for them. Do whatever it takes to get back to them.*

Some might have seen those travels as wasted time and wasted money. Not me. If I thought there was even a 1-percent chance that some pursuit might help me prove my innocence, there was no way I was going to pass it up. My questions about Laurie Evans—including how and why she was given so much power at the CAC—kept nagging at me. I couldn't understand it. Plus, I had nothing to lose. In my mind there was no way any of those pursuits could make my situation worse.

That was exactly the mentality I had as the snow cleared and I finally flew over to Newark.

More than a few people (including my husband) told me not to make that trip. Newark is a "scary city," they said. Their concerns fell on deaf ears. I feared nothing more than losing my children forever. Flying to some strange city, staying at the types of hotels that would accept cash with no credit card upon check-in—what I was going through was nothing compared to the agony I felt had been placed on my son and daughter.

On the first day, I failed to find the woman at the other end of that phone number. I questioned why I'd come. After sleeping in a cheap, rather seedy hotel, I woke up on the second day and was surprised to find a treadmill in the hotel's run-down gym. I went for a run and a prayer—and it paid off. I hit the streets of Newark once more, and I found her. I recognized her voice the moment we said "hello." I made sure my trusty little tape recorder was running as this woman ushered me back to her office, in a small space with a desk and a few chairs. That hidden tape recorder was my insurance policy. Always.

It turned out she was a chiropractor who ran her business from her home.

"Oh! You *called* me!" she said. "How could I forget that accent?"

I guess I hadn't done a very good job of disguising my voice when I tried to find out who she was originally. I tearfully asked if there was any information she had that might help me. It turned into a lengthy conversation resulting in tears from us both. I couldn't push too hard or she might have stopped talking to me. It was very strange. The whole thing was just *strange*. Although the content of the discussion didn't further my case in any way, the dialogue was congenial, and upon leaving, she hugged me and tearfully said that she wished me the best.

I thanked God for allowing me to experience that kindness in the midst of everything else—even on those days when my long-distance travels and dogged pursuits left me wanting.

Chapter 41

With a couple of days left to kill in the lovely environs of Newark, it suddenly struck me that I had failed to fulfill a mission I'd vowed to complete a few months earlier: to get some national media attention focused on my case. I called David from my hotel room and asked him, "Hey, how close is Newark to New York City?"

David laughed at me. He said, "Well, try looking out your window. You see those big buildings over there? That's New York!"

It felt like fate to me.

I didn't own a proper winter coat, so I bought one off a clearance rack and took a train into the big city. I trudged all over town in the freezing cold wearing dress slacks and a turtleneck sweater. I felt I needed to show up dressed in a professional manner so that people would take me seriously.

One of my primary targets was Anderson Cooper. I went to CNN and they wouldn't let me in, so I left a package for him. Then I found his home address, and I left a package for him there, too. I repeated the same mission all over town, with basically no luck at all. By the time I had dinner and found my way to the correct subway station again to catch a train back to Newark, it was 12:45 A.M. *What woman rides the subway in New York City alone at 12:45 A.M.?* A M.O.M.—that was who!

The next morning I trudged over to *Good Morning America* with a little handmade sign: "M.O.M.—Mother on a Mission!" I stood in line in the blistering cold and steady snow with others who I was told had gotten tickets months and even years in advance. When I reached the security guard, he must have seen the desperation in my eyes. He shook my hand as if taking my ticket and let me into the studio.

I stood with my sign held high, and Robin Roberts actually came over to me during a commercial break. I showed her the pendant with my kids' pictures on it and said, "If I can just have fifteen minutes of your time, I think you'll find this is a story you'll want to cover. I'm fighting for my life and for my children's lives." I gave Robin and one of her producers a business card with the Truth for Tonya web address on it.

Then I waited and waited for the phone to ring.

Back in Tennessee, it occurred to me that maybe I needed to start a little smaller. I decided to approach some of the regional media outlets to get my story out. The idea of it scared me because the local media had covered my story so extensively already. I was worried they might twist my words on the air in a way that might make matters worse. But something told me I had to do this. I just needed to find the right person to tell my story to.

That's when I met a producer named Melydia Clewell, from NBC Channel 3 in Chattanooga. Melydia wasn't really doing much on-air reporting anymore. She'd moved behind the camera pretty much full-time. But she and I met and had an off-the-record conversation, and she told me she was absolutely floored by my story. It was clear to me that she was listening to what I had to say and that she wasn't approaching this with any preconceived notions of what kind of a "monster" the DA's office had painted me to be. After hearing me out, she said she'd be willing not only to cover my story but also to do the on-air interview herself. She assured me she would help me to get the truth out to the public.

I'd learned to go with my gut, and my gut told me Melydia was the one.

I sat down with her and her camera crew for an extensive interview at my parents' home. I opened up about everything. My parents agreed to be interviewed. My attorneys Clancy Covert and Scott King both went on camera and discussed the case. Some friends came by to show support, and we all snacked and chatted in the kitchen while the cameras rolled. We basically gave Melydia carte blanche.

Then nothing happened. We waited a few days, and the interview never aired. I reached out to Melydia to find out what was going on, and she told me that the interview was so strong, they'd decided to hold it until March, and to tease that interview all through NBC's Winter Olympics coverage in February—when just about anyone with a television was sure to be tuned in. I realized that her ratings strategy was a good thing. I guess I'd grown fairly accustomed to waiting by then, too, but it still made me nervous. I'd given her the exclusive, and yet I needed my story to get out there. I felt like I was running out of time. *What if I've made a mistake?*

While I waited for the public to hear my side of the story, the trial clock kept ticking. On January 26, we got Laurie Evans's notes from all three children's sessions with her at the CAC. We also got a log of parents' notes, and the sign-in/sign-out records for parents and detectives and anyone else involved in the case.[54]

The notes were awful to read. They suggested my kids didn't want to see me. They suggested that the kids hated being around my parents and were said to be sad and miserable the whole time they were with them. None of it reflected the truth that had been relayed to me by the people I trust or by those who had been around the kids firsthand. Those notes showed that Laurie Evans had diagnosed my son, Tyler, with major depressive disorder, too—a serious condition that suggested he'd turned into a nonfunctioning member of society. Yet I knew that his grades were good, he was playing sports, he appeared happy and playful around my parents, and he even seemed happy at *my* house when he got to play with his friend Braden and others. That serious diagnosis was now a part of my child's medical record, even though a judge had found that woman "non-credible." It burned me up inside something awful.

I read every document, every line, every word of those notes. My attorneys said I didn't need to do that, but I knew that I did. There were times when my attorneys said I didn't need to be present for certain meetings, too. I insisted I did.

There were times when all of my attorneys would be gathered in a conference room with me, discussing the case, and they'd start making decisions about this or that without asking my opinion. I'd make a suggestion and they'd just keep talking and arguing while my words seemed to fall on deaf ears. Finally, one day when they were all bickering about some part of the case or another and dismissing my suggestions with hardly a nod in my direction, I slammed my hands on the table and stood up.

"Everyone shut the hell up!" I said. "I appreciate all of your hard work and guidance, but one thing needs to be clear. This is a business of sorts— and I am the CEO. I will consider everything I am told, but in the end the decisions are mine. It is *my* life on the line. Not yours. When that verdict is read, I could spend the rest of my life in prison. No matter how heart- broken and upset you might be about the loss, you will still get to go home and continue with your lives. So please remember: You work for *me*. And if you do not like that, there's the door."

They didn't dismiss me so much after that.

The day after we received Laurie Evans's treatment notes, ADA Chris Arnt posted this status update on his Facebook page:[55]

> **Chris A. Arnt** is wondering if Tonya Craft's Defense lawyers are really insane of just trying to jack uo her defense bill ?
> January 27 at 10:13 a.m.

I wasn't Facebook friends with Chris Arnt, but a friend pointed it out to me, and he'd posted it with a setting of "public." So anyone could see it. I was just beside myself. Ignoring the sloppiness and typos, all I could think was, *How could he write something so flippant in a public forum? Is Facebook the place for an ADA to be making comments—during work hours—about a major case in which a woman's life is at stake and three children have supposedly been molested? Is this some kind of a joke to him?* Just below the post was a little thumbs-up symbol, along with the phrase, "Holly Nave Kittle likes this." (Holly Kittle was the woman who had performed the fourth interview with Brianna Lamb.) *Where's the professionalism? Where's the seriousness with which child sexual-abuse cases should be treated?*

Chris Arnt eventually removed that Facebook post, but a friend of mine saved a screenshot of it for me. Lots of people were aware of it. The local media picked up on it and wrote about it. Bloggers in the legal community had a field day with it. It felt like yet another violation of trust. We were supposed to trust the courts and detectives and judges and assistant district attorneys. My trust was crushed.

My own father broke down in tears over his loss of faith in the system that was supposed to protect us, right in the middle of his interview with Melydia Clewell. I wondered if my daddy's tears would make the cut and be seen on TV when that interview finally aired. I'd have to wade through another long month of setbacks and preparations in order to find out—right before all of this would finally come to a resolution, one way or another, in a courtroom.

Chapter 42

It had always been do-or-die time for me, but February seemed to finally be do-or-die time as far as my attorneys were concerned, too. The whole month became all about our strategy in the courtroom.

Doc would be the lead attorney, handling opening and closing arguments, expert witnesses, and the cross-examination of many of the prosecution's witnesses. Scott would be the "bad cop" who'd go head-to-head with the witnesses we considered adversarial. Cary would be more of a "good cop" who'd deal with the direct examination of most of the witnesses for our side, with Clancy doing a couple of friendly directs as well. Clancy's a wonderful organizer and a fantastic thinker. I needed him at the defense table as much as possible, helping me to strategize and think about everything.

It was especially difficult dealing with Doc, who quite frankly is the most arrogant man I have ever met in my entire life. The more time he spent with us, the more I understood my team's initial reaction to him. We'd go grab lunch at some restaurant and after his interactions with waitresses I'd feel like I wanted to sink under the table and die. After one meal full of comments, I said to him, "Doc, what God gave you in intellect, he clearly took away in social skills."

I don't think anyone had ever spoken to Doc that way, but I couldn't help but be frank. All of my attorneys made the comment at one point or another that they'd never worked with anyone like me, and I'm not sure they meant it as a compliment. I really didn't care. I did what I had to do and said what needed to be said. What else could I do? I wasn't going to sit back and let any of them get lazy or make what I thought was a wrong decision concerning my case.

As we got down to brass tacks (as they say), Doc led us wholly in the direction of science and facts. We would need to try to refute everything the prosecution threw at us, not with theories or emotion or character attacks, but with how *wrong* these accusations were and how we had the science and facts to prove that beyond any doubt. That was the standard I demanded. We would hire people who we felt were the best experts in the field to come and review my case and testify on my side—true standard-bearers in the legal world. That, of course, would cost a lot of money and would stretch our budgets past the breaking point. But it was what we had to do. I couldn't take any chances.

By the middle of that February, we locked in the basic strategy that would help keep us focused, no matter what the prosecution tried to throw at us. The strategy was to prove three things to the jury: "It didn't happen; it couldn't have happened the way they said it happened; and it doesn't make sense." That was our whole case. That was what we needed to prove in order to prove my innocence.

I reminded my attorneys almost daily, "Don't let yourself for one minute think that you've got this thing won. Arrogance will send me straight to prison." I knew in my heart that we all needed to remain humble. We needed to keep cool under pressure, and we would have to fight with everything we had in order to present the truth no matter what happened in that courtroom.

The teasers for Melydia Clewell's interview started running, and all of a sudden, all of the *other* networks started calling trying to get interviews of their own. I made Melydia a promise that hers would be an "exclusive" until after it aired, and I stuck to my word. Melydia asked me something else once things heated up in the press, though: "When the trial's over, will you give me your first interview?"

"You keep your word to tell the truth about my story, and I will absolutely give you the first post-trial interview. You have my word on it," I told her.

On the inside all I could think was, *I'm pretty sure that interview is never going to happen.*

Chapter 43

By mid-February, we were running out of money like never before. David and I decided to hold a yard sale. Every dollar counted at that point, and bringing in a little extra cash felt good.

A young woman stopped by who showed great interest in some of my old classroom supplies. "I just started teaching," she said, and she went on about how much the kids would love some of this stuff. "It's such a struggle having to pay for supplies," she said.

This woman seemed to have no idea who I was. I mentioned that I used to be a teacher myself, and we talked for a while. I saw so much of myself in the enthusiasm of this young woman.

"Hold on a second," I told her, and I went into the garage. I grabbed all the big boxes full of classroom supplies that my attorneys had managed to retrieve from Chickamauga Elementary after my termination, and I gave them to her. All of them.

"I want you to have these," I said with tears in my eyes.

"Why are you giving me all of this?" she asked.

I handed her a Truth for Tonya card and told her to visit the website. "You'll understand," I said. I turned and walked into the garage, sat on the stairs, and cried.

That moment was a huge letting go for me. I knew I'd most likely never be allowed to teach again. *What school would ever hire me even if I'm acquitted?* The indictments and charges would show up on my background report. I couldn't deny that any longer. I'd kept those supplies and dreamed of putting them to use in a classroom again. Now at least a part of my dream would come true. Those supplies would get used in a classroom. They just wouldn't be used by children I was teaching myself.

Shortly before my trial, a grand jury indicted my private investigator, Eric Echols, on the "Intimidation of Witness" charges he'd been arrested for the previous summer. His trial was set to start the same day as my trial, March 15. It obliterated our plans to put him on the stand and negated our ability to introduce the interviews he'd conducted, too.

I was feeling pretty down about it all when my friend Jennifer showed up and said she had a surprise for me. She turned around and pulled her long hair up in the back to show me her brand-new tattoo.

She'd gone and had a Truth Cross tattooed on the back of her neck!

I cried like a baby. I could hardly believe that a friend would do something like that. She reminded me in that moment that the support I had from my friends and family was deep and permanent as could be.

No matter which way this trial went, I was innocent. That was the truth. That would never change. At times I felt like I was the only one who realized that, but the fact of the matter is I wasn't the only one. I had people all around me who knew the truth. Who believed in the truth. Who believed in me with all of their hearts.

It was right around the same time when another friend opened up a Truth for Tonya Facebook page to go along with the Truth for Tonya website. A few hundred people "liked" that site almost overnight. Another friend printed up "Truth for Tonya" bumper stickers in my favorite color, yellow, and people started putting them on their cars all over town. The love and support seemed to flow in from everywhere.

It was only the beginning.

On March 1, my interview with Melydia Clewell aired on NBC Channel 3. It started with a report on the five o'clock news, followed by a longer report on the six o'clock news, and a "closer look" at the charges against me on the eleven o'clock news that same evening.

Melydia promised to be fair to me, and to my absolute relief, she was.

"Nearly two dozen times since her arrest in 2008, we have reported on the charges against her, we have aired her mug shot, and we also covered her termination hearing," Melydia said live from her seat at the anchor desk just before that first five o'clock report aired. "Now, for the first time, Tonya Craft wants you to hear her side of the story."

It was a strange thing to watch myself on the news, in my gray turtleneck sweater with my silver pendant around my neck, pleading for some kind of understanding. It was difficult to hear my own words echoed back at me through the TV: "How can I go from being a mother, and a teacher, and a friend, and an aunt, and a daughter, to having a mug shot on television for something I did not do?" I had said.

I bawled watching my mother on that report, telling the world that she supported me and that she would be there no matter what, no matter how long it took.

Melydia stood in front of the Catoosa County courthouse and talked directly into the camera, telling the audience that I *did* understand the need to protect children, including my own, because of the nature of the charges. But she also noted that I felt that in this case I'd been "condemned without a trial."

"If I was innocent until proven guilty," I had said, "then I would have my children, I would at least have contact, I would have my profession, I would have my home that I've lost, and I've lost everything without a trial."

She went on to note my confidence that I would prove my innocence when my case finally went to trial and added that in the meantime, I hoped to change laws and perceptions of the accused.

"It could happen to anybody at any time," I had said. "All there has to be is an accusation, and that's it. You're stripped of your life, and your rights, and your children."

The piece went on to share a sound bite from ADA Chris Arnt. He looked to me like he had a little smirk on his face as he spoke about us attempting to "try the case in the media" and said he refused to reveal any facts of the case before he stepped into a courtroom. I guess he forgot the press conference *he* gave after my termination hearing, in which he revealed to the media that his office had "physical evidence" against me.

The hypocrisy is staggering, I thought.

The six o'clock report included news of the positive results of my two polygraph exams, quotes from my attorneys, and more—including the moment when my daddy broke down in tears. That shattered me. It broke my heart to think of what he and my mother had been put through, and how much they'd given—and given up—trying to defend me from these lies.

Melydia told me her reports received a massive response from Channel 3's audience. The station was overwhelmed with calls and emails, she said. They wound up doing a follow-up report the next night looking at the phenomenon. Overnight, the number of "likes" on the Truth for Tonya Facebook page shot up to more than 3,000.

The only reason I wanted cameras on this trial was to attempt to hold the judge and prosecutors accountable. I didn't want the attention for myself. My greatest wish was that I could just go back to being an unknown kindergarten teacher doing the job I loved. It was a wish with no possibility of ever coming true.

A few days later, my team got busy preparing for our final hearing in front of Judge Brian House before the start of the trial. That hearing would be so important that we decided we needed to bring Doc down from Ann Arbor to make the arguments himself. It would be the first time that the judge and prosecutors laid their eyes on Demosthenes Lorandos, and I could not wait to see their reaction. His scholarly presence, his quirky delivery, the matter-of-fact way he seemed to devastate opponents with research and facts was something I suspected no one in Catoosa County would ever expect.

That final hearing would determine a whole bunch of details about the evidence we would and would not be allowed to present at trial. It seemed like such a backward thing to have to argue to get more evidence into a trial as a defendant. From what I understood, the way trials normally go is that the prosecution argues to get all of their evidence in—the more evidence the better—while a defendant tries to get evidence excluded in order to keep the jury from hearing something that might be damaging. In our case, we *wanted* the jury to hear as much evidence as possible, because we felt the evidence all pointed to my innocence. It was the prosecution that seemed to be trying to keep evidence away from the jury's eyes and ears. It was sickening to me. I couldn't wait for Doc to make his arguments and hopefully put a scare into them about what they'd face in the courtroom.

Then it didn't happen. The prosecutors had a "conflict," so the hearing was postponed. Doc would have to wait, but Cary, Scott, and Clancy did as well as they could given what we were up against.

By the time we were ready to fly Doc down for the trial, money was so tight we realized we didn't have the funds to do it. Doc had tons of files that needed to come with him. The shipping expense alone was going to be hundreds, if not thousands, of dollars. We weren't sure what we were going to do.

Then word got out to supporters in my church, and lo and behold, someone offered to let us borrow their beautiful custom van to drive up to Michigan to pick up Doc and his files. David and I decided to make that trip together, and we could hardly believe the generosity. It wasn't until we started driving that I happened to open the glove box and find an envelope with my name on it. The envelope was stuffed with a beautiful note of support—and a bundle of cash. There was enough money to cover our gas up and back, and hotel rooms if we needed it, and meals—just about anything we'd need and then some.

I cried like a baby. I still do not understand the generosity and the outpouring of love from the community in the face of the horrible things I'd been charged with. There is no one that can tell me that God wasn't directly involved in that spirit of giving. *He was there.*

Doc rode with me in the van while we talked strategy the whole way back. David flew back because he could not be privy to the information we were sharing. The man that could save my life was in the van with me. The man who held my heart flew miles overhead to adhere to the rules of criminal procedure.

Chapter 44

Just days before my trial was set to begin, a family tragedy struck that none of us saw coming. A tragedy that would require every ounce of Attorney Scott King's attention. Out of respect for his family, I'm going to leave the details of that tragedy out of this story. The details were never reported in the media. I'll just say that it was one of those times when you wish the whole world would come to a standstill.

Temporarily losing a key member of our legal team at such a late date made it impossible for me to mount my defense. It was an argument we felt the court could not deny, and we were correct. Judge House postponed the trial to the end of the current session in Catoosa County. The trial would start on April 12. We all hoped it would be enough time for Scott to deal with the matter as best he could and rejoin us. I needed him. He knew that. We all wanted him to be there.

The month's delay did put an extra strain on our finances. By the time we were through waiting, we couldn't afford to put my team up in a hotel or to rent office space for a headquarters, so my parents generously offered to give up their house for the duration of the trial. We turned their home into a makeshift "war room." Each attorney could have his own bedroom. We cleared out the furniture in the living room and set up a big conference table just off the kitchen. We took the photos and decorations off the walls and hung up a big bulletin board, a white board, and my timeline. We had all sorts of friends and family over to help us move all the equipment and furniture in and out. We brought in an office-sized copy machine, a fax machine, and computers, and really turned that old family home into a live-in legal office.

My dad would stay at our house with David, while my mom and I both holed up with my parents' neighbors across the street, Karen and Walt. They offered me a guest bedroom in their lovely home. They gave me my own key. That bedroom was just upstairs from Karen's hair salon. Karen hates it when people make this comparison, but it was just like something out of *Steel Magnolias*, with the old-fashioned hair dryers that come down over your head, and the swivel chairs, and everything all done up in tasteful Southern fashion. As April came around, I started sleeping there almost every night. It saved me the drive from our house every morning, and it gave me my own private place to escape. It was perfect. It was just one more example of the love and support I had all around me.

Finally, the whole team was in place at my parents' house—including the addition of a top-notch jury consultant named Denise de La Rue. We stayed up almost all night on April 11, going over everything one more time.

My attorneys gave me all kinds of last-minute pointers and advice about what to do and not do in the courtroom during those final hours. Mostly they reminded me to keep my emotions in check: "But don't be too cold." "Don't be too emotionless." "You want to show the jury that you're human." "But you don't want to show too much emotion or the jury could be turned off . . ."

It was honestly too much information for any one person to take, so I nodded and let it go. I already knew I couldn't go in there and make a fool of myself. I knew I didn't want to come off as a crazy person. The less flailing about I did, the less angry I looked, the more I behaved as I normally would, the better off I would be. I finally resolved inside, *I will just be me. Nothing more, nothing less.*

Finally, I told everyone that we ought to get some sleep.

Other than Clancy, the members of my team weren't of the same faith. None of us went to the same church. Cary and Scott are Jewish. Doc often demeaned my faith, calling Christians "simpleminded." I believe it takes a stronger person to believe in something or someone bigger than yourself, but regardless: I asked all of them to say a prayer that night.

"Just pray for the truth," I told them.

I walked across the street in the darkness. It couldn't have been more than a couple of hours before sunrise, and I prayed as I walked under that sky: *God, I don't know why I'm going through this, but I thank you for staying with me. Thank you for watching over me. Thank you for bringing my team together and giving us all the strength we need. Thank you for watching over Tyler and Ashley. Thank you for watching over all of us.*

I made my way through the shadowy outlines of Karen's salon and into the quiet bedroom, alone. I closed the door and lay down on the bed with all of my clothes still on—absolutely terrified that my last days of freedom were now upon me.

Part III

The Fight

Chapter 45

I woke up at 5:00 A.M. I took a hot shower. When I came out of the bed-room, Walt had made me a whole pot of coffee right there in the salon. He had a mug already poured for me.

"Good luck, Tonya," he said.

"You know we're here for you," Karen added.

"Thank you," I responded. My head felt heavy.

I walked across the street, and everybody was buzzing and rushing around like the house was a hornet's nest that'd just been hit with a thrown stone. My mind started racing, going over checklists, making sure we had everything we needed. All of a sudden it was time to go. David, who was a witness and wasn't allowed to be privy to what went on in that house, came in only at the last minute to help us load all the files into my parents' van.

"You ready?" Doc said.

"Ready as I'll ever be, I suppose."

I didn't feel ready. Not at all. After all the time I'd spent ripped away from my kids, just praying for this day to come, I suddenly felt like I needed more time. I started racing through the list of people who I never talked to in my travels. I wanted to dig back into my laptop and read every line of every false-allegation case I'd ever found.

"Tonya," David said. I'd apparently been standing there quite a while without moving or saying anything. "Honey, it's time to go."

As we stepped out of David's truck, the cameras were everywhere. One girl with a still camera walked right beside me and jumped in front of me occa-sionally, just snap-snap-snapping away. She apologized for having to do that, and I said, "I understand, it's your job."

We went in through the back entrance and up the same elevator in which I'd previously been forced to face the back wall, to the familiar hallways under the fluorescent lights where so many awful twists of my fate seemed to have played out over the course of the previous two years. Only this time, we made our way into the main courtroom toward the front of the building. The biggest courtroom in the whole place.

Despite opposition from the prosecutors, Judge Brian House had agreed to media requests to place a camera in the courtroom throughout the trial. That morning, he made the decision to keep the camera off during jury selection. A few verbal spats ensued. I believe he even wound up fining one of the media crews for shooting footage on the front lawn. The media was restricted to sitting in a separate room just off to the side of the courtroom as it was, where they would watch the proceedings on a little TV. The publicity of it all seemed to be ramping up everyone's emotions, and the general stir in the air made me even more nervous than I already was.

A trial doesn't start with the slamming of a gavel and the calling of the first witness the way it does on TV. It starts agonizingly slowly and methodically with any last-minute motion hearings and perhaps the most important part of the whole thing: jury selection.

The court called in a special jury pool for my trial. They seemed to want to make sure they found jury members who hadn't read any of the press coverage, and clearly that wouldn't be easy. When I saw that group of hundreds of people, I thought the fix was in. I saw people I recognized, some of whom I thought might be friends with the Lambs and the Wilsons. I saw Joal Henke's father, my former father-in-law, leaning against the wall with his arms crossed. He was mixed right in with that whole group that we were somehow supposed to whittle down to sixteen—twelve jurors plus four alternates. (My understanding is there normally would only be one, maybe two alternate jurors, but Judge House decided we ought to select four, just in case.)

A couple hundred of the potential jury members were dismissed in the first hour, mostly because they had obligations that wouldn't allow them to sit for a potentially long trial. It was amazing to think that my life was on the line, but there were people who seemed to feel that they were too busy to be bothered fulfilling their civic duty. It sure changes your view of "jury duty" when you're sitting in the defendant's seat.

Incredibly, Joal's father and some other familiar faces were still there after lunchtime, so I was very glad we would have the right to remove certain potential jury members from the pool during "voir dire"—the Q&A portion of the jury selection process that literally means "to speak the truth." Paying attention to whom we let through, and whom we removed, was crucial. That was why we'd hired a jury consultant. We didn't want to get it wrong.

The first thing that happened in front of all of those people that day was the prosecutors read all twenty-two counts of my indictment, one by one. I had to sit there next to my attorneys, under the stares of all of those Catoosa County citizens, and listen to the prosecutor read all of those statements. The individual counts don't say the word "alleged." Each and every one of those charges say "Tonya Craft did" commit those grotesque acts to those girls. *How is that not tainting the jury pool right there?* I wondered. *How is that not setting them up with a bias from the beginning?*

The selection process was slow and tedious. Both Chris Arnt and Len Gregor seemed to be serious during the whole procedure. They appeared dark and cold. Doc was different. He came off like some kind of a mad professor. It's not that he wasn't serious. He was. But there was something about the way he spoke to the people in that room that appeared to make them feel more relaxed. I could see it, and I'm sure everyone in that room could feel it.

Much to my surprise, Doc brought up some pretty specific details during voir dire. For instance, he spoke about the fact that Brianna Lamb had played the part of an abused child in two different films. He wondered if anyone had seen those films and seen her performance. It was part of the strategy.

One woman raised her hand and wanted to be called up front. She gave her "voir dire" directly to me: "No offense, Miss Craft, but there is no way that if a child says it—I don't care what anybody else says, I'm *going* to believe it." That woman was removed from the jury pool "for cause," but all I could think was, *How many of the other jurors are harboring that same feeling and just not admitting it?*

There were more than a hundred potential jurors left by dinnertime, and all of those candidates filled out written questionnaires that were put together by the legal teams on each side.

It took a long time to get to that point. Judge House called a recess until the following morning—so we were able to take those questionnaires back to my parents' house that night and review them in tremendous detail.

Denise and I stayed up all night long sorting through every questionnaire and making notes on all of the jurors we hoped to pick—and those we wanted to do everything in our power to exclude. The bulk of the decision-making was all done by us two women.

Denise and I agreed that we wanted jurors who were well educated, who could listen to experts and discern which people actually know what they're talking about and which people don't. All I wanted were potential jurors who could put two and two together. Jurors who could potentially see the facts through a forest of what we believed to be lies.

The next morning, it took less than two hours to whittle the pool down to seven men and five women. I looked at those perfect strangers along with the four alternates and thought, *Those people hold my life in their hands. They hold my children's lives in their hands. No matter what I do or say now, it's all in their hands.*

All I kept praying was, *God, please raise them all up to this task.*

Chapter 46

The Truth for Tonya website, the Facebook page, the media coverage, the bumper stickers—none of those things were to be discussed in front of the jury, according to a pretty stern warning we received from Judge House during a pre-trial motion hearing. He didn't issue a specific order on those subjects, as far as I could tell, but we were all under the impression that those topics were out of bounds. Talking about public opinion wasn't a part of our strategy anyway, so we didn't really fight that point. But then another issue came up and a "jury-out" hearing became necessary just moments before we were set to start the actual trial.

We learned that the prosecutors planned to use some statements of mine from the day my doorbell rang, May 30, 2008—statements that were made after I had contacted an attorney and therefore "invoked my right to counsel," at which point it is now my understanding that the detectives should have stopped asking me questions. Suddenly, the jury was sent out of the room and we found ourselves in the middle of yet another hearing. Oddly enough, the ADAs wound up calling Detective Tim Deal to the stand to discuss his version of how things were handled on that day, which provided a brief glimpse of what was about to unfold in front of the jury.

Deal took that stand and described me not just as "upset" but "irate" on that day, saying that I got on the phone and was "yelling" about him and Detective Keith trying to force me to sign something. He then spoke about "not being welcome on the property" and said that he and Detective Keith went out and "waited by the curb" when Mr. Boggess came into my house.[56]

He talked about the "safety plan" that I signed that day and described it as a "non-binding" agreement.

It was downright surreal to hear that man talk. It was as if he were talking about somebody else, because almost none of what he described was as I remembered it.

When Scott got up there to cross-examine him, Detective Deal said that he didn't mention any children's names specifically when he first came and knocked on my door. He said he wasn't aware of any allegations made by Ashley at that time. Then, just a minute later, on that very same witness stand, he said that he specified to me that my daughter was one of the people the allegations had come from. *What? And how did I know to call Kim Walker the day they showed up if they had never mentioned her daughter's name?*

Is this how the whole trial's going to go?

"It was early on in the investigation," he said. "Detective Keith gave me a quick overview and summary of the case, but I'd only been involved for one day. And I wasn't present for the original interviews that occurred on the 27th. And, you know, out of respect for her position, just like I would a minister, or law enforcement, I really hoped that these allegations weren't true—until the evidence appeared to become so overwhelming that probable cause existed that indicated it had happened."

It was almost impossible to bite my tongue.

He went on to make more statements that confused me, saying on one hand that he was not aware that my attorney had left him messages at his office, because he wasn't in his office. Then he said that the second time he came back to my house, with Mr. Boggess in tow, that he told me that I had "invoked" my right to counsel. *Does he not remember telling me on the phone that he didn't "work for" my attorney and didn't care about anything that my attorney said? He certainly didn't tell me anything about invoking any rights. I had no idea what my rights were that day.*

In a way, I guess that last-minute hearing was good practice for me. I sat in my seat, with Doc to my right and Cary, Scott, and Clancy to my left at the defendant's table, on the left-hand side of the courtroom. It gave me a little time to absorb the green-carpeted, wood-paneled surroundings—and to get used to holding my feelings in as much as I could.

I took solace in the fact that none of this motion business was taking place in front of the jury, and that Judge House looked to me like he couldn't care less. He kept looking away, rolling his eyes, and tipping his head back—especially when my attorneys mentioned some case reference or point of law meant to bolster my side of whatever was going on. *If it doesn't matter to him, and the jury isn't in here, who does it matter to?* I wondered.

That whole business about when I'd invoked my right to an attorney apparently went in my favor. My attorneys seemed pleased. The prosecutors wouldn't be able to present anything that happened between me and the detectives during that second meeting on my porch, unless it was part of the testimony from Mr. Boggess (who, it turned out, would never be called to testify). Why any of that would make a difference, I wasn't sure. But I was glad my team was paying attention to the little minutiae and legal goings-on in that courtroom. And the fact that anything could seemingly go in my favor felt like the tiniest sign of something good on that second day of court proceedings.

My nerves were still all bundled up, and the muscles in my shoulders were so tight you could've hit 'em with a hammer and the hammer would've broken. Still, knowing my attorneys felt good about the outcome of that hearing was something. We all needed a little something.

<hr />

By the time that all got wrapped up, Judge House decided it was time to break for lunch. I couldn't eat. All I could do was think about that jury and what would happen if they listened to people like Detective Deal with the assumption that his version of things was the truth. It terrified me. I didn't understand how anybody on my team could eat or drink or make small talk like it was just some other day, when the battle for everything I'd ever lived for was just about to get started.

It was right around 2:15 that afternoon when the jury filtered in from a door over in the right-hand corner of the room, while everyone in the jam-packed seats behind us quieted down. *I've been schooled my whole life never to judge other people*, I thought, *and those twelve people are going to sit there and judge me.*

Judge House suddenly put on a jovial face. "Let me just remind you, you don't have assigned seats," he said to the jurors. "Most of you went back to the same seat. They're not assigned. But if you want to put your name on 'em, that's fine," he said, eliciting a few chuckles.

It felt like no more than two seconds went by before ADA Len Gregor got up and started making his opening statement.

This is happening now, I thought. *Oh, my Lord. This is it. This is my trial.*

My stomach tied itself into knots I didn't know were even possible until that moment.

Much to my surprise, that tall, thin, buzz-cut ADA Len Gregor got up there in his dark-colored suit and started talking to the jury about the "truth."

The *truth*!

"It is your job as jurors to speak the truth at the conclusion of this trial—and you do that with your verdicts," he told them. "That oath you swore is to the truth. It's not to find a reason to doubt, but to find the truth, simply."[57]

That sounded pretty right to me. But then he went on to tell them that in *this* case, "the truth is contained in the indictment."

"The bottom line is what is contained in this indictment, it is those charges for which this defendant faces in this trial," and he turned and pointed his finger right at me. "And those are for the offenses of aggravated child molestation, aggravated sexual battery, and child molestation, and those crimes are against the children of Brianna Lamb, Ashley Henke, and Chloe McDonald. Did the defendant do what she is charged with doing is the ultimate decision for you to make as jurors in this case."

I couldn't show my anguish. I wouldn't. I held it in.

"The truth that you are sworn to find in this case is not 'Tonya's truth.' It's not some website. It's not some slogan," he said. "It's not something on a bumper sticker. It's not some selfish, self-interested truth. It's an absolute truth. That's the truth you're here to find."

Well, hallelujah to that! I hoped and prayed for nothing more than the absolute truth. But my mind was already spinning trying to figure out what his strategy might be. *How is he going to use the website and the bumper stickers and the "Truth for Tonya" campaign against me?* It's like I was on the battlefield now, and no matter what my previous training had been, I had to be able to fight and react and move to wherever I needed to move in order to avoid the gunfire and hand grenades and napalm. My eyes and ears were running on pure adrenaline, and I couldn't wait for a break just to talk with my team about all I'd heard in those first few moments.

"The truth in this case is that in late May of 2008, Skyler Walker, a seven-year-old child, a child that had had contact with Ashley Henke, her friendship, the Walkers were friends with this defendant. Skyler Walker was at the home of DeWayne and Sherri Wilson out by the pool. Skyler Walker, out by the pool using sidewalk chalk that kids frequently play with and use, she wrote the words 'sex' and 'kissing' on the sidewalk, or the concrete area surrounding the pool. This was seen by Sherri Wilson. It was also seen by Sandra Lamb, who was there with her daughter, Brianna. Again, we're talking about people here who know the defendant, who are friends with the defendant, who have trusted the defendant with their children. All of the girls, all of the girls that were there that day ultimately end up being questioned by the parents.

"First there's Skyler Walker: 'Why would you write such words, Skyler? Where did you learn those?' We're talking about a seven-year-old child here. Sherri Wilson asked some more questions, and Skyler Walker ends up saying, 'Well, I learned those from Ashley Henke, because we play a game. That game is called boyfriend-girlfriend.' Ashley Henke is the daughter of Joal Henke and the defendant. And Skyler talks about this game that's been played between her and Ashley Henke. We're talking about girls that this defendant has had contact with. She says, 'We play this boyfriend-girlfriend game and Ashley kisses me on the cheek and she touches my privates.' Sherri Wilson hears that, and of course it's a shocking thing to be told by a child, and Skyler talks about the fact that Ashley plays this game with other children, too. Maybe Chloe McDonald, Brianna Lamb. Sandra Lamb is there with her daughter Brianna, and I will say this: Yes, Brianna Lamb has had two small parts, as you heard about during the voir dire during jury selection, that had nothing to do with child sexual abuse. Brianna tells her mother, Sandra Lamb, 'Ashley plays the boyfriend-girlfriend game with me, too. She kisses me and she touches my privates.' Brianna also told her mother that in addition to Ashley and the boyfriend-girlfriend game that this defendant, that Tonya Craft"—he pointed his finger right at me again—"had touched her privates as well.

"This is shocking information," he said. "This is something that no one wants to believe, particularly Sandra Lamb. A school mother in this defendant's room. A good, close personal friend of this defendant. This defendant was married . . . in Sandra Lamb's home. Sandra Lamb had trusted the care of her daughter with this defendant. This defendant taught the children, this defendant had the children spend the night at her house, and had slumber parties at her house, and had these children to her house for playdates. This was not something Sandra Lamb wanted or was ready to hear. She couldn't believe it and she couldn't hardly even take the fact that Brianna was telling her this. So she steps away and asks Sherri Wilson, 'Can you talk to Brianna for me?' Sherri talked to Brianna, and Brianna told Sherri about the boyfriend-girlfriend game, and she told Sherri about the touching by Tonya, and what stands out so shockingly for Sherri is that Brianna, at seven years old, is telling her about what this defendant has done to her: 'She touches me and she goes like this.'"

Len Gregor put his hand up in front of him and started moving it up and down, with his fingers all pressed together around his thumb, and he repeated that motion. "She takes her fingers, puts them in front of her, and moves them around to show Sherri Wilson how this defendant touches her."

He thrust his hand up and down, mimicking the motion Brianna had made in her fourth interview, making it look like my whole hand went up inside that little girl. It was *awful*. I felt sick.

"Again, at this point in time, no one wants to believe. It's hard to believe. How do you take in this information when it's someone that they love, that they trusted, someone who has been trusted with the care of children, and they're having to accept what they hear? They're not exactly sure what to do, though. There's not a call made immediately to law enforcement."

He talked about DeWayne Wilson coming home that night and recommending to Sherri that she call Catoosa County—in particular, that she call Detective Stephen Keith, "a detective that he knows."

The investigation wasn't to look into "Tonya," he said, but just to investigate the concerns about the children.

"Because Stephen Keith knows some of the individuals in this case, and because he has a daughter that attends Chickamauga Elementary School, he decides to bring in Detective Deal, and Detective Deal becomes involved in the case. The investigation proceeds."

I wanted to shout, "What investigation? What did they investigate? Detective Deal himself just admitted in this courtroom that he'd only heard about the case from what Stephen Keith had told him the day before he came knocking on my door!"

Len Gregor continued his opening argument by telling the court that Chloe McDonald's name came up "early on" in the investigation. He talked about Kelly and Jerry McDonald introducing me to friends in the community, helping me to move into my house, driving my children, and how Kelly cleaned my house for me. "This was a very close personal relationship. A relationship almost like sisters. They did so many things together," Gregor told that jury.

Sisters?

He then jumped into what the jury was going to hear and see in the trial, including the actual interviews with the children and testimony from the children themselves. "They will sit right here and tell you what the defendant did to each of these little girls. You will hear how the girls disclose the sexual abuse in the hands, literally, of the defendant touching—touching of their primary genital area, their vaginal area. You will hear from each of these girls how during the course of the investigation, it isn't as though it all comes out at once. These little girls are scared. These are children that [disclose] a little bit of information, and then as they get a little bit more comfortable they provide a little bit more information, and it takes sometimes a series of a couple of interviews for them to say everything. But they don't come into the first interview and have everything spelled out. They are scared, and they *say* they are scared. You will see when you see the video, you will see their demeanor on the video. You will see how they react. You will see what happens to them emotionally. Imagine, if you will, talking about your consensual adult sex lives, and that's what these children have to talk about.

"You'll get to see the children in the videos, and you will get to see them here in court."

I dreaded that last part more than anything.

"Ashley, in the first interview, disclosed that her mother had touched her privates, and that her mother had sexually abused her," Gregor said.

I grabbed a pen and wrote, "Can he just lie like that?" on a Post-it note—and slid it over to Doc. He read it without drawing attention to himself and gave me a little nod.

ADA Gregor then went on to say something I thought was really odd. "When you see and you hear from each of these little girls, there's something I want you to take notice of: how similar they are in some ways. Approximately the same age. Their appearance, how they look similar in their appearance"—*Those girls don't look alike*, I thought—"and how each of these little girls, no matter how scared they are, these are each bright and articulate girls. And *that* really, other than one other thing, is what binds these girls—other than one other thing. And that's *her.*"

He pointed his finger right at me again, and there was a part of me that wanted to stand up and break it off. "That's *this defendant. That's* what brought these girls here. That's what binds these girls together: *Her*," he pointed again, "and what she did to them."

He then got animated and talked about seeing and hearing "the meltdowns" these girls had during their interviews. *What meltdowns?* "You will see and hear about the nightmares these girls suffer from." I felt sick to my stomach. "You will hear about the therapy these girls have been involved in and need because of the defendant—therapy that continues to this day. That's because of what *she* did," he said, pointing at me yet again.

"This is a case in which it doesn't just end with the statements of these three little girls about what happened to them. Medical exams are performed on the children. It is a touching case, and touching cases don't always result in medical evidence. Nonetheless as part of the investigation, medical exams are performed when appropriate—and in this case it was appropriate to perform these exams . . . by a sexual assault nurse. By someone who is trained to perform sexual assault exams."

He talked about Chloe's exam being "normal," and Ashley's exam being "suspicious for abuse." I truly felt like throwing up. Then he talked about Brianna Lamb; how she had spent the night at my house "so many times"; that she had been "bathed by the defendant"; how Brianna discloses the "most" acts, discloses "the worst" acts, the "greatest number of acts over the greatest length of time"; and that her exam is "very, very suspicious for sexual abuse."

His whole opening statement was summed up by telling that jury, "You may not want to believe that a mother, that a woman, that someone who worked as a teacher could do such things, could do such awful things to children," but that they *would* believe it after seeing the evidence and knowing that the evidence would point to "the truth."

The fact that he used that word and tried to turn it on its head like that seemed like a cruel joke. *God, please tell me it's not possible that that twisted version of the truth is the "truth" that jury's going to believe.*

Chapter 47

Here appeared to be an immediate shift in the mood of the room as Doc stood up and Len Gregor sat down. I didn't realize until that moment just how stiff the jury seemed as Gregor made his opening statements. Yet as soon as Doc started speaking, I could almost feel them exhale. I hoped that didn't mean they were too relaxed. I hoped that was something that would work for us, not against us, because I had no idea what any of them were thinking. They were as poker-faced as I was trying to be as I sat there sweating under my tweed jacket—praying that my sweat wasn't making me look guilty.

Doc's approach was to tell the jury the story of what happened. I don't want to say he was "entertaining" to watch, because that seems like too light a word. He was incredibly serious, almost studious in a way, but he just talked to that jury like he was talking to a room full of friends—or maybe a room full of eager college students. He was authoritative, but he never talked down to them. And he was animated as he talked about how everything was just fine between me and the Lambs until "Ashley had a birthday party."

"Brianna, who's two and a half years older than Ashley, was invited with her friend Lydia Wilson, Sherri Wilson's daughter. And they played with Tyler, the older brother, and his buddy. But all the little girls got all made up, with makeup and hair and sparkles, it was really cute and they got in a limo and went to the party and it was excellent. And it was a sleepover: *One of the few that Tonya ever had,*" he said. "And the facts will show that Brianna and Lydia, the older girls, said, 'Oh, this is a baby party. We don't want to stay.' And Miss Tonya said, 'Hey, that's not very nice. You were invited to come to the birthday party.' And the facts will show the little girls got *ticked off*, and they called Sandra Lamb, and *kaboom*! Like a steel trap: One day you're up, next day you're down, you're dirt, never coming over again. As of January 2008, Tonya was dirt, Tonya was 'forget about it' to

Sandra Lamb. So when Sandra Lamb was grilling, questioning, repeatedly, over and over and over and over: 'Tell me what Miss Tonya did. Miss Tonya did something. Tell me what she did!' And she told this detective that she did it, and she told this detective she was OCD, and she told the detective that she bribed the kid—

"Oh!" he shouted, and stopped, and looked at the jury. "You didn't hear that, did you? Well, so they take Brianna for an interview." He came over and picked up a transcript of her interview from the table next to me. "And what does Brianna say? What's Brianna say? Sandra has previously called DFACS and said, 'I think there's child-on-child funny business going on between my daughter and whatever.' So before this, Sandra has already turned little Ashley in. So they take Brianna down to the interview place, and they interview her on May 27th, Part 1. And they talk to her about what's been going on. I've got it word for word. Anything about Miss Tonya doing anything? No. Was she scared? Oh, please. La la la la la. Having a nice time," he said as he turns the page. "Nothing about Miss Tonya. The interviewer goes out, and then comes back and says, 'Say, wasn't there something about a bath?' And Brianna goes, 'Oh yeah! Miss Tonya did this and Miss Tonya did that.'

"The rest of the story was, it wasn't enough to get an indictment. So what do the cops do? They've got to go searching for another victim. They go get Skyler Walker. You'll meet her. So in comes Skyler Walker. 'Oh yeah, me and Ashley and da da da da.' We're bringing in two professors of pediatrics from the best universities who will tell you that even though we may think little girls don't do that—yes, they do! Yes, they do. There's fifty years' worth of research. You'll hear that testimony. We've got boxes of science. So what does Skyler Walker say? 'Did Miss Tonya do this?' 'No.' 'Did Miss Tonya do that?' 'No.' No, no, no, no, no. D'oh! And what happens with Sandra Lamb when she finds out from her friend Detective Keith that Skyler Walker's not going to say anything about Tonya? 'Ooooh. Who can we get? Aha! Chloe McDonald!' How did that happen? We'll show you. We've got the evidence."

I couldn't tell what the jury thought, but I could sure tell they were paying attention. There wasn't one of them who took their eyes off Doc when he spoke. From what I could see, he was mesmerizing.

"What's Chloe do?" he continued. "She's on-script. But Kelly is a loose cannon, according to Sandra Lamb. They're worried about this. So Sandra calls Kim Walker, Skyler's mom, and threatens her. The cops call and threaten her: 'You better get your kid back down here, we're going to interview her again.' With no control for parental influences. With no control for rumor formation. No control for repeated questioning effects. No control for modification: 'Outside your clothes or inside your clothes?' 'Outside.' 'Okay, was she nice to you?' 'Yeah, she was nice to me.' 'Well, a minute ago you said it was inside your clothes, tell me how it felt when it was inside your clothes.'"

Doc started flinging his hands all around and shook his head. "*That's a modification!* She didn't say that. *You* said that! There was no control over modifications, no control over suggesting things to children. My goodness. We're bringing you the premier interviewer for the State of Georgia who testified for the prosecution hundreds and hundreds of times. She's a nurse, she's a PhD, she's a professor, and she says, 'Wait a minute. I teach this subject.' She will tell you, 'I've done this for decades. These interviews *stink!*'"

I felt like Doc had everyone in the palm of his hand. I was so glad we had him on board.

"The evidence will show the rest of the story: They take Ashley and Tyler away," he said. "And just a little while later, she gets a phone call from her little daughter, Ashley. 'I love you, Mommy, but I'm not going to see you for a very long time.' What?"

Doc got into the whole previous story about Ashley and Chloe maybe touching each other, way back in 2006, and Kelly smacking Chloe and screaming, "I told you not to do this!"

"So what does 'evil child sexual abuser Miss Tonya' do? She goes immediately to the physician and says, 'Please check my daughter.' Leaves the room and asks a pediatric diagnostic to examine her daughter. Ashley's fine. Okay. But the moms are talking, and the evidence will show, Chloe has done this before with other children," Doc said.

"Fast-forward, 2008, detectives show up and Miss Tonya, she's got a knack for picking guys. I don't know what happens. All that education. She had a very bitter divorce with Mr. Henke. The evidence will show that there is serious pathology in this family. Bitter divorce. And Ashley, little Ashley, when she had to go visit after Sarah—oh, yeah, Joal married Sarah. Sarah was Miss Tonya's *student* in Sunday school. *That's* who Joal picks to marry. Anyway—Joal and his family are so difficult, Ashley, when she has to go: chronic, routine diarrhea. Tonya asks [the] pediatric diagnostic what to do about it, and what does Tonya do about it?"

He described Ashley's diaper rash and how I put medicine on her to help her—the way any mother would.

"Ashley says to Tonya that Sarah, the young girl that Joal married, is showering with her. 'Okay.' Ashley who's having this chronic upset stomach, says, 'Sarah's showering with me and Daddy's in there, too.' Tonya goes, 'Oooh.' And she says, 'Oh, honey, okay.' She tries to figure out what to do about it. And Ashley says, 'She teaches me how to shave,' and she's shaving her pubic hair! Tonya says, 'Oh my God.' She calls her friend, the sheriff." Doc motioned toward the prosecutors. "They didn't tell you that, did they? She says, 'I think my daughter's been abused.' And she makes an appointment. The deputy that handles this, who'll come and testify, called her right back, and they set up a forensic interview that was scheduled to happen right after Memorial Day weekend in 2008. So when Detective Deal shows up, she had already set up an interview for Ashley! They didn't tell you that.

"So they take her in for an interview, and what does she say? Yeah, boyfriend-girlfriend game, yeah. And 'Mommy put medicine on me. Mommy put medicine on me, 'cause I was sore.' And despite all the attempts, repeated questions, sadistic questions, modifying what she said: 'She just put medicine on me.' And when she got hammered and hammered by this interviewer—oh, wait a minute, was the investigator investigating an alternative hypothesis to get to what was going on here? Nope. Just trying to get the goods. So what did little Ashley say? She asked her to stop questioning her like that. And then she got badgered and badgered and she started to cry! And she told the interviewer that her daddy, that this guy who the evidence will show has serious pathology, had been badgering her and badgering her about Miss Tonya and 'touching.' Oh, wait a minute, no control for parental influences before you come into the interview—"

ADA Len Gregor stood up right then and interrupted: "Your Honor, at this point I'm just going to object because we keep getting into argument. I don't like objecting during the opening, but I've given Mr. Lorandos a lot of leeway here, but we just keep going back to it. If he wants to talk about what the evidence he thinks will show or expects to show this jury, that's fine. But he keeps arguing now, and I want to object to arguing."

Doc never looked back. He never looked at Len Gregor at all. He never looked at the judge. He simply looked down at his notes on the podium until Mr. Gregor stopped speaking, and Judge House piped in: "Let's stick to what's pertinent to opening."

Doc started speaking immediately, without missing a beat.

"So the evidence will clearly show, the evidence will clearly show that Ashley didn't say anything about Tonya. However, the evidence will also show . . . that as soon as she got into the clutches of, into the custody of the dad, and with the 'therapist' that the cops put her with, that it got worse and worse and worse. No contact with Mom. None. Kept away from Mom for two years! [. . .] The evidence will show that the 'do-over,' the idea, the rationale that's used, is to say, 'Well, they were scared and they had to be in therapy for a while, and they had to *trust us* so they could tell the story.' And if that was true, if that was true, why would decades and decades of scientific research—"

Len Gregor stood up again: "Your Honor, again, we're going into argument."

Judge House said, "Let's quit the argument and get to the reason why we're here, for the opening statement."

Doc kept pacing back and forth and responded, "Opening statement *is* argument, but I'll try to confine myself to what the evidence will show. The evidence will show, and we're going to bring in a professor of child and adolescent psychiatry from Vanderbilt who wrote the guidelines, and he will tell you—he's been doing this for thirty years—he wrote guidelines, he's published gigantic amounts of research on these very issues, and the expert will come in and he'll tell you that when you do not control for parental influences, when you do not control for repeated questioning effects, when you do not control for rumor mills, you get very badly skewed and emotionally abused children."

Doc went on to talk about the physical examinations of the girls and how we would bring in experts who would show that those examinations didn't show any signs of abuse whatsoever: "The evidence will show it's not indicative of sexual abuse any more than a bump on your head is indicative of a car wreck."

Doc's opening was already longer than the ADA's. I knew he was only getting started in some ways. We had so much we wanted to say. We had so much we needed to share. It seemed to me that the difference in the opening statements laid out for the jury what the difference in this whole trial would be: The prosecutors were relying on the words of the accusers and their parents, the therapist (whom they didn't mention by name), and one nurse who'd examined the girls (who we felt wasn't nearly the "expert" she claimed she was), all built around the contradicting stories of Brianna

Lamb. Brianna seemed to be their biggest focus. We, however, were the ones who were going to bring that jury loads of evidence to consider, different voices, different experts, different friends and family who would all tell a very different story.

I hoped Doc wasn't talking too long, but from what I could tell, the jury seemed intrigued. They seemed to be listening. I prayed that their minds were still open.

Doc walked them through what we felt were the various outlandish allegations that Brianna made during her fourth interview. He walked through some of the names of my real friends and the children who were at my house every day and who would come to tell that jury the rest of the story that the prosecutors seemed to purposefully leave out. "The evidence will show that contrary to what little piece of the picture you're shown by the state, the defense wants you to see the *whole* picture," Doc said. "What matters is it didn't happen. It couldn't have happened the way they say. It doesn't make sense!"

He went on: "The evidence will show, very clearly, when you see it all, that the therapist—the therapist, quote-unquote, that they put these kids with before they were able to get Tyler and Ashley away from her, the therapist has serious issues."

Len Gregor stood up yet again: "*Again*, Your Honor, I'm just going to object. We're talking about argument, not facts, and I would just ask counsel to move on to an opening argument."

Doc started right up again, without a beat: "The evidence will definitely show that this therapist has serious iss—"

"Your Honor!" Gregor said. "I will rely on the previous ruling by this court."

"Let's stick to what the evidence is going to show and let's not get into any argument," the judge said.

Doc took a sip of water and walked over and placed it on the table right in front of me. He then turned and walked straight back toward the jury. I could see people shaking their heads on the other side of the courtroom, right behind those prosecutors. I tried to focus my eyes straight ahead so it wouldn't bother me.

"So," Doc said, "the bottom line, as we were told earlier, is the truth. The bottom line is the truth. In every case like this, every juror says, 'Well, if it didn't happen, why would they say it?' And every defendant is in the horrible position of having to climb that mountain and make explanations about, 'If it didn't happen, why would they say it?' That's backward. She's not guilty until proven on every piece of every element of the crime that you believe that she's guilty. She's innocent until then. So, I don't know why they did this. The parents, the children, the professors, they'll give you their ideas. But it's you that can only take those tools that you need and make the decision that you've got to make.

"So how do you defend yourself? How do you defend yourself from allegations that this happened in 2006, and 2005, and 2004? How do you get the information to defend yourself? The allegations are so horrible, you're toast before you even get into court. You have to go back and try to find things, so we're going to bring you—and the evidence will show—pictures. Pictures of what was going on. I wasn't there. You weren't there. Pictures of what was going on. People who were there. People that were actually there all the time who know Miss Tonya and know that this is the product of parents who went off the deep end. Maybe they were angry at Tonya, maybe I don't know what happened, but the kids were questioned over and over and over again. We will bring you *not* the people that depend for a living on finding child abuse, but the people who teach how you do it properly. Because in the final analysis, what we want is to spend our resources into getting the bad guys. Not divert them into witch hunts or hysteria. Because every time we spend our resources like this," he said, throwing his arms out wide toward everyone who was sitting in that courtroom, "we don't have 'em to spend on little kids who were really abused.

"So this is why it's *the rest of the story* that is so critically important," he said. "It didn't happen. It couldn't have happened the way they say it did. It doesn't make sense."

And with that, Doc gathered up his papers and very quietly said, "Thank you."

Chapter 48

I felt like there were a million things we needed to do and a million things we needed to discuss as we reviewed the opening arguments that night back at the war room. *What did we learn from Len Gregor's opening? Were there any surprises? What's their main focus? Who do we have to be careful of?*

We would talk about all of those things back at my parents' house, and the discussion would last for hours. We would focus especially hard on that hand gesture that Len Gregor made during his opening—that notion that I'd put my fingers together and put my whole hand into Brianna's privates, and our questions about when that first came to light. We didn't see it turn up until Brianna's fourth interview, but now they were claiming she'd been saying that since day one? It didn't make sense.

We spent almost as much time discussing the observations that came from the mouths of my parents, and David, and a couple of my friends who came by to see how I was doing. What I didn't realize until that evening was just how unfairly my supporters felt they were being treated in and around the courthouse. From what they were telling me, supporters on the other side were getting the red-carpet treatment compared to what my supporters were getting.

First of all, anyone who was going to be a witness wasn't allowed to sit in the courtroom. David, who vowed to be there every single day, was forced to sit out in the hallway on a wooden bench where he couldn't see or hear any of the proceedings. He tried to bring a book in with him so he'd have something to do for all those hours. They told him he couldn't bring it in. He tried to bring in a bottle of water. They confiscated it. They wouldn't let him have a phone, or a newspaper, or anything.

None of my supporters were allowed to carry anything into the courthouse. Nothing. Every one of my supporters and witnesses would have to come through the metal detector at the front door, too, which would take forever and a day. Then another metal detector right before entering the courtroom. Witnesses on the prosecution's side weren't forced to do any of that.

It turned out that the prosecution's witnesses—some of whom had already gathered in case they got called that afternoon—were all being put in a big room downstairs, right underneath the courtroom. A few of my supporters had been walking by at opportune moments and saw what was going on in that room. "They had laptop computers in front of them! They had newspapers! They had food and drink! It looked almost like they were having a party in there!" they told me.

To say it was upsetting was putting it mildly.

The fact was the judge had ordered that witnesses were not to have access to testimony. That was why David and all the other witnesses weren't allowed in the courtroom. We didn't even allow David to eat lunch with us because we didn't want him overhearing anything he shouldn't. With computers open in that downstairs witness room, what was keeping anyone from reading the media's live Tweets from the courtroom or reading quotes from the previous day's testimony or anything else?

Plenty of people also saw spectators on the prosecution side get waved right past the metal detectors. *That's not only unfair*, I thought, *it's not safe. There's a lot of high emotion running around. What if somebody decides to do something crazy?*

Joal's father, who came back as a spectator, walked through the front door with a cup of coffee in his hand at the very moment my husband was stopped and told firmly to throw his bottle of water away.

I tried to put it all behind me. I told my attorneys to stay focused on the trial. I told my friends and family to fight for what they could. They had rights, just like anyone else, to come and go from that public courtroom—and they had a right to demand that they were treated fairly. Some of them were sure to go to the media with these complaints, and that was fine with me. The media seemed fed up already. We heard Judge House told them not only to get off the front lawn, but to back away to a farther radius from the courthouse on that second day. It seemed like the judge and the media were going to be fighting the whole time. I just hoped none of these extraneous fights would affect my case in the wrong way.

I went to bed sometime shortly before dawn once again. I woke up at five. I got dressed. Walt made me my coffee. He and Karen wished me well. I rode over to the courthouse, ready to face the day—only to run headlong into a whole slew of craziness instead. Judge House came after our team that morning, without letting the jury in, to complain that there were vehicles parked on the courthouse square with "Truth for Tonya" bumper stickers on them. He fined David $300 for displaying that sticker on the van we used to bring the files to the courthouse. He said anyone parking anywhere near the courthouse with one of those bumper stickers would be fined, and he called out a number of spectators on my side of the courtroom and told them to go move their vehicles. He'd actually had law enforcement officers run down their license plates, and then he called out their names in the courtroom. So all of a sudden a bunch of those people, plus David, had to scramble around to go move vehicles to comply with the judge's order.

My friend Jennifer was interviewed by Melydia Clewell about the whole debacle. "I think it's their way of keeping us quiet," she said on the air.

All of it seemed like a nonsensical distraction to me. We were about to hear our first witnesses in the trial that could put me in prison for life. I wanted to focus on that.

The thing is, even without all that distraction, absolutely nothing could have prepared me for what I was about to face on the witness stand.

———————◆———————

We hadn't even taken our seats yet when Judge House came in and cleared the courtroom of all spectators. He ordered the camera turned off, too.

"What is going on?" I asked my team.

Judge House called the jury in. He asked the prosecution to call its first witness. Then Chris Arnt stood up and said, "The prosecution calls Brianna Lamb."[58]

From what I'd learned, it seemed that in most of these types of cases, the prosecutors would save the children for the end—so their words would be the last words the jury heard. I was floored to see one of the children so early on. I wasn't emotionally prepared for it. At all.

It was the first time I had laid eyes on Brianna in person since whenever I'd last passed her in the hallway at Chickamauga Elementary, all the way back in the spring of 2008. She came in wearing her Sunday best, a white dress, with her hair all done up nice. She carried a doll that seemed to be dressed like her, and she kept her head down, solemnly, as she walked in escorted by a designated adult and took her seat on the witness stand.

Brianna was nine now. She was visibly older than she'd appeared even in that last videotaped interview from April 1, 2009. She was remarkably composed as the prosecution asked her a few questions and basically had her repeat her allegations against me for the jury. She didn't get upset. She didn't cry. In fact, she smiled and seemed relaxed. She just sat there and spoke like it was just another day in her life.

The most shocking part to me was the fact that the prosecution asked her so few questions. It was over in no time. There were very few specifics asked of that child whatsoever. I think the prosecution wrapped up in less than ten minutes, then all of a sudden it was Doc's turn to cross-examine her.

Doc got up there and started pretty much where the prosecution left off. He asked Brianna what she thought of me, as a teacher and as a person, and Brianna answered that she didn't like me. He asked her about the abuse and pushed for more detail than the prosecution had pushed for on that stand. She told that jury, very distinctly and graphically, that I had fondled and violated her in the bathtub at my house. She said quite clearly that "in the bathtub" was the "only" place where I'd ever touched her.

Doc then shifted gears and did what he does best—putting his PhD in child psychology to good use. He developed a rapport with Brianna very quickly and spent a whole lot of time talking to her about her modeling and acting career. His questioning went on and on, for hours, with frequent breaks so Brianna wouldn't get exhausted by it all. He got her to talk all about the sorts of classes she'd taken and the type of acting she'd done and how she'd worked on memorizing lines and how proud she was of the work she'd done in the two movies she'd acted in.

By the time he circled back to the charges against me, Brianna was talking freely—and all of a sudden her story changed. Brianna started talking about the alleged abuse and said it happened "in the kitchen." When Doc pressed her to describe how I'd touched her, her story changed on that front, too. She described the alleged abuse entirely different than she'd described it the first time.

"Are you sticking to that story, or are you going to change it?" Doc asked her.

"I don't know," Brianna answered. She seemed puzzled and she thought about it for a moment before responding. "Yeah," she said, "this is right."

The jury was absolutely stone-faced. Not one of those people blinked an eye, shook a head, shrugged a shoulder, let out a sigh—nothing. I had no idea if they realized the depth of what just happened. I had no idea if they caught it. I had no idea if it would matter. All I could think was what some of those jury members must be thinking: *Any way you look at it, this little nine-year-old is up there recalling memories of how Tonya Craft fondled her. So what if it was in the kitchen? So what if it was in the bathroom? So what if her memory isn't clear? The fact that this girl remembers being fondled by Tonya Craft must mean it's true.*

Doc circled around again, this time going after the statements Brianna made about not liking me. He showed Brianna some of the gifts that Brianna and her mom had given to me when she was in my classroom and the cards that she had signed for me, telling me how wonderful I was and what a great teacher I was—reminding her that she wrote "I love you!" on those cards.

It was a very stark contrast to the "I don't like her" statements Brianna made at the beginning of her testimony, and she didn't have very much to say about it. So Doc let it rest.

He then asked Brianna if she remembered anything else about the "creepy" things Miss Tonya did to her, and Brianna answered: "No, but I do remember she used to mow the lawn and she'd wear really short shorts and a sports bra whenever she was mowing."

It struck me as such a bizarre thing for a little girl to say. A lot of women dress that way doing yard work in the Georgia heat.

Brianna's testimony was cut short late that afternoon. It came to light that one of the alternate jurors on my case was the husband of a woman who worked at Chickamauga Elementary. She was a teacher. Once I heard the name, I knew exactly who it was. I had never met her husband before or I would've spoken up during jury selection.

How can the husband of a teacher I worked with be sitting on this jury? Clearly that man didn't disclose his affiliations during voir dire. This man's wife could very well have alliances with certain families involved in the allegations against me, which means he's probably friends with them, too! So someone with a clear bias against me basically snuck himself onto my jury?

It caused enough of a ruckus that Judge House decided not to continue Brianna's testimony that day. We adjourned. So here we were at the end of day three of my trial, and all we'd heard were opening arguments and the partial testimony of the first witness. I was frustrated. Exhausted. And so was everybody else on my team.

We all went back to my parents' house that night wishing for nothing more than a little normalcy the next day. All we wanted was the chance to present our case and to start showing that jury the truth.

Chapter 49

———◆———

Just as surely as Walt made me coffee every morning (to which David joked, "Hey, Walt! You're gonna make me look bad!"), and just as surely as David drove us in and helped to truck all of our file boxes into the courtroom every morning, my father showed up bright and early to help and then took a seat in the very front row just behind me in that courtroom. Every single day.

David walked in with us beforehand and wished me well every morning, and as soon as testimony ended, he'd walk back in, put his arms around me (if I let him, depending on my emotional state), or lean over and smile and show me his love and support. The camera actually caught some of this on the third day and they wound up showing it on the news as background video while one of the reporters was talking. It was a really sweet moment that camera caught, and a lot of my friends took notice of the way David looked at me and the way he acted toward me. After all that time, I think some people who'd questioned why I'd gone back to him started to glimpse just how much love there was between us.

———◆———

The fourth day started with Brianna on the witness stand again, dressed in her Sunday best once more, with her hair done just so. Only this time, Doc played Brianna's original videotaped interviews for the jury while Brianna sat there. He noted how Brianna kept changing her story and asked her why she was doing that.

"I don't know," she said.

He asked her whether the interviewer in each of those interviews had maybe put ideas into her head.

"I don't know," she answered.

He asked her about whether her mother had talked to her about what to say in those interviews.

"I don't know," she answered.

He also asked her "when" she had first told anyone that Miss Tonya had put her fingers together and put her whole hand up inside of her privates. Remarkably, Brianna remembered. She was in the hallway, walking out of the interview with Suzie Thorne, she said, when she suddenly remembered that incident and told her about it.

The fact that she might have made that accusation outside of the video-taped interview, yet was never brought back inside to put it on the record, was a big deal. We were all blown away by it. We'd need to confirm what she'd said at some point later in the trial, when her mother was on the stand or when interviewer Suzie Thorne was on the stand.

We'd get back to that.

Overall, though, Brianna's lack of memories was more compelling at that early stage of the trial. The result of Doc's questioning, especially when coupled with the videos that showed her changing her story and her ever-evolving hatred of me over the course of the year, seemed devastatingly obvious to me.

Is it obvious to the jury? I wondered.

I expected the prosecution to call Chloe or Ashley to the stand after we wrapped with Brianna and got back from lunch. I thought they were going to lay it on thick, all at once, so the jury would see all three girls right away. But they didn't do that. All of a sudden the camera got turned back on and the courtroom filled up with spectators. And Chris Arnt called Sharon Anderson to the stand.

Sharon is the certified sexual assault nurse examiner (SANE) who performed physical examinations on all three of the girls. With the prosecutors' help, she walked the jury through the process of the physical exams, and they showed pictures of all three of the girls' privates on a big-screen television mounted to the wall. It was awful. I went right back to that sick feeling I had the first time I read Nurse Anderson's reports and could not hold back my tears. Cary handed me tissues.

As Anderson described what she saw as "suspicion of abuse" in Ashley and "strong suspicion of abuse" in Brianna, I had the sense that the jury believed her. Why wouldn't they? On the surface, Anderson seemed extremely qualified. She'd performed hundreds of these exams. She'd gone through specialized SANE training. She spoke in seemingly exact terms about her findings and about the hymen tissue and the way it was "rolled" and such in both Ashley and Brianna. And when it came to the question of how Chloe could have been abused without any physical signs of abuse showing up, she told the jury, "Because some of the touching and some of the things done to children don't leave any problems—they just don't leave any signs behind."

It wasn't until Doc got up and started questioning her that even a hint of doubt seemed to get raised. Doc talked in scientific terms about what it means for a child's vagina to appear "normal." He asked her how many "normal" vaginas she had compared them to. She didn't have an exact answer. He asked if she had looked at pictures and medical journals, and she said yes. Then he asked her again, how many children was she comparing Brianna and Chloe and Ashley against in order to determine that they were not "normal"? She said there wasn't an exact number, so Doc asked her to be general. Was it 500 children? 1,000 children? 10,000 children? To what was she making her comparison about what was "normal" and what showed "signs of abuse"?

Anderson's answer was that she was basing it on her training and basing it on a comparison against other children she had examined over the years.

Anderson was a gray-haired woman who had been at this job for quite some time. It seemed like a valid way to do those exams to a layperson like those folks on the jury. It wasn't until Doc started citing some major studies in the field that showed an incredibly wide range of hymen tissue that was "normal" in young girls that the atmosphere in the room started to shift. Doc asked Nurse Anderson if she had read those studies.

"No," she answered.

He asked her if she had read certain books that were standards in the field.

"No," she answered.

He asked her if she read up on the latest medical journals and studies that had been released in the years since she completed her SANE training.

"No," she said.

He went round and round with her and determined, without a doubt, that she had not read the latest studies or even some of the greatest studies that serve as the centerpieces of her field.

Those studies showed, he said, that "normal" could mean many things. Even a layperson understands that some girls' hymen tissue can be *entirely* missing for no immoral or abusive reason whatsoever. Girls lose their hymens from horseback riding and bike riding and gymnastics. Girls could simply be born with the tissue missing or shaped in a variety of ways. He pointed out that the position the children were placed in during the examination caused the vaginal area to look different than when the child was in a normal position, and Anderson concurred. Finally, he called into question whether the rolling and erosion of hymen tissue that Anderson had seen in two of these girls could have been caused by anything *other* than sexual abuse—to which she very hesitantly, after hemming and hawing, *agreed.*

Doc had done it. In the course of his questioning, he had called into doubt the only "physical evidence" the prosecution had for my alleged crimes. I was extremely impressed with his performance that day, and I just hoped and prayed that the jury was paying enough attention to see the truth.

———————◆———————

Back at the war room that night, I realized we had a problem. We were all taking notes during the trial—writing down the questions we had or ideas we needed to follow up on—and none of those notes were organized enough to follow once we got back home. So we sat down and took a few minutes to develop a system. We color coded questions, thoughts, and suggestions and matched them to each of the three girls' cases. We made sure to write our notes on colored Post-it notes so we could simply tack them onto the assigned attorney's folder for follow-up or to use during cross the following day, or the following hour, or whatever the case may be. It made a world of difference almost immediately and allowed our conversations to flow with some coherence, rather than exploding into a flurry of unrelated questions and concerns covering eight hours' worth of testimony. It shocked me sometimes that these top-notch attorneys hadn't developed a system like this already, but I was happy that we came up with something that worked for us.

———————◆———————

Next, Chloe McDonald walked into that courtroom looking almost exactly like Brianna: white dress, hair done up, carrying a doll and a stone for good luck. The prosecution got up and once again talked to this accuser for about ten minutes. Half that time was spent establishing who she was, where she went to school, and the fact that the therapist had given her that stuffed animal to help her feel "safe" at night and when she came into the courtroom that day.

Chloe didn't like sitting on the witness stand, so they let her move to the first row of the gallery, just behind the prosecutors' table. She sat there—and completely changed her story. She went from "it was something that happened one time" to saying it happened something like twenty-two times. It was a crazy number she came up with, and when Doc got up and developed a rapport, he asked her where she got that number.

"Well," Chloe said, "me and my momma were praying on it last night, and I just remembered when we prayed on it."

Doc spent a couple of hours that morning showing the jury her taped interviews—conducted by Detective Tim Deal—and asking similar questions to the ones he asked Brianna about why she'd changed her story. Chloe said that when Detective Deal kept asking her the same questions, she changed her answer because she thought she had answered "wrong" the first time.

Just like Brianna, she didn't show any emotion when she talked about the details of my supposed abuse. She said it like she was talking about going to school that day.

Doc had made a big point during his cross-examination of Brianna to note that she was rewarded with a "spa visit" for one of her interviews. He was able to highlight a similar moment with Chloe, when she revealed during her interview that she was going to get a toy if she'd "done good."

Doc had also turned a spotlight on Brianna's admission that her mother had questioned her about what happened with "Miss Tonya" multiple times and that she believed what her "momma told her" about some other things, too. We weren't able to highlight those sorts of moments with Chloe while covering her interviews, because there weren't any. To me, that was a problem. I made a note to myself to go back over her interviews and to listen to them again, just in case there was anything we missed. There were an awful lot of "inaudible" moments in her transcripts. I decided those moments deserved a closer listen. If nothing else, our showing a jury at some point later that those moments weren't really "inaudible"—no matter what they said—might show some of the basic incompetency I felt had taken place in the investigation.

I tried to focus on that as Chloe wrapped up and left the room. I tried not to think about what was coming next. I felt like crying long before the prosecutors ever stood up to call her, and I could feel the tears well up immediately when Chris Arnt stood and said, "The State would call Ashley Henke . . ."

There was nothing I could do to stop those tears from falling once my daughter walked into that room.

Chapter 50

A shley didn't even look like herself. I could hardly believe how much she'd grown up. She was six when I last saw her. She was eight now. The difference between my just-out-of-kindergarten daughter and this girl at the end of her second-grade school year was devastating. She'd sprouted right up. I'd always thought she might be taller than me someday, and she was well on her way. She looked *so* much older.

That wasn't all that bothered me, though. My baby girl didn't seem to sparkle like she used to. She seemed troubled to me. She seemed distant. Void. She'd requested that she not have to look at me, and we'd all made adjustments so I wouldn't be in her direct line of sight. They put a folder up in front of her on the witness stand.

My God, what have they done to her?

She came in wearing another of those white dresses, too, all "Sunday best"–looking with her hair done up. *Ashley would never have worn a dress like that by choice. Ever. What are these prosecutors trying to do?*

I tried to hush my cries so they wouldn't interfere with her testimony, but I could not shut those tears off no matter how hard I tried to compose myself.

Chris Arnt started questioning Ashley, and at first she just nodded yes—until he prompted her to say "yes" or "no" for the record a number of times. She seemed annoyed, but she was absolutely polite about it.

"Yes, sir," she said.

"Who have you got there with you in your arms?" he asked.

"My two stuffed animals."

"Do they have names?"

Ashley nodded.

"What are their names?"

"Coco and Tucker."

"What was the first one?"

"Coco."

"And do you have something around one of their necks in a little bag?"

Ashley said it was a Bible verse on a rock, which she had borrowed from Chloe for "good luck."

"Is that helping you today, that rock, to tell us the truth?" Chris asked.

"Yes, sir," she said.

He then asked about Chloe and whether she was a friend. Ashley said she was a friend "a long time ago." He asked her about where she goes to school, and where she used to go to school, and what subjects she liked ("math") and didn't like ("social studies"). He asked about what pets she had, and she talked about her dogs at her daddy's house and the dogs at her dad's parents' house, and then she finally mentioned Buddy and Candy Cane "at my mom's."

She talked briefly about her brother, Tyler, and when prompted by Arnt, she talked about the fact that she didn't live with me anymore.

"Okay. Did something happen and then you went and lived with your dad?" Arnt asked.

"Are you asking about, like, what she did or something?" Ashley responded.

"Well, did something happen?" he said.

"I don't know what you are asking," Ashley said.

"Let me back up a little bit and go a little slower. You were living with your mom, right?"

Ashley nodded. "Yes, sir."

Arnt went on to say that she was now living with her dad and asked her how long it had been. She said, "Two years maybe. I don't know," and Arnt made her narrow it down: "Two years or one and a half."

"And when you lived with your mom, how was things? How were things?" he asked.

"I had a lot of good friends, but I still always liked my dad the best," Ashley said.

Boy, oh boy, did that hurt.

She went on to say that life at my house was "okay," until Chris asked her point-blank: "Did anything ever happen between you and your mom that made you feel upset or uncomfortable?"

"Yes, sir," she said.

"Can you tell us about that?"

"She touched me in the privates."

"She touched you in the where?"

"Privates."

"The privates. What did she touch you with?"

"Her bare hand."

"Her bare hand. Did her bare hand touch your privates on the skin or on the clothes?"

"Skin."

I started to lose it. My tears turned into sobs. I buried my head to try to muffle the sound, but I was shaking. I couldn't stop.

"So her skin of her bare hand touched the skin of your privates."

"Yeah."

"Do you remember how old you were when that would happen?" Arnt asked.

"I really don't know how old I was. I don't know. Maybe like the last time I saw her or something, but I don't know how old I was. I'd say maybe six and a half. I don't know."

"You're not sure, maybe six, maybe six and a half," Arnt said, "but you were kind of shrugging your shoulders like you weren't really positive."

"I don't really know," she said.

"Okay. Did that happen a lot of times? Just once? A few times? Can you give us—"

"Maybe a few."

Arnt asked her where Tyler would be when it happened, and she said "different places," like "with a friend" or "with David." So he asked about David, whom Ashley described as "my mom's husband," adding, "He's nice to me." He continued with questions about how she liked staying with her grandma and grandpa on her mom's side, and Ashley said, "They were nice to me a lot, like, but sometimes they make me feel embarrassed or they would be mean to me sometimes."

I thanked God that the courtroom had been cleared of spectators for the children's testimony—and that my mom and dad weren't sitting there to hear that.

Then Arnt turned the questions back to the topic of "touching her privates" and whether everything in my house was usually okay other than that.

"Yes, sir," she said.

He asked her where it happened, and Ashley said, "Usually in her room."

He asked her whether I would say anything to her when I did it, and she said, "Sometimes, sometimes not, but I don't really know what she would say because I don't have the best memory."

"Chris." Doc spoke up. He wanted Arnt to repeat what Ashley had said, since she said it really softly.

"She said sometimes yes, sometimes no, but I don't really remember what she said because I don't have the best memory," Arnt repeated.

"Thank you," Doc said.

"Did I get that right?" Arnt asked Ashley.

"Yes, sir," she said.

Arnt mentioned to Ashley that the two of them had talked before. "Do you remember saying that you don't like to think about this and people like me asking you questions that makes you think about it?" Arnt said.

Ashley, of course, repeated that sentiment right back to him: "I don't really like to think about it," she said. "I've been trying to get it out of my mind. When I heard I had to talk, it made me feel worse."

Arnt then looked at Doc and said, "Your witness."

That was the whole prosecution side of Ashley's testimony. It was shocking how short their direct was. *Don't they even want to make it look like they've done some work? Don't they want to preempt even some of the most obvious questions we're going to be sure to ask?*

I'd managed to recompose myself a little bit. I wasn't sobbing at least. But every time I looked at Ashley, the tears welled up all over again. All I kept thinking was, *What have they done to my baby girl?*

Doc stayed seated at first. "I'm the guy back here writing notes. I get to talk to you. Okay?" he said.

"Yes, sir," Ashley answered.

"Is that all right with you? I work for your mommy. When was the last time you saw your mommy?"

"Like maybe two years ago," Ashley said.

"Two years ago. Okay. Where is your mommy now?"

"What do you mean by that? Where does she live or what do you mean?"

"Is she here?" Doc asked.

"Yes."

"Where is she?"

"Over there," Ashley said without looking.

"Over there. Have you looked at her since you came in?"

"I saw her face," she said.

"You saw her face. Have you looked at her since you came in other than just seeing her face?"

"Not really."

"No. Okay. Well, I'm going to ask a bunch of questions. Okay? And if I mess something up, I want you to tell me that I got something wrong. Okay?"

"Okay," Ashley said.

Doc went and handed her a part of the Christmas wrapping she'd given me just that past Christmas. It had a picture of Hannah Montana on it, and she'd signed it twice with the words, "To Mommy, Love Ashley." She said she'd signed it twice because she messed it up the first time.

Doc was careful to explain to her why he was talking to the court reporter and why there was a sticker with a number on it attached to that wrapping paper, because he was entering that exhibit into evidence and "Ms. Janet" had to type it down.

Ashley seemed to understand it all very quickly and was fine with it. She confirmed that she'd written those notes to me herself.

Doc then handed her another bit of evidence—some more of that Christmas wrapping, this time with the dollar bills attached. I'd kept it just as-is. It was so precious to me—I hated bringing it into the courtroom. I didn't want anything to happen to that gift.

"And who was the present for?" Doc asked.

"Tonya."

"Okay. And is Tonya your mom?"

"Yeah."

"When did you start calling her Tonya?"

"Ever since she did the bad thing."

I lost it. I started sobbing again. I couldn't hold it back. Cary put his arm around me and tried to comfort me.

"Okay," Doc continued. "Ever since she did the bad thing?"

"Uh-huh."

"And when was that?"

"Let me interrupt here," Chris Arnt said, standing up and addressing Judge House. "I've been very, very lenient. I think we do need to get people to gain control of their emotions in front of the jury. I don't know if we need to take a break to do that or not."

"No," Doc said. "I mean, this is the real world. She hasn't seen her in two years."

"I understand that," Judge House said. "Take the time and ask your client if we need to take a break," Judge House asked Doc.

"We set it up so there's no line of sight," Doc answered.

"I understand. I'm very sympathetic to that. That's the reason I ask," Judge House said.

"Thank you, Judge," Doc said. "No."

I'd stopped sobbing quite so hard by then, so Doc went on with his questioning. He confirmed that Ashley had wrapped that present, and he entered it into evidence. He also confirmed that Ashley had picked out a purse for me and a matching pair of shoes and had given me some other presents in the current year as well—little gifts like a cross and a ring that came from her hairdresser.

During part of that evidence introduction, Ashley made a comment in which she thanked "Chris" by his first name. Doc seemed to pick up on that real quick. He asked when Ashley had first stepped into that courthouse, and Ashley described coming in about a month ago with her dad and her stepmom, Sarah—specifically to meet with Chris, and, she noted, she'd even met Judge House.

I didn't know what to make of that.

Doc then turned his attention to trying to narrow down when the alleged touching of privates had happened.

"It didn't just happen in one year. It happened more than one year," Ashley volunteered.

"Yes. I want to know every single time that it happened," Doc said.

"I don't have the best memory," Ashley said.

"If we can figure it out. Okay? And I'm going to show you pictures of you to help see if they help you remember. Okay?"

"Okay," she said.

Doc explained that some of the pictures would be of Ashley and me together.

"Do I have to?" Ashley said.

Doc basically convinced her that she did, and then Arnt spoke up again—complaining that one of the photos showed Ashley as a baby, and "How can she possibly be expected to identify that one?"

"I have an indictment that starts just about when she was born," Doc said.

"Regardless of how the indictment is, how do we expect a six-month-old to identify a picture?" Arnt complained. "It's impossible. He's just making a show of it. I object to that."

"Well, okay," Doc said. "If they want to narrow the indictment down so the defense isn't looking at her entire life span, that would be fine."

I admired Doc's feistiness right then. It was one instance where I was absolutely *glad* that he could be such an arrogant pain in the butt!

"I object to the impossibility of the witness possibly identifying the picture," Arnt said. "It's just a show. I'm objecting to that."

Judge House finally spoke up: "If she doesn't identify it, then let's move on."

"Who are those two people?" Doc asked Ashley.

"Me and my mom," Ashley said without skipping a beat.

"And who are those two people?" Doc asked, showing another photo.

"Me and my mom."

Showing her the photo of me holding her as a baby—a photo that was now officially entered into evidence because of Ashley's confirmation—Doc asked, "Now, when you were this old, were the touching privates happening?"

"I don't know," Ashley said.

"Okay. Let me ask you about the next year." He showed her three pictures. "Can you identify those people?"

"I know they're all going to be the same people," Ashley snapped. "So that's me and my mom and that's Tyler in the background, if you can see my brother."

"Okay," Doc said.

"In the little round glasses."

"Thank you."

Ashley identified a couple of other photos, too—until Arnt stood up again. "Judge, I'm going to make a relevancy objection to this entire series of photos. The stated purpose is obviously not—she said she doesn't know. This doesn't jog her memory. That was the stated relevance on a whole host of these photos," Chris said. "What these really are is a back-door attempt to generate sympathy for the defendant."

Doc countered, "I have medical records fixed in time. I have reports from other people fixed in time. I'm trying to fix her in time as to when this happened."

As Doc continued with a well-reasoned counter to the objection, Arnt said, "I don't know if I'm speaking English or not. Apparently, I'm not."

Judge House went right along with him. He tried to get Doc not to enter all of the photos, and instead just ask Ashley about specific years of her life to try to narrow down when the incidents happened. Only after something relevant was established would he allow the photos to be entered into evidence, he said.

So Doc went through, year by year, trying to narrow down when the touching began, and Ashley responded, "I really don't remember when, but it wasn't when I was like a teeny, teeny baby."

"Got you," Doc said—meaning he understood what she was saying. Not like, "*Got* you!" He was just speaking casually and comfortably with her, which I hoped made her not feel threatened as she sat there.

Finally, she remembered something. He focused in a little more as Ashley took a big stretch. He asked about Chloe McDonald, and Ashley talked about going to her house "a lot."

"When was that?" Doc asked.

"The last time would probably have been like 2005 or 2006," she answered.

Doc asked her if she remembered being at Chloe's house one time when Chloe got in trouble. Ashley said, "No." He asked if she remembered an incident at Chloe's after which she went to see a pediatric diagnostic. Ashley asked what a "pediatric diagnostic" was, and once she understood she said, "No." He tried for a while to get her to recall that incident, until Ashley finally said, "Can I take a break?"

The judge allowed a short break. I'd made it a habit to leave the courtroom and give David a quick hug during breaks, but I didn't go out that time—so David knew I was in a bad place. He hesitantly came in and approached me. I sat at the defense table with my head down, sobbing. My body was shaking. David placed a hand on my back to let me know he was there. I shrugged it off.

I could barely breathe. Doc went over a bunch of notes, and we all talked very briefly before Ashley came back to the stand. Doc decided to go back with a new approach to the whole timeline question. When we got started again, he showed her a picture of Hunter, my friend Tammy's son. He asked her if he was around a lot. Ashley said he was at our home two or three days a week. He then showed her a picture of her and her then best friend, Danielle. He asked if Danielle was around a lot, and she said she was at our house a lot, yes. He then showed her a picture of another one of her very good friends from kindergarten, Hailey Lewis (my friend Shanica's daughter), whom Ashley also said was over at our house "a lot." In fact, Hailey was over "mostly all the time Hunter was. Tyler would have Hunter over and I would have her over," she said.

Her memory was perfectly clear when jogged by a few photos.

After going through a whole long list of friends and events, trying to pin her down to even a general range of dates, Doc showed her pictures from her January 2008 birthday party, with the limo. Ashley pointed out some of the people in the picture, including Chloe. When Doc asked her whether Chloe came over to the house very often, Ashley answered, "Not really."

After establishing that the party was at the beginning of 2008, he then asked her whether the first time I ever did a "private touch" happened before 2008 or after 2008.

"Before 2008," Ashley said.

"Before. Okay. How far before [that] 2008 limo party?"

"I honestly don't know what year," she said. "So I don't know, but I know it was before 2008."

"Okay," Doc said. "Did it happen after the limo party in 2008?"

"Maybe about one more time."

"Maybe about one more time. Okay," Doc said.

He continued this way, using photos and events such as the wedding to pin Ashley down to something specific, and writing the dates on a big white board. In the end, he basically got Ashley to confirm that the touching had "happened between April of 2007 and May of 2008, in there; is that right?"

"Yes, sir," Ashley agreed.

"Thank you. Boy, that was helpful," Doc told her.

Doc went on to try to get some details of May 30 from Ashley, and she remembered it incorrectly. He attempted to play the whispered phone message she left me that weekend, but Arnt objected, and Ashley said she had no memory of making such a call. So we weren't allowed to play it.

Doc then focused on whether or not Ashley recalled getting stomach-aches and whether I had put medicine on her during that same time period when the alleged "touching" took place.

"No," Ashley said.

"No," Doc answered. "Do you remember telling somebody that your mom put medicine on you?"

"I did not say my mom did. I did not say my mom did," Ashley said.

"You did not say your mom did what?"

"Put medicine on me."

"You did not say your mom put medicine on you. Okay. Do you remember saying that your dad put medicine on my privates?"

"No."

"You don't remember that?" Doc asked.

"He didn't," Ashley answered. "I can tell you I promise you that he didn't."

He asked her about whether she had ever told me about taking showers with Sarah, and whether she told me her dad was in the bathroom with them, and that Sarah would shave in the shower with her.

"I never said that, no," Ashley answered.

After listening to Ashley say "no" to a whole bunch of other things, including some details about the now-infamous limo birthday party and what I had said to Brianna Lamb and Lydia Wilson at that party, Doc decided to go to the videotape of Ashley's interview with Suzie Thorne at the Greenhouse.

"Do I have to watch it? I don't want to watch," Ashley complained.

"Well, I've got to ask you about it. You can listen, but I've got to ask you about it."

"I already know what I said," Ashley pleaded.

"Okay. But I've got to ask you about what you remember."

"I know I remember," Ashley said. "I know what I said."

"Okay. Did you say your mom put medicine on you to Suzie Thorne?"

"No. I said that my grandma did."

After some more back and forth, Doc started the interview. He kept starting and stopping the DVD as he went through it, asking questions that forced Ashley to address how she could have known that I was "lying," unless her dad told her. She said she didn't know. Then Doc played the portion of the DVD interview in which Ashley said that I had put medicine on her.

"Oops," Doc said.

"I guess she did do it," Ashley admitted. "I just don't have the best memory because, like I said, it was a long time ago because I remembered better because it was a shorter time. So I guess she did."

"You remember better back then, or you remember better now?" Doc asked.

"It was closer to when it happened," she said of the interview tape. "So I would have remembered it better."

"Back then?" Doc said.

"Yeah," Ashley admitted.

Well, hallelujah to that, I thought. *My daughter's smart enough to recognize that her memory would have been better closer to an actual event than it would be two years afterward. Why couldn't the prosecutors or anybody else realize that simple human factoid?*

Ashley went on to reconfirm that notion when Doc asked her about her belly aches and the need for the medicine: "I still don't remember, but if that's what it says then I guess that's right. But just like I said, I had a better memory back then than I do now."

"I understand," Doc said. "Thank you for explaining that to me."

Doc went back to the white board and added the date of that interview, June 3, 2008.

He played the portion of the tape in which Ashley talked about showering with Sarah, and while she tried to deny that she'd ever *told* me about it, she said that those showers happened "six or seven" times. "And then it stopped."

It had gone on longer than that. Sarah and Joal admitted as much in their depositions.[59] The Tennessee courts had to tell Sarah to stop after her February 2009 deposition—ten *months* after it first came up. It sickened me that Ashley was trying to protect the people that I felt had done wrong by her, and there was nothing I could do but sit there and listen.

When Doc asked Ashley about the shaving, she said she "didn't remember," but then added that it was like a "fake shaver when you pop off the razor. You use it . . . It's just fake."

Ashley also said, after viewing more of the tape, that she didn't know what the boyfriend-girlfriend game was. She said she had no recollection of that game at all.

At one point, Ashley asked if the tape was almost done. "How many more minutes?" she said.

Doc looked at the DVD player and figured there were eight minutes left.

"Then it's over?" Ashley asked.

"Yes," Doc said. He offered her some water. She refused. It was such a bizarre, conflicted feeling to sit there feeling proud of how strong and brave she was being and to know that she could barely look at me.

When they got to the portion of the tape where Suzie Thorne left the room and Ashley was seen sucking her thumb, she explained that she "always" did that. In fact, she said, she had done it for seven years. "They said if I stopped I would get an iPod Touch," she said. So she'd stopped. She had an iPod Touch now, apparently, courtesy of Joal and Sarah.

"An iPod Touch from stopping sucking your thumb? That is so cool," Doc said.

"I have to get braces," she added.

Doc started up a regular old conversation with Ashley right there in that courtroom. He talked about how he got braces when he was young, but not *that* young.

"I know a guy who just turned eight and he already has braces," Ashley said.

The fact that he could get Ashley to chitchat after sitting in a chair for that many hours was downright miraculous to me.

Ashley made a comment as we sat there about how long Suzie Thorne had left her alone. Doc tried to get some information about who she was talking to during that break, but Ashley just repeated that Thorne had left to talk with "someone she works with."

They finally went through to the end of the tape, and the judge ordered a bathroom break—during which Len Gregor stood up and said he wanted to note, for the record, "With each of these children we keep getting from counsel to the children, 'Well, we're going to be done in just a minute, I just have a few more questions for you on this.' He's leading these children to believe they're done and then we go in another area for another two hours. I mean, I think that there are little psychological games being played with these kids . . . I'm getting tired of it."

Scott spoke up in response: "Is that an objection?"

"Let's not get into this. I know it's late," Judge House said. "We're trying to get this witness done for everybody's sake. Okay?" Judge House offered to tell Ashley when she got back that we'd actually have about another hour of questioning, and he did so. "That's part of our procedure," he told her.

"No more than an hour," Ashley stated flatly.

Doc responded to her, "Yeah."

"She's telling you," Judge House said to Doc.

"If it's more than an hour," Ashley said, "I'm going to say, like, no way."

"Yes, ma'am," Doc said. "I promise, miss."

The last part of Doc's cross-examination started with questions about the interview she'd done with Ann Hazzard. Doc simply confirmed that Ashley hadn't left anything out of that interview, and she said she didn't think she had. He then asked some very specific questions regarding some of the allegations Brianna Lamb had made against Ashley during her own interviews.

"I'm just asking you about stuff that I've got to ask you. Did you—don't get mad at me. Did you stick your finger in your privates and put it in Brianna Lamb's face and tell her to smell it?"

"No," Ashley said. She looked completely shocked.

"Okay. Did you tell Brianna Lamb that she had to touch your privates or you would hurt her mom?"

"No. Where did you get that from?"

"Brianna," Doc told her.

He got it directly from Brianna's interviews, Ashley. I wish I could talk to you. I wish I could explain all of this to you!

"Didn't anybody ask you about what Brianna said?" Doc asked her.

Chris Arnt stood up and objected, but Judge House didn't respond and Doc went on asking questions, making sure they were specifically about what Brianna and Chloe had said on the record.

"Did anybody ask you about what Brianna said?"

"No."

"Okay. Did anyone ask you about what Chloe said?"

"No."

"Well, I'm going to ask you and I'll be done," Doc said.

"Because I don't know what they said," Ashley complained.

"I'm going to ask you. So did you put your hand down Brianna's pants?"

"No."

"Well, did you tell Brianna she has to put her hand down your pants?"

"No."

My stomach was in absolute knots. I never got a chance to ask Ashley if she actually participated in the so-called "boyfriend-girlfriend" game. What if she didn't? What if that story was false, too? What if Ashley wasn't involved with any touching with any of these girls outside of that incident in which Chloe might have touched *her? That one time. That one time that she doesn't even remember, which I'd tried to handle correctly so it wouldn't be traumatizing.* I wanted to stand up and tell everyone to stop. *Let my baby go. Just take me to prison. I don't want to put her through any more of this!*

"Did you take Brianna's hand and stick it in your pants?"

"No."

"Did your mommy make Brianna stay in your bedroom with no TV at your house?"

"No."

"Was there a TV in your bedroom at Mommy's house?"

"Yeah."

"Yeah. Did your mommy have kids over and then never let them have anything to drink or eat?"

"Uh-uh."

"Okay. That's a no?"

"Yeah, that's a no."

"We're getting through this pretty quick. So do you remember did you have—do you remember having a Halloween party at your house?"

"No."

He asked if she was ever in a bath with Brianna Lamb and Skyler Walker. Ever. And Ashley said, "No."

He asked if she hid under the blanket during her birthday party and touched all the little girls' privates.

"No."

He asked if she'd been in the bath with Brianna and "your mommy touching Brianna's privates and your privates in the bathtub?"

"No."

He asked about touching Chloe's privates ("No"), and again about Brianna touching her privates ("No"), and Ashley called him out for asking some of the same questions twice.

Doc apologized.

"Are we almost done?" Ashley said.

Doc assured her he was trying *not* to take the whole hour. He got a few more questions in, and Ashley pretty much refuted *everything* Brianna and Chloe had described during their interviews, *and* in the therapy notes we'd seen from Laurie Evans.

A few questions later, Doc wrapped it up.

"So we're done?" Ashley said.

"No, not until the judge says," Doc told her.

"Anything further?" Judge House asked Chris Arnt.

"No," Arnt said.

"Okay," the judge finally said. "Now you're done."

Ashley stood up.

"That was *so* not an hour," she said.

Len Gregor, Chris Arnt, and Ashley's assigned handler then whisked my strong, beautiful daughter out of the room. She didn't look back at me. I had no idea when I might see her again. If ever.

Doc made his way back to our table and the first thing he said to me was, "Wow. She's *you!*"

Under any other circumstances, I might have laughed at his sentiment. There's a line from *Steel Magnolias* that I have always liked. It says, "Laughter through tears is my favorite emotion." There wasn't anything favorite of mine about that moment, for sure.

The jury filtered out. The judge was gone.

David came in and tried to comfort me and I jerked away from him. I didn't want to be touched. Finally, I dropped my head to the table and just let it all out. In that dull brown courtroom drained of all its judging eyes, I cried without worrying how loud I was sobbing—and prayed once again for it all to just end.

Chapter 51

 My trial was estimated to last two weeks. The way things were going, suddenly everybody started saying it was going to take *four weeks* to get through all the testimony. I could hardly imagine keeping my composure that long. I could hardly imagine keeping up the routines of the all-night work, the full days in court, and hardly any sleep in between. Even after those couple of days away from the courtroom, the exhaustion I felt heading into day six was only matched by the adrenaline that rushed right through me when the prosecution stood up and called, "Sherri Wilson."

Lord, here we go, I thought.

Sherri came in and plopped herself into the chair on the witness stand and sort of slumped down a bit. She talked with a real somber tone in her voice that seemed completely false to me. She then went ahead and discussed the whole pool party incident with Skyler Walker and specified that Skyler had written the words "sex" and "kissing" in sidewalk chalk by the pool. She went on and on about how she'd questioned both Brianna and Skyler after that and made the shocking "discovery" that Skyler and Ashley had supposedly been touching each other in this game called "boyfriend-girlfriend." All in all, the prosecution wrapped up quickly, as they had with each of their witnesses so far.

It was Scott King's first chance to shine when it came to cross-examining Sherri, and he got up, stood strong, and called into question just about every word that came out of that woman's mouth. She appeared to me to be defensive from the get-go. She didn't answer the question of who called Detective Keith first to discuss the alleged pool incident, either her or her husband, DeWayne. She said she had no memory of any incident at Ashley's birthday party in 2008—despite the fact that she'd stopped being friends with me and stopped coming into my classroom. She said the only reason she was upset with me that March was because she had apparently "just learned" that her daughter wasn't going to progress into first grade.

When simple school records would show that we'd had meetings and discussions long before that. Basically, almost nothing she said matched the way I remembered it or the records and timelines we had gathered to back up the facts. None of it.

Sherri got up there and talked about how Brianna had come back to her house at some point after that chalk incident because she wanted to "talk to her" about something. Sherri said she "sat right down" on the driveway for that intimate talk with Brianna, and while they sat there talking is when Brianna revealed that "stuff happened" with Miss Tonya. It was so shocking, she said, that she immediately "sat down" because she could feel her legs going.

Wait a second, Sherri. You said you were already seated on the ground. How are your legs giving out on you if you're already seated? It's those kind of little, telling details that you hope a jury picks up on, and which in many cases my attorneys were quick enough to notice and highlight in the heat of the moment. In that particular case, I caught it. I wrote a note about it. But Scott didn't get a chance to mention it to her during cross.

What Sherri told that jury was that Brianna told her all about what I'd allegedly done to her: that I'd touched her in the bathtub *and* in the kitchen and that one time I had "touched" some other little girls when we were all under the covers together during a sleepover. Sherri testified that she then went inside the house and relayed all of that news to Brianna's mom, Sandra Lamb. Sherri testified that *she* was the one who told Sandra about it for the first time. *Well, that doesn't match Sandra's story at all,* I thought. *Unless Sandra's story is going to be different now, too.*

I found it strange that Sherri never shed a tear. This was emotional stuff we were dealing with. It's hard not to cry when you talk about it, even if you're talking about other people's kids. She looked like she was going to cry, or maybe *trying* to cry, but no tears ever fell. I could almost see her trying to spin everything to match the stories they'd been spinning from the very beginning—especially as Sherri put her fingers together and described the up-and-down motion Brianna made with her hand to show what I'd supposedly done to her. Under cross-examination, Sherri specified that Brianna said I had done that up-and-down hand-motion thing to her in the kitchen. *Only* in the kitchen. According to Sherri, Brianna made that motion to her during that very first conversation they had while they sat together on her driveway—even though it clearly didn't come up at all until much later in the official interviews with Brianna, and even though nobody mentioned that aspect of what I'd supposedly done to Brianna during the early months of the investigation whatsoever. To anybody. *It doesn't even line up with Brianna's testimony from just the other day!*

In the end, I wasn't sure that Sherri Wilson's testimony would really mean that much to a jury. She wasn't a parent of one of the accusers. Her kids weren't directly involved in any of this. A part of me wondered why the prosecution would even call her to the stand. The only thing she offered was an initial glimpse at the "origin story" of how their knowledge of all of this alleged "touching" had come about.

Trying to step outside of my own bubble and see it more objectively, I just kept thinking, *Is Sherri Wilson the most credible witness the prosecution could present when talking about the origins of a molestation charge? Isn't that the job of detectives to find out? Shouldn't they be trumpeting their investigation into these charges, instead of putting up a mom who's tangentially involved? And where's Stephen Keith? The detective who started this whole investigation? The friend of the Wilsons whom Sherri admitted she and DeWayne called? Why haven't they called him to the stand?*

I could tell you where Detective Tim Deal was: He was seated right over at the prosecution's table. The only thing between him and me was Doc and a little space between the tables. There's a statute in the Georgia legal system that allows a "lead investigator" to stay in the courtroom and observe the whole trial as part of the prosecution team (once a motion is filed, and if a judge agrees to it), even though he was going to be called as a witness. Prosecutors seem to *love* it. They appeared to use this to their advantage all the time, taking lots of notes and then using the lead investigator—who had had the great privilege of listening to everybody else's testimony—to get up there and close the case for them. In a sweeper position, he can clean up any messes, fill in any blanks, and leave the jury with an impression of exactly what the prosecutors want to prove.

So every time I glanced over to their side of the courtroom, I had to suffer a glimpse of that man's face.

Part of me wondered if I knew too much. Maybe this would be easier if I was blissfully ignorant. Maybe I'd read about too many of these cases. Every time I felt like we were doing okay, I immediately went back to thinking that I would be blindsided by a guilty verdict in the end. *Maybe Sherri was a better witness than I realized. Maybe the jury heard the "pain" in her voice and took it as real.* I told myself I needed to keep my emotions out of it. I needed to stay focused. I needed to take notes and pay attention to every word. I needed to remind myself that all that mattered were the facts. All that mattered was the truth. We weren't going to prove my innocence by proving that Sherri Wilson was out to get me. If we were going to prove my innocence (which I very seriously doubted), we would do it by proving that it didn't happen, it couldn't have happened the way they said it happened, and it simply didn't make sense.

Lucky for all of us, it seemed the State's next witness did a whole lot of that work for us.

"The State calls Sandra Lamb," Chris Arnt said.

Sandra Lamb came strolling up to the witness stand in a pair of dark tan slacks and a fashionable sweater that tied down low around her waist, over a blouse that was unusually conservative for her, based on my prior observations. Her hair looked freshly done, with blond highlights streaked over her dark brown hair. She wasn't somber and sort of meek or nervous looking like Sherri Wilson had appeared to me. She actually smiled a bit as she took her oath to tell the truth, and after introducing herself directly to the jury as "the mother of Brianna Lamb," I could see her sucking in her cheeks, as if she were trying to hide a smile or stop from laughing.

They spent the first few minutes of Sandra's testimony talking about how she knew the Wilsons and how she knew the McDonalds. They spent the next few minutes talking all about Brianna's movie roles and trying to make the point that neither film she was in dealt with any kind of "sexual" abuse—seemingly ignoring the fact that the films dealt with abuse and neglect of other sorts. The next few minutes were dedicated to her involvement in my wedding plans.

Then it got interesting. Sandra started talking about a time when I called her up to tell her that I thought Ashley was being sexually abused over at Joal's house—by Sarah.

Sandra talked about the conversation we'd had about this subject as if it were real. As if that call or that conversation ever happened.

"I said 'What?'" Sandra testified on the stand. "And you still let her go over there? She's like, 'Well.' And I said, 'It would be a cold day in hell before my child would go, I don't care. If I thought my child was being sexually abused at her dad's . . . she wouldn't go back.' And she said to me that it is very hard to prove 'female-on-female abuse.' Tonya told me that."

Chris Arnt asked her when that conversation happened.

"It was when Brianna was in kindergarten," she said. Arnt tried to narrow down whether it was the fall of 2005 or the spring of 2006 of that school year, and Sandra didn't hesitate for one second. "I would say 2006," she said.

So two full years before I had any inkling that anything might be going on at Joal's house? Two full years before Ashley mentioned anything to me about showering and shaving? She's telling this courtroom that I thought Ashley was being sexually abused in Joal's house way back when she was four years old? And I didn't do anything about it? Joal and Sarah weren't even married until December of 2006.

The ADA then moved on, asking Sandra when she first learned that something had happened to Brianna.

"It was toward the end of her second-grade year," Sandra said. "And honestly, I don't remember what made her start talking about playing girlfriend and boyfriend, and that Ashley had wanted her to play girlfriend and boyfriend. And I said, 'Well, Brianna, you know that's not right,' and she said, 'No, but Ashley told me if I didn't that she would tell her mommy, that Brianna wanted to and that her mommy would believe Ashley and then that Brianna would get in trouble.

"I actually called DFACS, it was May, around the 19th, and I actually called because I actually thought Ashley was being abused by Sarah. I wasn't really talking to Tonya anymore at that time," she said.

Arnt asked why she had stopped talking to me, and that was when the storytelling really got started. She told the jury that by the time my wedding reception was over, she'd discovered that I "wasn't the person" she thought I was. She said she had a problem with me at the Walker County Gala in November 2007, but then she never specified what the problem was. She then described the goings-on at Ashley's January 2008 birthday party (which Sherri had testified contrary to there being any problems at the party), and said that was when our friendship ended.

So our friendship was over, but she was calling DFACS about my daughter being molested by Sarah Henke? She and Joal didn't even know each other.

Arnt kept things moving quickly.

They dug into the whole "sex" and "kissing" sidewalk chalk incident with Skyler Walker, only Sandra said it was *three* words that Skyler wrote: "sex, love, and kissing." She testified about asking Brianna *all about it* back at their house, in her bedroom, while she stood in the bathroom. "Brianna was kind of shaking, and I thought, *Something else has happened to her,*" she testified. So she asked her if anything else had happened. "She said, 'Yes.' Ashley used to touch her in her privates . . ."

She testified to telling Brianna she hadn't done anything wrong and asking yet again if anything else had happened. "To be perfectly honest, I thought Brianna was going to say that Tyler Henke, Tonya's son, had been a part of this."

Don't you dare drag Tyler into this now. I was so mad.

"Is that what she said?" Arnt asked.

"No. She said that Miss Tonya had done stuff to her. She was, like, hysterical at that point. And I was in total shock. In total shock. That was the furthest thing ever from my mind. I would've never thought that was what she was going to say to me," she said, rolling her eyes.

She then said she gave Greg, her husband, the DFACS card and told him to call them right away. "We were both in shock. I can't even explain the shock," she said. Brianna was "hysterical," and yet, at some point in the next day or two or three, Brianna insisted that she wanted to talk to Sherri.

Okay, so now we're going to get a connection to that Sherri conversation on the driveway, I thought. But they never actually connected the dots. They never explained why Sandra was saying all of this happened *before* Brianna talked to Sherri, while Sherri had said that *she* was the one who first told Sandra all the awful things Brianna had told her about what I'd supposedly done to her.

Instead, Sandra said DFACS called her back and said that it would have to be handled by a detective. "They told me not to ask her another question, not to say anything else to her," Sandra said.

She said Brianna talked about "Miss Tonya" doing the hand thing, pressing her fingers together, pointed upward. She also said that Brianna was afraid that Sandra "was going to get hurt," because "Tonya had threatened to 'kill'" her if Brianna ever said anything. Sandra couldn't remember when Brianna said either of those things.

Sandra kept biting her bottom lip and shaking her head and rolling her eyes as she talked about Brianna having nightmares ever since that time. "She would kick and say, 'Don't touch me, don't touch me.' You could look at her, like you give kids a stern look, and she'd say, 'Don't look at me like that . . . That's what *Miss Tonya* used to do!'"

They began talking about Brianna's therapy with Laurie Evans, through which it became apparent that Brianna "has a real problem with the color yellow," she said. Brianna was still in therapy with Laurie, she confirmed.

"She said that that was Tonya's favorite color, and she just hated the color yellow. They have worked on that issue. She doesn't have as big of a problem [now]," she said in response to Arnt's questioning about it. "Honestly, it triggers at different times. We may be at a restaurant and there's a yellow-colored crayon on the table and she breaks it in half. And other times she doesn't."

We had all seen Brianna coloring with a yellow crayon in her very first interview—when all of this was freshest in her mind. That just seems completely made up right there. I wrote a note about that and passed it to Scott.

Sandra then went on to talk about the times she caught Brianna masturbating.

"She would sit on the floor, sometimes she would sit like Indian style, and sometimes she would sit with like her legs behind this part of her body, with like her privates touching the floor. I was like, 'Brianna, what are you doing?'" she said. Brianna wasn't using her hand, she was fully clothed, she was just contracting her muscles, she testified.

"Did you ever ask her where she learned to do that?" Arnt asked. *Do kids normally learn to do that from someone else? Is that how it works? Can they just make a statement about child behavioral issues without any kind of reference to back it up?*

Sandra let out a big puff of air and said, "I did. She said that's what Miss Tonya had taught them to do—*her* to do," she said, correcting herself with an exaggerated eye roll.

According to her testimony, it was some time after she got caught masturbating in a classroom in third grade that Brianna then told Sandra about an incident she hadn't yet mentioned. In fact, it was when Sandra walked in on Brianna touching her "anus" when she was getting out of the tub that Sandra said, "What are you doing?"

She testified, "And she started crying, and then she said, um, 'When Miss Tonya would put us in the bathtub,' that that's what she would do to them. That she would have soap on her hands and stuff and that she would stick fingers up their bottoms.

"The next day she had therapy, and I called the Advocacy Center and said, 'Brianna has remembered something else.' And I didn't question her a lot more about it because I knew she had therapy and I had already been told not to question. So, when we got to the Advocacy Center for her therapy, they were going to do like a taped interview."

Sandra claimed she had never seen any of the interviews with Brianna. Then Arnt said, "That is all the questions that we have at this time, Your Honor."

Scott popped up and walked over to the podium instantly.

He started by asking Sandra if she was a "caring mom" and if she would ever put her child in a situation that she thought was unsafe. She answered yes to the first question and no to the second question, of course. As any mother would.

He then worked very hard to try to pin her down about just how often Brianna spent the night over at Ashley's house and when.

"I couldn't give you a number," she said.

Scott pressed her. "More than ten?"

"Yes," she said, shrugging her shoulders and shaking her head.

"So if Brianna told us it was only one time, she would be mistaken?"

Sandra agreed that one time would be incorrect. She also said that she was never concerned about Brianna staying over at my house, adding that she had no indication that anything might have been wrong after she stayed at my house—ever.

Asked to describe whether Brianna showed any behavior that concerned her, Sandra said, "I had never had a little girl, but she would tell me that—if she got mad or got in trouble or anything—she would tell me that I didn't love her, and she wanted a new mommy because I didn't love her, and I had no clue where that came from. I never associated it at that point with anything else."

"But you do now?" Scott asked her.

"Yes, I do now," Sandra said, sternly.

"But she would only do that when she would get in trouble?"

"I guess when I may have spoken sternly with her."

Scott confirmed that those were the only times when Brianna would act out toward Sandra—when Sandra had spoken sternly to her or gotten her in trouble.

I don't think Sandra realized how important that statement was.

Sandra could not recall on that witness stand when she first let Brianna sleep over at my house. Scott pressed her for specifics, like whether it was soon after we met or during the first half of Brianna's kindergarten year, and she just repeated, "I have no idea. That wasn't something that I kept track of."

She visibly tensed up and appeared to get upset when Scott pressed her for specifics. Scott tried to ask her about what she'd told us on the record back in our depositions, and she got what looked to me like a nasty look on her face. She interrupted Scott. "You should allow me to finish my answer," she said, and she pointed a finger at him and stared at him.

"As soon as I'm done with my question, I will," Scott said.

The basic point Sandra eventually made was that her daughter spent the night at my home in Chickamauga when Brianna was in kindergarten and that she stopped spending nights at my house "at some point during the first grade."

I wasn't living in that house during Brianna's kindergarten year.

Sandra looked over at the prosecution table during this questioning. Her eyes kept darting over to them, and she even gave them a little shake of her head, which to me looked like she just couldn't *believe* the questioning.

Sandra couldn't pin down how many times she had come to my house to drop Brianna off, or to pick her up, or how many times I'd dropped her off after a sleepover.

She seemed to be forgetting that in her initial calls to DFACS, she told the person who took the call that Brianna had *never* spent the night at my house after the end of her kindergarten year. Scott pointed out that fact to Sandra. *We had the written records of that call.* She still said she didn't remember saying that.

Scott asked her whether Brianna ever seemed "nervous" or "apprehensive" or "scared" around me in all the time we were together, and she answered "no" to every one of those questions.

Then there was a turning point in Sandra's whole demeanor. Scott asked about the fact that Brianna really seemed to like me in kindergarten and wondered why Brianna would in later interviews say that she "hated" me during that school year. Sandra took a big long pause, and rolled her eyes a little, and started to use her hands when she spoke: "I can tell you right now if you ask me to tell you one thing about Tonya that's *good*, I couldn't tell you anything—although I know I felt good about her in kindergarten. Brianna right now has no good feelings about Tonya."

"I understand," Scott said. "Y'all call her 'the Evil One,' right?"

"Absolutely," Sandra said.

"Absolutely!" Scott repeated back to her.

"We're healthy, we can say her name is Tonya, but, um, the Evil One is just much easier for us."

"Talk about her rottin' in jail, right?" Scott said.

"Objection," Arnt called out.

"Sustained," Judge House said.

At that point Sandra scrunched her face up and looked at the prosecutors and shook her head, with a shrug and an angry-sounding laugh. She looked tense on the stand and from that point forward she appeared much more combative. She answered Scott's questions with what seemed like attitude to spare, whether she was confirming her daughter's presence in a series of photos in my classroom, or talking about Brianna's acting abilities, or talking about the cards and gifts she'd given me proclaiming just how great a teacher she thought I was before any of this started.

The thing was, along the way, Scott got her to confirm that Brianna was always smiling and relaxed around me and choosing to come into my classroom and visit me after school. Brianna was perfectly normal around me all the way up until that moment when I'd spoken "sternly" to her during Ashley's birthday party in January 2008.

Scott also got her to confirm just how much Brianna was out of town while she was working on movies during part of the same time period when they were alleging that she'd stayed at my house and I'd "done" these horrible things to her.

He managed to do all of that before lunch, and I don't think Sandra had any idea how much conflicting information she'd just shared in front of that jury.

By the time we got back from lunch, Sandra seemed even more annoyed at the whole thing. She snapped at Scott's questions any number of times, right from the start, and she even looked at Arnt and whispered, "I'm sorry," after one of those instances.

As Scott continued walking Sandra through the entire timeline of how much time I spent with her and with Brianna, including at my wedding, she made a big point of telling that courtroom that the only reason she let me spend my wedding night at her house was because I was too drunk to drive home. As if it were a last-minute decision. She also mentioned the big stain on her carpet from where I'd thrown up. All the while, all she really was doing was confirming that Brianna was around and that not for one minute did she act scared of me. In fact, just the opposite.

Even in 2008, Brianna was playing softball that spring, and Sandra testified that she would run into me at the Chickamauga ball fields through May of that year. Scott asked her how often she would see me, and she said, "I have no idea." He asked whether it was once a week, or twice, or more, and she adamantly answered that she had "no idea."

"Do you have any memory problems, ma'am?"

Sandra looked dumbfounded. She didn't answer.

"Have you been diagnosed with any problems with your memory?" Scott repeated.

"Are you kidding?" Sandra said.

"No, ma'am," Scott said.

"No, I haven't," she said, staring at the prosecutors. Her jaw grew so tight it looked like her chin might break off. Someone on their side of the courtroom even let out a big audible gasp, like they were horrified that Scott would ask such a thing. There would be a time later in the trial where someone on my side of the courtroom gasped, and Judge House stopped everything to have them thrown out. He didn't do that when folks gasped on the prosecution's side.

"Can I have some water?" Sandra asked the judge at that point.

Scott went on to get Sandra to admit that she was "angry" at me for reprimanding her daughter at Ashley's birthday party. "When somebody pushes me or messes with my children or my family, I have a horrible temper," she said.

Sandra could not "recall" what she'd told the person at DFACS during her first call to them, so Scott went to the written records of that call and reminded her. Reading from the report, Scott noted that the *reason* she'd started questioning Brianna about what "happened to her" was because Brianna was suffering from "night frights." Scott tried to pin her down on whether or not those night frights began around the time that she took Brianna and some friends to see the horror film she was in, which was also in January of 2008—a "scary" horror film that Sandra admitted she would never have taken Brianna to see if she weren't in it. She seemed appalled at the idea that Brianna could have been traumatized by watching an R-rated horror film and instead wanted to focus all of her daughter's fears on *me*.

I remember being so thankful in that moment that we'd done all the homework we'd done. I thought of Eric Echols and some of the details he'd managed to dig up for us, which were about to put a big wrinkle in the latest iterations of Sandra's story.

With a little help from the transcript of Sandra's very first call to DFACS on May 19, 2008, Sandra finally admitted that *she'd* been the one to start questioning Brianna about whether or not anything had "happened to her"—but she still tried to insist that she only did that after Brianna had told her about the boyfriend-girlfriend game. Using the transcript as a crutch (since she testified that she had "no memory" of any of this), Sandra confirmed that she then had asked Brianna whether someone "had done something to her," to which Brianna initially responded, "No." Then she had asked Brianna, "Did anything happen when you were with Miss Tonya?" To which Brianna responded, "No." Then she had asked her daughter whether she could think of anything else that made her uncomfortable, and Brianna had responded to that question: "Tonya was mean to me."

"So that's it?" Sandra had responded. And Brianna, she agreed, had said, "Yes. That's it."

Scott basically brought her right back to the original moment of her questioning Brianna and showed that jury that Sandra was the one who seemed to push the idea of "Tonya" doing something *to her* into Brianna's mind. As I listened, I thought, *As soon as Brianna confirmed to her that I had done something (by being "mean to her"), Sandra jumped right onto it, and wouldn't let go.*

Sandra looked all kinds of flustered to me as this questioning went on.

Scott got her to say that she'd questioned Brianna "at least four times" before Brianna came up with any accusations against anyone.

"I can tell that you're trying to confuse me," she testified, "and I understand that, and I knew you would . . . You act like I just asked Brianna all of these *leading* questions, and that's not what happened! I wasn't interrogating her!" she insisted.

"I'll rephrase for your sake. Did you consider for one moment that it might be better for you to stop repeatedly questioning her about this and allow somebody that was trained professionally to question her?" Scott said.

Sandra's only response was, "I had never dealt with anything like this in my life."

Hearing that answer, I once again had a thought about Sandra Lamb that I very much didn't want to have: I felt sorry for her. I was furious; I was livid that I had to look at her for all of those hours in that courtroom. Yet at the same time, I felt sorry for her. I truly did.

I felt even sorrier for her daughter.

Scott's questioning went on for hours. He went over every bit of everything that had happened, including how many times Sandra had spoken to the detectives in the case and how often she'd been in contact with Joal. Scott asked her about the various interviews and whether she had talked to the interviewers in between the questioning—and whenever he asked what seemed to me like a sticky question, Sandra simply said that she couldn't remember.

Scott then asked her about Brianna's undocumented June 4, 2008, charge of me putting my whole hand up into her privates. While Brianna had said she told Suzie Thorne about it while they were walking down the hall, Sandra said Brianna told *her* that she forgot to tell Thorne something, and then they went to find Thorne together. And let's not forget the story Sherri had told about being the first to hear of this disgusting "revelation."

I just hoped the jury was picking up on all of those little discrepancies. Those little differences mattered.

Near the end of the day, Sandra answered some redirect questions from Chris Arnt, and then some additional re-cross from Scott. In that short exchange, she mentioned a time that I supposedly had Brianna at my house all by myself without her knowing it, after my own kids had gone to Joal's for the weekend. She testified that she couldn't recall a date for that or an approximate time when "it happened." As far as my team knew, she had never mentioned it anywhere on the record before that moment. She didn't even allege that anything had happened on that particular occasion. She just mentioned it, as if she wanted the jury to fill in the blanks.

That never happened.

She also spoke of the fact that her husband had filed for a divorce and said that the stress of this situation—caused by me—was a factor in the divorce itself, despite the fact that there is no mention of my case in the divorce petition that Greg Lamb had filed. In fact, that petition—which we had a copy of and which Scott placed right in front of her—had Greg placing blame on Sandra's behavior.[60]

It was hard for me to imagine that Sandra might really believe everything she testified to. How awful that must be for her if it's the case. The fact that her marriage had fallen apart and that so much of the blame for everything in her life seemed to be placed on me, *the Evil One,* made me once again feel sorry for her.

When I stopped and thought about the truth, I went right back to feeling angry instead. But by the end of that day, the only thing I felt was exhaustion. Facing Sandra Lamb in the courtroom had been a long time coming. It was over now. Whether a jury would wind up believing her or me was in God's hands.

Chapter 52

O n the seventh day, my trial seemed to pick up steam. The Sandra Lamb testimony was referred to as a potential turning point by my team and my supporters the night before. I didn't see it as a turning point. I didn't feel more secure for one second about my chances. It did seem as if the prosecution side had grown increasingly annoyed at my attorneys' long, detailed questioning of their witnesses. It felt like they were starting to lose their cool.

I was proud of my team. All I wanted them to do was to keep pushing for the truth, to keep their composure, and to never lose their cool no matter how heated anything got.

The day started with one more "victim's mother" on the witness stand: Kelly McDonald. Kelly's presence was very different from Sandra's. She didn't seem to carry such an edge or an attitude into the courtroom. She came across to me as more down-to-earth. I wondered if the jury might find her more sympathetic because of that.

The prosecution presented Kelly as my former "best friend." She got up there and talked about how our friendship developed and how she and her kids used to spend time at my house frequently.

As far as I was concerned, the most important factor in Kelly's whole testimony was that she testified to questioning her daughter, Chloe, repeatedly on the way to both of her interviews with Detective Tim Deal. She didn't admit to "coaching" or planting ideas in her head. But she did say on that stand that she'd questioned Chloe before she sat down for her interviews—and we were prepared to use our expert witnesses later on in this trial to explain to the jury just exactly how damaging and influential *any* such questioning can be to a young child.

"I said, honey, if anything else has happened, you need to tell Mommy, because you're fixing to have to talk to the police," Kelly testified. "She was scared. She was crying. And I said, 'It's okay, you haven't done anything wrong.'"

Kelly also tried to make it sound like she had "no idea" any allegations were being raised against me before she took her daughter in for questioning that first time on May 29.

"I only knew I was there to talk about child-on-child," she insisted.

We had documentation to back up the fact that she absolutely knew that Chloe was going to talk about me during that first interview. She had filled out a child victim information sheet at the CAC when she brought Chloe in on May 29. On that form, she wrote, "I caught my daughter, Chloe, and Ashley Henke under the bed and Ashley was touching Chloe in her private area and then told her to do the same thing to her to make her feel good. Then when I confronted Chloe about the situation at Ashley's house the night in question with Brianna, Skyler, Chloe, and Ashley she told me Ms. Tonya had touched her in her privates and touched Brianna in her privates."

The jury hadn't heard much about Skyler yet. They hadn't heard that after the chalk incident, she had gone in to be interviewed and had made absolutely no allegations against me whatsoever. But they had heard from Brianna, and from Ashley, and neither of those two girls backed up Chloe's claim that they had all been present together when any touching was allegedly going on. *So where is Chloe getting this story from? Who is it that put that idea in her head?*

I hadn't had a chance to go back and relisten to Chloe's interviews yet. Now that I'd heard her mother's testimony admitting to the fact that she'd "questioned" her on the way to those interviews, I was determined to go back and review them to see if there was anything we'd missed.

———————✦———————

Next up for the prosecution was Suzie Thorne, the interviewer from the Greenhouse who had interviewed Ashley and then performed Brianna's third interview on June 4, 2008—the one that led to my arrest, despite the fact that Brianna made no mention of "penetration" whatsoever.

The prosecutors actually spent a long time with Suzie. They went through her educational history. They talked about her job. They talked about the fact that she'd been trained not to ask leading questions. On the surface, she seemed like a decent interviewer and somebody who could be trusted. She didn't seem like a mean person who would try to twist the words of a child. In fact, to the jury I bet she seemed pretty sympathetic. She had left the Greenhouse after four and a half years to go back to work as a detective, she said, because there was only "so much" you can hear from little kids who've been molested. *I can't imagine a more difficult job*, I thought. *The trauma of that, day in and day out, must do something to a person.*

Of course, I also thought, *If you messed up these interviews with Ashley and Brianna this badly, how many other times have you done that? How many children have you traumatized? How many other families have you helped to destroy?*

The prosecution actually went ahead and showed the entire videotaped interview with Ashley while Thorne was on the stand. I had to sit there and endure that videotape of my daughter. Again. They played it all the way through her crying and protesting that she wanted to leave at the end, and I supposed that they wanted the jury to see that as an example of the "breakdowns" that these girls supposedly had when they were talking about the abuse at my hands. At least, that was how Len Gregor had presented it in his opening argument.

When Doc got up to question her, he took a similar approach to the one he'd taken with Sharon Anderson. He went back through Thorne's educational history and training on dealing with child sexual abuse. He asked her about some well-known studies on the ins and outs of child interviews, none of which she was familiar with. He asked her about some well-known false-allegation cases that anyone in the field should be aware of, including the Michaels case in New Jersey, which was one that I read about online in some of my very first Google searches because it was so well-known and well documented. Thorne testified that she hadn't heard of it.

He then took Thorne line by line through her interviews, and the discussion got pretty heated at times. He tried to make her admit that *she* was the one introducing ideas in the interviews: terms like "good touch" and "bad touch." He pointed out the fact that she had grilled Ashley "sixteen times" to see if she had anything else to say, even though she said "no" each and every time.

Thorne countered that she wasn't trying to introduce ideas into the girls' heads; she was simply trying to get information. The prosecution made a point of saying that everyone's interview techniques are different, but Thorne simply didn't seem to be able to refute what Doc was saying.

It went on for a very long time, and I hoped the jury was getting the gist of it all—without getting so tired that they'd have some kind of a backlash reaction to the flood of information and detail.

Then Doc finally came to the crux of the Suzie Thorne problem: When it came to Brianna Lamb's accusations, she hadn't captured everything on tape. In fact, it wasn't revealed until the trial, right there in that courtroom, that Brianna's most egregious accusation—the mysterious charge of "penetration" that led to my first arrest—had originally been made to Suzie Thorne. It was just *after* Brianna's June 4, 2008, interview when Brianna supposedly made the assertion that I'd put my fingers together and stuck my whole hand up inside her privates.

"That wasn't videotaped. It should have been videotaped and followed up on, but it wasn't. That was my fault," Thorne said on the witness stand.

"It sure *should* have been videotaped," Doc said in a tone that came pretty close to a reprimand, "because that's a major felony that *you* say, and *she* said, that *she's* not talking about [on the tape]."

"You're correct," Thorne said.

"Major felony!" Doc added.

"You're right," Thorne said with a contrite look on her face.

Thorne went on to testify about how it supposedly happened. She said Brianna had already gone back to her mother after the interview was all over. Then Brianna wandered back to Thorne's office all by herself, she said, to tell Thorne that she'd "forgot to tell her" that Tonya had stuck her whole hand up inside her vagina.

Her story about the details of that moment didn't match Brianna's testimony or Sandra's testimony. But it turned out that wasn't the biggest issue.

Thorne testified she "thought" that a "deputy" who was present was writing down the accusation, but she clearly had no idea where that documentation had gone—which to me made it sound like maybe it never really existed. We asked who that officer was, and she said it was Detective Stephen Keith. *The personal friend of the Wilsons*, I thought. *The man who started this entire investigation. A man whom the prosecutors have still not called to testify.*

Doc pointed out that the prosecution didn't present any documentation for that charge in the entire case history. It is the *law* that any accusation of child molestation *must* be videotaped in the state of Georgia, he noted. Doc made the point that there was no good reason that Thorne couldn't have immediately taken Brianna back in front of the camera and asked her about the incident on the record—but for some reason, she didn't do that.

Thorne didn't have any good explanation as to why.

My team and supporters might have thought that Sandra Lamb's testimony was a turning point in the trial, but *that* was a bigger turning point to me. That revelation in that courtroom, which took all of us by surprise, called into question the very reality of the penetration charges for which I had been arrested in the first place, and at the very least called into question whether that accusation was properly obtained.

I sure hoped the jury was letting that revelation sink in.

More than that, I hoped the prosecutors were letting it sink in. *Aren't making up charges or arresting someone on undocumented charges both FBI-investigation-worthy offenses? Couldn't an ADA get disbarred, or even arrested, if that's what happened?*

Most of all, I hoped Judge House was paying attention. *Is he going to ignore this, too?*

Given the disclosure that just happened in that courtroom, he had every reason to stop the trial and to dismiss Brianna's penetration counts of the indictment right there. *He* should have been the one to demand an investigation into why that accusation wasn't videotaped, why no written documentation of that accusation was put into the record, and how that nonvideotaped accusation had been allowed to move forward as a part of my original arrest warrant.

But he didn't do it.

I thought I was gonna scream. I held it in. I listened to my attorneys. They said we would request a dismissal of those charges when the appropriate time came. Not now, but later.

That night we decided to try to get all of Suzie Thorne's testimony thrown out, since she seemed to have knowingly broken protocol by not videotaping Brianna's accusation. But when it came to the rest of the charges, for now, we'd just have to go on breaking down the prosecution's case as best we could—and once again hope the jury paid more attention to the law than the officials in that courtroom whose job it was to uphold it.

Chapter 53

There wasn't a chance of me sleeping that night. I was fuming. I still had my friend Jennifer's key that she'd given me way back when I was staying in the motor home. She continued to tell me that her door was always open. So I grabbed some of my files and my trusty black laptop and I drove over there to find some solace on her downstairs sofa.

For days I had been thinking that I hadn't spent enough time micro-analyzing Detective Tim Deal's interviews with Chloe McDonald. So I sat on the couch in the middle of the night and listened to those tapes on my black laptop with the volume up loud and my headphones plugged in. I listened and listened, and every time there was an "inaudible" in the transcript I pushed pause and wrote down what I heard. It was actually pretty easy. *Whoever did these transcripts wasn't very good at their job.*

It was right around 2:00 A.M. when I started all the way back at the beginning of Chloe's very first interview and gave it another listen. I looked at the transcript, at one of the questions right near the top—shortly after Tim Deal introduced himself and reminded Chloe that he was a police officer who had known her family for a long time.

"And you're not in any trouble and you're not here to get your friend in any trouble . . . I just need to know the truth. Uh. Do you remember anything about that?" the transcript read.

"Yeah, uh, I just remember a place and, uh, uh, (INAUDIBLE) where they touched me . . ." Chloe said.

I paused the recording.

Oh my gosh. What she said wasn't "inaudible" at all. I backed it up and listened to it again, and wrote down Chloe's words *exactly*. What she said, clear as day, was, "Yeah, uh, I just remember a place and, uh, uh, my mom told me which is which and where they touched me . . ."

My mom told me which is which and where they touched me.

"My mom told me" changed the meaning of the entire interview that followed, in my opinion. And it wasn't muffled or distorted at all. I listened to it a whole bunch of times in a row, and I couldn't understand how none of us had caught it before. Her words were clear as day! I didn't adjust the tape. I didn't alter any settings. I didn't have it enhanced by some professional in order to bring it to light. All I did was listen. Really listen. *The way any professional transcriber who's working for the Catoosa County detectives on an alleged child-molestation case should surely be listening themselves*, I thought.

I called Doc right away. He didn't pick up. I called Cary. I called Scott. I called Clancy. Everybody'd gone to sleep and must've turned off their phones. This was a key piece of missing evidence for our defense against Chloe, and really, in a way, our defense against everything. It seemed to me that all *three* of the girls' interviews had very clear mention of directions and ideas they were given by either their mommas (in Brianna's and Chloe's cases) or their daddy (in Ashley's case). To me, it felt like I'd found a missing piece of the puzzle—and it was sitting right there in front of us the whole time.

I drove back to the house at about 6:00 A.M. I didn't even shower first. I just ran in and said, "Guys, you've got to listen to this and tell me what you hear." I didn't tell them what I thought it said. I made each one of them put the headphones on and listen for themselves, independently. I had them write down what they heard and then fold up the piece of paper and hand it to me. I wouldn't let any of them speak a word of it to each other. Somebody got the coffeepot going.

As I unfolded the pieces of paper, I held them up for everybody to read. Every single member of my team heard the same words that I did. They all wrote down the exact same thing: "My mom told me which is which and where they touched me."

———————————◆———————————

Judge House started day eight of my trial by denying our request to throw out Suzie Thorne's testimony. *Of course.* Then the prosecution called their next "expert" interviewer, Stacy Long—the woman who'd conducted the very first interviews with Brianna. They presented Long basically the same way they had presented Thorne, by listing her credentials and training, and Doc got up and broke all of that down again, getting Long to admit that she didn't read peer-reviewed journals on the subject about which she claimed to be an expert and that she didn't know about certain cases that were very prominent in the history of child interviews, etc.

Doc then questioned her for several hours about the way she interviewed Brianna. He especially seemed to hammer her on the moment when she asked Brianna if "Tonya" had asked her to touch me back.

"Had the child brought up a*ny idea whatsoever* about Tonya requesting to be touched by a child?" Doc asked her.

"No," Long said.

"That idea came from you," Doc said.

"That's a common question to ask in a forensic interview," she said. "Reciprocal touches—but, yes, I brought it up."

Doc used more examples directly from her own interviews with Brianna to ask whether her "introducing ideas" into the discussion could have caused the child to then incorporate her words and ideas into the child's memories and descriptions of what happened.

Long's basic response was the same as Thorne's: She didn't think so, and it wasn't her intent.

This was certainly one of Doc's biggest areas of expertise, going all the way back to the "mousetrap studies" and more. He'd stood in front of that jury three times now, with all three of the State's biggest experts, and in my opinion had shown that they really weren't the authorities they claimed to be.

He also asked Long extensively about the possibility of parental influence on the interviews. "Possible parental influences?"

Long threw her hand up in the air. "I don't know," she said. "I mean, I don't know where she got it from."

"Possible rumor formation?"

"Possible," Long said, shrugging.

Well, d'you think you might've mentioned that there were signs of parental influence and rumor formation when it happened? How could you not include any of that balancing information in your summary of that girl's interview?

I wished I could've stood up and yelled at her. Luckily, I had Doc there to stick to the facts without ever losing his cool.

When the prosecution called Detective Tim Deal to the stand next, I felt like I was going to fall right off my chair. *Could this be it?* I wondered. I expected they'd call him to the stand last. *What about Joal and Sarah? Are they skipping right over them?*

Deal got up there in a gray suit with a blue diagonal-striped tie, looking very official, and he put reading glasses on to read his own reports of the day he came and knocked on my door. He then proceeded to testify to details that drastically contradicted my memory of what happened that awful day, right from the very beginning—just as he'd testified during the motion hearing at the start of the trial.

He told that jury that when he mentioned the allegations to me, I turned so "beet red" that my face was almost "purple."

"She became just flushed, almost like a fight-or-flight type syndrome reaction," he said. "She started becoming very nervous," he added. "I thought she was gonna hyperventilate."

Even if that wasn't an overblown exaggeration of my reaction, I thought, *wouldn't that be a perfectly fitting reaction for someone who's just been accused of something so horrible? It's almost like there's no correct way to react. These prosecutors and detectives will spin anything you do just about any which way they want. If I had stood there calmly, they would have called me "stone cold."*

All in all, I didn't think there was anything unexpected or telling about Deal's testimony. He recounted the story that the prosecution had seemed to try to paint from the start. He basically stuck to the story that Len Gregor had laid out during his opening statement.

It seemed to me that wherever there was something that had gone unexplained in the prosecution's case, Deal was right there ready to explain it. For instance, he recounted the way Detective Stephen Keith had told him about the charges Brianna made at the Greenhouse—and then the prosecutors produced a copy of the written report that Keith had supposedly written to document Brianna's whole-hand-penetration charge that she made to Suzie Thorne. A document that had never appeared before that moment, in nearly two whole years. My attorneys went nuts over that one. They demanded an original copy of it so we could have it ink-dated. They demanded an immediate investigation of the prosecutors' and detectives' computers to confirm the originating date of this "newly created evidence."

Of course, none of that would come to pass. The judge would simply note our objections but never order any kind of an investigation whatsoever.[61]

As the hours ticked by, the judge ordered a recess until the next morning. Deal would continue on the witness stand. He showed up in a light gray suit this time, with a dark red shirt, and he went over the timelines of the interviews he conducted.

He actually sat up there and had the audacity to tell the jury that he proceeded with "caution" as the case went forward, because he was aware of the "sensitivity" of the case—because I was a teacher, he said.

Under cross-examination from Scott, he admitted that he'd seen cases where children had been influenced and essentially given false memories by adults. He said that it usually happened in drawn-out custody cases, as far as he had seen. We put some former testimony in front of him, from a case where he himself had testified that younger children are "more susceptible" to suggestion.

He agreed that parents questioning their children before a forensic interview could sometimes taint a child's recollections.

He agreed that when it comes to small children, it is his responsibility to work hard to "investigate" the allegations and to look for "evidence"— not simply to rely on the words of the accusers.

He agreed that forensic interviews should be unbiased, that they should not be suggestive or leading—and then Scott went through his entire investigation and pointed to all of the points where my team believed suggestions and parental influence and an overall lack of investigation could be shown.

When it came to differences that showed up between transcripts of interviews and the summaries of interviews and the number of "inaudibles" in the transcripts of Chloe's interviews, Deal chalked it up to simple "typos" and other "clerical" errors. He talked about those errors in what sounded to me like a very nonchalant voice, as if those differences were of no real importance—as if they didn't change the outcome or allegations at all.

Then Deal testified on that stand that if he had known that Chloe's mother had been questioning her on the ride over to the interview, he would have been concerned about what she said and would have perhaps asked some questions differently in order to discern any witness tainting.

Finally, after a whole long day of cross-examination, Scott asked Detective Deal to take a look back at page 5 of his original May 29, 2008, interview with Chloe McDonald. Scott asked him whether he remembered hearing what was written as "inaudible" in that one particular "inaudible" moment that I'd discovered two nights earlier. Detective Deal said he didn't remember it, "No."

Everyone turned to page 5 of that interview transcript as Scott asked the court to replay that portion of the tape. Detective Deal had to step off of the witness stand in order to see the video, because there was a technical error of some sort with the big screen. It took a few minutes to get the DVD playing. So there was a big long pause in the courtroom before it happened. My stomach got all tied in knots as we waited for it.

Scott turned the volume way up, so everyone in the courtroom could hear the voice of that little girl. It struck me just how tiny Chloe sounded.

The video finally started back on page 4 of the transcript somewhere, so it took a few minutes more to get up to the moment. And then it happened.

"This is the part I want you to pay attention to," Scott said.

"Do you remember anything about that?" Detective Deal had asked Chloe on the tape.

Chloe had responded in that little voice of hers, after looking at the camera for a moment and appearing as if she were thinking real hard: "Uh, uh, and my mom told me which is which and where they touched me."

"Okay stop," Scott said. "Did she just say, 'I think my mom told me which is where they touched me'?"

Deal answered, "I heard her say something about 'mom.' I'm still having a hard time."

Scott followed up: "If she had said, 'I think my mom told me which is where they touched me,' would you consider that a suggestion that might taint her interview?"

Deal didn't hesitate. "From her mother, yes," he said. "But I can't be sure that's what she said."

"I understand," Scott said. "Nothing further, Your Honor."

Chapter 54

Sarah Henke, my ex's new wife, got up on that stand and immediately testified concerning the allegations with my daughter. The showering did happen. She didn't deny it. But she seemed to try to talk her way around the shaving part when Chris Arnt asked her about it. She said that she gave Ashley an old razor of hers that never had a razor blade in it. She claimed the whole idea was Ashley's and that it was just for "pretend."

Sarah then described how she'd taken Ashley to a doctor's visit before the start of the past school year, saying that Ashley got upset and wouldn't allow the pediatrician to even "peek" down her pants. She sat there describing how traumatized she thought my daughter was. *Is she implying that Ashley was traumatized by me? If Ashley was traumatized by anything, she was traumatized by the physical examination she'd been put through because of these charges—the exam that Sarah had stood witness to, and which her own father allowed.*

I felt like I was going to throw up.

Arnt then asked Sarah whether child services had removed any children from her and Joal's care, to which she replied, "No." And that was it! She wasn't on the stand for five minutes.

By putting her on the stand for those five minutes of testimony, which in my opinion didn't seem to do anything for their case, the prosecution opened the door to us asking Sarah Henke whatever we wanted in front of that jury. *Why would they do that?* I could not wrap my mind around what those prosecutors were doing.

Scott got up and jumped quickly to the question of why she'd been showering with my daughter in the first place.

"Ashley had been coming to our house," Sarah said. "Her hair was dirty. It was matted. When she was sitting there, I could smell her. Joal and I, we both could. And Joal said, 'Will you please teach her how to bathe?'"

My daughter was never dirty. We have tons of witnesses who were with her every day who can testify to that. Sarah hadn't mentioned *any* of this during her depositions the previous year, and in fact said on the record that she had no concerns about me as a mother.[62]

After going through a couple of other allegations concerning Ashley's health, Sarah admitted on that witness stand that she was "angry" about the allegations I'd made about her and Ashley. I figured everyone listening in that courtroom could make up their own minds about what this witness's motivations might be.

She was done with her whole testimony in about half an hour, and then Joal took his oath, looking his full-on charming self in a sharp suit with a crisp white shirt and a rather peaceful-looking green tie. He started out by telling the court that we'd had a completely peaceful, "uncontested" divorce and had come to a custody agreement without any troubles. *A complete and total lie after the very first question*, I thought.

Christ Arnt then asked him whether I'd ever brought any kind of female-on-female pornographic materials into our marriage.

My whole body clenched so tight I thought I was going to implode.

"When we first started dating she went to her father's house and, uh, got a pornographic VHS tape and brought it to a date that we had," Joal said. "We were actually at her brother's house when they were out of town, that's where we were," he said.

Arnt asked him again if it was female-on-female pornography. "That particular tape at that time was a female-on-female tape. Mostly just women," Joal said.

The follow-up question was whether or not there was ever a night during our marriage when I went out with my friend Jennifer. Joal said there was. Arnt asked if there was ever a night in our marriage when I didn't come home.

"Yes, there was. Tonya . . . indicated that she was going to have a girl's night out with Jennifer"—meaning my good friend Jennifer, with the Truth Cross tattoo, who was there supporting me every day during this trial. "They went out. Tonya turned up the next afternoon. I had not heard from her, and when I did hear from her, Tonya had indicated that her and Jennifer had gone to a bar on Brainerd Road, and, uh, had drinks and that's the last she remembered. She said she woke up the next day at Jennifer's house, in Jennifer's bed, and said, 'I think maybe we were drugged and something was slipped to us.'"

Arnt reiterated that I woke up "in Jennifer's bed," and Joal said, "Yes, *in* her bed."

If I had allowed myself to react whatsoever, I think my jaw would have broken right through the table as it dropped to the floor.

My attorneys were as shocked as I was. I had told my attorneys everything I could think of about *every bit* of my past. I had told them about the sex I'd had outside of marriage. I wanted them to know everything "bad" I'd ever done, just so they wouldn't ever get blindsided in the courtroom. I never expected in a million years that I'd be accused of something so outlandish as having a lesbian affair with my friend Jennifer.

Arnt seemed to move on from that line of questioning just as quickly as he'd brought it up. He asked briefly about Joal's interaction with the McDonalds and the Lambs, whom Joal claimed not to have spoken to until May 30, 2008, and then he focused in on what Joal talked to Ashley about that same night.

"That night I sat down with Ashley in her room, and I asked Ashley, 'Has anyone ever touched you inappropriately?' She said, 'What do you mean?' And I said, 'Has anyone ever touched your privates? Anyone,' is the way I phrased it," he said.

"She said, 'Mommy did,'" Joal continued. "When she said 'Mommy did,' I said, 'How did Mommy touch you?' And she said, 'Mommy put medicine on my bottom.' And I said, 'Ashley, you know the difference between putting medicine on and being touched inappropriately. She touched your bottom or your vagina? Where were you touched?' And she said, 'She touched my vagina.'

"At that point I asked, 'Well, how did she touch you?' And she demonstrated for me. She stood up, and she put her hand between herself, and she started rubbing herself. She started rubbing her vagina, up and down, [in an] up and down motion," he said, standing up and acting it out for the courtroom in a very dramatic manner, moving his hand up and down and up and down between his legs. It didn't look sexual to me. It looked painful.

Scott got up and immediately asked Joal about our "uncontested" divorce, which Joal basically agreed was actually quite contentious. He then asked Joal about the fact that nowhere in his divorce petition did he ever mention female-on-female videotapes or my alleged "incident" with Jennifer. He asked Joal about the fact that he didn't mention those alleged incidents in the emergency custody petition he filed after the detectives rang my doorbell, either. He asked Joal if he ever mentioned any of that, at any time, until he came into this courtroom—despite the fact that it would have been important for the court to know and for the detectives to know when he first met Detective Keith and Brandon Boggess in early June of 2008. He asked Joal why he never even brought it up in the *hours* of depositions we'd put him through in the Tennessee custody dispute over the course of the previous year.

"We asked you to share every complaint you ever had against Tonya as a mother," Scott reminded him, and Joal agreed that all of that was true.

So Scott finally asked my ex-husband why he hadn't mentioned it in all of that time, and Joal said—I kid you not—that he'd just remembered it that morning when he was on his way into court.

We could hear the media folks laughing from the room next door. The judge was furious. To some people, it was funny. To me, it was sickening.

Scott went on questioning Joal for quite a while, as he did most witnesses. It seemed to me that he showed pretty clearly that Joal's story had changed over the course of the last two years. It seemed filled with holes in his memory. It appeared to be filled with new memories that he'd suddenly remembered at various points along the way. We put his phone records into evidence, showing dozens upon dozens of calls between those other families around the time of my arrest and in the months following my arrest, and hundreds of calls with Sandra Lamb alone. We didn't use the word "conspiracy." We didn't allege that he and Sandra Lamb and Sherri Wilson had done any of this because they were out to get me. The goal was to show the jury that these parents had acted hysterically, and that their hysteria and clear hatred of me influenced their decision-making abilities. We believed that we could illustrate them questioning their children in a way that would influence the children's answers, and maybe even plant false memories in these kids' heads. I, of course, felt that there were darker motives behind much of it. We just didn't want to lose the jury by talking about those motives—especially since they would be free to draw their own conclusions from the factual evidence we were putting into the record.

All I ever wanted was to be able to present the facts and let the jury decide.

Chapter 55

The prosecution put the principal of Chickamauga Elementary up on the stand, plus two teachers from that school, all of whom wound up testifying that they'd never witnessed any inappropriate behavior between me and any children.

Brianna's third-grade teacher got up there and talked about Brianna masturbating in her classroom. She said she'd called Sandra Lamb in to talk about it, and Sandra told her that "Tonya" had taught those things to her daughter.

I started to wonder if there was anyone Sandra *didn't* spread rumors to.

My team expected that the prosecution would rest their case by the end of that long afternoon. But instead, they said they were planning to call some more witnesses at the start of the following week.

What else are they still holding on to? I wondered.

The first witness they called Monday morning was Holly Kittle—the interviewer who'd conducted Brianna's fourth interview back on April 1, 2009. Kittle got up there and started talking about certain studies. She seemed to show some knowledge that the previous interviewers had not. Then Doc stood up and ripped that knowledge apart. Under his cross-examination, she testified that she had never read those studies or articles until the prosecutors gave them to her to read. Her overall lack of knowledge about the field of child interviews seemed just plain embarrassing.

Doc went after her personal connections with Len Gregor and Chris Arnt, too, noting that she was Facebook friends with both of those prosecutors. He brought up the fact that Holly had "liked" Arnt's Facebook comment about my defense team back in January—the one that called them "insane."

When Doc asked her why she "approved" of that post, she tilted her head a little and gave him what I would describe as a bit of attitude. "Well, I can say that for six years I worked for the Georgia Bureau of Investigation, I've worked death-penalty cases, I've worked high-profile cases, I've worked

311

cases that have made *national media*," she said, giving a little side glance to the jury, "and I had never in my career seen anything like this before."

Doc paused for a moment.

"So, what has that got to do with whether the defense lawyers are 'insane'?" he asked her. "Anything?"

"No," she said, putting her head down—meekly, I thought—and averting her eyes.

Doc then went in for the kill, pointing out all of what he'd deemed points of "suggestion" during the interview she'd done with Brianna Lamb. He also pointed out the fact that she couldn't name the authors of any research in her field or describe the findings of any studies in the research in her field.

She had heard of the Michaels case in New Jersey, she said. She seemed real proud of her knowledge, too—sitting up tall and talking really clearly. When Doc asked her what forensic interviewers had learned from that case, she turned to her left, looked directly at the jury, and started what sounded like a lecture about it with an air of confidence.

"Well," she said, "I think the thing to remember with the Michaels case is that, um, he was not convicted, and the children never gave a disclosure in their forensic interview."

"Well," Doc corrected her, "by the way, it was a *she*."

Kittle looked confused.

"Margaret Kelly Michaels," Doc said.

He tried to get her to clarify whether Margaret Kelly Michaels had been convicted or not, and she didn't answer with any certainty at all. Doc pointed out that Margaret Kelly Michaels was wrongly convicted and spent years in prison based on interviews filled with what he referred to as leading questions and clear examples of contamination of children's memories—*just like the interview Holly Kittle did with Brianna.*

Kittle showed no comeback or attitude for that.

The State's next witness was Jerry McDonald, Kelly's husband—and Chloe's father.

Jerry always seemed like a real nice, hardworking guy to me. There are people who just seem sincere and who have a way about them that makes you like them. Jerry's one of those guys. His work as a paramedic with a flight service is a testament to who he is, and when I could separate myself from the fact that I knew there was no truth to the allegations he was up there talking about, I could see that this man was hurting, and I could see that his testimony was heartbreaking.

His descriptions matched Chloe's story line on the witness stand pretty well. He described Chloe having nightmares after coming home from a "Halloween party" at my house, and her not wanting to go to school anymore. He testified that it wasn't until May 2008 that his wife called him and asked him to meet her at the CAC, because Chloe had alleged some child-on-child touching, which eventually escalated into allegations that "Tonya" had touched her as well.

"We didn't know what to think," he told the court. "It was just mind-blowing."

Jerry went on to say that he didn't question his daughter about any of it because he wasn't comfortable with it. He said he didn't want to move forward with any prosecution, but that his wife, Kelly, did. Jerry also testified, in front of all of those people, that he had suffered at the hands of a child molester when he was young.

"I know what it's like for people not to believe you," he said.

Jerry broke down on the witness stand. He started shaking and crying as he described asking his daughter whether she was "one hundred percent sure it happened," and his daughter "stopped and looked me dead in the eyes," he recounted through tears, "and said, 'I know it did, Daddy.'

"I told her, 'That's all I need to know.'"

After Jerry took a short break to compose himself, Clancy Covert stood up for the cross-examination. It was the first time Clancy spoke in the whole trial, and he did great. He was confident but familiar, without being pushy. He handled Jerry just right, I thought.

I also thought that my case was all over. I was sure that Jerry's tearful, heart-wrenching testimony alone would put me in prison.

Jerry admitted under cross-examination that if he could, he would go back in time and do things differently. He said he would have talked to me directly about Chloe's allegations. He recalled telling my private investigator that he didn't want to be a part of "this thing." He said he meant "the trial" when he said those words, but it sure made me wonder if he meant something more—especially since he testified that it was Kelly who told him that he "had to" be a part of the investigation whether he liked it or not.

Clancy then handed Jerry a transcript of his daughter's first interview with Detective Tim Deal. He cued up the DVD, turned up the volume real loud, and asked Jerry to confirm what his daughter said in the portion of the interview marked "inaudible" on page 5.

Jerry McDonald, Chloe's own father, confirmed what we'd all heard on that tape. He confirmed that what his daughter said was, "My mom told me which is which and where they touched me."

To me, Jerry looked surprised by it. He testified that he had never seen that interview tape before. He tried to explain what Chloe said on the tape, saying Chloe might have meant that her mother told her what her different body parts are called. But when that little girl's dad confirmed that Chloe had said her "mom" told her "where they touched me," I felt like it sent a powerful message to the jury.

Lastly, Clancy asked him whether any investigator for the prosecution side had ever spoken to him about his daughter's story. Jerry answered, "No, sir."

After a couple of quick follow-up questions by Len Gregor, the prosecution rested their case.

After eighteen witnesses and weeks of testimony against me, the onslaught was over. My attorneys immediately filed a motion to drop sixteen of the twenty-two counts against me. In our opinion, even after all of those witnesses, the State had shown no concrete evidence to support *any* charges of "penetration," Scott argued. Scott also tried to get the judge to dismiss the five counts that accused me of abuse during a time period before I lived in Catoosa County.

Chris Arnt stood up and argued that it didn't matter if some of the charges had occurred outside the county—they still fell within a statute of limitations.

Scott was impassioned, he was thorough, and I was positive that his arguments met the letter of the law. But Judge Brian House didn't even take one minute to consider our request. He denied the motion right there on the spot. He said the State had presented enough evidence to move forward with all twenty-two counts.

And so it continued. Just like that.

Judge House ordered a break, I conferred with my attorneys, and twenty minutes later we began our side of the fight for everything I am.

Chapter 56

The prosecution started their whole story with the sidewalk chalk incident that supposedly began at the hands of my friend Kim Walker's daughter, Skyler. So that was where we started, too. From our perspective, there were some pretty major differences between the way Sandra Lamb remembered that story and the way Sherri Wilson remembered that story. Kim herself got up there as our very first witness and recalled a story that was significantly different from *either* of those women's recollections.

Kim testified that when Sherri Wilson called her that evening, Sherri told her that Skyler had "written the word 'sex' in sidewalk chalk."

Kim said, "I asked her how she used it, in what context . . . and she said that she had written a little boy's name, a little girl's name, had drew a heart and written the word 'sex.'"

Kim and her husband, Joey, were already on the way to Sherri's house to pick up their daughter when the call came in. Sandra and Brianna were already gone by the time they arrived. Sherri walked them down by the pool to show her that sidewalk-chalk drawing. Sure enough, Kim testified, it had a little girl's name, a little boy's name, a heart, and the word "sex."

That was very different from the words "sex" and "kissing" that Sandra and Sherri described. When questioned about the difference, Kim said very plainly that the word "kissing" wasn't there—and it couldn't have been there because her daughter wouldn't have been able to spell that long a word at her young age. Skyler had just finished kindergarten when this incident happened, she said.

When it came to the word "sex," Kim testified, she told Sherri that "she may have heard it from her [older] brother, my son, Evan." That was when Sherri told Kim what she'd heard from Sandra Lamb: that Chloe and Ashley had been playing a "boyfriend-girlfriend game," and that Sandra thought Kim had better ask Skyler about it.

Sherri's husband, DeWayne Wilson, arrived home around that time, Kim recalled, and the adults took their conversation out to the deck—where the conversation "basically became a Tonya-bash," Kim explained. Instead of talking about any alleged child molestation, Kim testified that the Wilsons stood there calling me a "bitch" and "whore," and claimed that "Tonya" called their child "stupid."

For the first time, Kim was able to articulate the way Sandra and the Wilsons "hated" me to that jury. She testified that Sandra Lamb made threats to her after that day, trying to force Kim to make Skyler press charges against me. She even described a time when Sandra said she wished I would "die a slow death."

The prosecution's cross-examination didn't put up any sort of a factual counterpoint to call Kim's statements into question. They didn't do anything to call Kim's character into question, either. I suppose they might've had a hard time doing that, since Kim's statements and stories had been consistent from the beginning—and because those prosecutors and investigators had never actually interviewed Kim Walker themselves before that day.

Instead, the ADA got up there and pressed her on why she refused to bring her daughter in for a second interview. Kim testified that it was because she believed her daughter when she said that "nothing happened with Miss Tonya." She didn't want to put her daughter through the "trauma" of a second interview.

Kim added that if she had been asked to do an interview on the topic herself, she *gladly* would have done so. But the investigators never asked.

I was surprised how little the prosecution seemed to fight back against Kim's words. *Maybe they know they can't refute them.* I was also surprised at how quickly it all went. Kim was all done, and court recessed until the next morning.

Once my defense witnesses started talking, the whole trial felt like it'd crested a hill and rolled forward without any brakes on.

———————◆———————

I'm not sure if something changed overnight, or if the prosecution had been preparing all along to grill our next witness with an entirely different demeanor than the way they'd questioned Kim, but when we called my friend Dee Potter to the stand, things turned ugly.

This was finally Cary King's moment to shine. Unfortunately, the pros-ecution interrupted him pretty early in his direct examination of Dee and objected to Cary asking about some simple background material concern-ing my interactions with other kids. Cary got really offended and got into a bit of a spat with Len Gregor over the whole thing, right in front of the jury.

I pitched a fit later that night when we all got back to the house. "Any-body on my side that acts inappropriately in front of that jury, you're fired," I said.

"They pissed me off!" Cary argued.

I said, "Cary, don't you think I'm pissed off in there? If I can keep it together, you can certainly keep it together."

He eventually apologized for it, and that was the only moment when anyone on my team would break the rule of decorum I set. I knew that keeping our cool would matter to the jury—and I knew so doubly when the other side started interrogating Dee on that stand.

Instead of countering all of the factual information we'd given them about how often Dee and her kids were over at my house or vice versa, or how Dee never saw Brianna or Chloe at my house during any of those extensive time periods, Len Gregor stood up and asked Dee if she had ever observed my "intimate sex life."

"No, sir," Dee said. Dee kept her cool. She answered everything with "yes, sir," or "no, sir," even when Gregor asked her if she or her husband had ever had sexual encounters—with *me*.

He asked Dee if the two of us had ever been naked in bed together!

We never could have prepared Dee to answer such questions because we never imagined this line of questioning. She denied anything of the sort, of course. Then Gregor started asking her about how important my appearance was to me—specifically whether I was a "narcissist"—and a whole series of questions that implied that I was a heavy drinker.

Cary finally stood up and objected, calling it an "assault on the defen-dant's character."

Judge House allowed the questioning to continue.

Gregor's next question was, "Do you think Brianna Lamb is a slut?"

On direct, Dee had described seeing Brianna dance in what she con-sidered an "inappropriate manner" during my wedding reception. A bunch of people witnessed that behavior from Brianna.[63] She was basically pole dancing by the pool to the song "My Humps" by the Black Eyed Peas.

When Dee responded that Brianna is far too young to ever be considered such a thing, Gregor said, "So you are saying she is a pre-slut?" There was anger in his voice.

He then turned his attention back to asking all sorts of questions about all kinds of supposed incidents and observations of me that hadn't been introduced during the whole trial to that point—prompting my attorneys to object, and then to object again. Judge House let him keep on going. He seemed to take on a combative tone when he asked what kind of bathing suits I wore. Dee told him I wore bikinis. He asked if it was true that I wore "thong" bikinis, to which she answered that she'd never seen me in one, "No."

He asked Dee about her involvement in the "Truth for Tonya movement"—once again bringing that gag-ordered subject into the courtroom discussion. *Apparently the gag order only applies to my team. It has nothing to do with not "tainting the jury." It only has to do with keeping us quiet.*

Dee testified that she was there to "tell the truth" in that courtroom. A few minutes later Gregor asked her, "Which one of Tonya's truths do you believe?"

"That she is innocent," Dee responded without missing a beat.

When that prosecutor finally sat down, Cary stood up and apologized to Dee for what she'd just been put through on that witness stand—only to have Judge House reprimand *him* because that *apology* wasn't an appropriate thing to say in front of the jury.

The whole thing just floored me.

I was scared to death of what they might ask our next witness, Dee's twelve-year-old daughter. Thankfully, after she testified to witnessing Brianna's "pole dance" herself, and said she had never seen Brianna at my house, ever, and that I never played rap music or kept any kids from eating while they were at my house, Chris Arnt stood up, asked a few short questions, and let her step down without any Gregor-esque remarks or accusations.

———◆———

We decided it was a good idea to move away from the "friends" side of our witness list for a moment when we got back from lunch on that bizarre twelfth day in the courtroom. We didn't want to incite anymore false cries of lesbianism or any other intimate encounters with my friends from the prosecution. In fact, we tried to get Judge House to bar the prosecutors from entering any further allegations of my contact with adults into the record.

Once again, Judge House denied our request.

So we called to the stand Dr. Nancy Fajman, an associate professor of pediatrics at Emory University and a renowned specialist in the field of child sexual–assault examinations. The prosecution objected and asked for a pre-interview to determine what Dr. Fajman was going to say on the witness stand before they allowed her to get up in front of the jury. It seemed like a ridiculous request. She was on our potential witness list. She's a well-known expert in her field. Yet Judge House granted their request anyway, and the prosecutors took Dr. Fajman downstairs to interview her.

When she was finally allowed to take the stand, Dr. Fajman explained to the jury that it was standard practice in physical examinations of sexual abuse in young females to make a finding of either "normal" or "abnormal." The word "suspicious," which Nurse Sharon Anderson included in her reports, is not a word that is commonly used in the field whatsoever.

Dr. Fajman then shared her assessment of the photos that Anderson took during her exams. Dr. Fajman said she found that in those photos, all three of those girls' private areas appeared "normal." Even Brianna's, which Anderson had deemed "very suspicious," appeared "normal" to this woman who we felt was a much more highly educated and renowned expert in the field. She explained in great detail what "normal" actually meant and how the examination photos she had seen did not show any "abnormal" features that would be consistent with the alleged digital penetration of a child—and certainly not a "fisting," which is the slang term for what Brianna and those mothers had alleged I'd done with my hand.

Dr. Fajman described the tiny diameter of a six-year-old girl's vagina. Doc then asked me to hold up my hand so the jury could see just how big my hand was, proving that it would have been near impossible for me to do that—and was certainly impossible to do without severe physical damage being done to a child.

The whole discussion horrified me. I could not believe I had to sit through that kind of talk concerning six-year-olds and four-year-olds and my *hands*. I felt sick to my stomach, again.

Chris Arnt got up, and it looked to me like he tried to pull some of Doc's techniques on our witness during cross-examination, asking Dr. Fajman about a series of studies and research—but unlike the prosecution's witnesses, Dr. Fajman was able to answer every one of those questions, and even spelled the name of one particular study's authors for Arnt. That seemed to only establish her further as a true expert in her field and very much a "credible witness."

In any case, the attorneys and ADAs were supposed to verify the credibility of whoever was on the stand. *Did they really consider Joal Henke to be a credible witness, considering how many times his stories had changed, even on the very day of his testimony?* We had decided not to put some of my good friends and acquaintances on the witness stand ourselves because some of them had questionable moments in their backgrounds. Nothing to be ashamed of, nothing awful. But still, under the law, it was our duty to verify the credibility of our own witnesses, and we took that duty seriously. *Even if it weren't a legal duty, wouldn't it just make sense for attorneys on either side to use the most credible witnesses possible in order to prove their case?*

We wrapped up that day by putting Mike Potter on the stand, just to corroborate Dee's timelines and stories, which also matched their twelve-year-old daughter's testimony. He testified that there was a very long period of time in which his kids were with me *every day*. He picked them up at the house often, he said, and not once had he seen Brianna or Chloe at my house. Mike made that point well, just as Dee had done. He also shared with that jury just how much he trusted me with his kids.

Len Gregor stood up, once again, and started verbally attacking poor Mike on the stand. He said all sorts of disparaging personal things concerning me and my history. He asked Mike about a trip to Vegas I'd made with the two of them at one point, in which we'd shared a hotel room—implying that I'd shared their bed with them. He did so using a snappy remark: "What happens in Vegas doesn't get to stay in Vegas." Mike wasn't flustered by it. He told the court, "Yes, we went to Las Vegas together," but as "friends," and there was nothing particularly interesting to share.

Gregor asked if I'd ever worn a thong bikini at Mike's pool.

Mike said, "No."

Gregor kept getting louder and sounded angrier to me as he spoke. He flailed his arms about as he accentuated his points. It seemed almost like he was fighting some ghost in the room, because Mike wasn't fighting back at all. He then asked Mike whether his wife had ever bought a dress for me, and Mike said he thought Dee had loaned me some money for a dress once. Gregor seemed to make a big deal out of this, and we had no idea where that question was leading.

We wouldn't find out until near the end of the trial.

Chapter 57

W e rocketed through our witnesses on day fourteen. We called up a
series of former colleagues from Chickamauga Elementary, including my original principal and others who worked with me on a daily basis,
all of whom backed up the truth about my relationships with kids and,
specifically, my relationship with Brianna. We called in the school nurse,
who saw no evidence of anything unusual with any of the girls in question
during my time with them and who also testified that she would never
consider a mother putting medicine on her child's bottom and vaginal area
a potential sign for concern or "abuse." We called the investigator for the
Walker County Sheriff's Department whom I'd first called about my concerns over Ashley and Sarah, who backed up my timeline of events and the
descriptions I'd shared from the very beginning.

Chris Arnt and Len Gregor switched off their cross-examinations,
and Gregor was remarkably calm and polite throughout the entire day.
I wondered if he had been reprimanded out of court or something,
because he was even apologizing in advance of asking any sort of tough
question of any witness. The thing that struck me as really odd was that
both of those prosecutors asked nearly every single one of those witnesses if they'd visited the Truth for Tonya website or Facebook page.
Some had; some hadn't. *Aren't they making that page seem like a very big
deal to the jury?*

Just to throw it back at them, Cary got up during one of his redirects
and asked if our witness had ever visited "Chris Arnt's promotional Facebook page." It wasn't too subtle, but I think he got his point across.

The prosecution talked about the fact that I took pictures of kids in my
classroom at school, and that I took pictures at my kids' birthday parties. It
seemed that they were trying to insinuate that taking photographs meant
that I was a child molester—because child molesters are known to take
photos of kids in public places. It was just awful.

Another question that Gregor asked every witness during cross was if they knew that I had once been a "fitness instructor." He never followed up with anything, he just got a "yes" or a "no" and moved on.

Finally, he asked almost every single one of our witnesses, "Do you know what a narcissist is?" He would sometimes follow it up with, "Does anyone you know *in this room* fit that description?"

It didn't take a brain surgeon to figure out who he was talking about. Of course none of my friends thought I was a narcissist. I didn't think I was a narcissist. I might be a lot of things, but a narcissist is not one of them. What none of us could figure out, though, was *why* he was trying to paint me as a narcissist and what in the world that had to do with the charges against me.

Hour after hour those prosecutors got up there and attacked my character. Only God knows how I was able to hold back and keep most of my emotions in check. I suppose the adrenaline of holding in the anger might have helped keep me energized and focused. There simply wasn't time for a breakdown.

I didn't look good, though. Whenever I caught a glimpse of myself in a mirror, it scared me. I was dropping weight like crazy and didn't have a moment to step on the treadmill. I couldn't have run even if I wanted to. My energy was too depleted.

Somehow, God kept me going.

On Thursday, April 29, a full eighteen days since we first stepped into that courtroom, my trial became national news. NBC's *The Today Show* sent a crew down and ran a report in the early morning, when the viewership numbers nationwide are at their highest point. I'd learn sometime later that Melydia Clewell herself was responsible for pitching my trial to the powers that be. My gut was right about her.

We rolled through a bunch of our witnesses once again, delivering firsthand, long-term observations of my "normal," "loving" relationship with Ashley to the jury's ears—along with more backup that Sandra Lamb and Sherri Wilson had both been publicly trash-talking me long before any allegations arose. Shanica Lewis; Courtney (my lifelong friend); Courtney's son, Hunter; two other children who were friends with my kids; and Kim Walker's husband, Joey, all got up and held their own against the relentless questioning of the prosecution.

Courtney summed up the overall feeling pretty well when asked if she would be comfortable leaving her son alone with me after hearing all of these allegations: "She can take him right now!" she said.

We brought up Courtney's mom, Frances, who relayed the Ashley Christmas–present story firsthand and testified to Ashley asking her and my mom why she couldn't see "her mommy." We brought up Karen, my parents' neighbor with the hair salon, and she relayed similar stories about Ashley's demeanor, as well as her longtime observations of me as a loving mother. We also brought up the original DFACS representative who took Sandra Lamb's earliest phone reports, just to verify everything Doc had already asked Sandra about when she was on the stand.

In my opinion, the other side didn't offer very much in the way of cross-examination for any of them—nothing beyond what I considered character assaults and the repeated questions about my being a "fitness instructor" and "narcissist" who wore "thongs."

It wasn't until Friday that our relatively rapid pace came to a screeching halt. That was the day we were set to call Ann Hazzard—the forensic interviewer from Atlanta who'd found no evidence of abuse with my daughter and who'd previously testified in front of this very judge that my daughter and I should be allowed to see each other.[64]

The prosecutors fought to keep her off the witness stand. Len Gregor made what all of us felt was a bogus charge that morning, stating that he hadn't received our summary of Ann Hazzard's expected testimony. As far as we knew, that summary had been emailed and properly marked as "received" by the court.

We were all gathered up in front of the judge's bench when Gregor claimed he "never received it."

"Are you accusing [that] an officer of the court has falsified documents?" Doc asked.

Judge House reprimanded Doc for raising his voice. He hadn't reprimanded Gregor for raising his voice over and over throughout the trial.

In the end, Judge House ruled that Ann Hazzard could testify, but that we wouldn't be allowed to ask her about *any* of the key points of our original witness summary. She wouldn't be able to talk directly about her findings with Ashley at all, let alone what we felt were her revealing interviews with Joal and Sarah. I was devastated.

Doc wasn't devastated, though. I swear that man could think on his feet in a courtroom faster than Deion Sanders could run a football down the field. He managed to ask Dr. Hazzard all sorts of questions about "hypothetical" cases involving children and tainted interviews. Almost like magic, he made most of our points to the jury without ever violating the judge's ruling.

It seemed to drive Gregor nuts. I could see him steaming.

Dr. Hazzard told that jury how easily kids' interviews can be "contaminated" and talked about cases in which children were wrongly influenced by "leading questions" into believing that they had actually been abused. She talked about children's tendencies to want to please their interviewers, and their tendencies to answer multiple-choice questions with one of the *provided* answers. Even as adults, if we're given a question on a test and a choice of four answers, we tend to answer a, b, c, or d. We don't buck the system and write in "none of the above" if "none of the above" isn't one of the choices. And if we don't know the correct answer, we choose one because we think that one of them must be correct. So of course *children* respond with one of the answers that's been provided for them, she testified.

That's what happened during the interviews in my case.

Len Gregor seemed all kinds of feisty again that day, and he kept objecting to Doc's asking "leading" questions of the witness. In response, Doc immediately and very purposefully asked Dr. Hazzard a "leading question" about tainting children's interviews with "leading questions." Dr. Hazzard actually laughed out loud on the witness stand.

I'm not sure Gregor even got the joke.

Doc asked Dr. Hazzard a couple of questions to guide the jury toward a later witness of ours, too: He probed about whether it would be bad for a child to receive therapy from a "hypothetical therapist" with a mental illness and whether it would be bad for a "hypothetical therapist" to lie to a court. Both answers, of course, were "yes."

After all of this, Gregor got up on cross that afternoon and asked Dr. Hazzard who had paid for her lunch. He also asked her how much she'd been paid by *me* to appear that day.

Dr. Hazzard is an extremely respected legal expert in the state of Georgia. The prosecution readily agreed at the top of her testimony that they knew her credentials, and that "both sides" know and respect her. Why is he asking her those questions?

If I were watching it on TV, if it were somebody else's trial, I might have thought that Dr. Hazzard's testimony put a point in the "win" column for the defense. But the jury couldn't have kept a better poker face through any of it, and I kept thinking back to that last bit of tearful testimony from Jerry McDonald. I wondered how much that had stuck in the hearts and minds of the jurors.

I doubted very much that I'd ever see my children again.

———————◆◆———————

On Monday morning, we called to the stand Dr. Nancy Aldridge—a trained RN with a PhD in social work and psychology and the founder of the Georgia Center for Children. From what my attorneys had told me, there is hardly a more respected expert anywhere in the fields of forensic interviewing and the abuse of children. The fact is, Dr. Aldridge spends the vast majority of her time in courtrooms presenting as a witness for the prosecution.

On the stand, she admitted that when Cary King first called her to testify for this case, she promised him nothing. She said she would evaluate the interviews and present "the facts" no matter which side they benefitted. It was nearly impossible for anyone to argue that she was not only a credible witness, but also a fair and unbiased witness.

Doc walked Dr. Aldridge through the specific interviews in my case, and one by one, she broke them down for the jury.

During Stacy Long's interviews of Brianna, she said, Stacy asked leading, suggestive, and inappropriate questions. She explained that when children get asked a question repeatedly, "the child believes the answer they've given is incorrect and they should change it."

She said it was wrong for Detective Tim Deal to tell Chloe that he had already spoken to her mom about the "problem" before they sat down together in the first interview. She said his second interview with her was just plain confusing and not done correctly at all.

Doc then asked her specifically about the moment during Chloe's second interview in which she said "my mom told me which is which and where they touched me." Dr. Aldridge told the court that the only way that could possibly have been marked "inaudible" is if it was done "on purpose." We were all shocked that she would make such a bold statement on the witness stand.

"Well, what would be the significance of the cops leaving that out?" Doc asked her.

"It didn't fit with their theory," she said.

I could sense the temperatures rising at the prosecution table. The fact that she so publicly reprimanded their investigative behavior was astounding. The legal world would jump all over it—and so would the media. There were bloggers who are known as "watchdogs" in the legal community who turned all of their attention to my trial at that point and who used Dr. Aldridge's testimony as a chance to spotlight questionable behavior in Catoosa County.

As Doc turned his questions again to a hypothetical case of a therapist with a mental illness, Chris Arnt stood up, slammed his legal pad loudly on the desk, and objected, asking to approach the bench. The media went nuts for the drama. The fact that *The Today Show* kept a crew in town meant other national media outlets started following suit, too. My parents and attorneys started fielding calls from producers trying to pin down an "exclusive" first interview with me when the trial was over. I already knew who my first interview was going to, and I was oblivious to most of these other goings-on until long after they'd happened. Whenever we were done with preparations at night, I'd lock myself in the bedroom at Karen's and try to make myself disappear.

From my understanding, it was the first major trial in this part of the country that had ever played out in real time over social media, and I was glad to have so many eyes watching over my case. I suppose that could be one of the great saving graces of our justice system someday—that even judicial systems in small-town corners of America can't hide behind an iron curtain of anonymity anymore. Not that it seemed to be having much of a positive effect on the behavior of anyone in my trial. It's definitely not enough just to make this stuff public. People have to get active and make their opinions known. People need to voice their displeasure by voting out the DAs and others who make a mockery of the justice system.

The sad fact is it will take a lot more than a little bad publicity to change this system.

Airing dirty laundry doesn't make it clean.

Chapter 58

Just to hammer it all home, we put one more nationally recognized expert on the witness stand the next morning: Dr. William Bernet, professor emeritus of psychiatry from the Vanderbilt Kennedy Center in Tennessee. He had testified in more than 400 trials and was about as highly published, quoted, and regarded as anyone could possibly be in the area of forensic interviews of children in alleged sexual-abuse cases.

Dr. Bernet's studies found that the way a child is *interviewed* is often one of the most telling indicators of whether or not the alleged abuse actually happened. "Ninety-five percent of what matters is what was said," he told that jury—and in his reviews of the children's interviews, just as Dr. Aldridge had testified, he found far too many faults to believe that the children's interviews hadn't been tainted in a major way by their parents.

"You're saying that parents wanted to hear their kids were abused?" Doc asked him.

"No, I think they wanted to get to the bottom of it," Bernet answered.

He wasn't advocating a "conspiracy" but instead stating the fact that widespread evidence of parental influence was present in the pages of those interview transcripts. The parental influence had been ignored in Detective Deal's "shoddy investigation," he testified. The result of that "shoddy investigation," he said, was the terrible consequence that led to this very trial.

So how did the children get drawn down a path of pointing a finger specifically at Tonya Craft? Doc asked.

"Inept interviewers, inept therapist," Bernet said.

Judge House didn't like that much. He told the jury to ignore Bernet's comment. Still, Bernet's own studies show that kids can have false ideas implanted in a single, relatively short interview if that interview isn't done correctly. These kids had endured multiple interviews, had multiple parental influences, and had "therapy" influences drilled into them for the course of a year or two, and Bernet pointed to that as a huge mistake.

The really sad part was that all of that "ineptness," he said, was what led these children to falsely believe that I might have actually done something to them.

Dr. Bernet seemed to speak about this subject in a manner that was as close to an objective truth as a person can get. *Isn't the truth all that matters here?* I thought.

It angered me to think that Len Gregor had questioned my friends on "which of Tonya's truths" they believed. *There isn't more than one truth*, I thought. *There is truth, and then there isn't.*

All I had wanted, all I had expected from the law enforcement officers and judges and prosecutors and everyone else in the system from the beginning was for them to conduct a fair search for the truth. Not *a* truth. *The* truth.

For all the notes I'd read, all the places I'd traveled to, all the fretting I'd done to prepare ourselves to show a jury the negative and potentially tainted influence that Laurie Evans had on all three of these children, that woman came into the courtroom and basically buried herself in her own "ineptness" (to borrow a word from Dr. Bernet).

First of all, since she was the court-ordered therapist to all three accusers, I wondered if it struck anyone on the jury as strange that *our* side called her to the witness stand. It soon became clear why the other side hadn't wanted her up there.

It took Doc a full half hour to get *one* answer out of her. The question was simple, about when she was first informed that Judge Williams in Tennessee had filed an order to have her removed as my children's therapist. Doc tried to help her by giving her the actual documentation, just as we had done in this very courthouse once before, but it took her forever just to flip through her own pages of notes and records. Even after reading a specific note about a date or a time from a transcript or a motion filed by the guardian ad litem during the December 11, 2008, hearing that Laurie herself had attended in this very courthouse, she couldn't answer a simple "yes" or "no" about seemingly *anything*.

"I'm not sure that I follow the question," she said, even when Doc took it real slow to make sure she got it all.

Laurie Evans couldn't "recall" even the simplest details, such as whether she had been sworn to tell the truth at her own depositions with my attorneys on December 30, 2008. Doc had to show her a transcript to confirm that she'd been sworn in. Doc then asked her to read from a portion of the transcript of that deposition in which my attorney Scott King had asked her, "Have you ever had a complaint filed against you by a patient or family member of a patient?"

"No," she had answered. "Not that I'm aware of."

Scott had followed up. "Have you ever been treated for any mental illness or psychological disorder?"

"No," she had answered.

"Have you ever been treated for depression?" Scott had asked her.

"No," she had answered.

Doc stopped her right there in the transcript. He then asked her whether her answer to the psychological disorder question was "true." Evans sat there and thought about it for a few seconds, pointing her eyes up to the ceiling, before finally answering: "For me, yes," she said.

"What do you mean by that?" Doc asked her, as her mouth broke into a crooked smile.

"What do I mean by that?" she echoed back to him.

"For *you*, yes. Do you have a truth that's different from other people's truths?" Doc asked.

"No," she said. "When I was thinking of mental illness, I was thinking of something like bipolar, schizophrenia, those kind of mental—chronic mental illnesses."

"But this says *any* mental illness or psychological disorder, doesn't it?"

"Yes, that was what it says," she answered.

"So when you said no . . . that wasn't quite right, was it?" Doc said.

She pondered that again, for a very long pause, before shaking her head a bit and saying, "I'm not sure."

Her entire testimony went on this way. Questions about her PTSD led to nothing but confusing answers.

I was hoping we'd pull some real "aha!" moments by putting that woman on the stand. Instead, all we got from an entire day's worth of testimony was reinforcement of that very apt description Bill Bernet had already placed on her.

For the life of me, I cannot figure out how that woman keeps her job, and how on earth she'd been allowed to serve as the therapist for all three of my accusers. Why had the court listened to her recommendations? Of all people?

———————◆———————

We'd been at this trial for just about four straight weeks—and by the end of that day, we'd gone through all of the witnesses we wanted to call except for two: my husband, David, and me.

My attorneys didn't want me to take the stand. "It's too risky," they said. "Len Gregor is too much of a loose cannon. He could throw anything at you up there!"

My parents didn't want me to subject myself to that torture. David didn't want me to do it, either.

I just plain wanted the chance to speak the truth from my own lips. "I've waited two long years to look into the eyes of those jurors and tell them that I did not do this," I argued. I also thought there was a very important point the prosecutors had been making along the way, and I was very afraid they would turn it against me if I didn't get up on that witness stand myself.

The seemingly unexplainable questions about whether so many of our witnesses were aware of the Truth for Tonya campaign and websites, to me, seemed like a weapon they were getting ready to use. I had a bad feeling that if I didn't get up on the stand and speak, they would call that into question during closing arguments. I could just picture Len Gregor in that exaggerated Georgia drawl he put on when he talked real loud, saying, "Tonya Craft has a website. Tonya Craft has a Facebook page dedicated to her cause. Tonya Craft had the audacity to go on TV and talk all about her innocence, and all about the 'truth.'" Legally, the prosecution isn't supposed to draw attention to the fact that a defendant doesn't testify in their own defense. It's not supposed to matter. But who would stop him from mentioning it? Judge House? Ha. I could imagine that question loud and clear: "When it came time for Tonya to speak her mind here in the courtroom, where was she?"

I couldn't let the jury think that I didn't respect them enough to get up there and speak directly to them. Plus, I didn't think there was one thing left in the world that they could throw at me that would break me down any more than I was already broken.

When I stood up and that verdict was read, I wanted to know that I had done everything I possibly could have to fight back. I needed to know that not one stone was left unturned. If I got convicted and *hadn't* taken the stand, I never would have forgiven myself—and I told that to my attorneys.

Scott and Doc and Clancy and I got into a very heated argument about it. "You cannot testify," they said.

"If you testify, you're going to wind up going to prison."

"I did nothing wrong!" I said. "You cannot keep me off that stand. I need to talk to that jury."

"If you testify, then you're going to sign something saying that we're not accountable if something goes wrong."

"Fine," I said.

I was in the fight of my life and suddenly fighting worse than ever before with my attorneys, who I felt were trying to cover their own behinds. Everyone around me wanted me to listen to their advice. I was the only one left to stand up and go against them, and I don't know if it was my gut, or my stubbornness, or my resolve, or if it was just plain God, but I was not going to stay silent. In the end, on what felt like the last night before we'd have to make up our minds for certain, I simply would not budge.

"I am getting on that witness stand," I said. "There's no more arguing. There's no more talking about it. So get yourselves ready."

I broke the screen door off its hinges as I stormed out of my parents' house.

Chapter 59

The anticipation over whether I might be getting ready to testify hit a frenzy point on trial day nineteen. A whole slew of people showed up at the courthouse. Perfect strangers tried to get into the courtroom. Tons of supporters had somehow spread the word to wear yellow just to support me. There were yellow shirts everywhere.

We still had one more witness to get through before I took the stand, though.

David walked in wearing a blue and white striped shirt with a button-down collar over a plain white T-shirt, all neatly tucked into his light-colored khakis. He looked good. I was so nervous for him as he took his oath that I worried I was visibly shaking.

Scott was the attorney we'd chosen to do the direct examination with David. The two had a good rapport, so it felt like the right choice. In a way, David was our last line of defense, and we still had plenty of hurdles to jump over.

I prayed he'd stand strong no matter what came his way.

At the start, David talked about how much he loved Tyler and Ashley and how he got to see them just about every other weekend now. He relayed to the jury that they always had a good time, whether playing ball or playing video games or eating together. He also echoed the words of some other witnesses, in that Ashley would ask about me often: "'How's she doing?' Things like that," David said. "General questions."

"Does she ever say, 'I don't want to see my mom again'?" Scott asked.

"Never," he said.

He talked about me, and how much he loves me, and how we first met. He answered Scott's questions plainly about our separation, and explained that it had nothing to do with the case against me. He blamed himself. He said he was the one who "gave up" on the marriage—that I "never gave up" on him.

He testified specifically that Brianna Lamb had never spent the night at my house in the whole time he'd known me. His whole testimony was very matter-of-fact and easygoing. Scott questioned him about whether I had given any kids a bath (other than Ashley), and David said plainly, "No." Continuing with the bathing questioning, he asked whether Ashley would ever be sent to Joal and Sarah's house for visitation all dirty and smelling bad, with "matted hair." David looked truly surprised to hear something like that and said he'd never seen Ashley appear that way—"ever."

Scott worked through all of the various terrible things that people had said about me during the trial. He even asked David about some of the more outlandish allegations that seemed to come out of nowhere, like whether or not I ever wore a thong bikini.

"No. She doesn't even own a thong bikini," he said.

Scott asked whether I liked or kept pornography around the house.

"No! I get in trouble if I say 'damn.' There's not gonna be any *porn*," David said, eliciting a few laughs in the room.

David answered "no" to all of those crazy things. Poor David had been forced to sit in the hallway on a hard wooden bench for all those weeks. He hadn't been able to listen to any of the testimony, and I wasn't allowed to talk to him about any of the testimony. So all of this stuff was truly a shock to him. I think anyone watching him could tell he wasn't putting on a show. He wouldn't be capable of putting on a show, anyway. David is who he is. You can read the plain truth on his face.

He spoke the plain truth about our wedding reception, which the prosecutors had attempted to turn it into some sort of an awful example of what kind of a person I was. He talked about the fact that at one point, he and I jumped in the pool. At one point I tripped and fell by the pool and skinned my knee, when Greg Lamb was chasing me around. He admitted openly that I had too much to drink that night and got sick all over the Lamb's carpet. He didn't think any of it was a big deal—because it wasn't.

Scott then asked him about the friendships that the prosecution kept trying to paint as something more.

"Did you think she was having an affair with Mike Potter?" Scott asked. "No."

He asked him whether he thought I'd had an affair with *Dee* Potter. "No," David said.

"You ever joke about it?" Scott asked. "Or—"

"No," David insisted. He reasserted that we were all just "good friends."

David answered a whole slew of other questions aimed at backing up our earlier assertions about what *really* happened at my house with sleepovers and various visits from other children. Most of all, I think what he did was firmly establish his view of me, as the wife and mother and teacher I truly am—or at least *was*. It was quite a thing to watch my husband get up in front of all those people and say how he felt. It was about as public and moving a proclamation of his love for me that any man could make.

Scott sat down.

That was when some new fireworks began in that courtroom.

Len Gregor stood up and started asking a series of hypothetical questions that seemingly had nothing to do with David whatsoever. He did so in a loud, angry-sounding voice. For instance, he asked David if he knew from therapy evaluations that "yellow" was something that caused psychological harm and was a trigger for a child; and if he knew that, whether David would approach a child on the witness stand, wearing a yellow tie, flipping some yellow legal-pad pages in front of that child, and telling the child to look at a photo of Tonya Craft in a yellow dress on the screen.

"I don't understand," David said.

Is Len Gregor insinuating that Doc somehow tried to intimidate Brianna while she was on the stand because her mother said she's terrified of the color yellow? That's absurd. There are yellow legal pads all over the courtroom. Doc's tie may have had a pale yellow background that day in court, but it certainly wasn't some purposeful weapon used to harm a child. Gregor got so animated about it that he accidentally smashed his hand into the big TV monitor mounted on the wall. I thought he was going to break it.

"Scared of 'yellow'?" David said at one point. "I don't understand."

David wasn't in the room for any of that testimony! We weren't the ones who brought up Brianna's psychological aversions to yellow in the courtroom. Sandra brought that up after all the girls were long finished with their testimony. Gregor's behavior in that moment—especially directed at David, of all people—seemed way out of line.

Of course Judge House didn't stop it.

"Would you agree with me that it's just wrong? That it's not a good way to get to the truth?" Gregor asked my husband.

David pointed out that it wasn't his job to question a child, and he didn't understand why Gregor was asking him the question, but said that he would never do anything to purposefully hurt a child, no.

"Okay," Gregor said, taking a breath and seeming to calm himself down. "Okay."

Gregor then took on a mellow tone. He started talking about how his "daddy" always took him out fishing. He said he wanted to talk to David about fishing, which led to questions about his friendship with Greg Lamb and how long they'd been friends. He didn't pull out anything disparaging, he just established that David had known, or at least known of, Greg Lamb for about twenty years—because they competed against each other in fishing tournaments and eventually started hanging out sometimes.

Then he switched gears again.

He made a point of telling David that it was "silly" to think that he was around me 24/7 during our relationship, to which David responded, "We all know that." He then asked about Brianna, and whether David considered Brianna a "worldly-beyond-her-years girl who pole dances."

"I would say she's very advanced for her age," David said. When pressed, he agreed to the term "worldly."

Gregor then tried to define the word "worldly" as meaning "someone who gets around a lot."

"She doesn't '*get around*,'" David said "She's ten!" Gregor sort of laughed about someone describing her that way in the courtroom. "It wasn't me," David said.

Gregor apologized for having to ask certain questions (of course with no reprimand from Judge Brian House). He seemed to keep trying to tone it down. But then he'd ask David something outrageous and completely unfounded: "Didn't you tell a variety of people that the defendant is an alcoholic?"

"I never said Tonya was an alcoholic," David answered.

"Is one of the things that she drinks a vodka mixed with red-raspberry something or other?"

"She's drank that before," David answered.

Gregor pressed on about my drinking. He asked David whether he'd rented a steam cleaner to try to clean up the Lambs' carpet after I threw up on my wedding night. David told the truth about all of it.

Out of the blue, he asked David whether he'd caught me doing a "strip-tease nude dance" in front of my friend Tammy one time and whether he had told people about *that*.

"No," David said.

David had a look on his face like, *What in the world is this guy talking about?* And I wondered when, if ever, they were going to bring up something relevant to the actual allegations. Gregor went on for more than an hour about my alleged lesbian tendencies and my drinking too much on a couple of occasions. The scary thing to me was just how many of the assertions Gregor made about me during his questioning of David were completely untrue and how many times David was forced to say "no" to those assertions.

The ADA didn't even seem to hide the fact that most, if not all, of his information about those things came from Sandra Lamb and Joal Henke. He referenced their names more than once when asking whether David had "said" certain things.

The ADA then went off on a long speech about how David knew "the real Tonya Craft" better than anyone. He knew the "real" me, not some made-up "television Tonya Craft." He said David knew what I was capable of, and *that* was why he left me in April 2008. He said that was why, when Greg Lamb first called David and informed him that "Tonya Craft had molested their daughter," David had said, "It all makes sense now."

"I never said any of that," David said.

"That's as true as anything else you've told us," Gregor said. He sat down and ended his questioning.

Did he just insult my husband and call him a liar? Is he allowed to do that?

———◆———

Scott jumped up real quick for his redirect, and asked David to clear up a laundry list of Len Gregor's insinuations. David did what I knew he'd done from the beginning: He told the truth about everything. As uncomfortable and awful as it was for him to get up there and have to refute the filth they were spewing about me, David sat there without flinching and stood up for me when it counted most.

I thought about the fact that Sandra Lamb's husband had filed for a divorce from her in the middle of all of this. This whole ordeal wasn't just awful for me. These false allegations, the changing stories, the media, the stress—all of it was destroying marriages. I felt very blessed that it hadn't destroyed mine.

Chapter 60

Doc stood up and so boldly spoke the next five words that it sent a shiver down my spine.

"The defense calls Tonya Craft."

The electric feeling in that courtroom was something to behold. Oddly enough, there was an ambulance going by outside, and the siren wailed right through that courtroom as I stood. Not twenty seconds had passed since David stepped off that witness stand. Here I was about to fight for my life, to fight for my kids, and I actually felt sorry for David having to go out there and sit on that bench again.

I did everything I could to keep my knees from giving out as I made what suddenly seemed like a very long walk to the witness stand.

I'd chosen a simple black-and-white dress jacket to wear over a black blouse, and black pants. I don't think that I made that choice consciously, but the idea of "black and white" was certainly fitting.

I wore my pendant necklace with the etchings of Ashley and Tyler around my neck, close to my heart and prominently displayed against the black background of my shirt.

Doc said, "Tonya. Raise your right hand. Do you swear to tell the truth, nothing but the truth, so help you God?"

"Yes," I said. My voice was shaky. I could barely breathe. He asked me to state my name, and my throat sort of choked up between my first name and my last name—but I managed to get the words out.

I tried to settle in. I took a deep breath. It's impossible to explain what it feels like to have everything on the line like that and for it all to come down to that final moment. I guess the overwhelming thought—more of a feeling, really, that sinks into your bones and drives a nail into the pit of your stomach—is, *This is it. This is my last chance.* The bell had rung and the clock was now ticking on the biggest test I'd ever take in my life. I had to get this right.

Doc asked his first question before I even had time to exhale.

"What are you doin' up on that witness stand?" he asked me.

"I'm here because I have been falsely accused," I said, slowly and clearly.

I was about to go on with that thought, but he cut me off, rather forcefully.

"Don't you know that you have a right to sit there and make them prove every element of their case?" he asked.

"Yes."

I looked right into the eyes of Chris Arnt.

"Don't you know that they're supposed to *not* have to hear from you?"

I took another slow, deep breath as Doc asked that question.

"Yes," I said.

I looked at that jury.

"Don't you know that you have a right to remain silent?" Doc asked.

I looked Doc right in the eyes.

"Yes," I said, as Len Gregor stood up and objected. I could hardly believe he was interrupting already, before I'd even had a chance to take a few breaths. I felt he was doing that on purpose.

"Your Honor," he said as I reached for my water. "This is a direct examination, and I object to leading questions—"

"Don't lead the witness," Judge House said.

"Do you know that you have a right to remain silent?" Doc asked, rephrasing the question.

"I know that I do have that right," I said, taking one more breath as I tried to slow my heart rate down from the panic it was clearly in.

Doc looked at the prosecutors and asked me if I had any idea what I "might have in store [. . .] from this happy group of wolves."

I looked right at Gregor and said, quietly, "I can only imagine."

"Have you been listening to what this charming procession of questions has been to your friends?"

"Yes, I have," I said.

Doc asked if I knew there were things I may *not* say—and the ADA objected again. It turned into a whole big deal, with Judge House accusing Doc of playing "to the media," and my testimony was interrupted so we could all go into chambers to discuss the matter.

This was not how I wanted to start my time on the stand.

Ten minutes later, we were back in front of the jury.

"So, here you are," Doc said. "Seven hundred and six days. What does that mean?"

"Seven hundred and six days," I said, slowly, "since I have had contact with my daughter."

He asked me to speak up, so I repeated: "Since I have had contact with my daughter."

I was still having a hard time talking. I could feel my heart racing. I could hardly believe how out of shape I'd become and how out of control of my body I felt as I sat in that chair. I grabbed the arms of it just to make sure I didn't fall out.

"Seven hundred and six days," Doc said. I could tell he was trying to give me some time to calm down. He left big spaces between his questions. He asked about where I grew up, and where I went to school, and whether I played any sports, and I told the court about my running and playing softball.

He asked about my growing up—and just as an aside asked whether I was an abuse victim. "No, I am not," I said.

I told the story of my "normal" upbringing, with my father's job at a corrugated box company and my mother's mostly stay-at-home-mom role.

"Is that big guy right there your daddy?" he said, pointing to my dad in his front-row seat.

"It is," I said. I choked up pretty bad. I could see my dad was choked up, too.

"Where's your mom?"

"She's out in the hall," I said, "because we weren't sure if she'd have to be a witness."

Doc started his questions in earnest right then and there. He asked what this whole "fitness" thing was about, which the prosecutors had clearly asked many of my friends. And I told the story. My parents and brother had always struggled with their weight, and I'd seen how hard it was. So when I was in ninth grade, I took up track and field and running, because I'd made up my mind that I wanted to live a healthy lifestyle.

"It was more of a prevention thing," I said.

I spoke about going to college and getting my BS in multidisciplinary education, which is elementary education. I spoke about my first marriage when I was around twenty-one. "We were just kind of young and dumb and in love and thought, 'high school sweethearts, let's get married,'" I told the court. We were together for approximately four years, but we just "grew apart."

I gave my history with Joal, explaining how we'd met through my work doing fitness competitions.

"Were you a narcissist?" Doc asked me.

"No," I answered.

"Are you a narcissist now?" he asked.

"No. I do take care of myself and try to be healthy," I said.

The pace of Doc's talking finally got me calmed down a little bit, and I was thankful neither of the prosecutors jumped up and objected about anything for a few minutes. I knew this was going to be a long haul. I needed to find a pace. I needed to get my body in tune with what we were doing. It would just take some time to catch my stride.

Responding to Doc's questions, I talked openly about starting my relationship with Joal before I was divorced from my first husband. I told the truth about it. I took a sip of water. I spoke about living with Joal before we were married.

"Uh-oh," Doc said. "Does that make you a child molester?"

"No," I replied.

We continued going through my history and started to get into some of Joal's family history—and Len Gregor stood up again and objected to that line of questioning, calling it hearsay and inquiring about the relevance. Doc came back pretty strong. He hadn't even asked the questions yet, but Judge House sustained the objection.

Is this how my entire testimony's going to go?

So instead of getting into Joal's family history, we talked about the pornographic materials that Joal brought home one day.

"This was right whenever we got married," I said. I had never had any kind of pornography in my home before that. "It bothered me," I said.

"The way I've been portrayed, I hate to even say the word 'Christian,'" I explained, "because of all the things I've done that are not perfect." But I talked about how I was bothered internally and wanted to change and become a Christian at that time. "I got pregnant with Tyler three months into our marriage," I explained. "When I got pregnant, I knew that I was not going to have anything like that [pornography] in my house."

Doc and I had talked about a lot of this the night before. We were very worried that a jury could possibly believe my ex-husband's allegations against me and that it might taint their view of everything I was as a human being. They could convict on their emotions based on the fact that he'd described me as far less than a moral person. So like it or not—and I swear,

I did not like it one bit—I needed to tell them about who Joal was and to let them make up their own minds who to believe.

I told them how Joal kept making comments about "making sure I lost the weight" after Tyler was born and the whole condescending, controlling way that I felt Joal treated me. "It wasn't the way I saw my dad treat my mom," I said.

Doc asked me whether I'd ever blacked out and woke up in my friend Jennifer's bed, as Joal had claimed on the witness stand. "No," I said. I explained that there was a night when we'd had some drinks, and we wound up sleeping at her mom's house that night. It was nothing like Joal insinuated. I was still in my twenties. It was a sleepover, nothing more.

"Does that make you a child molester?" Doc asked.

"No," I said.

He kept coming around to those questions that related directly to the prosecution's case against me every so often, and the whole time, all I did was try to be as open and honest as I could possibly be. I am not a perfect person. I wanted the jury to know that. I never pretended to be some sort of a perfect person. I've made mistakes.

As we went on, I went through the whole history of the divorce. I explained to them that whenever Joal came to pick the children up for visitation, he would say, "Look at your children. You're never going to see them again." *That* was how contentious our divorce was. From my viewpoint, the only reason he signed custody over to me was because I had hired a private investigator who found proof of an affair Joal had right in the middle of our split.

I basically gave a whole sordid history of my relationship with Joal and how I'd dropped all of my fights about money with him "because it was not worth arguing about." The only thing I was willing to fight for is my kids, and I let that jury know that I would fight for them relentlessly.

At that point, Doc brought out the timeline I'd put together, which David had printed for us on his professional printer at work. He put it up on a stand so the jury and everyone else could see it. We started talking about how busy I was when I worked in Chickamauga—going for my master's degree and juggling the kids' sports program.

"Well, so how did you work out that you're going to school four nights a week, you're teaching a room full of kindergarteners all day," Doc said, "how did you work in sexually abusing children into that hectic schedule?"

The question caught me off guard and quite frankly ticked me off, but I turned and looked right at the jury as I spoke: "I did not and have not sexually abused any child."

I started to panic again. It was so upsetting to have to say those words out loud. I was exhausted already. I was still trying to take deep breaths to calm myself down. In my mind, I asked a question of my own. *Dear God, help me. Please tell me why I have to proclaim my innocence when I'm innocent? Why am I here?*

It was right at that moment when Doc asked me a question about how I managed to squeeze in studying for exams on top of everything else I was doing back then.

"I read when I'm on the treadmill," I said. "So I would get up and run on the treadmill before the kids got up. And—"

"How many miles can you run on the treadmill at one time?" Doc asked.

"Well, right now none, because I haven't been able," I said.

"At that time how many miles were you running?" he asked.

"I would do about six miles a day," I told him.

The thought of being on that treadmill helped calm me down. It helped me get centered. I couldn't have been more thankful for that.

Doc jumped on that detail about my running and ran with it. He noted for the jury that I was running at 5:00 A.M., five days a week, then teaching five days a week, then going to school four nights a week, on top of the kids' sports and activities, all through that 2005–06 school year, with the master's degree schedule going through the end of 2006; Tyler's baseball continuing into July for All-Stars, with multiple day practices and weekend tournaments and more; and Ashley coming along with me everywhere I went—just hammering home how full my days were.

That led him to ask how in the world I ever relaxed, and that led to talking about my friendship with the Potters, which began that spring of 2006. That led to the detail of my watching the Potters' kids during the summer.

"Every single day?" Doc asked me.

"Every single day," I said.

"We can't say that enough, can we," Doc said.

I didn't move to Chickamauga until approximately May 25, 2006, which was right *after* the end of that school year. We laid everything out, plain as day for the jury to see and hear. I spoke about Mike and Dee dropping in to my house to pick up the kids, unannounced, at any time, just to make a point about how I was never trying to hide anything. And more.

We were definitely hitting our stride.

I'd already been up on that stand for almost two hours when I related the Chloe and Ashley story, of the touching and "losing it" that happened at Kelly's house. The whole time I was talking, I just hoped and prayed that the jury was seeing and hearing me as the reasonable human being I am. As absolutely stressed out as I felt as I sat there, there was a part of me that felt good to finally speak the truth in front of all of those people.

Of course, right as I was feeling like it was going pretty well, Len Gregor stood up again. He objected to us entering a "good conduct" teacher evaluation into evidence from my first year of teaching at Chickamauga Elementary.

Much to my surprise, Judge House allowed it. I felt like shouting, "Hallelujah!" It was the first bit of any kind of a decision that had gone our way in what felt like forever. I didn't think the tide might be turning or anything like that. But it was almost five thirty in the afternoon, and right after we put that document into evidence, Doc asked the judge if we wanted to break and continue the next day—and Judge House agreed.

All of a sudden the courtroom burst into a rush of commotion like it was Grand Central Station or something. Everybody started talking and yammering. My attorneys got up to try to take the timeline off the stand so we could take it back to the house with the rest of our boxes. The jury filtered out. Everybody milled about.

I got up on my feet and just stood there at the witness stand. Everybody in the courtroom was going back to their lives, back to their homes, back to their children. Some of those people seemed to be there just for the spectator sport of it. It sounded almost like people leaving a baseball game or something. People sounded happy. People sounded alive.

I touched my face and could feel that my cheeks were all hot. Knowing me, they were probably bright red. David hadn't come in yet. I had no one to talk to. No one was asking me anything.

I stood there in the middle of all that commotion, knowing there were people gathered outside who had come just to support me, and knowing there were TV news satellite trucks parked up and down the street outside planning to talk about me. And in that moment, standing in the middle of all of it, I felt alone.

Chapter 61

I hardly slept at all before coming in for that second morning of testimony. I think it showed, too. My face felt tired. I knew my hair wasn't quite right. I really didn't care.

I'd put on a black-and-gray striped jacket over a white blouse this time. I wore my pendant inside my shirt, where I could feel the metal on my skin—right close to my heart.

I stood in the witness box as the jury filtered in, taking deep breaths, once again trying to slow my heart down to some reasonable rate. I just couldn't seem to get it calmed down. And then all of a sudden, we started again.

"That was tough yesterday, wasn't it?" Doc asked me.

"Yes," I said.

"Did I go too fast?" he asked. He was good about catching me off guard with odd questions now and then, almost to distract me from my own fear.

"Sometimes," I said. I smiled for a second. Not a full smile, just a quick one.

"And how are you feeling today?" he asked, while I gulped a few more breaths.

"Um," I said. I shook my head trying to put it into words. "The same way as yesterday. Scared, and I know I'm being questioned and grilled and it's—it's very difficult for me to get up here because I feel like I'm fighting for my life and my children's lives and any child that believes something that didn't happen to them, and that's why I have to get up here. It's the personal attacks. It's very scary," I said.

Doc gave me some instructions, telling me to stop him if he was going too fast or if he was being flippant. I was half-surprised that Len Gregor didn't jump up and object to him coaching me or something.

"This is your trial," Doc said, "not mine."

He then instructed me to speak a little louder.

"Okay," I said. And off we went.

Doc continued walking through my whole timeline, bringing up every bit of my busy life, every friend who'd been over to my house, talking about Shanica and her daughter Hailey, and Tammy and her son Hunter, and the Potters, and all of the people who were truly there, truly spending time with us, and who rarely, and in some cases never, saw Brianna or Chloe spend any time at our house at all.

We used the visual of the timeline for what felt like a very long time, walking the jury through absolutely everything.

We rolled through the details of my "love at first sight" with David and went into the basic detail of the wedding-reception stories from my point of view—but not that much. David had covered it accurately, and I let the jury know that. Plus, I felt like Doc kind of nipped that whole thing in the bud just perfectly with one series of questions: "Did you eat the food? Did you drink a lot? Did you dance around? Did you puke in the middle of the night?" I answered yes to all of that. And then Doc said, "So what?"

He moved right back to the timeline.

We covered the specifics of how few times Chloe and Brianna had been over at my house. Ever. We went through the details of the *High School Musical* party that had been brought up during the trial, which happened in August 2007.

"The girls played dress-up, the boys ran around doing boy stuff," I said, and we talked about the fact that David was there. Chloe was there, and she spent the night, along with a whole bunch of other girls, and Chloe's older brother was there, too.

"Nobody took a bath," either that night or the next morning, I confirmed. There was nothing unusual that happened other than children having fun. Nobody complained about anything that night. "Maybe David [complained] a little bit," I said, which got a chuckle out of Doc.

We made the point that David was there at my house every night, unless he was traveling on business trips, which were pretty few and far between. Basically, we added up the whole timeline, all the way through the end of 2007, and explained what we felt were the inconsistencies with Brianna's and Chloe's stories.

Someone's cell phone went off on the prosecution side of the courtroom somewhere, right in the middle of my testimony. It was shocking, since everybody who came in on my side was practically body searched on their way in. Even my attorneys couldn't bring phones in. And yet, no one was escorted out. It was a beeping electronic reminder to me that the bias I perceived in Judge House's courtroom was as strong as ever.

After Doc and I talked through the fact that I never gave baths to any other kids at my house, ever, we turned the corner into 2008. I relayed the details of what happened at Ashley's birthday party and the moment when DeWayne Wilson threw a notebook across the table at me and said, "Somebody's gonna pay!" We walked through my concern over Ashley and Sarah showering together. We then went through the awfulness of May 30, 2008. Judge House had ordered me not to talk about anything anyone said to me on that day, including the detectives. So I couldn't tell the whole story. I wasn't allowed to tell the "whole truth." I kept having to stop myself to say, "Oh, I can't say that."

We *were* allowed to play the tape of the whispered message Ashley left for me that night. I got choked up on the stand when Doc played it, just thinking about my baby girl.

I talked about staying with my friend Diana for the very first time in any public forum whatsoever. I walked through my arrests, noting that I'd turned myself in both times. I walked through my termination hearing in August 2008, and when Doc asked whether I had called the media to that hearing, I told that jury the absolute truth: "No!"

In fact, looking back on it now (and I didn't say this in court), I wondered if the DA's office had been the ones to call the press. After all, it was an election year. Now here they were complaining about all the press and trying to turn it on me as some sort of evidence of my guilt.

The hypocrisy sure runs thick in this place, I thought.

Finally, Doc asked me point-blank if I'd ever touched any of those girls. "Did you do any inappropriate touching with Ashley?" Doc asked me. "No," I said.

He asked me if I'd done anything inappropriate to Chloe.

"No."

He asked me the same of Brianna.

"No," I said.

He went on to ask me if I'd scrubbed Brianna in the bath, or neglected to feed her, or whether I listened to rap music with her in the car. I answered "no" to every one of those allegations.

"Do you have any idea why Brianna Lamb is saying these things about you?" Doc asked.

Len Gregor tried to object to my answering that question. He said it was speculation. Doc pressed it, and the judge let me speak.

"In my mind," I said, "I've listened to the experts, I've listened to the different influences and how things can play out, and *how* she got to the point to where she believes it, I don't know. I think it's just horribly sad for any of these children—for them to think that something happened to them that did *not* happen to them."

I left the detailed breakdown of the girls' interviews to the experts we'd already put up as witnesses, but I thought it was important for the jury to know that I'd done that legwork myself, too. It was important for them to know that I wanted to understand how on earth this could possibly happen.

We talked openly about all the research I'd done, and the traveling I'd done, and how I wanted to get lots of people's opinions about my case, and advice about my case. I certainly didn't see any need to hide that part of my story from anyone.

Doc even asked me why I'd gone so far as to hire a team of expensive attorneys. I thought about my kids, and I made the best analogy I could: "If your child has a brain tumor, you take 'em to a specialist. You don't take 'em to a walk-in clinic."

"The last thing I want to go through," Doc said, "I want to ask you about the things that Mr. Gregor has been asking. This is the 'You're a child-molester *if*' list."

I nodded. I was more than ready to finally speak up for myself.

"Tell me about wearing a thong," Doc said.

"I do not have a thong bathing suit. I never have," I answered.

"Tell me, if you were to wear a thong, does that mean you're a child molester?"

"No," I said.

"Now tell me about wearing a bikini."

"Yes, I have."

"Does that make you a child molester?" Doc asked.

"No."

"How about changing clothes in front of other women. Have you done that?"

"I'm sure if I went shopping or if we were at the house and going some-where it could have happened."

"Does that make you a child molester?" he asked.

"No."

"What about gettin' drunk? Does that make you a child molester?"

"No."

Doc took on a bit of a Georgia drawl as he said these things.

"What about mowin' the lawn in shorts and a tank top. Does that make you a child molester?"

"No."

"What about having premarital sex, does that make you a child molester?"

"No."

"Have you done that?" Doc asked.

"Yes."

"Have you mowed the lawn in shorts and a tank top?"

"Yes."

"What about puking on the carpet after you eat food and drink alcohol. Have you done that?"

"Yes, I have."

"Does that make you a child molester?"

"No."

"If you have pictures of your children's birthday parties, does that make you a child molester?"

"No," I said.

"But we heard that child molesters have pictures of kids and parties," Doc said.

The listing of all of these things in succession was making me feel sick.

"If you had sex with men that you didn't marry, does that make you a child molester?"

"No."

"If you had sex with women—have you ever done that?"

"No."

"If you had done that, would that make you a child molester?"

"No."

I kept taking sips of my water. My throat felt so awfully dry.

Doc asked me about my having kids do sleepovers with my kids, my babysitting kids, my choosing a career centered around children—all of those things that the prosecution seemed to insinuate would prove that I was a child molester.

He asked me if drinking at the wedding and jumping in the pool made me a child molester, to which I answered "no."

Then he asked me if Sandra was drinking at my wedding.

"Yes."

"How much?"

"I didn't watch her."

"Does that make *her* a child molester?"

"No."

"If you're a Boy Scout leader or a teacher or a priest and in a position of authority, does that make you a child molester?"

"No."

"You're a teacher. You *were*."

"I am a teacher, and I am not a child molester."

Doc asked me what happened to all of my classroom supplies, and I told that jury about the yard sale—giving it all away so it would go to a classroom where it was meant to be.

"How many years did it take you to assemble all of that stuff for your students?"

It took me a moment to find the strength to say it.

"Fifteen years," I said.

I started to tear up. I didn't want to lose it. I didn't want to cry.

Doc then asked me how much money I'd had to raise in order to put on a defense for myself in this case, and that sobering thought dried my tears up pretty quick.

"I don't know exactly, but between my parents cashing in their inheritance, and my parents refinancing their house . . . and having garage sales—it's been over $500,000."

"$500,000 of your parents' inheritance, and refinancing houses, and garage sales to deal with this," Doc said. "So if you raise and borrow and refinance and hocked an inheritance up to $400,000 or $500,000, go all over the country, and do everything you did to get ready for this trial, does *that* make you a child molester?"

"No, it absolutely does not."

"What about these lesbian affairs that Mr. Henke suddenly remembered on the way to the courthouse? Any truth to that?"

"No. And—"

"What a guy," Doc commented before asking me if I'd had affairs with

Tammy, or Dee, or Jennifer, or an affair with Mike Potter—and even if I had, would it make me a child molester?

I said "no" to all of those things.

"Is there any more mud I could throw on you and ask you about that you can think of?"

"I'm sure anybody could think of something more," I said. "I don't know."

Doc looked me in the eyes. He paused for a second. And then he said, "That's all I have, Your Honor."

That was that. That was the end of my direct testimony.

You know what I needed to do at that moment?

I needed to pee.

I unceremoniously asked the judge for a bathroom break, which he granted. I used that moment away from the courtroom to try to prepare myself for the attack I was surely about to endure.

Chapter 62

"Miss Craft," Len Gregor said. "You realize that money, no matter how much—money doesn't buy the truth, correct?"

"It shouldn't," I said.

"It shouldn't affect the truth, should it?"

"No, it shouldn't."

"And the truth isn't some sort of a commodity, a product that you buy?"

I just sort of looked at him for a moment while gathering my thoughts, and he took it to mean that I didn't understand him or something.

"You know what a commodity is?"

"I do, I—"

"It's not something you *buy*."

"No, you don't buy the truth."

"The truth simply exists, right?" he said.

"*Yes.*"

"As it relates to that, why did you and Mr. Lorandos have a discussion for the benefit of the jury about how much money you've spent on your defense?"

"It is seemingly impossible to defend yourself against allegations such as this, and I will do everything I can to prove the *truth*," I said, reiterating that same brain tumor/child analogy I'd made less than an hour earlier.

He went on making a speech about how the amount of money either side spends on a case should have no bearing on the outcome of a trial. He then brought up the media attention this case was getting and compared it to other cases that have caught the attention of media—in which a lot of money has been thrown at a defense.

He didn't have a question for me, so I had no response.

"And as it relates to the Gregor list, there really is no list, is there?" he said.

Again, I didn't answer. *Doc hadn't called it the Gregor list.* I just looked at him.

"You're a child molester if you molest children. If someone inappropri-ately touches a child's genitalia, they're a child molester," he said, and then paused.

"Are you asking me a question? What's the question?" I asked.

"Yeah, do you agree with that or not?" he said.

"Restate that, please?"

He restated that someone who inappropriately touches a child's geni-talia is a child molester, and I agreed—looking right into his eyes: "If you do that, yes."

He then accused me of making a prepared "speech" at the beginning of that second day, when Doc had asked me how I was doing. "Absolutely not," I told him.

My attorneys had told me to keep my answers succinct during cross: "Keep it to just yes or no as much as possible," they said. So that was what I did. I wanted to show them, "See, I can follow orders. I don't go against *everything* you say!"

Gregor then spent some time talking about some literature that he'd found on a website dedicated to "false allegations." I wasn't sure where he was going with it. At all.

"We've asked people this, but, narcissism. Do you know what narcis-sism is?"

"Um, I guess I've learned during this trial," I said.

After spouting off a long, dictionary-type definition of "narcissism," Gregor then talked about the literature he'd found on that website, quoting the author of that literature and stating, "The number-one thing that he has found in research that links individuals to being pedophiles is being narcissistic," he said. He paused. I just looked at him and waited. "It cites a study by 'Lee-hee' or 'Lay-hee,'" he said, struggling with the pronunciation of somebody's last name. And then he read from a printed page: "The most common diagnosis of the child abuser is the narcissistic personality disor-der. They're seeking intimate encounters with children as some affirmation that they are both loved and desired," he said.

He asked if I was familiar with that research.

"I had not read that, no," I said.

"[The author] cites unsuccessful marriages as part of narcissists and relationships to narcissists and pedophilia."

"Okay," I said.

He went on to keep talking about it, and Doc finally objected to his reading a study into the record when I'd already answered that I wasn't familiar with it. Judge House overruled the objection, and Gregor kept right on going.

"Interestingly . . . [the author] lists as one of the top links between child abuse [and] pedophiles is substance abuse. A history of substance abuse. And more often than not there's alcohol issues with those who commit acts of pedophilia," he said.

He tried to insinuate that I fit both of those descriptions—of a narcissist and of an alcoholic—and Doc objected again and approached the bench. Finally, Gregor agreed to move on.

"Now, we're gonna go through a variety of things, but whatever the time period was, I can tell you I'm not going to keep you up there as long as Brianna was up there, okay?" he said.

"Okay."

"And, um, as it relates, I bet you at $460 an hour you were pleased that he didn't keep Dr. Bernet up there that long either, correct?"

"I just wanted him to tell the truth. It didn't matter how long it took," I said.

Doc called over to me and told me to speak up a bit more. My voice was definitely fading. I sipped some more water as Gregor went on: "I look behind me and to my left and it looks like people in support of a team out here with yellow. Is it a game to you?"

"Absolutely not."

"I look behind me and see spectators and 'Team Tonya.' Are they gonna do a wave here in a moment?"

"No."

He went on about the Truth for Tonya website, talking about the pictures of me that were on that website and confirming that my favorite color is yellow. He then asked about our questioning of Brianna on the stand.

"Did you instruct Mr. Lorandos to wear a yellow tie?"

"No."

"Was it your idea for him to stick yellow stickies in Brianna Lamb's face?"

"He uses yellow stickies everywhere."

"Was it your idea to point out some yellow crayon being utilized when she was interviewed?"

"No."

"Your defense is that this is a conspiracy, right?"

"No."

"I mean, that's what's promoted on the website, right?"

"It's not my website."

"It's not your website," he said with a little laugh, making a reference to Diana (who created it) and going on for a bit about what else that website professed. "At the beginning of the trial we were told that this is a frame job, a setup, a witch hunt. Correct?"

"I don't recall hearing those words."

"Well, I do. I wrote 'em down," he said.

He then listed the "primary" conspirators, including Brianna, Chloe, "your own daughter," he said. "And they all are conspirators and liars."

"No."

"Under your theory they have to be. Right?"

"No."

The attention then turned once again to my attempts to defend myself, the hiring of my team, the "aggressive" civil action we took in my custody case in Tennessee. He talked about the "extraordinary number" of people I deposed in that case, and then asked me how many people we deposed.

"Joal. Sarah. Laurie Evans," I said.

"That's it? Because I've got boxes and boxes downstairs that's just a part of what we have."

"I don't remember anybody else," I said, wondering whether he had read any of the "boxes and boxes" of material we'd sent him in discovery. He went on and on about the number of phone records we'd subpoenaed and said we had threatened lawsuits. We hadn't threatened anybody with a lawsuit. It simply wasn't true.

"What about your investigator, Eric Nichols, and the charges of influencing a witness as it relates to Jerry McDonald?"

"It's Eric Echols," I corrected him. "He talked to a willing individual and he was arrested."

He turned back to the "aggressive media campaign" and referred to a "five-part puff piece" I had done with Melydia Clewell, basically making a speech again until Doc stood up and asked, "Is that a testimony or a question?"

"Overruled," Judge House said immediately.

"You engaged in the aggressive media campaign, right? Part of the strategy?"

"No. I went on television and told the truth," I said.

"So the television dragged you, and you were on the television?"

"No. I want to tell of my innocence."

Pounding his podium, he spoke at length about the "aggressive tactics" and asked whether it was all meant to try to make him "quit." He asked who I had practiced my cross-examinations with, and I told him it was Dr. Lorandos. And then he asked me, "Is that where you learned to tell a *Tonya truth*?"

"The truth is the truth," I said.

"When the jury wasn't around, you seemed to like to catch my eye and stare at me. Was that part of what you learned somewhere, an intimidation stare?"

"No."

"Did you talk about when the jury's around, maybe not to do that because that's sort of a mean face, and maybe cry at the appropriate moments?"

"Did I what?"

He asked whether I'd been coached on what faces to make. I hadn't. I told him "no." I didn't deny the fact that I'd stared him down when the jury wasn't there. I did stare him down. *He deserved to be stared down!*

At this point, it seemed to me that Gregor had finally let us know why he asked so many witnesses about my "narcissism," and he'd also managed to get in some good speeches about the "conspiracy" and the "Truth for Tonya" website, so I was waiting for him to bring up my "fitness pageant past" at some point, too. He finally did. He talked about my having to wear certain outfits and do certain poses and routines in front of judges.

"How long have you been doing that?" he said.

"I did for a number of years. I haven't been, in a long time," I answered.

He asked an odd question about whether my first husband had hired Joal to be my fitness coach. He hadn't, and I said so. He asked if I had paid Joal to be my fitness coach. I told him that wasn't true, either. "Nobody hired Joal."

He went on and on about the workouts and routines and what my diet was—for no apparent reason. He then stated something completely false: "[Your first husband] was married to you and caught you in the act with Joal Henke, correct?"

"No."

"And you said it was just a 'massage'?"

"No."

As that whole line of questioning went on, it was certainly not difficult for me to discern where Gregor got his information. *It's classic Joal. I guess Doc was right. I guess it was important for us to bring up all of my history with Joal before the prosecutors questioned me about it.* I hoped the jury believed me over him. I closed my eyes for a moment in the middle of this, just praying that the truth would win out.

The next attack on the list was a bit of a surprise. He asked me about my trip to see that woman in Newark, New Jersey—the one who had shown up on Joal's phone records so many times.

"You got on a plane, you went up to New Jersey, and you *accosted* [this woman]—who was a real-estate customer of Joal's—because her name was on his phone records," Gregor said. "Right?"

"No," I said.

"Well, explain it to me, then."

"I talked to her."

"At her home?"

"At her office," I said.

"And at her home."

"I went to where her office was and knocked on the door. Her office is in a home."

"You hopped on a plane and went to New Jersey . . . because you saw there was 115 minutes of conversation between her and Joal."

"No, actually there was thousands of minutes," I said.

"So you didn't bring up that there was 115 minutes over and over again, and you wanted to know who she was and why she was talking to Joal for 115 minutes?"

"No," I said.

"She asked you to leave, didn't she?"

"No. I have it recorded," I said.

"Did you have anything recorded where she said, 'I felt scared—a woman going to great lengths about getting information on me, harassing me, my friends, my office, I feel like she's a stalker.'"

"No. I have the whole conversation on tape," I said.

Chris Arnt called Len over and whispered something in his ear. Gregor then shot straight up and asked me, "So, when you went up to [her address] and you say you had the whole thing on tape?"

"Yes."

"Did you tell her you were taping the conversation?"

"It's a one-party state," I said.

"So you felt like you could be sneaky and tape the conversation and see what kind of *dirt you could git*?" he said in a greatly exaggerated Southern twang.

"No," I said, looking straight back at him. "I felt like something like this could happen and my words could be twisted."

Gregor seemed to stumble a bit after that. He asked me a couple more questions about the conversation, but I think he realized that he'd better be careful. Since he brought it up in court, I would definitely be allowed to enter that tape into evidence and play the whole thing, which would have shown how wrong he was about that whole line of questioning. I had never been so thankful for tape-recording conversations over the last couple of years than at that very moment.

I wondered when, if ever, this ADA who was prosecuting me for offenses against children was going to ask me about the actual charges. He went on a long line of questioning about whether I was "holding hands" with Eric Echols when we ran into David at the Bonefish Grill and even made reference to us going into a hotel room afterward.

"Was Mr. Echols getting his *bonus* for threatening Jerry McDonald at that point?"

I answered his disparaging innuendos with a firm "No."

He asked about the details of May 30, using Tim Deal's descriptions of me "turning purple" and "hyperventilating" and more. I said yes to what was true and no to what was false. He asked me to describe my "relationships" with Jennifer, Tammy, the Potters, and more.

My voice kept fading. Doc asked me again to speak up so the jury could hear me. He asked the judge if he could place a piece of paper with the words "Speak Up!" in front of me on the witness stand so I wouldn't forget. I took a deep breath. I drank some more water. I think my nerves were getting the better of me. I've never had trouble talking before, that's for sure. And it wasn't a problem with answering the questions. Telling the truth is easy. My mouth was just all dried out, and my throat felt tired. I felt like my exhaustion was catching up with me at the worst possible moment.

During the questioning about the Potters, Gregor went back to the whole issue of whether Dee had helped me pay for a dress one time. The fact was she *had* paid for a dress. It was a different yellow dress than the one they kept showing a picture of, but she'd paid for a dress nonetheless.

Gregor then said that Dee had also testified that she bought me some "Venus swimwear."

"No, she didn't say that," I told him. *He's misquoting something that we all heard directly from Dee on the witness stand. She didn't say she had bought me "Venus swimwear." She specifically said "no" to that whole line of absurd questioning. I was positive of that. I'm sure anyone who'd been paying attention was positive of that.*

If they put me in prison, if I wanted to appeal, I would have to fight about the mishandling of the trial and anything that looked like prosecutorial misconduct. So I was paying attention. To everything. Little things could make a big difference. I knew that.

And yes, even as I sat on that witness stand being grilled about every intimate detail of my personal life, even as he went on about the "lesbian porn" and accused me of "borrowing it" from my father—disparaging my daddy in front of that whole courtroom—even as I sat there taking what felt like abuse, I was actively thinking about how I was going to fight for my freedom from inside a prison. I refused to be shocked and unprepared for a guilty verdict. I did not for one second believe that I was in the clear.

I looked at that poker-faced jury. I knew I was running out of time.

Chapter 63

During a break, Doc, Cary, and Scott all told me that they didn't mean for me to take their "stick to yes and no" advice quite so literally. They told me to go ahead and expand a little bit more in my answers to Len Gregor.

In most cases, I didn't have to explain. Especially when Gregor tried to imply things without actually saying them, like when he talked about my work as a fitness instructor and asked about an email I'd once registered that had the word "Kidfit" in the email address. Yes, at one point I gave some seminars about kids' nutrition and exercise. I had an email address registered with a "Kidfit" address. Yes, I did. *So what?*

Yes, I drank too much at the Walker County Gala in 2007 and danced with some other men. I wrote an apology letter to some friends and acquaintances because I was not proud of my behavior. But no, my zipper did not break and my "rear end" was not hanging out, as Gregor kept declaring in front of that jury.

"You wear thong underwear, right?" he asked.

I looked directly at the jury for that one: "Yes, I do," I said. *What does any of this have to do with this case?*

The ADA tried to attack the timeline we'd presented, saying there's "no way" that I could account for everything I did and put "everything" on that timeline.

"That's correct," I said. "There's nobody that's followed me around twenty-four seven."

"It'd be silly to think that! Correct?" Gregor said, rather loudly.

"Yes," I answered.

When he finally got to talking about Brianna and Chloe, Gregor said that "depending on which of your witnesses we listened to, Brianna Lamb was either over there all the time, or she was never over there. Chloe McDonald, according to which witness of yours testifies, is either over there all the time, or she was never over there. Did you hear that?"

Doc shot up like a rocket. "Object to the form of the question. That's not the testimony. That's not the testimony at all! It's a *rank* mischaracterization of the testimony of the defense witnesses."

"That's for the jury to decide if they heard that," Gregor said, and he offered to rephrase things a little bit. Then he asked the same questions all over again.

"I don't recall hearing absolutes either way," I said, but I told him that neither of those girls was over all the time. I was perfectly clear about how many times they'd been over. I felt we'd shown evidence throughout the trial to show that the number of times they were at my house had been grossly exaggerated by the prosecution's witnesses.

"What about some of the jurors"—I'm pretty sure he meant to say "witnesses," but I let it slide—"who said that Brianna went home with you every day?"

"I don't recall hearing that Brianna went home with me every day," I said. *Where is he getting this from? Was he in the same room for this trial? Has the jury heard the same things he was hearing?*

He asked me whether I disputed the fact that Brianna had spent the night at my house numerous times. Of course I disputed that. He asked me if it was my assertion that Brianna had only ever stayed at my house one time. "Yes," I responded.

"You're saying that you never gave Brianna Lamb a bath?"

"That is exactly what I'm saying."

"How often did Chloe McDonald spend the night?" he asked.

"Chloe McDonald spent the one night, in August, at the *High School Musical* party."

"Not at the after-Halloween party?"

"No, sir." *There was no after-Halloween party.*

"And not on any other occasion?"

"No, sir."

"Your daughter and Chloe were friends, though, correct?"

This seemed to be an occasion that called for me to say more than yes or no, so I did. "They had gotten to know one another. After the incident between Ashley and Chloe, there was not as much. We would see them at the ball fields and things like that, but we wouldn't get together." I reexplained the whole friendship with Kelly and the kids' friendships with Chloe and her older brother, and explained that we did keep running into each other at other people's birthday parties and the like after the incident as well.

I quietly wondered why someone on their side, anyone on their side, hadn't asked these same questions of me two years ago.

He got real specific about Sandra Lamb's assertion that I had once kept Brianna at my house after the kids had gone to Joal's on a Friday night. He added a detail, too, saying that Sandra had said I kept Brianna until around nine thirty at night. To all of it, I said, "No. She wasn't over there when my children weren't there."

"So again, to sum up, Brianna Lamb: never bathed her, never spent more than one night, was over at your house some but not that much," he said.

"Correct."

"Chloe: one night, not the after-Halloween party night, the *High School Musical* party night, and not really over at your house that much either."

"Correct."

Why weren't these questions asked before I was arrested?

Gregor spent a lot of time going over the details of Ashley's January 2008 birthday party. He said he was "confused" about the fact that I didn't yell at the girls, and so why would I tell David that I thought I just "ticked off two influential families"? I walked him through the whole thing, wishing once again that someone had sat down and simply asked me about all of this two years ago.

After a moment when he mocked Doc's voice and asked some more about Ashley, he asked me, "How long do you think it would take to touch a child's vagina inappropriately?"

"I haven't done it, so I don't know," I answered.

"Well, I think you do," Gregor said. "How long do you think it would take?"

"I don't know." He pressed me on it again, demonstrating various motions with his hand in front of the jury, so I said, "Seconds. Sure. I would say that the appropriate and the inappropriate could take the same amount of time."

"We've heard all of this about your busy schedule and you were asked the question, 'When did you fit in molesting children?' Well, you didn't really have to make a lot of room in the schedule to do that, did you?"

"I didn't molest any children," I said, "and I didn't have a video camera, unfortunately, on me twenty-four seven."

"How often do you think a child molester molests a child with video running?"

"I didn't molest any children."

He repeated the question, and I answered: "I can't tell you what a child molester would do."

After some talk about the unfortunate fact that no one "expects" anyone to be a child molester, and yet it happens—a statement to which I agreed—he said, "It's not some creepy guy in a trench coat always, is it? That stereotype doesn't even really exist."

"You're exactly right."

He then asked me if it was my "testimony" that I had "never" told anyone that I had been sexually abused myself. I confirmed that I had never said such a thing, ever, and I looked over at my poor father, who had to sit there and endure this line of questioning about the "cycle of abuse," and the notion that "someone" who was touched by their "mother" might repeat that "learned behavior."

"Sir, are you implicating my *mother*?" I asked.

"No, I'm asking general questions," he responded.

I took a drink of water. *When is this going to stop?* I had put myself up there. I knew the risks, and I knew with some certainty what I was going to endure. It just never occurred to me that Gregor would drive his cross so far into the dirt. The thing that changed in that moment, for me, was that I got angry. I was tired of this man saying whatever he wanted. *It's fine if he wants to say things about me, but for him to stand up there and misquote people who've come into this courtroom, to disparage my friends, to disparage my parents—I feel like I need to stand up for the people I love, the way I would stand up for them in response to any common bully.*

Even as I looked him in the eye and countered all of the attacks with the truth as strongly and assuredly as I could while still remaining respectful to that court of law, that man continued in this manner for another solid hour. I could barely stand it. *He's jumping from one subject to another, misquoting testimony that we've all heard, insinuating that our expert witnesses are lying simply because they were paid, asking me about the men I've dated in my past, wrongfully accusing me of being physically abusive to one of my old boyfriends (without either evidence or source; in fact, that former boyfriend is still a friend of mine, and had shown up in court to support me on previous days), incorrectly claiming that I'd dated a married man when the man he spoke of was clearly divorced (and his divorce decree is public record), misquoting me multiple times by using much harsher words than I've actually used in documented testimony, and more. How far can this go?*

He then seemed to mock Doc's delivery and the way he pronounced DeWayne Wilson's name. At one point, his questioning made it sound like Doc and I together had made disparaging comments during my testimony about Jerry McDonald—as if we were somehow poking fun at Jerry for working three jobs and trying to support his family.

"Isn't it kinda just cheap and silly to try to humiliate someone," Gregor said, "with a name or the fact that they had to work three jobs or struggle financially?"

I glanced at the jury as he uttered those words, and then I looked Gregor straight in the eyes and said, "I think that it's ironic that you're talking about humiliating someone."

He went on for so long about so many disparaging things that Doc finally stood up and said, "Cut it out!" He asked to approach the bench. Judge House didn't stop any of it, of course, but the ADA finally moved on—and started talking about some of the research I'd done into other false-allegation cases.

"None of these children had accused you of turning them into a mouse," he said. "Right?"

"Okay. No."

"None of those children have talked about being molested in secret tunnels, right?"

"Correct."

"Or about ritualistic sacrifice of babies—"

"No, that's not in the Kern County case," I said.

"Or that you could fly, or any of those cases from the 1980s that we've all learned from—McMartin, Kerns . . . right? I mean, they haven't accused you of any of these outlandish allegations in those classic cases."

"I would say there are some outlandish things in this. Throwing a child down a flight of steps with the mother in the driveway, and not feeding, and—"

"Now if we really—" he attempted to interrupt, but I continued.

"False allegations are awful in and of themselves," I said, "for everybody involved. From the accused to the children."

He seemed to try to disparage the experts who spoke on my side, making an analogy about how it's easier to "blow up a bridge than to build one." He said, "You paid people a lot of money to blow up a bridge."

"No," I said. "I paid money to experts to tell the truth."

His final line of questioning was all about the manner of questions Doc asked in the courtroom. He went on about how Doc asked leading questions, made suggestions, and offered closed-choice options when Dr. Aldridge was on the stand.

"Okay," I said. "She was an adult. And he would, kind of like you're trying to lead me?"

"That's what you do on cross-examination. That's one of the rules of court—do you understand that?"

"And not what you're supposed to do whenever you are trying to get to the bottom of a matter of a child that's been abused or not been abused," I said.

"Okay, is that how you're gonna answer that one? You gonna stay with that answer?"

"Yes, that's how I'm gonna answer."

Gregor seemed to finally be reaching the end of his rope. He kept pausing longer and longer between switching subjects. He repeated himself, flipping through the pages of his legal pad, trying to cover the same material over and over and throwing in what seemed to be one last notion he caught in his notes: "What did you mean when you said it was hard to prove female-on-female sexual abuse?"

"I have never said that," I said.

"So let me sum it up," he said. "The children are incorrect about what happened to them, and everybody but Tonya and her witnesses are incorrect and liars and part of this 'gotta get Tonya Craft,' right?"

"I did not call anyone a liar," I said. "I don't know how—well, from some of the expert testimony, it makes *sense* about how the investigation was handled, about how parental influences and different things that they discussed, how it *can* happen. I don't know how it *did* happen, but I did not molest any children. I did not molest Brianna Lamb, I did not molest Chloe McDonald, and I did not molest Ashley Henke. So how it happened, I don't know. But it has happened, and unfortunately these children are just as much of a victim as I am."

He went once more back to words he apparently found on a website, and he went once more back to his apparent anger about the "conspiracy" theory, and spoke forcefully, thumping his podium about how "the system . . . these authorities just had to get *Tonya Craft* . . . 'We want this kindergarten teacher!' Right?"

"I don't know what you want," I said. "I want the truth."

Gregor looked back at Chris Arnt, and Arnt shook his head.

"That's it," Gregor said.

Doc immediately stood up.

"Nothing further," Doc said. "Thank you, Tonya. The defense rests."

Chapter 64

Istood up as the judge recessed the trial until nine o'clock Monday morning, and the whole gallery exploded into a sea of commotion once again.

My heart raced something fierce. I tried to take some deep breaths. I wasn't sure how I would make it through a whole weekend of running that testimony through my head over and over, worrying about every word I said and every word I *didn't* say. *Have I said my piece? Did they hear me? Does it matter?*

I wouldn't have a chance to defend myself again in this trial. I wouldn't have another moment to get in front of that jury and tell them that I was innocent. Ever. It was done. Other than doing what I could to help Doc prepare his closing remarks that weekend, I was finished.

My own freedom wasn't in my hands anymore.

Maybe it never was.

I threw myself into closing preparations that weekend. My whole team did. Doc needed every key moment, every key detail, every key piece of evidence and testimony and background material at his fingertips at a moment's notice while he composed his final argument meant to save my life and the lives of my children.

Somewhere in the back of my mind, I wondered if either side's closing arguments would matter. After four long weeks of testimony, what more was there to say? Still, I could not rest. I could not give up. I had to give it everything I had, and I did.

The courthouse was a madhouse that Monday. There was more media from all over the country than I'd ever seen before in one place. There were so many people that showed up to hear the closing and quite possibly a verdict that day that poor David barely made it in. He was all sweaty from running and pushing through the crowd.

There was a sea of people left standing in the hallways and outside the building. The court even opened up the media room just so some of those spectators could watch over the reporters' shoulders and see what was going on through that little TV.

Normally each side would have two hours for closing arguments, but there seemed to be nothing "normal" about my case. Judge House decided to limit it to ninety minutes each that morning. Not one of my attorneys had ever seen a judge do that. Ever. We'd worked up a Power-Point presentation, which of course suffered a major computer glitch when transferring from Mac to Windows at four in the morning and had to be copied without half of the professional look we'd developed. Then we got to court and had to scrap a huge portion of it to help Doc fit into the newly allotted time.

The prosecution had the advantage. They'd go first, then Doc would go, then the prosecution would get to finish out whatever portion of their ninety minutes was left. So Chris Arnt and Len Gregor would have the first word *and* the last word before that jury started their deliberations.

I prayed to God for fairness. I prayed to God for truth. I prayed for my kids. I prayed for Doc. I sat there trying to hide my shaking, trying to hold off the tears—basically trying to keep breathing as Gregor stood up. The courtroom fell silent as he started his speech aimed at putting me in prison. Forever.

———◆———

"I got to thinking," he said, "you know, when you're bass fishing, you use a lot of colorful lures. You change those colors and you use those to try to attract the fish. The colorful lures, to me, are like conspiracy theories. And like those lures, there really isn't any substance to those colorful conspiracy theories."

He turned on an overhead projector and put up a series of slides that he referred to as "Tonya Truths." He started with *Tonya "Truth" #1: The Wilson Conspiracy Theory*. He went on to *Tonya "Truth" #2: The Brianna Lamb Conspiracy*. And so forth. Naming my husband as one of the conspirators. Naming Chickamauga Elementary as a conspirator. Naming Chris Arnt as the "architect of evil" and himself as "even more evil than that," continuing all the way through #12, naming all of Catoosa County (and the surrounding area) as a conspirator because it included everyone in the whole mix of numbers 1–11.

He repeated many of what we felt were the same half-truths and untruths that he'd asked me about during cross-examination, using them as the basis for each of his so-called "truths." He added some fresh accusations, too. I don't think it's worth repeating any more of his awful claims than I already have here, except for one: With David sitting right there in that courtroom, he talked about our "miraculous" reconciliation in November 2008—and basically called it a sham.

"What she *has* on him, or what power she has over him, I don't know," he told that jury.

As he completed each "truth," he took the piece of paper it was printed on from the projector and laid it on the rail right in front of the jury. He commented that each "Tonya Truth" was a "color," and he wondered aloud whether the jury would "go for that one."

Gregor told those jurors to think back on my testimony and to think about all of the "lies" I was caught up in: "How do you know when Tonya Craft is lying?" he said. "When her *lips* are moving. Just lie after lie after lie."

"And don't let packaging fool you," he said. "Unfortunately in this world, evil comes in attractive packages. More often than not you can't identify 'evil' by appearance, or else we'd be able to stamp it out."

He referred once again to this "ridiculous, shameless, disgusting conspiracy defense."

"If this was motivated by anything other than people wanting to get to the truth and wanting this defendant to be held accountable for what she's done, don't you think they could have come up with bigger, better lies than the evidence that was presented in this case?" he said.

He explained what those lies would be, too: about eyewitnesses, confessions, and more. "There is plenty of evidence to prove this defendant's guilty beyond a reasonable doubt. If it was a conspiracy, there would be a lot more," he said.

"There is an absolute and actual truth out there," he added. "It's not a *Tonya Truth*. It's simple. It's black and white. It's not a bunch of pretty colors," he said, forcefully grabbing up the printed paper "Tonya Truths" one by one from the jury rail and dramatically crumpling all that paper in his hand. "It's not variations on it," he said. "It's simply the truth. As sad, despicable, and cruel and distasteful as it might be, it's the truth. It's like what's contained in this indictment. It's black and white. It may be unpleasant, but it's the truth."

After hitting once more on the "overpaid" experts and my attempts to "buy" the truth, he asked that jury to find "a truth that is real, for Brianna, for Chloe, for Ashley, for our community, and for justice."

I tried not to shake my head. I tried not to throw daggers with my eyes. I'm not sure I successfully held it in. After listening to all of that, I was floored that they'd only used up thirty minutes. They'd have almost a full hour left on their ninety-minute clock for Chris Arnt to present at the end. *What else are they planning to say about me?*

Doc got up looking very tired. In some ways, I think he had already given everything he had to my defense. But slowly and surely his adrenaline kicked in, and he ramped up his fully animated self in front of that jury. He recounted absolutely everything that mattered. He walked through my whole timeline. He talked about the experts and the interviews. He somehow managed to squeeze all of it into three-quarters of the time he'd been preparing for all weekend.

He showed the jury a tattoo on his wrist, a Greek word that means "essential truth," and he talked about the fact that it was the State who held the burden of proving each part of the alleged crimes "beyond a reasonable doubt"—not the other way around. He reminded the jury that it was up to *them* to discern the truth: "The only thing that matters is what you believe in your hearts to be true."

He verbally fought back against what we felt were a few of the more ridiculous claims Len Gregor had been harping on for days in that courtroom. He defended the experts we'd hired, saying each one of them had studied the evidence from a professional and unbiased point of view. They weren't going to come participate in a trial that was based on "conspiracy theories," he said. Why would they risk their entire professional reputations for *that*? They studied the evidence, they saw the "shoddy" investigation and the "tainted" interviews, and "they came here to put a *stop* to this," he said. "Because they care about the truth."

Doc spent most of his time going over what we saw as problems with the investigation. He reminded them of how hard we had worked to bring in the best people we could find to show them why, in reality, "it didn't happen, it couldn't have happened the way they said it did, and it doesn't make sense."

"Tonya Craft was a respected, wonderful, award-winning teacher. *Is* a respected, wonderful, award-winning teacher," Doc said. "I hope to goodness she will be a teacher again." He got a little quieter, and walked in front of the podium, and stood right in front of those jurors. "She wasn't guilty of ever hurting a child. She didn't ever hurt a child. She'll never hurt a child," he told them. He was almost whispering at the end. It was difficult to hear him from across the room.

"Look at what's happened. Look at what's happened in this community," he said. "It has to stop. You're the only people that can stop it," he said. "Thank you."

———❖———

Chris Arnt's final hour of closing wasn't as fishy as Len Gregor's on the surface. He started calmly and professionally, using a PowerPoint presentation to talk about evidence and the jury "putting together the pieces of a jigsaw puzzle" without knowing what the picture was from the cover of the box. He said evidence was like that, too. The jury was to keep hearing evidence, just the way the detectives kept looking for evidence, until they could discern what the picture was—beyond a reasonable doubt. They might not have all of the pieces of the puzzle in place, but there comes a point when there is no more reasonable doubt as to what the picture on that puzzle is going to turn out to be.

I sat there wishing with everything in my heart that the detectives in my case had done what he described.

Arnt's closing statements didn't look quite as fishy, but they were. At one point, he said that Kim Walker had got on the stand and confirmed that Chloe was at the after-Halloween party sleepover at our house, and that I'd contradicted her during my testimony—which was enough for Doc to jump up and object, "No. She did not say that."

Judge House overruled it and said, "He's on closing."

"Whether I tell, or they tell you," Arnt said, pointing back at our table, "it's *your* memory that controls it."

Let's hope they all have good memories, I thought. That jury wasn't allowed to take notes. This "refresher" from the prosecutors might have been messing with their memories all over the place.

Apparently in Judge House's courtroom, anything could be said during closing or cross, whether it was factual or not. That's not the way a court is supposed to work. I've read the statutes! There is supposed to be a basis established for any charge or accusation or evidence that is presented whatsoever. Why is the prosecution being allowed to bend that rule over and over again?

For all I knew, the jury was listening to them and taking it all in, hook, line, and sinker.

Arnt got more animated as he went along.

He said if the girls were making up lies about me, they'd have said those lies in the very first interview. He tried to prove this by drawing a reference to the Bible, and the story of Jesus's resurrection, and the Roman guards—a story that was confusing to me. I couldn't make sense of it.

He called into question the words that Ashley said on the phone message she left me the night of May 30—even though it had been played twice for that jury, and everyone heard those words themselves. He insinuated that she actually said something different from what we'd all heard, but then didn't confirm what it was she might have said.

He dropped to his knees to show the "level" I was on when I reprimanded Brianna Lamb and Lydia Wilson at Ashley's birthday party. Then he dropped down again moments later and said, "Think back to Brianna's testimony. She said she was just like this, on her knees, when she molested her."

He even talked over his allotted time by a few minutes. Judge House didn't stop him. Arnt berated Doc, talking about him "prancing" over to embarrass their experts by showing them books that they hadn't read. He compared me to "Tiger Woods" and Tiger's "secret image" that nobody knew about.

Then he made a big point to remind the jury about the tearful testimony of Jerry McDonald: "Would he have put his kid through this if it wasn't true?"

"You need to send a message to the Dream Team over there that this ridiculous conspiracy is a bunch of garbage," he said. "You need to protect the innocent and hold the guilty to account for what *she* did in this case. You'll also send a message to Chloe, Brianna, and Ashley that they will be protected. Their strength is worth it. You do that by filling out the verdict form: guilty on all counts."

I was a wreck. I wasn't sobbing or showing very much in that courtroom, but I thought for sure those final words, combined with the girls' testimonies, combined with the remembrance of Jerry McDonald's testimony were going to put me away.

As soon as Arnt's closing was finished, the judge reread all twenty-two counts of my indictment to that jury. Every one of them struck me all over again, like twenty-two shotgun blasts to my stomach. He gave that jury a long list of very detailed instructions about their obligations and duties.

Then he sent them off to deliberate my guilt or innocence.

Chapter 65

My team took me back to the house while Scott waited at the courthouse. I walked across the street and collapsed on the bed at Karen's. I closed my eyes and tried to block out the world.

Scott called us around 4:30 P.M. The jury didn't have a verdict yet, so Judge House sent them home for the night. They wouldn't be back until nine the next morning.

That's when I got up and left. I couldn't take the waiting around doing nothing while everybody chitchatted and talked about what they thought went well or didn't and what the jury might be thinking. I didn't want to hear any of it. No one knew what that jury would do except the jurors.

For the first time in two years, there was nothing for me to do. There were no more arguments to prepare, no research that needed to be done, no folders that needed to be organized. Nothing.

So I left. I didn't tell anybody where I was going. I just climbed into my old SUV and drove away. The way I saw it, this was the last night of freedom I might ever get. I wasn't sure where I was headed. I just drove around for a while. I'm sure some of them were scared to death for me, so I called David just to let him know I was okay and not to worry.

I wondered if anybody saw me as I drove. I don't think they would have believed it if they did. *What the heck would Tonya Craft be doing out driving around when her trial's about to end?*

I eventually stopped at a Holiday Inn Express just off the highway. I decided to get a room. I checked in. I went up. I sat on the bed. I turned on the TV and watched some reruns of *Friends*. I didn't want to think anymore. I didn't want to be bothered. I turned my phone off. I knew there was nothing anybody needed to talk to me about until the next morning.

At some point I walked across the parking lot and over the divider to a little Italian restaurant that had been there for as long as I could remember.

I'd eaten there with my family in the past. It felt like I was choosing my last meal. I ordered a large serving of lasagna, saturated grease and all, to go.

Sitting in the hotel room alone, watching TV and eating with a plastic fork, I made my peace with what was about to happen. I truly felt I had done everything I could to fight these allegations. I gave all I had to give. So if God wanted to keep testing me, I'd somehow find the strength to keep on fighting.

I knew I'd be walking out one of two doors the next day: I'd either go back out the door I came in and start working on getting my kids back, or they'd walk me out through the door behind the jury, in handcuffs on my way to prison.

At that point, honestly, whichever door it was, I was prepared to face it—because I knew that God would be right there with me. I knew the truth, and he knew the truth, and that was all that mattered. Either door would be hard. Either one would have a whole lot more fighting left on the other side. I wanted to go home. I did. But I knew my life was never going to be the same again. Not one bit of it.

Nobody was upset with me when I got back to the house early the next morning. No one said very much at all. I went back over to the bed at Karen and Walt's and waited. I told everyone to leave me alone unless it was crucial.

David walked into the bedroom at one point that afternoon to tell me that Scott had called from the courthouse. The jury was still out, he said, but somebody had called the court and made a death threat against me. The court was going to provide me with protection—law enforcement officers to lead me in and out of the courthouse, which was the absolute last thing I wanted.

"I don't want protection," I said. "I don't care what happens. I don't care if there was a death threat!"

Judge House was planning to lock up the courtroom whenever the jury came in with a verdict, and he planned to limit the number of spectators inside. I'd be limited to about thirty people.

"Who do you want?" David asked. "We need to give Scott a list of names, like, right now."

"Out of all these people who love and support me? Are you kidding me? No. I'm not going to do it," I said. "Get somebody else to do it. Go!"

I have no idea who chose those thirty people.

I couldn't close the curtain tight enough in that room at Karen and Walt's house. I couldn't make it as dark as I wanted. I lay down on the bed and tried to enjoy the comfort of it. I tried to enjoy the fact that the bedroom was bigger than where I was headed. My body was so ravaged, I couldn't help but fall asleep.

"Tonya? Tonya," my friend Tammy said, gently waking me late that afternoon. She was talking real calm and peaceful, like she didn't want to scare me. David and Jennifer were both standing there with her, and I immediately knew why they'd come.

"There's a verdict," Tammy said.

I stood up like a ghost. I brushed my teeth. I changed into a pair of plain white cotton panties and a sports bra with no underwire. I walked out of that room and through the salon and across the street, where a bunch of the people I cared most about in the world had gathered with my team while I slept. I got into a car with Doc, Cary, and David for the drive down to Ringgold, down Highway 41, past the jail where I'd already suffered. I knew it was nothing compared to what I'd face in prison.

We drove past the hordes of media and hundreds of people all gathered outside the courthouse. It looked like a sea of yellow. It bothered me to think how many people were going to be saddened and disappointed when that jury convicted me.

We filtered back into the courtroom and an officer locked the doors. Judge House came in. The jury walked in. They all took their seats as I tried to breathe. I tried to slow my heart rate down, but I couldn't. Not one of those jurors gave me an indication of what their verdict might be. Most of them were looking down or to the side, and if I had to guess, I'd say they looked pretty morose.

"I understand you have reached a verdict," Judge House said once they were all in place. "Will you please hand that verdict form to the bailiff."

The form got passed to Judge House first, and then he handed it over to a white-haired gentleman in a suit and glasses who positioned himself right in front of our table.

"Mr. Stone, will you read the verdict?" Judge House said.

Mr. Stone spoke in a booming voice, with a deep Southern drawl: "In this Superior Court of Catoosa County, State of Georgia . . . number 2008-SU-CR-534 . . . the State of Georgia versus Tonya Craft . . ."

He took a pause that felt like forever and a day as he turned the page and arranged it just so in his hands.

"Verdict," he said. "We the jury find the defendant, Count Number One: Not Guilty."

I heard screams and shouts of joy erupt from the hallway and then again from outside the building as the news spread, like a wave.

I tried to block it out. I stared at Mr. Stone's lips, not wanting to miss one word. I could not cry. I did not breathe. There were twenty-one more counts left to go.

"Count Number Two: Not Guilty."

My knees wavered. Scott put his hand on my back to support me.

"Count Number Three: Not Guilty."

"Count Number Four: Not Guilty."

"Count Number Five: Not Guilty."

"Count Number Six: Not Guilty."

"Count Number Seven: Not Guilty."

Scott grabbed my shoulder. I could feel him bouncing all nervous in his shoes. Doc stood to my right, rocking back and forth a little bit.

"Count Number Eight: Not Guilty."

"Count Number Nine: Not Guilty."

I started to cry a little. I couldn't hold back anymore.

"Count Number Ten: Not Guilty."

"Count Number Eleven: Not Guilty."

"Count Twelve: Not Guilty."

"Count Thirteen: Not Guilty."

"Count Number Fourteen: Not Guilty."

"Count Number Fifteen: Not Guilty."

I heard more cheers from outside on the front lawn. I started shaking.

"Count Number Sixteen: Not Guilty."

"Count Number Seventeen: Not Guilty."

"Count Number Eighteen: Not Guilty."

"Count Number Nineteen: Not Guilty."

I bowed my head. *Thank you, God. Thank you. Thank you . . .*

"Count Number Twenty: Not Guilty."

"Count Number Twenty-One: Not Guilty."

I started sobbing.

"Count Number Twenty-Two: Not Guilty."

My head fell into my hands. Scott squeezed my shoulder, and Doc threw his arm around me and hugged me to him. I nearly collapsed. Scott and Doc held me up.

"This Eleventh Day of May, Two Thousand Ten, Signed . . ." Mr. Stone continued.

"Let's go," Doc said. He and Scott nearly lifted me by my arms and tried to rush me right out of that courtroom. If the death threat were real, that was when it would have come.

The judge had ordered everyone to stay seated until the jury and everyone was out of the building, but a few people stood up, and he yelled, "Wait. Sit down! Y'all have a seat."

A female court officer put her hands on me and turned me back toward the table. I felt violated. I felt woozy. I wanted to push right past her and leave. *Why should I have to stay even one second longer?*

Doc yelled to the judge, "May the defendant leave, Your Honor?"

"I've already said that, yes," Judge House said.

Doc looked at the jury and shouted above the crowd, "Thank you, ladies and gentlemen."

He half-held me up as we exited to the left, and I spotted Detective Stephen Keith standing by the door. Even in the middle of that rush, I paused to give that man a look of death. I was shocked to see his face in that courtroom, and in that split second of recognition, I wanted him to *know* what he'd done. I wanted to remind him that I'd had the guts to take the stand and face the jury, and he had not.

I could hear the words of Judge House's voice booming over everything as I made my exit. "You do not have to talk to anyone . . ." he said, talking to the jurors.

My sobs were so big and I was shaking so badly, I barely remember getting down the stairs and out to the car. The media was a mob scene. People were cheering. We drove past them all and I thanked God for every one of them. I thanked God for seeing me through this. I thanked God for those jurors, who were given the ability to see the truth through all of the confusing mudslinging and character attacks. I prayed that God watch over Chloe and Brianna. I prayed that God keep watch on my baby girl, Ashley. I prayed that God keep watch over Tyler, too.

Mommy's coming, I said to them both in my mind. *Mommy will be there soon.*

Part IV

Freedom

Chapter 66

It was very strange to go from thinking I would sleep in a prison cell that night to getting whisked off in a limousine to catch a flight to New York City. After giving my first interview to Melydia Clewell in a room at my parents' house, I followed through on a request to fly to New York for an exclusive interview on *The Today Show*.

I barely had a moment to breathe. I barely had a moment to think about what I wanted to say. Suddenly I was on the air on live television, sitting across from Meredith Vieira on a stiff sofa surrounded by blue walls and all sorts of cheering people on Rockefeller Plaza—in the city I'd come to in January with my handmade sign just trying to get anyone's attention. It was, in the truest sense of the word, absolutely surreal.

Meredith asked me what was going through my mind as the bailiff read "not guilty" on those twenty-two counts. I told her, on the one hand, it was a relief, and it was. But, I said, "It wasn't a victory. There's nobody that wins in this situation. And my whole heart had been taken, and I got half of it back, but until I get my children, I won't have my entire heart back."

Meredith asked me if I was the victim of a witch hunt. I explained it a little more fully.

"I believe I was possibly a victim of a perfect storm, as the children were as well," I said. "I think that there are many attributes to this. One being there already were some friendships that were no longer friendships," I said, "and whenever there was a certain situation between normal childhood behavior and pointing and touching, and then my name immediately got put into the mix, and then it turned into parental phone calls back and forth, and my name being brought up, 'Didn't Miss Tonya do this?'"

Looking back, I think that was a pretty decent characterization of it all, especially considering how soon it was after the verdict. I'd barely had time for anything to set in, let alone to come up with the right words to say to an audience of millions of people.

In the coming days, I'd make the rounds to *Good Morning America*, and *The View*, and *Larry King*, and *Nightline*, and all of those big TV shows. Some people misinterpreted that "media tour" as me looking for publicity for myself. That's just plain false. I wasn't the one calling the media. They were calling *me*. I'm not sure why I'd want or need any publicity after enduring that public trial for all those weeks. But people like to think what they like to think. The fact is, I had a message to share: This could happen to anyone. We need to pay attention to what law enforcement officials are doing when it comes to cases of false child-sexual-abuse allegations, to make sure they're doing their jobs as investigators in order to help sift out the real accusations from the false ones. We need to make some changes to the legal system. We need to be careful what we do and say with kids, and how we question kids, and how we as parents can overreact to things we don't like in a way that does more harm than good.

The media wanted my story, and I thought my story might help people. After all, what is it that so many people tuned in for? Why is it that so many perfect strangers from all walks of life supported me? I had to ask myself that question. *There has to be some bigger purpose, right? Why else would God let me go through it?*

I think I'm still searching to find the true meaning and purpose even as I write this book. But I know the gist of it: I went through this so that I can help people. I went through this so I can not only help individuals who face charges similar to mine, but also so I can help stop kids from being put into these situations in the first place—where they wind up being abused by those who are supposedly trying to protect them.

A big group of friends led by Diana showed up to meet David and me at the airport when we got back from New York City. They all held signs as we came out of the gate area. It felt amazing to have my extended family there. It truly did. Jennifer, Tammy, Courtney, all these people who'd shown up in court for me or championed my story on the local news and who in some cases were torn to shreds in that courtroom—they never walked away. We all grew closer through the horror of the ordeal.

I'm not sure if I could ever thank any of them enough for what they did. It felt good just to hug them, and to feel so much love as we returned home to Tennessee.

Everyone was relieved and celebrating that I wasn't going to prison. There were congratulations and lots of tears. I accepted their hugs with gratitude. But my mom and dad and David all knew that I wasn't happy.

Was I happy to be free? Yes. But I wasn't truly free. I wouldn't be free for a long time.

Once the whirlwind was over, I came back to a quiet house with no kids. David went back to work. I found myself all alone with no one but Buddy and Candy Cane to keep me company. All I thought about, all day, every day, were my children.

The Circuit Court in Tennessee made a decision back in June of 2008 saying that Tyler and Ashley would remain in Joal's custody until the "conclusion of the investigation" in the criminal case in Georgia. We had reached the ultimate conclusion of that so-called investigation: A court of law and a jury of my peers concluded that I didn't do it.

"Let's go get your kids!" my attorneys all said. They actually filed a petition for custody to be returned to me the same morning that I was on *The Today Show*. I knew in my heart that it wouldn't fly—at least not immediately. I knew it wouldn't be that easy. I'd have to fight. It might even turn into another war, for all I knew.

I had to go to court to force Joal to let me have a couple of extra hours with Tyler each week, and eventually the court made a decision to allow me to see Ashley, but only under strict supervision in the offices of the court-ordered therapist.

I tried going to Tyler's baseball games, trying to dip a toe into some kind of normalcy again, and instead found that Joal and Sarah and their families were just horrible to me. They would stare at me and give me nasty looks. They rushed the children away as soon as the games were over. I wound up in the public bathroom at the park, sobbing. They made me feel like a monster all over again.

When will the suffering end? I prayed. *When?*

———————◆◆◆———————

From the moment I walked out of the courthouse, almost everyone around me started asking when I was going to sue the pants off all the people who had done this to me. I told them I didn't know. I couldn't focus on that. I needed to stay focused on my kids. I was fuming mad, of course. The immeasurable losses I'd suffered because of these misbegotten allegations crushed me. Those people needed to pay.

Thankfully, I had attorneys who could focus on it for me.

On May 26, Scott and Cary King filed a $25 million federal lawsuit on my behalf, going after every person and every entity that had harmed me through "fraud, corruption, perjury, fabricated evidence, and/or other wrongful conduct undertaken in bad faith."

The people I wanted to sue the most—including Len Gregor, Chris Arnt, and Judge Brian House—I couldn't. We aren't allowed to sue those people. They work in the bubble of protection of the judicial system, which is only penetrable by higher entities, such as the FBI. I would bring my case to them soon enough.

Those whom we named in the lawsuit were Sandra Lamb, Sherri and DeWayne Wilson, Kelly McDonald, Joal and Sarah Henke, Detective Tim Deal, Catoosa County, Catoosa County Sheriff Phil Summers (who was Tim Deal's boss), Suzie Thorne, Stacy Long, Laurie Evans, the Children's Advocacy Center of the Lookout Mountain Judicial Circuit, and the Greenhouse Children's Advocacy Center.

I barely talked about the details with Scott and Cary before they filed, but I knew that these people and these organizations needed to be punished. They deserved to pay for what they had done to me and my family, not to mention those kids. We would go after them for both compensatory and punitive damages, for coaching these kids and for moving ahead with criminal charges that were not corroborated and actually were contradicted.[65]

The suit itself was fifty-two pages long. It detailed everything, including that the plaintiffs manipulated Ashley into the role of a sex-abuse victim. Key parts of it said that the "extreme and outrageous conduct of defendants was designed to subvert the parental and familial relationships between the plaintiff and her family."

I didn't care about the money. I wanted to be able to pay my parents back. I wanted to make up for the career that they took from me. But the rest of it? It was about accountability. Sadly it seems the only way an individual can hold people accountable through the court system is with dollars. We thought $25 million was an appropriate response—to hold them accountable, not to destroy or tear apart. I didn't want to do that. There had been enough suffering already. I just wanted these people to know that their actions were wrong and that these organizations needed to change the way they do things. But I always knew that no amount of money could ever make up for the destruction that had taken place.

My first visit with Ashley happened in a closed room, under controlled circumstances, with her court-appointed therapist present the entire time. I wasn't supposed to initiate conversation with Ashley. I wasn't supposed to touch her. That therapist had to be the one to initiate all contact and conversation between us. How could that not make me feel like I was being treated like a guilty person?

Ashley played with the games and did some coloring while her therapist talked and tried to get Ashley to say how it felt to see her mother. It was awkward. It was awful. It was exactly the opposite of what Ashley needed after all of the trauma she'd been put through, and I sat there with tears streaming down my face.

At one point, Ashley got up and brought me some tissues. She was cordial, but never affectionate in any way.

Seeing my baby girl again—even though it was the only thing I wanted in the whole world—almost made it worse. The same way it did with Tyler that first time he came to my birthday party at the restaurant. The distance. The lack of eye contact. The coldness from your own child is enough to break any mother's heart.

———◆———

The fact that a jury found me not guilty didn't clear my record. If a potential employer were to do the most basic background search on me to this day, the first thing that would show up are page after page of felony charges for child molestation. *Aggravated* child molestation. One day, I pulled a background check on myself just to see what it looks like, and all twenty-two counts are at the very top of the report. At the very end of that long list of repulsive charges, there's one line in small print that says "acquitted."

The way it works now, that's the way my background report will read for the rest of my life. Right then and there, I decided I would work to change the laws. I wasn't qualified to do that yet. I could advocate for change as a citizen, and I'd certainly found some success getting my word out through the media. But I wanted to do more than that.

A seed was planted. A seed that would eventually lead me down a new path in my life.

Chapter 67

Five months passed. Five more months of occasional supervised visits with Ashley, with the therapist taking notes the whole time, and mandatory psychological evaluations and legal hoops that required tens of thousands of more dollars in fees to attorneys—still with only limited visitation with my son. Finally, I was allowed a handful of supervised visits with Ashley at our home. But I didn't have Ashley back in any way. I didn't have either of my kids back home the way they should be.

Then one day, I decided to take things into my own hands. To do what I do best. I brought a book into our visit with the therapist and simply started reading, aloud. Wouldn't you know it, Ashley came and sat down right next to me so she could see the pictures. She laughed when it was funny. When I asked her questions about the book, she answered.

When she left, her therapist seemed shocked. "Wow, she was just sort of—normal," she said.

Ya think? I'm her mom. I know what she needs better than you!

All I said out loud was, "Well . . ."

About a week before Thanksgiving, I walked into a courthouse in Tennessee for the most important custody hearing we'd had so far. We'd prepared for weeks, my team was assembled, we'd made our opening arguments, and we were right in the middle of it all when I finally reached a new breaking point. It became clear to me that Joal was going to put our children in front of that judge and make them say out loud which parent they wanted to be with the most. I couldn't let them suffer that horror. They'd suffered the preposterousness of a court's idea of their "best interests" for too long. I was sick and tired of this justice system that wasn't doing any of us any good. So I told my attorneys that I wanted to talk to Joal, one-on-one, face-to-face, with nobody else in the room.

And that is what we did.

We went to an office just across the street from the courthouse. Joal sat down across from me. We shut the door. There was a lot of press there. There was still tons of interest in my case, and the custody fight was a whole new ratings boon for the local affiliates. The camera crews would've followed us right into that room if they could have, but it felt good to keep them and everyone else out.

For two years I'd woken in the middle of the night from those awful dreams in which I stood in front of my accusers and confronted them.

Joal was the first person I was able to confront in real life.

When he sat down, the first thing I said to him was, "I want you to look at me, and I want you to tell me that you think I did this."

Joal paused and then let out a big sigh.

"I know you didn't," he said.

My only reaction was tears.

Joal started fumbling around a bit. I think he remembered that there was a $25 million lawsuit pending with his name on it. He also might have been smart enough to guess that I'd have a tape recorder running in my purse—because I did.

He hemmed and hawed a bit. He said he knew I was innocent "now," but he would not explain why he had become a part of this. He eluded questions and talked in circles.

Whatever. It didn't matter. I bawled.

"Well," I said, wiping away my tears. "I forgive you."

Joal seemed really, really shocked by that. To tell you the truth, I was, too!

I can't fully explain how that forgiveness came to me. I had been carrying around so much anger and hatred toward that man. I knew it wasn't right. He's the father of my children, and I *needed* to forgive him—for me, but most importantly for *them.*

Joal knows what he's done. He has to live with the consequences of that for the rest of his life. I don't need to carry that burden. It's not my burden to carry.

I swear God was in that room with us that day. There was just a feeling of wonder and forgiveness that is too thick and enormous to describe. It's like right in that moment, right after I forgave him, I was able to put all of my focus on the children. God reached down and plucked any anger I had toward Joal right out of my heart. I forgave completely, with no strings attached. And it felt good. I felt free from chains that had bound me for far too long.

Joal and I agreed to a plan in which we both would not only parent our children but also do it together, as mother and father. (Not maritally, of course, but as "parents.") We agreed to work out a schedule that works for both of us.

Before we left the room, I told Joal, "The worst day of my life is when my daughter got up and was forced to testify against me. But the second worst day was when the father of my children got up and testified against me. It's one thing to be divorced and for you to hate me as a person. But you getting up and testifying against me hurt me more than anything ever could, except for seeing Ashley testify."

He nodded. I think he got it. I think he knew.

"Still," I said, "I forgive you."

When Joal and I walked out of that courthouse side by side, people's mouths dropped. When we stood in front of those cameras as two parents who'd come to an agreement, I felt like peace was radiating off my skin. It felt good to be on the news for something positive. If I could make peace for the sake of my children, I'm pretty sure anyone could make peace for the sake of their children! I wish I could explain how it happened. All I can say is that the immediate and lasting peace that comes from forgiveness is a gift. I wish I could share that feeling with anyone who holds on to bitterness or hatred.

I thought those twenty-two not-guilty verdicts would mean freedom. They didn't. The day I began to truly forgive was the day I felt my freedom for the first time.

———————◆———————

Just before Thanksgiving, David and I met Joal and Sarah and the kids at a park. Joal and I talked to the kids together that day about how "the schedule's going to change, and we're both going to spend time with both of you kids now, and we're going to occasionally do some things together, and we want you to know that we both love you."

I gave Joal a hug. I gave Sarah a hug, too. Joal and Sarah both hugged David. And then the whole lot of us hugged Tyler and Ashley. It felt like a miracle. It truly did.

Just like that, just as the Christmas season was starting, I had my kids back.

I remember taking Ashley up to her room for the first time. She stood there and read the words I'd written on her mirror all the way back on my 295th day without her.

"I can wash it off if you want, if it bothers you or anything," I said.

"No," she said. "You can leave it."

Those words have remained on her mirror to this day.

Ashley seemed cold to me in those first few weeks. She seemed distant. When it was time for her to go to bed, she would go up into her bedroom and lock the door. The sound of that lock made me cry every darned time. I didn't blame her. She didn't put those thoughts into her head herself. I knew she was confused by it all. But I also refused to push her.

Tyler was still a little distant, too, even after all of the visitation we'd spent together. He still refused to call me "Mommy." I refused to push him, either. Both of those kids had been pushed enough.

Ashley would sit next to me sometimes, but rigidly. She wouldn't tell me she loved me. I would say it to her, all the time. I always had. It was nothing new. Her lack of response was the only new part. And it hurt. Every single time, it stung. I didn't blame her. But it hurt.

When it comes to my forgiving Joal, the hardest thing to this day is dealing with everybody else. I get grief. Really *bad* grief about forgiving him. What I want people to understand is that I didn't do it for him. I did it for me and my heart, which affects my kids. And I did it for Tyler and Ashley.

The Today Show was so intrigued by the fact that he and I came to a custody agreement, they called us up and asked if Joal and I would fly up to New York to talk about it. So there we were, two formerly bitter exes, sitting on a couch on national TV talking about forgiveness, and talking about doing what's right for our children. Once again: surreal.

I shared something with Joal on TV that day. I'd decided to drop the lawsuit against him and Sarah. I'd made up my mind to remove their names from the whole contentious thing. My attorneys were really angry at me for that, but I told them: "How can I forgive him and tell my children I've forgiven him when I'm suing his pants off? It doesn't make sense!"

I dropped the lawsuit against Joal and Sarah "with prejudice," which means I would be unable to refile that lawsuit at any time in the future. I did that because I wanted them to know I meant it. Mostly, I wanted Tyler and Ashley to know, someday when they're old enough to understand, that when I said I forgave their father, it was real.

It was also just a matter of being practical. How could I possibly try to develop a working parental relationship with my ex at the same time I treated him as an adversary in court? Dropping the lawsuit against them made getting on with our lives seem a whole lot easier. In fact, it made everything feel easier.

The relief I felt, the weight that it took off my own shoulders and put squarely back on his, where it belonged, allowed me to have more honesty and good feelings with my kids. *It was that forgiveness that allowed me to get my kids back!*

For a number of weeks after that *Today Show* appearance, I kept asking myself, *If forgiveness is that powerful, where else do I need to apply it?*

As the lawsuit against the rest of them kicked into high gear, it became a constant source of anger and bitterness for me. The feeling of wanting some kind of justice for the pain those people had brought on my family, that overwhelming urge to see those people pay for what they'd done, was all-consuming—and at times, overwhelming.

I talked to Cary about all of it. I had questions about who it was we had listed in the lawsuit. I had questions about the action we could and could not take against the detectives and various officers of the court whom I felt were the true perpetrators of the crimes against me. Finally, he set me up with a meeting with a top civil attorney to go over every detail of what was to come in what was sure to be a long, drawn-out case bombarded by intense media interest and months, maybe years, of throwing daggers at others.

The fact was, no matter how we looked at it, there seemed to be no way to make the judges, detectives, prosecutors, and those responsible pay, in any way. They were all protected by "the system." The more it was explained to me, the more it seemed unlikely that we'd be successful in our pursuit of the other court-appointed therapists and such, too, simply because "the system" protects its own. That meant the most vulnerable parties in my lawsuit were the families of the children who'd been presented as my accusers.

That didn't sit well with me. At all.

I remember asking that civil attorney and Cary and everyone I trusted, "If the people who are responsible are not the ones I can hold financially responsible, who am I really harming with this lawsuit?"

The way I saw it, hurting those families would hurt those kids. I felt that the system had already abused those children by putting them through this ordeal, and I did not want to be a part of abusing those kids in any way.

On top of that, the entire process was taking me to a very angry place. I felt a physical weight on my shoulders, a pressure in my head, a twisting in my gut. I didn't want to be focused on punishing anyone else. I didn't want to be focused on making anyone pay, no matter how "right" or "just" that intention may seem. What I wanted to focus on was my own kids and my own family.

All along I had prayed that there might be something positive that could come out of this horrible situation. Pursuing the lawsuit didn't feel like trying to do something positive at all. It almost felt like I was trying to make something worse out of an already horrible situation. That just didn't seem right to me.

The more I prayed about it and the more thought I put into it, the more the answer to my forgiveness question became obvious.

I called Scott and Cary and told them to drop the federal lawsuit.

"Drop the whole $25-million thing," I said. I sat in the quiet of my house, with my eyes closed, with Candy Cane and Buddy cuddled up to my lap, and I forgave all of those people who hurt me. I forgave Sandra Lamb and her husband, Greg. I forgave the Wilsons. I forgave the McDonalds. I forgave Judge House. I forgave Judge Van Pelt. I forgave Len Gregor. I forgave Chris Arnt. I forgave Tim Deal and Stephen Keith. I forgave Laurie Evans. I forgave the women who conducted those terrible interviews and exams with the kids. I forgave everyone in the whole system who had wronged me and those children.

I had never blamed the girls. Brianna, Chloe, and my daughter, Ashley, had not done this on purpose. It wasn't their fault. So in their cases, there was nothing to forgive.

I will never let go of the belief that justice needs to be served. The judges and prosecutors and detectives who in my opinion moved forward without the required evidence, who accepted conflicting stories from witnesses, who seemed to manipulate their summations of evidence and interviews and charges to fit their desired outcome—all of them will some-day get what's coming to them, whether it's getting fired or getting put in jail. I have no doubt that the attorney general, the FBI, and more will have a field day in Catoosa County eventually. (As of the writing of this book, the entire Lookout Mountain Judicial Circuit was under review for conduct in other cases.)

Maybe they won't get the justice they deserve based on my case alone. Maybe it'll happen in some other way. It may not come until they meet their maker. But it will come.

That was the point I reached in early December of 2010, eight months after my trial ended. That's pretty much where I am today, too. People still need to be held accountable, and I'm taking steps to make sure that happens. I spent the entire year after my trial continuing to do research. The thing was, after being in such a powerfully focused state of awareness for two years, obsessing over every detail, losing sleep, fighting every minute of every day—it was difficult to slow my body, brain, and heart back down to a normal pace. So I used that energy. I used that drive. I poured almost as much effort as I'd poured into trial preparation creating a 1,200-plus page PowerPoint document that breaks down and analyzes everything that went wrong in my case. The entire "perfect storm," in a readable, understandable document that shows everything that I felt was done improperly (and perhaps illegally) in the "shoddy investigation"—and everything that I felt was done incorrectly (and perhaps illegally) in the courtroom.

I've given a copy of that PowerPoint to the FBI in Georgia. It is now up to them to take the next steps. I didn't do it vengefully. I'm not doing anything out of bitterness. But I am doing *something*. Things need to change. The system needs to change. If it takes me twenty-five years, mark my words, the system is going to change.

Chapter 68

Christmases aren't very pretty in Chattanooga. I don't remember it ever snowing on Christmas my whole life. But when we woke up that Christmas morning of 2010, everything was covered in a fresh blanket of snow. I could not have ordered a more perfect Christmas morning from God himself. It was a gift, and we all knew it. David and Ashley and Tyler and I wound up running outside, throwing snowballs at each other, and sledding down the little hill in our front yard. Ashley actually climbed into a sled with me, and when we knocked into the curb and tumbled into the street, the two of us laughed and laughed.

My parents came over and we cooked a full turkey and ham dinner. Tyler helped make the homemade gravy. Ashley helped me cut up the vegetables and put the corn in. It was absolutely perfect.

That night as she stepped into her bedroom, Ashley said, "That was the best Christmas ever."

She still didn't tell me she loved me. But for the first time in a long time, I think I felt it a little bit.

I didn't wallow in the Christmases I'd lost with my children. I didn't think about them once that entire day. I was just so thankful to be where I was. Just to *be* there. Instead of sitting around looking back and having sad feelings, I filled up with thankfulness and gratefulness like I'd never known.

It seems my children had been told that it wasn't okay to love me. That was not easy to overcome. Both Ashley and Tyler were convinced I was going to prison and they were never going to see me again. I think they both found ways to disconnect in order to protect their hearts. Tyler's thing, still, was he would not call me "Mommy." He wouldn't call me Tonya, either. It was always "you" or "hey." It was horrible. It was gut wrenching for me.

Then one day, sometime after that wonderful Christmas, Tyler said, "Mommy, can you grab my . . ." whatever it was that he'd left somewhere, as kids tend to do. It was completely nonchalant. I'm not even sure he noticed he said it. But from that day forward, I was "Mommy" again.

Even now, Tyler's in his mid-teens, and we'll be at a ballgame and he'll say, "Mommy, can you go get me a Powerade?" He's well past the age when most kids, boys especially, stop calling their mothers "Mommy." But it's the sweetest thing. I try not to make a big deal out of it because I don't want it to ever stop.

Tyler had said some awful things to me when he was feeling angry. But I completely understand where his anger came from, and I felt it had grown from the confusion and things he had been told. So I forgave him for it. It wasn't hard to forgive him at all. He's my son. Forgiveness is a given.

The hardest person for me to forgive, and the only person I didn't forgive that December, was my husband. With David, the fact that he'd abandoned me and the fact that he was (for lack of a better word) in "cahoots" with Sandra Lamb for a while—using her attorney in our divorce proceeding, allowing himself to open up to her in dozens of long phone calls—absolutely killed me. Those were the last things I ever expected from him.

Yet as the days went by, I watched him with my kids. The three of them are as close as can be. I saw the way he continued to look at me with those eyes that Cary noticed way back in our deposition. And eventually, I forgave David, too. I hope he forgives himself someday. Maybe he already has. I'm not sure. I don't ask him about it. I don't need to. I know that he loves me with all of his heart. And I love him with all of mine. The forgiveness has just made everything better between us.

<hr />

One night, sometime in the first part of 2011, Ashley allowed me to come into her bedroom and tuck her in. I had been praying for that for months. Soon afterward I asked if it was okay to read to her, and she let me read from the corner of the bed. One night at a time, I asked and she allowed me to sit just a little bit closer, until finally she let me sit propped up on a pillow right next to her, just like I used to.

When I was all done reading a few nights after that, I said the words I always said: "I love you, Ashley."

"I love you, too, Mommy," she said right back. It came out of her mouth just as naturally and easily as it had before they took her away from me.

Of course I started crying.

"Ashley," I said, "I really appreciate you saying that."

"Mommy," she said, "I've always loved you."

I gave her a great big hug. And as I held Ashley in my arms, I knew that those particular tears would never fall from my eyes, ever again.

"I know you have," I said to my daughter. "And I've always loved you, too."

I was finally, finally, all the way back home to my baby girl.

Epilogue: *Revelations*

The ripple effects of forgiveness are too numerous to count.

In the five years since the trial ended, I have been blessed with more revelations and positive interactions with unexpected individuals than I ever could have imagined.

It started just after my children came back, toward the end of 2010. The foreman from my jury reached out to me and asked if he and a group of jurors could come see me. I made some coffee and welcomed them into my home with open arms.

The conversations that followed that day were tearful, as you can imagine, but also filled with some shared laughter, and some shared understanding the likes of which no one else in the world will ever understand. We all went through that trial together. They were thrown into it with no warning, no idea what they were going to encounter in that courtroom—but then they went through every bit of it. Every emotion, every heartbreak, every hatred, everything that I had encountered and that those three girls had encountered, and that my friends and family had encountered. The jury experienced all of it compressed into four and a half weeks. Talk about an emotional ride. I had never considered just how taxing it was on them emotionally. Intellectually, yes. I can still only imagine the pressure they must have felt, holding a woman's life in their hands, and those children's lives in their hands, and, really, as Doc put it in his closing, the strength and foundation of that whole entire community in their hands. But I didn't realize how emotionally involved they would become, and how much they would grow to care about those girls, and about this case.

The news tended to report on my case as a "community divided." Sure, we all agreed it was divided. But it wasn't cut down the middle. To me it was like there was this whole great big giant community that supported me, that saw what a miscarriage of justice this whole trial was. And then there was a small, powerful, vocal minority that appeared to want to see me burned alive. At all costs. They got so far into it that they just wanted to win.

The jury seemed to understand all of that. But that's not the reason they voted "not guilty." They said they were moved by the merits of the case itself. They said they were moved by the facts. They were moved by the expert testimony. They were moved by the conflicting stories of the little girls. They were moved by the conflicting stories of the mothers involved. And they were extremely moved to act because of the arrogance displayed by the prosecutors, they told me.

In short, they said they were moved by the truth.

They also said they were not moved by the media. They were not moved by the "Truth for Tonya" campaign, which they would not have known anything about had the prosecutors not kept sticking it in their faces. They all followed orders, they said. They didn't watch the news. They didn't Google "Tonya Craft" on their laptops in bed at night. They didn't discuss the case with their families. This was a solid group of individuals who actually said a prayer together every day before they walked from the holding room to the jury box.

These same jurors said they'd offered to go talk to Chris Arnt and Len Gregor about the case after the verdict. It never happened. Imagine how much Chris and Len could learn from those people. *Why would a prosecutor who lost a major case not want to find out why they lost? I'll tell you why. Arrogance. They thought the jurors were tainted by the media. They weren't. They thought the jurors were "manipulated" by the experts and the fancy schooling of Doc and his courtroom tactics. They weren't. In fact, just the opposite was true.*

The jurors I spoke with said they were offended by the way Len Gregor raised his voice and flailed about. They were offended by the way both of the prosecutors attacked certain witnesses, especially female witnesses, with unfounded accusations of lesbian affairs and unseemly threesomes in Las Vegas hotel rooms—none of which had anything to do with whether or not I'd molested those girls.

They weren't "fooled" into thinking I *couldn't* have done it because I had a detailed timeline showing how busy I was. They weren't "fooled" into thinking I was innocent because I came in some sort of a "pretty package."

The truth of the matter is they weren't *fooled* by the shenanigans of the ADAs. Toward the end of the trial, and especially in closing arguments, when Len Gregor started misquoting witnesses' own testimony, the jurors noticed.

There was a jury member who said she wished she could look at me toward the end of the trial and give me a thumbs-up or something, to let me know it was going to be okay. They all agreed they could see how terrified and worried I was.

I thanked them for not doing that. I thanked them for remaining stone-faced. I thanked them for being more professional than Judge House or the prosecutors. I thanked them for giving me back my life.

In the end, the trial left many of them filled with fear. One member of the jury said he doesn't let kids sit in his lap anymore because he's afraid somebody's going to misconstrue something.

"That's *awful*!" I said. None of us should have to feel that kind of fear in our daily lives. But I shared with them my own ongoing fears. I shudder every time a friend asks me to drive their kid somewhere without another adult in the car. I know they trust me. I just don't want anyone to misconstrue anything ever again. I haven't used Facebook because I know that anything I write there could be "used against me in a court of law," even though I know there will be a time I will have to reach out publicly.

I spilled coffee all over the kitchen counter one day, and I started writing a text to David, saying, "I think I'm losing my mind!" But I never sent it. I erased it, because I don't want a written record floating around that might be used as evidence that I'm "losing my mind" if someone takes me to court over something. It's awful. But I don't let any of that fear overwhelm me. I deal with it. Little by little. Day by day.

I think they appreciated hearing that.

A whole year later, one of the jurors ran into my mom's neighbor Karen at church. She remembered her from the trial. "How's our girl doing?" the juror asked of me.

The fact that an unbiased juror could walk through those courtroom doors, go through a trial like that, and come out thinking of an accused child molester as "our girl" is a testament to the good that exists in people's hearts. It truly is. I cried when Karen relayed that story to me. I tear up just thinking about it now.

———————————◆◆———————————

About a year and half later, Jerry McDonald and I got the chance to sit down with one another. I had heard through the small-town grapevine that Jerry and Kelly went their separate ways after the trial ended. They eventually got divorced. By the time he came over to join me and David for dinner at the house, on a night when the kids weren't home, he had a new girlfriend. She was lovely. David grilled up some hamburgers and we sat down to eat, just small-talking and chitchatting.

Finally I looked at him—this man who'd cried on the witness stand and broke everyone's heart, including mine—and I said, "Jerry, I really want you to look at me and tell me that you think I did this, or that you think I didn't do this. Do you believe it?"

He started crying.

"No," Jerry said. "I know you didn't. And I'm so sorry."

I started crying, too. To know you're innocent is one thing. To hear it from the father of someone who'd accused you is something else. It was overwhelmingly emotional, for both of us. We both sobbed right there in my kitchen.

I could tell the weight of it had sat on him the way the weight of the charges had sat on me before the trial. Maybe it wasn't quite that heavy, but it was heavy nonetheless.

Once we broke through that wall, Jerry admitted to basically everything that I knew in my heart. He said he now believed that Kelly had pushed Chloe into saying those things. He was confused about it back when it happened. He said he didn't realize what his wife had done. The abuse he had suffered himself might have clouded his judgment and his ability to see the truth, he said. He desperately wanted to come talk to me about it and ask me what happened for himself, he said, but Kelly wouldn't let him. She was his wife, and he chose to believe in her.

It wasn't until Chloe finally came to him one night, long after the trial was over, crying and upset, and told him that she "just couldn't take it anymore," he said, that he truly came to believe that it was more than confusion and hysteria that drove Kelly's actions. Chloe told him, "I don't remember Miss Tonya doing anything to me. Mom told me," he recalled her saying.

That night at my house, Jerry, through tears, said, "I just need to ask you to forgive me."

"Jerry," I said, "I forgave you a long time ago."

He cried a whole lot more when he heard that. I think he was having a harder time forgiving himself than I'd had forgiving him.

Jerry and I still speak, and I respect him as a man, as a father, and as a friend. He's even offered to help me in bringing my case to the FBI. He's willing to talk about what really went on behind the scenes, openly. He never wants to see something like this happen to anyone else, ever.

Truly it is my prayer that each and every one of these people—from Sandra Lamb to Stephen Keith to Len Gregor—that every one of us could sit down and work together to help get it right the next time, to protect the innocent and convict the guilty.

David still rolls his eyes at me at times. "Tonya," he says, "you know that's a pipe dream that will never happen."

I just point up to heaven and say, "With God all things are possible."

The next revelation nearly knocked me flat on my back.

Through a mutual acquaintance, I agreed to meet Judge Ralph Van Pelt Jr. for coffee in downtown Chattanooga.

When I first sat down with that man, I asked him the big question right away. I didn't need to have any small talk with him. I didn't want any small talk with that man.

"I want you to look at me and tell me whether or not you believe I did it, and whether you ever did, and why?"

His response was, "No. I one hundred percent know you didn't. I know that now."

Of course I had a tape recorder on me the whole time. There was no way I would sit down with that judge without taping his every word. I expect he was smart enough to realize that.

My conversations with Judge Van Pelt that day were shocking. He told me about events that transpired behind the scenes in the Lookout Mountain Judicial Circuit over the course of my two-year ordeal that I never could have imagined. I told him a few things, too. For instance, he seemed to be under the impression that I had been uncooperative with investigators from the start. When I told him that I had been willing to sit down with the ADAs at any time whatsoever and even take a lie-detector test as long as my attorney was present, he seemed dismayed.

In fact, he seemed distraught.

Before that conversation was over, he asked me for forgiveness.

"I've forgiven everybody," I said, "including you."

Judge Van Pelt and I have had numerous texts and conversations since that day. He treats me like a good buddy now. I'm happy to keep talking to him because I learn more and more every time we talk.

If I had continued to move forward with the $25 million lawsuit, I never would have had any of this. If I hadn't forgiven everyone, I wouldn't have any of this information or any of this closure.

Forgiveness is powerful.

In my opinion, Judge Van Pelt still has plenty to answer to in his own heart. As I said to him one time, "One day, you may have to answer some *really* hard questions—when Ashley decides to seek you out and ask you a few questions of her own."

In 2012, I enrolled in law school. Ever since then, I've made the two-hour drive each way to Nashville for classes two to three nights a week. I get home around 2:00 A.M. I'm exhausted. Constantly. But I know it's what I'm meant to do.

I think I went through all of this for a reason. God's going to lay the path out for me. I know the credibility of a law degree is important. The knowledge behind it is important, too. I might not ever litigate a case. I might just keep doing what I'm doing now, consulting on individual cases—pro bono. I had plenty of credible and talented attorneys working for me along with very qualified experts and team members, but no one would help without a substantial paycheck. I always said I would never be like that. It's not about the money to me. It's about doing the right thing. I've consulted on several false-allegation cases so far, and I gave my all to each one. Hopefully my law degree will allow me to do that work with even more effectiveness in the coming years. It's an emotional experience, following another falsely accused individual through their ordeal. It's hard. But I know the strains on me are nothing compared to the struggles those individuals have faced, and I thank God for allowing me to do that work, to help in whatever way I can. Plus, it's important that my children see me help others and make a positive change through very negative circumstances.

I feel blessed to have been given the chance to speak and share my story with the public as well. I hope to do a lot more of that while I continue trying to change laws in order to put the focus where it belongs.

In my opinion, it's the prosecutors, interviewers, detectives, and judges who are responsible for allowing these misguided cases to move forward. You are always going to have an angry ex, or a jealous enemy, or a disgruntled parent making accusations. That's not going to go away. It's up to the professionals to figure out what's real and what's true *before* slapping the handcuffs on and throwing someone's mug shot on TV. I want to help make sure that's the case as often as possible going forward.

I miss teaching more than anything. This past summer I was helping out in the snack shack at one of Tyler's baseball games, and a little five-year-old boy climbed up on a chair and wanted to see how to work the register. His parents were there. They were comfortable with the situation, so I helped him. I talked to him about the money: "Now, if this costs two dollars, and this costs one dollar, how many dollars does the man owe us?" The kid said, "Three dollars, please!" to the man at the counter, and I nearly broke down. Teaching kids is what I'm meant to do. It's what I was born to do. And they took it from me.

For the most part, people have been wonderfully kind to me. Kinder than I ever imagined possible. But I'm still treated like a monster in certain situations. For example, in my continued quest to give back and do good for other people, I volunteered for a prison program to help people cope with life behind bars. I did this through a church group. But the prison warden nixed it.

They wouldn't let me into a *prison*.

I cried and felt like a monster all over again.

I dream of doing *The Amazing Race*. It's one of my favorite shows. I've been hesitant to complete the application because one of the very first questions I saw was, "Have you ever been arrested?"

Things like that seem to come up all the time. But I deal with them. And I move on.

In November of 2013, I finally asked David to reconnect the doorbell on our front door. He did. And it still gives me a start each and every time I hear it. But I'm facing it. I'm dealing with it. And each day it gets a little easier.

Of all the people who've opened up to me and shared the truth with me since the trial ended, none has brought me more love and light than my daughter, Ashley.

Something changed in the fall of 2013. The floodgates opened. After saying nothing about the trial for all that time, she came to me one day, out of the blue, and shared some things that she said went on behind closed doors at that courthouse. Through her words and our tears, we addressed her experiences, and the ordeal that *she* had endured. I learned startling things from her, and she asked me a few questions that I answered, openly. Out of respect for my daughter I will keep that conversation private. I always want her to feel safe when she speaks to me. But there have been many more times that she's opened up to me since, answering so many of the questions that I had during the two years I went without seeing her— and gaining answers from me about what really went on, both in the court- room and elsewhere. I let her speak. I never want her to feel like I'm grilling her. Ever.

When she is ready to share her story with the world, she will do that. And believe me, it will be powerful.

Tyler still doesn't talk about the trial at all. If he never speaks of it, I'm never going to hand him this book or the courtroom videotapes or any- thing else to look at. It's all up to them to find their comfort level and decide how they want to deal with it. I've prayed about this and I've listened to my gut, and the only thing I know to do with any of this is to be patient—to let it unravel and unfold in its own time.

Some people seem to think that response isn't "natural." I don't know what to say to that, except that my gut and my faith in God are what carried me through this entire nightmare ordeal. They're what brought me to my place of forgiveness. They're what brought me back to my babies. And after everything we've been through, seeing just how far we've come, I think it would be pretty foolish of me not to rely on those things to carry me through anything and everything else life has in store.

So that's what I'm gonna do.

Acknowledgments

As I count the many blessings in my life, those family and friends who stood by me in my season of pain are front and center. There were tears, heartache, and great loss—but my battlefield was full of warriors who fought right beside me. I could never fully express my gratitude for their resolve and their faith in my innocence. Someone told me when this all began, "Well, you are going to find out who your friends are." It could not have been a truer statement. I am truly blessed to be surrounded with more loving, caring, and loyal individuals than I ever believed possible.

I would not be here today without my amazing legal team. Dr. Demosthenes Lorandos, Cary King, Scott King, and Clancy Covert all brought unique skills to the table that created an unbreakable chain. I am eternally grateful for all of the hard work each and every one of them put into my case. Most of all they should get a gold star (I was a teacher ☺) for hanging in there when I know I was very difficult to handle at times.

Additionally, I want to thank the rest of my legal support team: Private Investigator Eric Echols, Jury Consultant Denise DeLaRue, and the many staff members who worked on my case, as well as Dr. Nancy Aldridge, Dr. Nancy Fajman, Dr. William Bernet, and Dr. Ann Hazzard. I want to thank you all not only for my own sake, but for the sake of my two children, who have their mother home because of all of you!

In the midst of my ordeal, I traveled near and far to seek out individuals who would help bring this injustice to light. The many doors that I was unable to open did not deter me. After thousands of miles traveled and refusal after refusal, one person took the time to listen to my plight. Melydia Clewell, a local news reporter and investigator, gave me the opportunity to do the one thing I implored others to do: to defend myself against the horrific war being waged against me. She listened without preconceived notions, investigated from a nonbiased position, and presented the facts discovered. Her tenacity and determination has had a lifelong impact not only on my life, but also on the lives of my children.

Around that same time, Kevin West at WGOW in Chattanooga allowed me to speak my mind in the public forum of talk radio as well. Both of those chances to finally share my story meant the world to me.

My church family, led by an amazing man, Dr. Mike Chapman, truly illustrated what it is to be the hands and feet of Jesus Christ. Many sermonize, but few actually practice what they preach. I shed many tears at the altar in prayer, but I was never alone. Jesus touched me through Pastor Chapman, the remarkable church staff, and the members of City Church of Chattanooga.

My story and this book would not be possible if my agent, Michael Wright, had turned me away when I showed up unannounced at his office. His dedication has made this all possible. I appreciate his gentle spirit and divine guidance. Additionally, I want to thank everyone at BenBella Books for believing in my story and me. In a world too often filled with fear, the team at BenBella stood up with courage to share the whole truth of my story.

Walking by my side through this literary journey is Mark Dagostino, who is not only my colleague but someone I am now privileged to call my friend. Mark's skill set is impeccable. When you couple that with the passion he has conveyed in his work, the results are astounding. Being able to collaborate with such a talented and brilliant writer and person has been an honor.

I want to extend a heartfelt thank-you to each and every person who has approached me in public. I've been at restaurants eating dinner with my family when some stranger has paid our bill. At the grocery store, individuals I've never met have come up with tears in their eyes to ask if they can give me a hug. I've been window-shopping in the mall only to hear an unfamiliar voice shout my name and to have that person come running over to meet me to share how my experience has touched their life. Each word of encouragement, each tear, each embrace, and each prayer means so very much to my family and me.

My strength to endure this ordeal came from two people I love dearly: my mother and my father. They raised me in a loving home, and both exude traits that I have carried into adulthood and that I hope to extend to my own two children. They stood by me in every way imaginable, and I hope I can make them as proud as they both have made me.

There are twelve people who were prayed for even before we knew their names. They sat in the seats of that jury box and watched my life unfold. I have their faces etched into my memory, and I will never forget their impact on me. Each and every hug I receive from my children, each laugh I share with them, each miraculous moment of healing—none of that would be possible without each and every juror. God bless them all!

David Craft is a man I am honored to call my husband. Although perfect he is not, he is perfect for me. I doubt many things in life; however, I do *not* doubt that my husband loves me, I do *not* doubt that he loves my two children, and I do *not* doubt that our marriage is wonderful today because of who he is. It took losing him for me to appreciate him fully. I count each and every day as a blessing with my life-mate, my friend, my husband.

Lastly, I want to thank my two precious children. Without the love I feel for them, I would not have fought the fight it took to win the war. Those times when I broke down and felt like I could never get back up again, two things kept me going: my son and my daughter. My resolve to love my children unconditionally and protect them as fiercely as I could picked me up when I thought I was broken beyond repair. They were my lifelines when they did not even realize it. The strength, integrity, and faith I see in them makes me as proud as any mother could be.

There is no amount of gratitude I can express to each and every person that would suffice. Thank you, my dear family, friends, colleagues, and legal entities. Each person has a special place in my heart.

Notes

1. The description of this incident is reconstructed from Kelly McDonald's own testimony at the criminal trial (State of Georgia v. Tonya Craft).

2. This statement is reconstructed from my testimony at trial; the fact that Jerry McDonald was molested as a child was confirmed by Jerry himself during his testimony in that trial.

3. Kim Walker and Dee Potter both testified at trial to witnessing these incidents and hearing these statements; Sandra Lamb also admitted to this behavior during her testimony at trial and in an interview under oath with Detective Tim Deal, which we obtained during the discovery process.

4. This description is reconstructed from Kelly McDonald's testimony in State of Georgia v. Tonya Craft.

5. This conversation between me and Detective Deal was referenced in my testimony during the December 11, 2008, bond modification hearing in State of Georgia v. Tonya Craft and is augmented by my personal recollection of that day. Detective Deal's description of what occurred differed from mine, as described in his testimony during a pre-trial motion on the first day of State of Georgia v. Tonya Craft and during his trial testimony, portions of which are recounted in Chapters 46 and 53 of this book.

6. The details and conversations from this birthday party are reconstructed from my testimony in the December 11, 2008, bond modification hearing and from my testimony during the trial itself.

7. The details of Ashley's discussion of the shower and shaving incidents are reconstructed from my testimony in the December 11, 2008, bond modification hearing.

8. Ashley confirmed she had taken showers with Sarah Henke during her testimony in State of Georgia v. Tonya Craft; Sarah Henke also confirmed during her testimony in that trial that she had taken showers with Ashley.

9. This conclusion is reconstructed from my testimony during the December 11, 2008, bond modification hearing.

10. Sarah Henke denied the incident, describing it from her own point of view during her testimony in State of Georgia v. Tonya Craft, portions of which are described in Chapter 54 of this book.

11. The descriptions of the actions I took after hearing about the showering and shaving incidents from my daughter are reconstructed from my testimony at the December 11, 2008, bond modification hearing.

12. The events of this meeting with the Wilsons are reconstructed from my trial testimony.

13. Kim Walker testified to this at trial. Dee Potter, Kim Walker, and Shanica Lewis all discussed these incidents under oath during their videotaped interviews with P.I. Eric Echols. Sandra Lamb also admitted to this behavior at trial and in an interview under oath with Detective Tim Deal.

14. The details of Ashley's stomachaches, rash, and treatment are reconstructed from my testimony at the December 11, 2008, bond modification hearing, as well as my testimony at the trial itself.

15. My bonds were entered into evidence at the December 11, 2008, bond modification hearing.

16. Sarah admitted to showering naked with Ashley during her February 2009 deposition in the Tennessee custody case, as well as during her testimony in State of Georgia v. Tonya Craft.

17. The details of the termination hearing were reconstructed from a transcript of the proceedings.

18. My private investigator, Eric Echols, confirmed this in a conversation with the director of Four Points, Melissa Gifford, which was recorded and transcribed; Joal also described this call from Chris Arnt to Four Points concerning my visitation rights during his deposition in the Tennessee custody case, February 2009.

19. Kim Walker and Dee Potter testified to these incidents during State of Georgia v. Tonya Craft and talked about this incident under oath during a videotaped interview with P.I. Eric Echols; Sandra Lamb also admitted to this behavior in her testimony at the trial and in an interview under oath with Detective Tim Deal.

20. Kim Walker testified to this during her testimony in State of Georgia v. Tonya Craft and under oath in a videotaped interview with P.I. Eric Echols.

21. Although their recollections of some of the details differed from one another, Sherri Wilson, Sandra Lamb, and Kim Walker all described this same sidewalk chalk incident during their testimony in State of Georgia v. Tonya Craft.

22. Kim Walker testified to all of the above (two paragraphs) at trial and also during her interview with P.I. Eric Echols.

23. David denied telling the detectives that he had any suspicions about me in any way during his testimony in State of Georgia v. Tonya Craft.

24. Joal testified during the bond modification hearing on December 11, 2008, and again in his deposition in February 2009 that he felt forced by his attorney in Tennessee to

make the agreement to let me see the children, after which he testified that he called the ADA in Georgia to try to keep that meeting from happening.

25. Per filings and rulings in Joal Edward Henke, plaintiff v. Tonya Faires Henke (Craft), defendant, in the Circuit Court of Hamilton County, Tennessee, at Chattanooga.

26. Joal testified to this in his February 2009 deposition.

27. I would later discover that Laurie Evans testified in her deposition that Joal had, in fact, accused my mother of molesting my daughter. Laurie Evans also wrote about this in her treatment notes, which we would acquire through discovery.

28. This entire section is reconstructed from transcripts of the December 11, 2008, bond modification hearing.

29. Joal later testified during his February 2009 deposition that he had no knowledge of the phone message from Ashley until he heard about it in the courtroom.

30. Per the December 30, 2008, order in Joal Edward Henke, plaintiff v. Tonya Faires Henke (Craft), defendant, in the Circuit Court of Hamilton County, Tennessee, at Chattanooga.

31. Sandra confirmed that she was close personal friends with Detective Stephen Keith during her trial testimony and also spoke of their daughters' friendship in her deposition during my divorce case; Detective Tim Deal also testified to the personal relationship between Detective Keith and Sandra Lamb during his testimony at my trial.

32. Joal testified to this in his February 2009 deposition in the Tennessee case.

33. The therapist would admit this to me at a later date, in a taped conversation after my trial had ended. She would also discuss basing her decisions about my daughter's treatment on the information she was getting from Joal during her deposition in Tennessee (after my trial ended, but before the custody dispute was resolved) and in her treatment notes.

34. This remark and the description of the encounter between Sandra Lamb and Eric Echols is reconstructed from the video footage that Eric took at the scene.

35. Per State of Georgia v. Eric Echols.

36. Jerry McDonald confirmed that he had been interviewed by Eric Echols during his testimony in State of Georgia v. Tonya Craft.

37. This fact is referenced in our July 27, 2009, Motion for Continuance, Special Setting, and Pretrial Scheduling Order in State of Georgia v. Tonya Craft.

38. All of the interviews with the girls were played in open court during State of Georgia v. Tonya Craft and can be found in the trial transcript and videotapes of the proceedings.

39. The fact that Brianna's mother was waiting for her outside of this interview was testified to by Brianna, Sandra Lamb, and Stacy Long during State of Georgia v. Tonya Craft.

40. Stacy Long testified that the second interview happened on the same day during her testimony in State of Georgia v. Tonya Craft.

41. This information was gathered by our private investigator initially, and Detective Tim Deal would confirm his employment and training history during his testimony in State of Georgia v. Tonya Craft.

42. During her testimony in State of Georgia v. Tonya Craft, Kelly McDonald confirmed on the witness stand that Chloe and Brianna are not cousins.

43. Suzie Thorne confirmed her background and education during her testimony in State of Georgia v. Tonya Craft.

44. Holly Kittle confirmed her background and employment information during her testimony in State of Georgia v. Tonya Craft.

45. This fact was summarized in the same New York Times article, "Studies Reveal Suggestibility of Very Young as Witnesses," by Daniel Goleman, published June 11, 1993.

46. My opinion that the interviews in my case were tainted in this way was reinforced during the expert testimony of Dr. Nancy Aldridge, Dr. William Bernet, and Dr. Ann Hazzard during State of Georgia v. Tonya Craft.

47. Joal Henke's phone records were entered into evidence in State of Georgia v. Tonya Craft, and portions of the phone records were reviewed in open court during the trial. Those phone records were also entered into evidence in the custody case, Joal Edward Henke, plaintiff v. Tonya Faircs Henke (Craft), defendant, in the Circuit Court of Hamilton County, Tennessee, at Chattanooga.

48. Laurie Evans's divorce records were obtained from the public record in Hamilton County, Tennessee.

49. A motion was filed in State of Georgia v. Tonya Craft for Brian House to recuse himself due to a conflict of interest. House denied that motion.

50. All of the details from this November 23, 2009, hearing are reconstructed from transcripts of the court proceedings.

51. Frances Woodard recounted this story during her testimony in State of Georgia v. Tonya Craft.

52. The wrappers and these dollar bills were entered into evidence during State of Georgia v. Tonya Craft, and Ashley confirmed during her testimony that she had signed those packages herself.

53. The details of these examinations are drawn directly from the medical examination reports of all three girls, which were entered into evidence during State of Georgia v. Tonya Craft. All three reports were vetted extensively in the courtroom during the testimony of SANE Nurse Sharon Anderson, and again during the testimony of Dr. Nancy Fajman.

54. The details revealed here come directly from Laurie Evans's notes, which were entered into evidence in State of Georgia v. Tonya Craft.

55. This Facebook post was drawn directly from the post itself, a screenshot of which was entered into evidence during State of Georgia v. Tonya Craft and read into the record during Holly Kittle's testimony in that trial.

56. Tim Deal's motion-hearing testimony is reconstructed directly from the videotape of those proceedings in State of Georgia v. Tonya Craft.

57. Opening statements from both sides are reconstructed from the videotaped proceedings of State of Georgia v. Tonya Craft.

58. Actual trial testimony and observations of goings-on in the courtroom are reconstructed from the videotaped proceedings of State of Georgia v. Tonya Craft, with the addition of transcripts wherever they were available.

59. In their February 2009 depositions, Joal and Sarah Henke both said that Ashley had been showering with Sarah since just after they were married. (They were married in December of 2006.)

60. Greg and Sandra Lamb's divorce record is public record in Catoosa Country, Georgia, and Sandra read portions of that divorce filing concerning the reasons for the divorce into the record during her testimony in State of Georgia v. Tonya Craft.

61. This moment in the trial concerning the newly produced document was reconstructed from a jury-out hearing that was held with the court reporter present.

62. This information was reconstructed from Sarah Henke's deposition in February 2009.

63. Dee Potter, Kim Walker, Shanica Lewis, and David Craft all testified to Brianna's inappropriate dancing at the wedding reception during State of Georgia v. Tonya Craft.

64. Dr. Ann Hazzard testified to this at the November 23, 2009, motions hearing in State of Georgia v. Tonya Craft.

65. Details here are drawn from the lawsuit itself, which was filed on May 24, 2010, at the Federal Court in Rome, Georgia.

About the Authors

Tonya Craft was born and raised in Chattanooga, Tennessee, by two wonderful parents. Immediately following high school, Tonya attended the University of Tennessee at Chattanooga with the desire to become an educator. Tonya obtained her Bachelor of Science in Education and began teaching at the middle-school level, but quickly found her niche with elementary students. Soon, Tonya faced life as a single mother, creating a personal-training business and taking a position as a literacy trainer with UT Chattanooga. She earned her Master's Degree in Education with a reading and literacy specialization while teaching kindergarten full-time in northern Georgia.

Since winning her court battle and being acquitted on all twenty-two counts, Tonya has served as a consultant on a variety of child-molestation cases. She is pursuing a law degree and is committed to helping others. She lives near Chattanooga with her two children.

Mark Dagostino is a *New York Times*–bestselling coauthor and former senior writer for *People* magazine. As a journalist, he was on the scene when JFK Jr's plane went down, reported from Ground Zero in the aftermath of 9/11, and stood witness to the Miracle on the Hudson. He also cut his teeth in the courtroom, learning valuable lessons from the Pamela Smart case in his home state of New Hampshire, covering Rosie O'Donnell's $100 million lawsuit with publisher Gruner+Jahr, and more. Along the way, he quietly became one of the most respected celebrity journalists in the business. Today, he's back in his home state, where he lives a somewhat quieter life with his two children.